THE NEW OWNERS

THE NEW OWNERS

The Mass Emergence
of Employee Ownership
in Public Companies
and What It Means
to American Business

Joseph Raphael Blasi

Douglas Lynn Kruse

With the assistance of

Lawrence R. Greenberg, Shane Williams,
Mary Tyrone, Inge Herre, and Elana Hyman

HarperBusiness
A Division of HarperCollins*Publishers*

The authors gratefully acknowledge permission to reprint excerpts from the following material:

"Workplace: Pepsi Offers Stock Options to All, Not Just Honchos," by Jolie Solomon, *The Wall Street Journal,* June 28, 1989. Reprinted by permission of *The Wall Street Journal,* © 1989 Dow Jones & Company, Inc. All Rights Reserved Worldwide.

"Storming the Barricades with a Proxy," by Randall Smith, *The Wall Street Journal,* May 25, 1990. Reprinted by permission of *The Wall Street Journal,* © 1990 Dow Jones & Company, Inc. All Rights Reserved Worldwide.

"Lockheed's Board Votes to Amend Poison Pill," by Rick Wartzman, *The Wall Street Journal,* September 25, 1990. Reprinted by permission of *The Wall Street Journal,* © 1990 Dow Jones & Company, Inc. All Rights Reserved Worldwide.

"The Bad News Is Wrong," a chart that appeared in "Real Wages Went Up in the 1980s," by Robert J. Myers, *The Wall Street Journal,* August 21, 1990. Reprinted by permission of *The Wall Street Journal,* © 1990 Dow Jones & Company, Inc.

International Standard Book Number: 0-88730-509-1

Library of Congress Catalog Card Number: 91-11045

Printed in the United States of America

Library of Congress Cataloging-in-Publication Data

Blasi, Joseph R.
    The new owners : the mass emergence of employee ownership in
public companies and what it means to American business / Joseph R.
Blasi, Douglas L. Kruse.
      p. cm.
    Includes bibliographical references and index.
    ISBN 0-88730-509-1
    1. Employee ownership—United States.   2. Corporations—United
States—finance.   3. Consolidation and merger of corporations—
United States.   4. Corporate goverance—United States.
5. Corporate culture—United States.   I. Kruse, Douglas.
II. Title.
HD5660. U5B58 1991
338.6—dc20   91-11045
                                              CIP

91 92 93 94 PS/HC 9 8 7 6 5 4 3 2 1

To Angelo, Jean, and Christina Blasi

and Lisa Schur

Contents

Acknowledgments   ix

Introduction   1

Chapter 1   Corporate Finance   33

Chapter 2   Restructuring Wages and Benefits   88

Chapter 3   Takeovers   139

Chapter 4   Corporate Culture/Governance   211

Conclusion   242

Appendix A   The Employee Ownership 1000   257

Appendix B   Employee Ownership and Stock Buybacks   307

Appendix C   Employee Ownership and Cashing
out Large Shareholders   311

Appendix D   Employee Ownership and Newly Issued
Shares   313

Appendix E   Public Companies Going Private
with Employee Ownership   319

Appendix F   Employee Buyouts (and Some Spinoffs)   320

Appendix G   Wage and Benefit Restructuring   325

Appendix H   Takeovers and Employee Ownership   330

Index   339

Acknowledgments

The research and production of this book would not have been possible without the dedication of many students who worked as research consultants and research assistants. We are especially indebted to our research consultants, Lawrence Greenberg and Shane Williams, whose energy knew no limits, and our research assistants, Mary Tyrone, Inge Herre, and Elana Hyman, who monitored key databases and conducted interviews. Vielka Harrison, Reena Tewari, Rathna Natarajan, and Paul Hempel took responsibility for important projects with the aid of our administrative assistant, Donna Lebowitz. We are grateful for timely and crucial financial support that came from Robert Beyster of the Foundation for Economic Development. Dr. Beyster is Chairman and CEO of Science Application International Corporation in La Jolla, California. We also received significant financial support from the RGK Foundation of Austin, Texas, and are most appreciative to its President, Mrs. Ronya Kozmetsky, for her continuing support.

Our editor, Martha Jewett of HarperBusiness, guided, strengthened, inspired, and saved us many times over, and we will never forget her belief in us. Elena LePera edited the book with brilliance and perfection and managed the thousand details of the project with solicitude. It was a miracle she took this project. HarperBusiness cut no corners in supporting us, especially Mark Greenberg, the president, Barbara Wilkinson, our publicist, Elyse Zucker, Lee Watson, Pat Cabeza, the managing editor, and Ann Rudick. We thank Publication Services, especially Catherine Albright, Annette Wall, and Maria Victoria Paras for their speedy work on book production.

We collaborated with Professor Michael Conte of the Center for Business and Economic Studies at the University of Baltimore on the analysis of market values and employment of public companies with employee ownership. Together with Michael we will publish a more in-depth study of the financial and other characteristics of these firms and acknowledge Michael's advice and contributions. Michael's research assistants, Bret Salazar and Mike Funk, assisted us with several projects during a real time crunch. This study was completed under the auspices of the Technology and Employment Research Center at the Institute of Management and Labor Relations (IMLR), Rutgers University, New Brunswick, New Jersey. We are grateful to all our colleagues at the Institute for providing us the tremendous time and resources, goodwill, and patience necessary to complete this study, especially, James Begin, Director at the time the study began, James Chelius, Steven Director, Barbara Lee, Jeff Keefe, David Bensman, Betty Lou Heffernan, and John Burton, Director at the time the study was completed. The Institute's IBM computer and database facilities, a gift of the IBM Corporation, were a significant asset in completing this project, and we wish to acknowledge their generosity and the support of Charles Fay of IMLR. Preparatory work for the study was done at the California Polytechnic State University School of Business in San Luis Obispo, California, where the first author was a member of the Department of Management. The support of the entire faculty is appreciated. We would especially like to thank the former Dean, Kenneth Walters, who played a key role in gaining initial financial support for this project. Dr. Walters is now Dean of the Anderson School of Business at the University of New Mexico. We also wish to thank: George Kanzler, Jeff Katz, Eugene McElroy, Mamata Datta, and the IMLR library staff, Betty Derco, Steve Wachtel, Jeris Cassell and Judy Gardner and other members of the Reference Division of the Kilmer Library. Mr. Ka-Neng Au and the entire Business Reference Division of the Rutgers School of Management Dana Library, the reference division of the Kennedy Library at California Polytechnic State University. Others worked with the research team on various short-term research projects including: Claire Harnsberger, Jim Finwick, Juan Herrera, Nathan Maas, Danica Curcic, Jeremy Vaugn, Elizabeth C. Reilley, Dawn Kapalski, Tristen Typographers, Frank Klatil, Keith Sproul, Rusty Kat, and Rachel Hyman.

This study would have been impossible without the gracious cooperation of hundreds of public corporations whose managers and employees answered letters and telephone calls, shared materials, and expressed interest in our work. Members of several other organizations were most helpful including the staff of the National Center for Employee Ownership, Dan Beller of the U.S. Department of Labor, Ann Yerger, Virginia Rosenbaum, Bill Sander, and Peg O'Hara of the Investor Responsibility Research Center, David Binns and the ESOP Association, Kevin Reilly of Ernst and Young, Michael J. Rosenthal of M. J. Rosenthal & Co., the research departments of the three major Stock Exchanges along with David Burnett of the National Quotation Service, and the staffs of most of the major investment banks and compensation consulting firms who gave many hours to us in confidential interviews.

Several people offered criticisms of earlier drafts: Steven Hester of Arnold and Porter, Corey Rosen of the National Center for Employee Ownership in Oakland, California, Lee Smith of the Industrial Cooperation Council, and Malon Wilkus and Adam Blumenthal of American Capital Strategies, who helped enormously with corporate finance. We look back and remember Brigitte Jacob's suggestion about the richness of SEC filings and Ann Yerger's idea that we should write to all the large corporations and ask directly how much employee ownership they have.

To a great extent this book can be seen as a review of the contributions of two men who have played the major roles in the development of employee ownership in the United States, Louis Kelso and former Senator Russell Long. Louis Kelso invented and popularized the ESOP (employee stock ownership plan) with his tireless work and deep idealism. He passed away in February 1991 and will be missed for his energetic leadership. Senator Russell Long has been responsible for the legislative development of ESOPs and whatever worthwhile political leadership has existed in Washington on the important issues they raise. He guided the adolescence of employee ownership in the country. Hopefully, he will have new ideas to guide its adulthood.

We owe a lot to many other colleagues and friends who wished us well and are by now thoroughly sick of this book. We salute their forbearance. Joseph Blasi would like to thank Angelo, Jean, and Tina Blasi for always being there and Philip Warburg and David Bloom for early guidance that had a decisive impact. He also wishes to thank William Foote Whyte, Karen Young, Tamar Warburg, and Lakshmi Reddy Bloom. Douglas Kruse would especially like to thank his wife, Lisa Schur, for her remarkable and profound strength and support. He also wishes to express his deepest appreciation to Lowen and Ruth Kruse, Jorika Anna, Janet Schur, and Rita and Michelle Link.

Joseph R. Blasi and Douglas L. Kruse
Princeton, N.J.

THE NEW OWNERS

Introduction

There are so many misconceptions about employee ownership. We found people are very confused about why ESOPs are being done, how they are being used, and what they are doing to the company. I also find the fact that how complicated ESOPs (Employee Stock Ownership Plans) are makes people scared. Working with employee ownership is not "Here's a cookie cutter. Here's your ESOP." It's how do you want to structure your benefits for the 1990s and beyond to get the best bang for your buck.

—Paul Mazzili, Morgan Stanley & Company

"It was only six months ago that I began to realize the very big macro impacts went outside of the pension community. Most of the discussions I have with people about this I have with myself," says John Mulligan, a vice president of State Street Bank & Trust, one of the largest administrators of defined-contribution plans. Future retirees . . . like their employer's stock, if it has been performing well. When companies offer their own shares as a 401(k) option, for example, employees tend to put about a third of their assets there. "If you run it out long enough, its very easy to see there will be firms, maybe without ever intending to, that will be 25–30% employee owned. Employee ownership is going nowhere but up," Mulligan predicts. And he notes, he's not even including the effects of ESOPs.

—Barrons, July 27, 1989

Employee ownership is expanding in public companies. As a result, the shape of American capitalism is being transformed. Employees, by odd turns of events generated by unforeseen social and economic changes, are becoming significant owners and investors in American corporations. They are serving as capital banks for their own companies. Like any basic change, this raises profound questions: Will this affect the role of employees in companies? How does it influence managers? Must it change corporate governance? Today, there are over 1000 publicly traded corporations in which the employees own substantial

1

stock in the company. In this book, we look at the engines propelling this expansion.

- Employee ownership of stock is a normal method of corporate finance affecting almost every kind of conventional transaction.

- Employee-held stock is starting to replace and restructure the system of fixed wages and benefits that have dominated the wage economy since the end of World War II.

- The employee block of shares has emerged as a strategic objective of companies that want to defend themselves against break-up raiders, encourage long-term patient investors, and give their employees a voice in corporate governance.

- The employee shareholder has the potential of being more involved in cooperating with management, improving the performance of the company, and playing a role in the corporate governance of the firm.

This transformation is in its toddler stage. It is part of a larger shift in the structure of ownership in public companies toward the concentration of economic and political power among a smaller and more stable group of shareholders, including institutional shareholders such as pension funds, mutual funds, and insurance companies—large holders who are not part of management or a founding family. According to the Columbia Institutional Investor Project, institutional investors currently control 45–50 percent of the stock market in the United States, 48 percent of the top 1000 corporations.

Whose assets do these institutional investors manage? Surprisingly, the most potent group among these institutional investors is public and private pension funds of American workers, which comprise 43 percent of this capital. About 30 percent of the top 1000 corporations are more than 60 percent owned by institutional investors. The top 20 pension funds alone hold over 15 percent of the top ten corporations.[1]

In the early part of this century, Adolph Berle and Gardner Means (*The Corporation and Private Property*) said that the public company had shareholders spread all over the country who were splintered and fragmented and, as a result, had little say in how their capital was managed. They criticized a monolithic management that owned little stock but controlled the company in the absence of any real involvement by its real, but powerless owners. Now, the new shareholders are becoming more active investors.[2] We cannot say for sure how every minuet of employee ownership and participation in America's corporations will play itself out. The discoveries presented in this book make it crystal clear that this is not a passing phenomenon. It will profoundly affect what the twenty-first century corporation looks like and how the tensions and uncomfortable relationships develop between those many sets of twins that coexist in our modern corporations: shareholders and management, workers and managers at all levels, and boards of directors and senior executive teams.

By the year 2000, more than a quarter of the companies traded on the New York Stock Exchange, the American Stock Exchange and Over-the-Counter Market will be more than 15 percent owned by *their* employees. Most corporations will also be more than 25 percent owned by pension funds, representing large segments of the population, and larger corporations will continue to be 50 to 70 percent owned by institutional investors as a whole. The public corporation will be a partnership among public shareholders represented by pension managers, other institutional investors, employee-holders, small and large individual investors, senior managers with significant holdings, and foreign investors. Further, the boards of these companies will begin to more fully represent these diverse interests.

Shortly before the year 2000, there will be more workers in companies that are more than 15 percent employee held than in the entire U.S. trade union movement. The property rights of workers will dwarf labor laws as an option for influence in corporations. For the first time since the 1930s, America will see a new wave of employee activism—one more likely to be low key and business oriented than the early trade union movement. But this time unions will be joined by company-wide employee associations—ad hoc and coordinated—asking for a say because they are either the dominant shareholder or the second major shareholder in the firm.

Employee ownership is taking place in an incredible number of ways that are not dependent primarily on leverage alone or junk-bond financing, which plays a very minor role in employee-ownership capital markets. Company pension funds of all kinds are simply using their cash reserves to buy up and hold their own stock. No debt is needed here. Companies are encouraging employees to contribute part of their salaries to 401(k) plans and invest it in company stock. This is not debt. Companies are giving profit-sharing payments to employees in the form of company stock. That is not debt. Employees are buying stock directly through employee-share purchase plans, with the company offering a discount and paying brokerage fees. That is not debt. Workers are being asked, or required, to take a proportion of their salaries and benefits in company stock or to trade wage and benefit concessions for stock. That is not debt. Employees are also purchasing their firms' stock directly on the stock market, and more companies are offering stock options throughout the organization.

This transformation is not going to be all peaches and cream for managers and rank-and-file employees who are in the same boat on this trend: most of this stock amounts to the bulk of their retirement. They may have more potential shareholder power, but the price is enormous risk. The new retirement plans—ESOPs, 401(k)/savings/investment, profit sharing, stock bonuses—provide the worker *only* the investment performance of the assets when he or she retires. There are no more promises. In one big gulp, employees are getting what William D. Partridge of the Wyatt Company sees as four major kinds of risk: investment risk, longevity risk, contribution risk, and inflation risk. Investment risk means if the stock does poorly, you end up with less money. Longevity risk warns that you may live longer than the assets will last. Contribution risk means you must contribute substantially to the retirement fund, now and for the long haul, to ensure a good benefit. And inflation risk cautions that you, not the company, have to absorb the fact that money is worth less with inflation, thereby reducing both the value of your pay increases and the value of any employee-held stock.[3]

Therefore, the move toward employee ownership is part of a broader shift in the economy away from defined-benefit pension plans that are the sole responsibility of the company and pay a fixed income for life, which is a high proportion of the worker's recent salary—no matter how the company has performed nor what the worker's savings have accrued. Businesspeople do not like defined-benefit plans because they cannot control and predict their costs. If the plan's assets are invested in the stock market and incur losses, the company's costs escalate. If the company hired more older workers, the benefits cost more. Since a company cannot control changes in the stock market nor the ages of the employees it hires, among other things, it cannot accurately assess how much these plans will cost. Although few people welcome the change, these defined-benefit plans are being replaced by defined-contribution plans. To conserve capital for companies, these retirement plans are more and more investing in company stock. In fact, when credit markets tighten, an increase in this type of employee ownership can be expected, because companies are in effect borrowing from their pension plans! The federal government has tried to limit this risk by saying that generally no more than 10 percent of the assets of most benefit plans can be invested in the company's stock, although many defined-contribution plans, like profit-sharing plans, can skirt the 10-percent rule. But less than 10 percent of the assets of many benefit plans represents a sizable chunk of the company's market value, and many plans with Employee Stock Ownership Plan provisions are not affected. In short order, the U.S. retirement system and employee ownership are becoming inextricably linked.

The chief insight of our book is that a tremendous gap exists between a public corporate employee-ownership sector, which has emerged right under our eyes, and the mindset or worldview—ideology, if you will—people have about it. There are two views. We call one Trusteeship, and the other Rights. They are sincere, and both can degenerate into extremes.

Trusteeship asserts that employee ownership may seem to be there, but it is really ownership held in trust for employees. It's like the trust you set up for your children. CEOs may say they want employees to take more responsibility and act like shareholders, but they do not mean it. The reason is that its main goal is to provide employees with some extra money. Thus, companies can set up and eliminate employee-ownership plans, and it is not employee participation that matters, but the money they get. Trusteeship realizes that the concentration of wealth has not changed much since the thirties, but it is an attempt to broaden the wealth-holding. Trusteeship is a sincere position for many individuals. Employees really do own the stock "in a beneficial way," and they do get money for it in return. But anything beyond that is viewed as unrealistic.

Trusteeship can degenerate into Paternalism. Paternalism does not really care about the broadening of wealth and expects that capitalism will always be feudalism. If there is any difference, Paternalism argues, it is that in capitalism employees and the middle classes *think* they're getting somewhere. Well, if that makes them feel good, so what. When they are finished with this artificiality, this "trust," they'll do away with it. Some companies seem to move in and out of ESOPs and other employee-ownership "programs" on all kinds of pretexts. It's always a front for something else.

Paternalism is cynical, insists that things never really change; just their appearance *seems* different. It says that corporate management must be a strictly militaristic hierarchy because that promotes efficiency.

The other point of view, Rights, maintains that the evidence we will present adds up to a substantial change. When the extent of employee ownership as well as its varieties and uses becomes so compelling a force in the flagship corporate sector that employee-owners dwarf other significant shareholders in many companies, this result confirms *some* change in both attitudes and behaviors. Rights is money plus influence. As Arnold & Porter attorney Steven Hester puts it, "In addition to giving you some rights when you retire, we're going to give you some rights while you are still working." Rights agrees that people in power just don't want to give it up, but says that persons in power recognize other people who have power and will make deals with them, accommodate them, work with them. Rights says that, perhaps, employees can strike a deal to be viewed as capitalists.

Rights is not an antimanagement point of view because it believes in well-paid, well-trained, professional, powerful senior manager leaders. Another reason Rights is not antimanagement is that a main proponent of Trusteeship, and even Paternalism, can be employees themselves. Employees, after all, have gotten very used to the fixed-wage system, thank you, and many of them are not anxious to have risk, employee involvement, performance-based pay, and so forth. But some employees want management to simply play by the rules: shareholders choose the board, which sets the policies and strategies that management implements. The message from shareholders to management is "You get us where we want to go and we reward you. You do not, and we fire you."

Rights goes further. It says that corporations can benefit by aligning the shareholder interests of all the stakeholders including employees. And perhaps, employees, who after all are on the premises more than those shareholders in Idaho, can take more responsibility to aggressively collect information, identify key problems, and work with management to solve them. Rights realizes there is a management hierarchy, but it sees employees as citizens rather than as wage-slaves.

Rights also has an extreme, which is called Control. Control tries to replace the managerial hierarchy with a worker hierarchy. Control does not understand that groups in a company or organization need to find ways to cooperate rather than solve problems of dominance. Control says now that employee shareholders finally have a chance to push the other people around, let's see how they like it. Control is the French Revolution in corporations. It is interesting that the worst fear of many corporate citizens about employee ownership, Control, is actually completely absent from the employee-ownership scene. The employee-ownership world is heavy on Trusteeship, well represented with Paternalism, and tending towards Rights in some companies.

We wish we could subscribe to either point of view—Rights or Trusteeship—at the outset, so that half of our readers could put the book down and half could go forward with us. Our goal is to walk you through the facts and the evidence and reflect on which makes sense.

This is a fact-driven book, and our goal is to offer as many of the facts as possible, so that you can apply them to your own situation and reach alternative conclusions, if they seem plausible to you. Recently, Blasi's comprehensive examination of past research and critique, *Employee Ownership: Revolution or Ripoff?* appeared in paperback and will be referred to routinely for more background on the subject.[4] In this book, each chapter underscores the public companies relevant to our inquiry and contains opening cases, illustrating the main points of that chapter.

The Employee-Ownership World: Detective Work

The writing of this book is the result of our own surprise when we searched for a bird's-eye view of the employee-ownership world: there existed no complete analysis of what public companies were doing in this area. For the last two years we have systematically assembled every piece of openly available information on employee ownership in publicly traded corporations from 20 different sources. These include references to the subject in every published newspaper or magazine in the country through a national clipping service; the Securities and Exchange Commission filings and annual reports of all public companies since 1986; a computerized record of every Internal Revenue Service Form 5500 filed by public companies on their employee benefit plans; articles in the *Wall Street Journal* and all major news magazines, newspapers, and news services; all corporate press releases available on the Press Release Wire and the Business News Wire; and a number of other specialized sources described in Appendix A.

There are two kinds of information in this book: experiences with employee ownership and amount and types of employee ownership. The *Public Company Employee Ownership Database* has information on these firms' uses and experiences with some form of employee ownership. We will analyze the data issued by public companies and interpret pivotal trends in detail. In some of these cases the precise amount of employee holdings cannot be determined or estimated. The *Employee Ownership 1000* lists every public company with significant employee holdings over 4 percent, based on best available sources. In some instances, the role or use of employee ownership also cannot be determined.

Employee ownership is ownership of common or preferred stock of a publicly traded corporation exceeding 4 percent of the total market value of these equities held by a group of employees, which includes substantially more employees than the senior executive team and key middle manager. Many public companies adopting ESOPs in the last few years have tended to include most of their employees, although many companies still exclude their unionized employees. The reason is simple. The tax incentives of ESOPs are a percentage of the total compensation of employees participating in the ownership plan. The goal of our definition is to include most relevant employee ownership in American society in our examination. This does not mean that these companies are "employee owned." We reserve the term *employee owned* for a corporation that is more than 51 percent owned by its employees versus a corporation that "has significant employee ownership or is employee held." Such a firm must include most of its employees broadly represented.

The Public Corporation

We are concentrating on the 7,000 corporations whose stock is publicly traded in a market on a Stock Exchange because these 7,000 corporations dominate the U.S. economy. These include Over-the-Counter companies traded mainly on the NASDAQ Exchange. Moreover, we estimate there are an additional 10,000 corporations whose stock is traded less heavily among brokers "over the counter." They are often called "pink-sheet companies" because information on their securities are available primarily in a pink telephone book published by the National Quotation Bureau in Jersey City, New Jersey. These corporations are included in the Employee Ownership 1000. Table 1 gives an overview of the three major exchanges.

As public companies these corporations are also watched more closely by the government, whose role is to ensure that all relevant information is accessible to investors and shareholders. Securities laws enacted by Congress require that

TABLE 1 *The Three Major Stock Exchanges*

Market	Number of Companies	Percent	Total Market Value (billions)	Percent
New York NYSE	1762	25	$3034	86
American AMEX	833	12	$ 116	3
Over The Counter OTC	4277	62	$ 373	11
TOTAL	6872	100	$3523	100

Source: The Exchanges, July 1990

these companies make "public disclosures" about significant events and facts surrounding their business operations and financial performance in regular filings to the Securities and Exchange Commission and in annual reports to their shareholders.[5] Investors and bankers almost daily issue votes of confidence or no-confidence in these companies by buying and selling their stock, by lending them capital, financing their bonds and debt offerings, and by mounting hostile takeovers, tender offers, and proxy battles to force their management teams to deliver more value to shareholders. Public companies are in contrast with what is commonly called privately held, or closely held, companies or even sole proprietorships, which have a small group of owners or just one owner whose ownership interest does not trade hands regularly in an investors market and who do not raise funds from the public.

A dramatic source of the public corporations' strength is that they can raise capital by issuing stock and other securities in a public capital market. They are where the big money of capitalism is given to the key managers to make the big profits. The substance of a public market is that supposedly, investors can easily get information on the financial and related performances of these corporations, and they use this information to make decisions about where to invest, which managers to hire and fire, and which industries to develop or abandon. Information is the lifeblood of this market, at least that's the theory, but we have in fact discovered that most investors, and most workers and many managers actually know very little about the employee ownership that exists in the public market.

Table 2 shows why the focus on public corporations makes sense.[6] Despite the fact that they are less than one-fifth of a percent of total businesses, they are the flagship business sector. Public corporations make up 60 percent of the market value, 50 percent of the jobs, and are estimated to command a wide majority of the sales in the nation. The significance of the Employee Ownership 1000 is that these companies, in which employees are substantial and often top shareholders, now include almost a third of the market value and sales of the entire publicly traded corporate sector! The transformation of ownership in this sector has reached the center of the economy.

The Employee Ownership 1000

About one thousand public companies are in the forefront of employee ownership in the American economy. Remarkably, these companies in the Employee Ownership 1000 constitute 29 percent of the market value, 27 percent of the sales, and provide 20 percent of the jobs in the nongovernment economy in the United States. Appendix A provides a complete list of these companies, ranging from Weirton Steel Corporation (NYSE), which is 73 percent employee owned, to K Mart Corp. (NYSE), which is 4 percent employee held. This represents a modest change in the ownership structure of American corporations in slightly more than 15 years. How are these companies grouped in terms of stock

TABLE 2 *Publicly Traded Corporations in the U.S. Economy*

	No. of Businesses (actual)	%	Market Value (billions)	%	Sales (billions)	%	No. of Jobs (millions)	%
Whole Economy	7 million	100	$5607	100	N/A	100	86	100
Publicly traded Corporations	7,000	.1	$3340	60	$6021	N/A	43	50
Employee Ownership 1000	1,000	14.28	$965	29	$1664	28	8.6	20

[a] Note that the percentages for the Employee Ownership 1000 are expressed as % of publicly traded corporations.

Note: This table is based on gross estimates. Number of total businesses is from Trinet Inc. of Parsippany, N.J. Total market value of all business units is from the Balance Sheet of The U.S. Economy, Flow of Funds Section, Federal Reserve Board for 1988. There is as yet no basis for estimating the total market value and sales and employment of closely held corporations that have significant employee ownership.

Source: Public Company Employee Ownership Database, 1990; Blasi, Conte, and Kruse 1990 and selected data sources

FIGURE 1   *Employee Ownership 1000: Distribution Among the Exchanges*

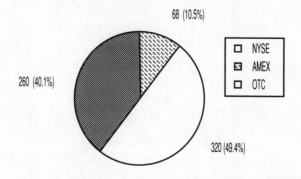

The New York and OTC Exchanges Are Dominant

Companies Shown by Stock Exchange

68 (10.5%)

260 (40.1%)

□	NYSE
☒	AMEX
□	OTC

320 (49.4%)

Source: Public Employee Ownership Database; Blasi, Conte, and Kruse, 1990. Chart by Lawrence R. Greenberg

exchanges, business sectors, regions, market value, sales, and employment? Figure 1 begins to tell the story. The analysis of the Employee Ownership 1000 is based on a sample of 648 companies examined in October 1990.

In which publicly traded business sectors are *companies* with significant employee ownership most concentrated? The evidence reveals density in the financial, transportation, utilities, and consumer products, and thin dispersion among such business sectors as services, equipment and instruments, oil and gas, and material production. But, except for services, there was no business sector in which less than 7 percent of the companies had significant employee ownership. In order to get a more accurate picture of employee ownership, we assessed companies with significant employee ownership according to the total market value of the companies, the number of employees in the companies, and the value of the employee-ownership stake in current dollars in all the companies as a group.

When all three criteria are taken into account, the top four employee-ownership business sectors are utilities, oil and gas, consumer products, and financial services. Together they account for almost 90 percent of the total value of significant employee holdings in publicly traded corporations. Significant employee ownership has a negligible presence in services, construction, material production, transportation, and equipment and instruments. These sectors as a whole account for only about 10 percent of the total value of significant employee holdings among publicly traded companies.

What does all this mean? First, significant employee ownership, while concentrated in certain business sectors, is still a fairly broad-based trend. Second, when the companies were sorted geographically, we discovered that employee ownership is concentrated mainly in the East and Midwest. Third, the popular conception that significant employee ownership is used mainly to rescue failing firms in mature industries, which are often unionized, is disproved by this evidence. Rather, it is a negligible factor in material production and equipment and instrument industries in which unionization is high, whereas it is highly concentrated in business sectors where unionization is quite low or unevenly distributed, such as financial services, utilities, consumer products, and oil and gas.[7] But until we examine the financial condition of the Employee Ownership 1000 compared with other companies in their industry, we will not know the full answer to this question.

In 1974, only 13 public companies reported that employee benefit plans were their largest stockholders, and only one plan, Sears, Roebuck & Co.'s profit-sharing plan attained 20-percent ownership. Five others—Ford, U.S. Steel, Textron, McDonnell-Douglas and Burlington Industries—averaged 12 percent.[8] The employee-ownership holding is probably the largest holding in most of the Employee Ownership 1000 companies. By 1981, employee investment funds were among the top stockholders in 69 of the Fortune 500 companies and attained close to 20 percent ownership in just 11 cases. Thus, in a space of eight years employee ownership in these companies increased fourfold. But the extent of employee ownership was not notable. Twenty-percent ownership was surpassed in just six companies. This has now radically changed as Table 3 indicates.

By our measure, employee ownership has grown enormously in just ten years. Over 20 times more companies are more than 20 percent employee held. *If one assumes that a 15-percent holding is typically the dominant holding in a public company, then 41 percent of these public corporations either have 15 percent or have said that their employee plans are the dominant holder.* There are a few companies with substantial employee ownership. Six companies have over 50 percent of their stock owned by employees and 54 companies, or almost 9 percent, have more than 25 percent of their stock held by employees. The numbers point to a remarkable consistency between the Exchanges, regarding the average and median amounts of employee holdings. The total estates of employee holdings in public companies are $99 billion, or 2.9 percent of the market value of all public companies and 10 percent of the market value of the Employee Ownership 1000.

Table 4 shows who the employees are in these firms and how the Employee Ownership 1000 compares to the employee-ownership sector in the U.S. economy, which has about 10,000 firms with more than 4 percent employee ownership. Only 10 percent, or 1000, of these firms are publicly traded corporations, but they account for about 40 percent of employee holders, while 9000, or 90 percent, of these firms are closely held companies, which account for 60 percent of the employee holders. Note that the total number of a company's employees is not the same as the employee-participants in employee-ownership plans. Most

TABLE 3 *The Size of Employee Shareholding*

	All Corporations	NYSE	AMEX	OTC
Average Significant Holding (%)	12.19	13.29	12.14	11.78
Median (%)	9.8	9.8	9.7	9.9

Percent of Companies with Holdings:	Total No. of Companies	Total Percentage
Less than 10%	340	52.3
10 to 20%	222	34.2
Greater than 20%	88	13.5
Below 25%	595	91.5
Over 25%	54	8.3
Over 50%	6	.9

Total Value of Employee Ownership Estates in Public Corporations: $99,946,805,950
(99 billion dollars)

As a Percent of the Market Value of all Public Companies: More Than 2.9%

As a Percent for the Market Value of the Employee Ownership 1000: More Than 10.3%

Source: Public Company Employee Ownership Database, 1990; Blasi, Conte, and Kruse, 1990

plans typically exclude a variety of employees, especially union and part-time employees.

The startling news is that 12.5 percent of the private-sector workforce, or 10.8 million American workers, own stock in companies in which the employee ownership exceeds 4 percent of total company market value. There are now more employee-owners in these firms than in the entire trade union movement in the United States, which has only 12.2 percent of all private-sector workers as union members. Two surprising conclusions emerge from these facts. First, the total employee-ownership sector is largely a nonunion sector, because over 87 percent of the private-sector workforce is already nonunion and because previous research suggests that even where a company has union members, they are generally excluded from the employee-ownership plan. Second, we predict that by the year 2000, there will be many more employees in firms that are *more than 15 percent employee held* than in the entire private-sector trade union movement. This will raise profound questions for employees, companies, and unions as a national institution. A key question is whether employees who are the core shareholders in their firms will see their ownership stake as entitling them to some involvement in corporate governance. In other words, corporate ownership rights have the potential not only of replacing collective bargaining

TABLE 4 *How Employee-Owners Are Distributed in the U.S. Workforce*

	No. of Persons (millions)	Percent
Total Private-Sector Employment in U.S.	86	100
Total in Public Corporations	43	50
Employee Ownership 1000		
Total employees in the companies with more than 4% employee holdings	8.6	10
Employees who are participants in employee-ownership plans	4.3	5
Total companies: 1000		
Total in closely held corporations	43	50
Total Employees in the companies with more than 4% employee holdings	10.8	12.5
Employees who are participants in employee-ownership plans owning more than 4% of co.'s stock:	6.5	7.5
Total companies: 9000		
Total employees who are participants in employee-ownership plans in both publicly traded and closely held corporations	10.8	12.5
Total employees who are members of trade unions in private sector workforce	10.5	12.2
Total employee-ownership companies with more than 4% holdings: 10,000		

Note: Total private-sector employment and union memberships are from the Bureau of Labor Statistics, U.S. Department of Labor 1989 figures. Total employment in publicly traded corporations is based on the total employment in Compustat companies for 1988, plus an estimate for the number of employees in smaller OTC companies not listed on Compustat. Closely held companies include all other employer types. We have computed the percentage of employees who are participants in employee-ownership plans by using an estimate supplied by the National Center for Employee Ownership (NCEO), which assumes that the exclusion of part-time employees, short-term employees, excluded union employees, and other excluded employees will on average constitute 50 percent of the workforce in publicly traded corporations and 40 percent in closely held corporations. Blasi (1988: 44, 146) cites a study by Kruse showing 52.7 percent of all employees were excluded from all ESOPs, while the General Accounting Office in 1986 found that 50 percent of all ESOP firms excluded 26.7 percent of employees. NCEO views GAO's data on exclusion as too low because they are based on the median. NCEO has more confidence in numbers closer to Kruse's estimates, which have been confirmed by NCEO's statistics on public and closely held firms, although public companies seem to include fewer employees in employee-ownership plans than in closely held companies. Data on total closely held companies are from the NCEO.
Source: Public Company Employee Ownership Database, 1990

and labor-law rights as the basis for employee voice in companies but also of strengthening collective bargaining in unionized firms.

Finally, Table 5 shows how significant employee holdings are represented among Fortune 100 and Fortune 500 companies: Employee ownership is having an impact on the central corporations of the nation.

TABLE 5 *Significant Employee Holdings in the Fortune 500 Companies*

The Fortune 500 Largest U.S. Industrial Corporations—27.2%
The Fortune 100—33%

Name of Company	Fortune Rank	% of Employee Ownership
Ford	2	11.73
Exxon	3	9.35
Texaco	10	10.00
Chevron	11	16.00
Amoco	12	6.23
Procter & Gamble	14	24.50
Occidental Petroleum	16	4.73
Xerox	21	11.00
Atlantic Richfield	22	9.00
McDonnell Douglas	25	32.60
Rockwell	29	4.10
Phillips Petroleum	30	16.17
Allied Signal	31	15.80
Sara Lee	34	10.40
International Paper	35	7.30
Unocal	40	20.00
General Dynamics	44	8.10
Lockheed	45	18.91
Anheuser-Busch	49	14.50
Motorola	52	9.00
Coastal	54	12.50
Monsanto	55	5.53
Ashland Oil	58	23.00
Textron	61	19.30
TRW	62	16.20
Honeywell	65	5.00
Ralston Purina	69	9.40
Reynolds Metals	75	5.84
James River	81	11.40

(continued)

TABLE 5 (*Continued*)

Name of Company	Fortune Rank	% of Employee Ownership
PPG	83	14.00
Kimberly-Clark	86	5.30
Quaker Oats	87	4.00
Abbott Labs	94	6.50
Northrop	98	16.40
Cooper Industries	101	5.00
CPC International	102	5.10
Colgate Palmolive	103	11.00
Mead	110	4.77
Boise Cascade	112	15.00
Eaton	115	7.00
Inland Steel	117	11.30
Whitman	118	10.20
Gillette	124	6.20
Johnson Controls	126	12.00
Grumman	129	42.85
Times Mirror	131	7.30
Cummins Engine	132	11.60
FMC	133	25.60
Kerr-McGee	144	5.00
Ingersoll Rand	146	4.95
American Petrofina	148	4.54
Owens-Corning	149	13.60
Universal	155	6.00
Upjohn	156	5.20
Armstrong	158	10.00
Brunswick	159	7.70
Union Camp	161	6.40
Ethyl	162	7.12
Rohm & Haas	167	17.59
Quantum	168	12.50
Olin	175	23.60
Parker Hannifin	177	5.21
Armco	178	7.80
Corning	181	22.00
Tribune	182	16.40
Knight-Ridder	189	14.00
Westvaco	193	14.00
USG	198	18.80
Sherwin-Williams	203	16.30
Diamond Shamrock	206	13.29
Louisiana Pacific	208	11.67

(*continued*)

TABLE 5 *(Continued)*

Name of Company	Fortune Rank	% of Employee Ownership
Mapco	209	7.40
Gencorp	211	12.60
Stanley Works	212	15.20
Cabot	216	11.00
Polaroid	218	19.37
Willamette	223	12.00
International Multifoods	224	5.30
Cyprus Minerals	229	13.90
Square D	234	5.20
Harcourt Brace Jovanovich	237	27.70
Avery International[a]	244	5.90
E-Systems	248	22.30
Arvin	251	9.94
Timken	258	5.20
Clark Equipment	273	18.26
Crown Central Petroleum	279	5.58
Weirton Steel	288	73.00
Data General	290	10.90
Nortek	291	11.80
Deluxe	293	4.97
Hartmarx	294	11.50
Federal Paper Board	295	4.00
Nucor	297	4.23
McCormick	299	26.30
Potlach	301	4.00
Ball	307	10.00
Wheeling-Pittsburgh	310	33.00
Rorer	311	4.08
Pentair	317	14.70
Ferro	327	7.80
Savannah	328	10.80
Nalco	329	6.80
Federal-Mogul	330	9.00
ITT Rayonier	331	10.30
Bemis	333	4.05
Worthington	346	5.20
Aristech Chem	348	23.50
Leggett & Platt	350	6.84
Consolidated Papers	353	13.00
Valero Energy	361	6.40
Interlake	362	10.50

(continued)

TABLE 5   (*Continued*)

Name of Company	Fortune Rank	% of Employee Ownership
Intergraph	365	14.10
Cooper Tire	367	16.66
Cincinnati Millacron	370	9.90
Crystal Brands	372	21.79
Herman Miller	386	35.00
Vista Chemical	392	6.10
Dennison[a]	394	18.67
SPX	397	12.00
Avondale	419	44.00
Imperial Holly	434	22.50
Toro	441	18.00
Lukens	443	12.00
Phillips-Van Heusen	444	5.15
Media General	464	9.87
Reynolds	466	13.61
Tyler	468	34.00
Kimball International	470	12.90
Chemed	471	19.40
Butler Manufacturing	477	18.80
Mitchell Energy	482	7.23
Allied Products	492	10.70

Fortune Service 500 — 19.4%
The 100 Largest Diversified
Service Companies

Wetterau	15	10.10
Ensearch	22	5.60
CBI Industries	60	22.40
Commercial Metals	77	11.70
Key Jewlers	85	8.50
Perini	87	16.00

The 100 Largest Commercial
Banking Companies

Manufacturers Hanover	5	8.00
PNC Financial	22	4.00
MCorp.	23	17.07
Norwest	24	10.08
Bank of N.Y.	27	12.89
Barnett Banks	28	13.63
Citizens & Southern	30	5.00
First Fidelity	34	10.20
Ameritrust	46	14.81

(*continued*)

TABLE 5 (*Continued*)

Name of Company	Fortune Rank	% of Employee Ownership
The 100 Largest Commercial Banking Companies—*continued*		
Northern Trust	59	16.70
Society Corp.	61	9.31
Huntington Bancshares	65	4.51
Baybanks	67	7.80
Meridian Bancorp	72	8.00
Commerce Bancshares	90	10.20
First Security	94	4.57
South Carolina National	99	13.90
The 50 Largest Diversified Financial Companies		
American Express	2	4.50
Aetna Life	4	4.30
Merril Lynch	5	25.00
Cigna	6	8.89
Travelers	8	4.80
Morgan Stanley	9	57.20
Transamerica	16	5.45
Paine-Webber	17	12.13
Household International	19	4.00
Fireman's Fund**	22	6.10
St. Paul Cos.	25	5.00
Chubb	28	5.00
SAFECO	31	4.08
Home Group	32	5.86
GEICO	37	8.00
Old Republic International	38	10.10
Alexander & Alexander	42	4.91
Marsh & McLennan	48	10.10
The 50 Largest Savings Institutions		
CityFed Financial***	12	16.40
Empire of America	17	5.60
TCF Banking	19	6.20
Northeast Savings	29	19.00
American Continental***	30	23.00
Old Stone Corp.	36	25.60
American Savings	37	4.70
Far West Financial	43	9.00
Great Lakes	48	11.70
Valley Federal	49	8.40

(*continued*)

TABLE 5 *(Continued)*

Name of Company	Fortune Rank	% of Employee Ownership
The 50 Largest Retailing Companies		
Sears	1	19.70
K Mart	2	4.00
Kroger	4	34.60
J.C. Penney	5	24.70
American Stores	6	4.62
May Department	10	13.10
Dayton Hudson	11	6.20
Melville	20	6.10
McDonald's	23	9.80
Carter Hawley Hale	24	40.00
Tandy	29	16.41
Lowe's	36	24.24
Mercantile Stores	40	5.70
Long's Drugs	46	15.60
The 50 Largest Transportation Cos.		
Delta Air	8	14.00
TWA	12	10.00
Pan Am	13	13.00
Federal Express	14	10.00
Consolidated Freightways	15	19.54
US Air	17	5.00
Yellow Freight	18	13.00
Roadway Services	19	17.22
Southwest Air.	28	8.34
Kansas City Southern	38	7.90
Preston	40	4.95
American Carriers	41	6.74
America West	45	20.00
The 50 Largest Utilities		
GTE	1	4.12
BellSouth	2	7.11
NYNEX	3	9.57
Bell Atlantic	4	5.90
Pacific G&E	5	12.80
Southwestern Bell	7	5.00
US West	8	13.50
American Info Technology	9	4.60
American Electric Power	13	4.03
Texas Utilities	15	6.00

(continued)

TABLE 5 *(Continued)*

Name of Company	Fortune Rank	% of Employee Ownership
The 50 Largest Utilities—*continued*		
FPL Group	20	9.30
Enron	26	17.12
Ohio Edison	28	5.96
Niagara Mohawk	29	9.92
Carolina Power & Light	30	7.80
Central & SW	32	17.31
Columbia Gas	39	14.25
Pacificorp	40	4.29
Baltimore G&E	46	5.69
Transco Energy	47	12.90

[a] Avery and Dennison have merged and would now be 178 on the fortune list. The merged company is called Avery-Dennison and has significant employee ownership.
Note: Additional Fortune firms have established employee ownership since this list was compiled. Appendix is updated to January 1991.
**Company has recently been sold.
***Both thrifts have been taken over by the Resolution Trust Corporation and transactions involving employee ownership by the firms are under inquiry. American Continental is parent to Lincoln Savings and Loan.
Source: Public Company Employee Ownership Database, 1990 and *Fortune*, April 1989

The Future

Employee ownership has become socially acceptable. When some of the big companies started putting in ESOPs, it was oh no, they are afraid they are going to be taken over. Now we have a lot of companies putting in ESOPs who are not even close enough to the amount of employee ownership that would give them any protection. But now it has become more of an acceptable business practice to do it. It used to be you could not open a newspaper and see that a company is implementing employee ownership. Now, there are more plans than before but you do not see anything in the paper. It is not sensational but it is still happening.

—*Ken Lindberg, Hewitt Associates, compensation consulting*

In terms of future trends, there is reason to believe that public corporations are steadily increasing the amount of employee ownership they have. Our information shows many additional public companies have employee ownership stakes of 1 to 4 percent, and there are several other public companies with less than 1-percent employee ownership with a market value of over $50 million.

We estimate the dollar value of employee holdings under 4 percent equals at least another 1 percent of the total market value of all public corporations. As the idea becomes more common, the number of corporations with majority employee ownership expands, and "that encourages expansion of the number with more than 25-percent employee ownership, and that encourages the expansion of employee ownership of more than 4 percent, and that encourages more companies to entertain the idea of employee ownership."[9]

Varieties of Employee Ownership

How does the publicly traded stock of these corporations get into the hands of employees? The bottom line is employee benefit plans serve as the main vehicle for most employee ownership, which is financed by both retained earnings and leverage.[10] There are two reasons the employee-ownership environment has turned out this way: First, employee benefits represent a large amount of the average American worker's compensation, which has become a fixed part of the country's pay system. As a pool of capital contributed by corporations to employee benefit trusts that qualify for federal tax incentives, employee benefits are the obvious source of major capital outlays for stock purchases for the benefit of employees. Second, the average American worker beneath the senior management level could not fund significant purchases of company stock out of savings, because this employee needs the money for immediate expenses. Indeed, economists have pointed out that, on average, real wages adjusted for inflation have declined for this group over the last 20 years.[11]

Most investors have achieved significant stock ownership, not by investing savings in a piecemeal or even a systematic way. They borrowed money to buy stock in corporations, or the value of their equity increased as corporations borrowed money to make profits and retire the debt, or they borrowed money to undertake partially or fully leveraged buyouts of companies and gained tremendous wealth as the debt was repaid. Applying just these insights, investment banker Louis Kelso first popularized using credit to leverage stock ownership in major corporations for regular employees through their benefit plans, and former Louisiana Senator Russell Long designed ESOP legislation to address exactly these problems.[12]

The federal government encourages corporations to provide for their employees' retirement security by allowing companies to deduct from their corporate income for tax purposes contributions to these retirement plans up to certain limits, typically 15 percent of the W-2 wages of participating employees. The upper limits increase to 25 percent of W-2 wages for ESOPs, plus interest. The basis for this deduction is clear: the federal government wants to encourage private companies to sponsor retirement programs to supplement the narrow benefits of Social Security. Retirement benefits are viewed as deferred compensation and therefore a reasonable deductible expense for companies.[13]

Companies are not obligated to set up retirement plans, but when they do, the Employee Retirement Income Security Act of 1974 stresses that the retirement plans must be administered for the exclusive benefit of the employee-participants and that the plans' investments must be prudent and in compliance with several fairness standards. We will discuss these issues in Chapter 4, Corporate Culture/Governance.[14]

Two Kinds of Pension Plans

A *defined-benefit plan* is a retirement plan commonly referred to as a pension plan. For the corporation, the cost of this benefit is undefined and less predictable, while for the employee the benefit is clearly defined and is usually a fraction of the average of the last few years' salary. The employer agrees to contribute funds to an investment trust. The assets of the trust are invested in a combination of stocks, bonds, cash equivalents (cash, money-market funds, CDs), and real estate and the growth of these assets funds the benefit the employee gets. The company agrees to put an amount of money in the trust required to produce the income necessary to fund the benefit. When these investments are performing well, the company can handily contribute less to the trust, but the company may have to contribute hefty sums to the trust when investments perform poorly. A fixed-benefit plan, like a fixed wage, does not vary with the performance or profitability of the company. It is commonly a sure thing, because the U.S. Government's Pension Benefit Guarantee Corporation (PBGC) actually insures the value of these benefits under most circumstances. The company assumes all the risk, except the insurance, which is subsidized by the taxpayer.

Defined-contribution plans are the opposite. For the corporation, the cost of the benefit is totally predictable—the exact dollar amount it reports to the employee will be contributed annually into the investment trust. For employees who may also contribute to this trust, the ultimate benefit is undefined and uncertain, although they can remove the funds and change how they're invested. This access offers employees some control. These funds are essentially investment accounts for workers. Employees or the company invest the assets in a combination of stocks, bonds, cash equivalents (cash, money-market funds, CDs, etc.). When the employee retires, he or she receives the assets plus the appreciation and income they generated. This investment income accumulates tax-free to employees until they withdraw it from the plan at retirement.[15] This may or may not be enough to cover retirement expenses, and no proportion of existing salary is guaranteed. The benefit the employee ends up with depends on how well the investments perform. Conceivably, if the pension funds are poorly invested, they could decline in value to the point that the employee could actually lose everything. The employee bears all the risk. Defined-contribution plans are any individual investment account plan with these characteristics, the most common being ESOPs, profit-sharing plans, savings, or thrift plans, and 401(k) plans.

Leveraged Employee Stock-Ownership Plans (ESOPs). A leveraged ESOP creates employee ownership by borrowing money to purchase company stock for employees while paying back the loan from ongoing operating profits. Described in the Internal Revenue Code Section 4975,[16] an ESOP is a defined-contribution plan that invests primarily in the stock of the corporation in which an employee works. The source of the capital is money borrowed by the Employee Stock Ownership Trust from a lender usually for five to ten years. Employees may also make contributions. No other defined-contribution plan can borrow money using the company's credit for buying stock. A company sets up a trust fund—the Employee Stock Ownership Trust—which uses the capital to purchase existing or newly issued shares of stock. As the loan is paid back, the shares of stock are allocated to employees' individual investment accounts. While the amount of stock assigned annually to each employee is typically based on relative compensation, it can be based on any principle that is not discriminatory, such as profits, thus turning the ESOP into a type of profit-sharing plan! In a public company, employees can sell the shares for cash when they retire or leave the firm.[17]

Various tax incentives make ESOPs more desirable to public corporations. The company receives a tax deduction for the repayments of the principal of the loan each year, because this credit is used to purchase a benefit for employees, namely, shares of company stock. The allocation of shares to employees is viewed as deferred compensation, a benefit expense to the company under the Employee Retirement Income Security Act (ERISA). When we discuss the policy implications of ESOPs later, it is important to keep in mind that this

FIGURE 2 *Employee Ownership 1000: Distribution of Employee-Held Assets in Employee Benefit Plans*

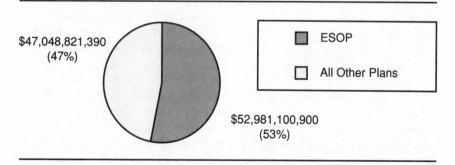

$47,048,821,390
(47%)

ESOP

All Other Plans

$52,981,100,900
(53%)

Source: Public Company Employee Ownership Database, 1990. Chart by Lawrence R. Greenberg

focal ESOP tax deduction is not special: it is a version of the tax deduction allowed for corporate expenses for salary and benefits in general. In this case, the deduction is for the amount of the purchase cost of the stock. But with the ESOP, the upper limit of this deduction is 25 percent of the W-2 compensation of participating employees—much higher than with other employee benefit plans—and also depends on the existence of other employee benefit plans.[18]

Dividends paid on the employee-held stock are also tax deductible under Section 404(k) of the Internal Revenue Code. In public companies they are the core ESOP tax incentive. It is usually the dividends paid on the employee-held stock, which actually pays back the loan that purchased the stock. These dividends can either be paid out to employees in cash or used to repay the ESOP debt more quickly, thereby freeing up shares for allocation to employees' accounts. Because corporations can deduct their contributions to other employee benefit plans for tax purposes, the pivotal special employee ownership tax deduction is the dividend deduction. As two financial analysts remarked in *Financial Management, "Ceteris paribus,* the greater the payout of dividends on ESOP shares, the greater the corporate tax benefits."[19] ESOPs have also been exploited to allocate interest payments domestically to free up foreign tax credit limitations (Section 861 of the Internal Revenue Code).[20]

401(k) Plans.   A 401(k) plan creates employee ownership by purchasing company stock with employees' savings, which are deducted from their salaries, plus the corporation's matching contributions and bonuses to employees through the plan. A defined-contribution plan like the ESOP, the name *401(k)* refers to its section in the Internal Revenue Code. This is a rapidly growing source of employee ownership.[21] These plans are now replacing conventional thrift (savings) plans, which encouraged employee savings before 1978.

The 401(k)s are remarkably flexible. When all the funds come from the employee's existing salary, this accumulation does not saddle any additional cost to an employer's payroll other than that of administering the plan. Corporations set the rules of each plan. For example, employees can be given the options of deferring all or part of a bonus, of making voluntary after-tax contributions through additional payroll deductions, or of receiving employer-matching contributions—typically 50 cents on the dollar—as an incentive for encouraging them to participate. Also, employers can base their matching contributions on profits, thus turning a 401(k) plan into a type of profit-sharing plan.

Here's how this approach makes employees owners. The corporation chooses the ways that employees may control how their funds are invested. While not common, at one extreme, the company can mandate that a large amount of capital in the plan be invested in company stock. Or the company can simply provide employees company stock as one of many investment options. Usually, the company uses company stock as its matching contribution or as special (called nonelective) contributions, based on its profits or some other formula.

The corporate tax incentives for 401(k) plans allow the company deductions for contributions up to 15 percent of the W-2 income of participating employees. Both employer and employee contributions, except for voluntary after-tax contributions by employees, are considered company contributions. Finally, a 401(k) plan can be combined with an ESOP, creating one plan often called a KSOP. In this case, a leveraged ESOP can use borrowed funds as the source of capital to purchase company stock, which may be used for the company's matching or additional contributions.

Deferred Profit-Sharing Plans. Deferred profit-sharing plans create employee ownership by investing all or a portion of the company's profits shared with employees in a retirement trust fund that buys the company's stock. Over 80 percent of profit sharing plans are of this type, namely, defined-contribution pension plans based on profits, and are not to be confused with a cash profit-sharing plan that gives employees a current bonus in cash.

The source of the capital in this arrangement is company profits, although this may be based on almost any profit-sharing formula, such as corporate-wide earnings, or profits earned in a specific operating unit, or plant, or store. Companies may also make contributions when there are no profits and employees can make after-tax contributions to their accounts, using a profit-sharing plan as a savings plan. Profit-sharing plans can also be combined with 401(k) plans, so that they can receive pre-tax employee contributions.

Most of the original profit-sharing plans established in the early 1900s used stock rather than cash in their plans until 1973, when the downturn in the economy caused profit-sharing plans invested in company stock to lose serious money. Nevertheless, many public corporations, whose stock may be a sound long-term investment, continue to invest large amounts of their profit-sharing assets in company stock.

Profit-sharing plans have substantially the same tax breaks as 401(k) plans, allowing employer deductions for contributions up to 15 percent of total W-2 compensation for participating employees.

Employee Stock-Purchase Plans. Employee stock-purchase plans create employee ownership by simply selling shares to employees, based on the belief that stock will mean more to employees if they pay for it directly with current savings. The source of the capital is the cash of employees, or gradual salary deductions, although many companies sell the stock to employees at a discount. They also match employee purchases of stock or pay the brokerage fees involved. In this case, the plan is really a combination share-purchase/stock-bonus plan.

There are generally no special tax incentives or contribution limits for this approach.[22] Since any matching stock bonus given to employees is a salary expense, obviously corporations can get a deduction for this. A key problem for corporations is figuring out a way to encourage a wide range of employees to participate, especially lower income workers who pay tax on the appreciation of any shares or discounts they are given. Most share-purchase plans have not led to extensive employee ownership, although many companies have been strikingly innovative about these plans.

Stock-Bonus Plans.   Stock-bonus plans generate employee ownership when a company contributes stock, or cash to purchase stock, to a defined-contribution retirement trust fund for employees. Giving employees shares enables a company to provide a bonus without using cash. The source of the capital for the shares is company cash, although the company may contribute newly issued shares, which dilutes the stock of current shareholders. Sometimes a company will repurchase shares on the open market to use to fund stock-bonus plans.

An ESOP that does not borrow money is essentially the same as a stock-bonus plan. (These are often called nonleveraged ESOPs.) Corporations obtain a tax deduction for the value of the shares they contribute up to 15 percent of the W-2 earnings of participating employees.[23]

Defined-Benefit Plans.   A defined-benefit plan, or conventional pension plan, creates employee ownership by simply investing some of the assets in the trust in company stock. Typically, public corporations choose professional investment managers to manage these investments. The managers may decide on their own that the company's stock is a good investment, or the company may ask them to invest in its stock. This results in a double-economic advantage for the company: it derives a tax deduction for contributing the capital to the plan in the first place, and the capital flows back into the company's coffers for use as working capital. Obviously, if all pension plans bought company stock with their assets, the risk in these plans would increase substantially. The government therefore says that no more than 10 percent of the assets of a defined-benefit plan can be invested in employer securities. But, please note, 10 percent of a pension plan's assets in an old established company with a huge fund could easily amount to more than 10-percent employee ownership of the company! Most corporations invest less than 1 percent of their defined-benefit pension plan assets in their own stock, but this practice is now changing as they begin to use their capital more efficiently and increase employee stock ownership through multiple means.

Individual Purchases of Stock by Employees.   Employees can become owners by purchasing stock on their own in public companies through brokers. The main drawback to this type of employee ownership is the limited discretionary income for stock purchases of middle- and low-income employees. It is interesting to note that no federal tax incentives exist for this simplest form of employee ownership. In fact, employees get taxed on both the capital appreciation on the shares and the dividends they receive, so they'd have to conclude that their investment return will more than compensate for these taxes on income. It is unfair to workers and taxpayers that the employee ownership that would be most direct for workers and least costly to taxpayers has no tax advantages.

Stock-Option Plans. The National Center for Employee Ownership points out that stock-option plans[24] have traditionally been the most popular form of providing executives with an ownership interest. Options give participants the right to purchase shares of their company's stock between certain dates, at a price fixed by the company at the time the option is granted. The amount of stock each individual may purchase is generally tied to a percentage of compensation, and the employee is under no obligation to act on the option. The Internal Revenue Service distinguishes between nonqualified-stock options (NSOs), incentive stock options (ISOs), and a Section 423 plan.

In an NSO, the duration of the option and the exercise period, as well as participation in the plan, are flexible. Additionally, the price of the option can be set at, below, or above current market value. An incentive stock option plan has more restrictions than this. The option price must be at least 100 percent of the fair market value on the date it's granted. This figure increases to 110 percent of the fair market value for owners of 10 percent or more of the company's stock. The life and exercise period of a plan may not exceed ten years and there's a $100,000 maximum on the amount that can vest in any one year. Finally, to qualify for an incentive stock option, the stock must be held for at least one year from the exercise date, and two years from the grant date. In brief, with an NSO the employee is taxed when he or she exercises the option while the company reaps a tax deduction.

Under a Section 423 plan, options must be granted to all employees who have been employed with the company at least two years, who work more than 20 hours per week, and who work a minimum of five months in a calendar year. Highly compensated employees may be excluded from the plan, however, and employees who own or after the granting of options will own 5 percent or more of the company's voting shares may not participate. The price of the option may not be less than the lesser of 85 percent of the fair market value of the shares at the time the option is granted or at the time the option is exercised, and an option cannot be exercised more than 27 months following the granting date. But this time may be extended to five years if the option must be exercised at 85 percent or more of fair market value. These plans are particularly helpful for companies interested in granting broad-based options, but the short time period for exercising the options makes them less of a vehicle for long-term employee ownership. In an Incentive Stock Option Plan (ISO) the employee incurs no tax, but also the company receives no tax deduction. As a result, ISOs are more closely regulated. We shall consider examples of broad-based options in Chapter 4.

What are the various vehicles for employee holdings in public companies? Although we do not have specific information for each employee benefit plan for every company, the available data indicate that the plans are almost evenly split between ESOPs and non-ESOP plans, with both holding substantial assets (see Figure 2).

The implications of these findings are that nonleveraged employee benefit plans are a significant factor in promoting employee ownership. The seemingly "quiet" purchases of stock in a variety of non-ESOP defined-contribution and defined-benefit plans constitute almost half of the employee ownership in public corporations. This lack of dependence of public company employee ownership on leverage means that the employee-ownership sector is far more flexible than previously thought.

A Note on Taxes and Employee Benefits

There is a popular notion that public corporations set up ESOPs just "to reduce their taxes" or "to give employees incentives and benefits." This is simplistic and inaccurate. Myron S. Scholes and Mark A. Wolfson of the Graduate School of Business at Stanford University suggest the case is thin that tax provisions and employee incentives alone are the primary motivations in establishing an ESOP. Contributions to other employee benefit plans are also tax deductible, so this deduction is neither magical nor unique to the ESOP. If a company's only goal is to reduce its taxes, it has many other options. In fact, straight salary and other business expenses are also tax deductions.

What's unique to the ESOP is that it allows corporations to group both ESOP and non-ESOP tax incentives in combination with taking an action that the company believes has other advantages, such as cashing out a large shareholder or buying back its own securities. Although taxes may be a relevant factor, the corporate finance uses of employee ownership are motivated mainly by the ability of employee ownership to make possible financial transactions, which corporate boards of directors wish to complete.

The same reasoning is true for employee benefits and incentives. ESOPs are not necessarily the perfect or most desirable employee benefit. Many moderately and low-paid employees would prefer more cash over fancy benefits designed by professors, investment bankers, and human resource staffs. Benefits come in many forms, and there is no evidence that employee ownership is a preferred form of benefit. Besides, as an incentive to reward productive behavior, cash profit sharing or other forms of gain sharing or commission may well be more immediate and effective than employee ownership.

Conclusion

Each chapter will focus on a different engine of employee ownership in publicly traded corporations and will have the same format: case studies, the uses of employee ownership with detailed evidence of what public companies are doing, and a discussion of relevant issues and their implications for decision-makers. One important note about our method of collecting evidence. We have constructed the Employee Ownership 1000 to provide a list of the top companies with employee ownership over 4 percent. But the basis for our analysis of public corporations is our survey of all publicly available SEC filings, news reports, press releases, and other information made available by these companies on the way they make use of employee ownership—the Public Company Employee Ownership Database. You will notice occasionally that both lists are not identical because we know how much employee ownership some companies have without knowing the kind of transaction they used to achieve it, while, on the other hand, sometimes we know how a company structured its employee ownership without knowing exactly what percentage of the company is employee held.

This intensive exploration finally gives us a true picture of employee ownership in the United States. Employee ownership is taking place not because it is the right or perfect benefit but because it fits smoothly with the changes in the economy and in companies and because Congress has facilitated its launching into the corporate world.

Notes

1. Carolyn Kay Brancato, The Pivotal Role of Institutional Investors In Capital Markets: A Summary of Economic Research at the Columbia Institutional Investor Project. (New York: Columbia University Center for Law and Economic Studies, July 18, 1990).
2. We have adapted and expanded the thoughts of Ira M. Millstein in his "Remarks to the Corporate Governance Workshop." The Wharton School of the University of Pennsylvania, May 23, 1990: 27–28.
3. William D. Partridge, "The Benefit Side of Employee Stock Ownership Plans," The Wyatt Company. In *ESOPS: Building Equity and Growth For America's Future* (Washington, D.C.: The ESOP Association, 1990): 162–167.
4. *Employee Ownership: Revolution or Ripoff?* Joseph R. Blasi (New York: Harper Collins/Harper Business, 1990, paperback). Douglas Kruse served as the key research associate for this volume. For reference, see also Douglas L. Kruse, *Employee Ownership and Employee Attitudes: Two Case Studies* (Philadelphia, Pa.: Norwood Editions, 1984), reporting on a detailed survey of employee opinions; Michael Quarrey, Corey Rosen, and Joseph R. Blasi. *Taking Stock: Employee Ownership at Work* (New York: Harper and Row, Ballinger Books, 1986), a book of case studies; and *Employee Ownership Through ESOPs: Implications for the Public Corporation* (Scarsdale, New York: Work in America Institute, 1987), a brief research review.

5. The public can now get immediate access to much of this information by dialing into a computer database or by ordering documents over the phone for FAX or next-day delivery. For a handy pocket-guide to what information is reported to the government you can get a free copy of *A Guide To SEC Corporate Filings* (Bethesda, MD: Disclosure Incorporated, 1990) by calling 1-800-843-7747 or 212-581-1414. They will also send you a list of all public corporations called, *SEC Filing Companies 1990* (Bethesda, MD: Disclosure Incorporated, 1990). For a guide of corporate documents for which you can order quick copies, request *The Doc Guy's Doc Guide: FDR (Federal Document Retrieval) Information Centers Index to Frequently Requested Documents from Government Agencies, Legislatures, and Courts* (Washington, D.C.: FDR Information Center Headquarters, 1990) from 1-800-874-4337 or 202-789-2233.

6. The market-value numbers for Table 2 differ from those of the previous chart because Table 1 is based on August 1990 figures from the Exchanges, whereas the numbers in this chart are based on the sum of all market-values of individual companies from Compustat, from which the individual market-value numbers were used to calculate employee holdings.

7. Pie charts are available from the authors, as are the Standard Industry Classification Codes (SIC numbers) used to categorize industries. In the oil and gas industry, for example, there are many unionized workers, but many of them have been excluded from participation in employee-ownership plans, which have been offered only to salaried employees or offered in nonunion companies.

8. U.S. Congress, Senate Committee on Government Operations, *Disclosure on Corporate Ownership* (Washington, D.C.: Government Printing Office, 1974).

9. Ken Lindberg interviewed by authors in August 1990.

10. For an excellent "how-to" guide, see *Employee Ownership: Alternatives to ESOPs,* prepared by Sue Steiner (Oakland, CA: National Center for Employee Ownership, 1990.) In closely held companies there are other possibilities for employee ownership, such as cooperatives, which we will not discuss here.

11. A detailed analysis of how much stock different income groups in the United States actually hold, how they deploy their assets, and what their attitudes are toward taking financial risk can be found in Blasi: 1988: 107–115. Footnote 19, p. 302 will refer the reader to in-depth Federal Reserve Board studies, which dissect the finances of American families. The case that wealth is becoming more concentrated while real income is declining was most recently made by Kevin Phillips' book, *The Politics of Rich and Poor: Wealth and the American Electorate in the Reagan Aftermath* (New York: Random House, 1990).

12. For an extensive analysis of the writings of both men and the development of employee stock ownership plan (ESOP) legislation and employee benefit

legislation affecting employee ownership, see Chapter 1, *The Birth of the ESOP,* in Blasi, 1988: 1–31.

13. For a national overview of these plans, see Blasi, 1988: 8–15.
14. Blasi, 1988, provides extensive criticism of the loopholes and misuse of these plans in structuring employee ownership by corporate managers. See pp. 38–59, 111–118, 122–188, 239–251.
15. If employees leave the firm, they can typically roll over their defined-contribution plan assets into an IRA (Individual Retirement Account) in order to defer paying tax on the assets until their retirement.
16. "Primarily" has never been defined by the Internal Revenue Code, but it is commonly taken to mean at least 50 percent of the assets of the trust. However, a majority of ESOP professionals believe that most ESOPs hold the bulk of their assets in employer securities. In order to cushion older employees against the volatility of the corporation's stocks, which would adversely affect their "ESOP nest egg" close to retirement, at age 55 employees, who have been in the ESOP for ten years, can take 25 percent of their assets or demand three diversified investment options for this same amount other than employer securities. This increases to 50 percent after age 60 and applies to stock acquired after December 31, 1986. Blasi, 1988: 37.
17. Death or disability allows an earlier sale.
18. See also, "Above the Limit: How to Contribute More Than 25% of Payroll to an ESOP," *Employee Ownership Report* 9, no. 4 (July–August 1989): 3–4.
19. See Susan Chaplinsky and Greg Niehaus, "The Tax and Distributional Effects of Leveraged ESOPs," *Financial Management* 19, no. 1 (Spring 1990): 29. It is true, however, that companies can deduct up to 25 percent of the W-2 compensation of participating employees from their corporate income for tax purposes in a leveraged ESOP, while they can deduct only up to 15 percent for other defined-contribution plans. But for ESOPs, the dividend deductions are not counted in this 25 percent ceiling. This raises the issue of the tax implications to employees of ESOPs. The investment in company stock and the income from its possible appreciation and from dividends accumulates tax free within the ESOP, just as in an IRA (Individual Retirement Account). However, if dividends are paid to employees in cash, they are immediately taxable. Dividends used to repay ESOP debt are not taxable to employees.
20. Taken directly from an article by Myron S. Scholes and Mark A. Wolfson, "Employee Stock Ownership Plans and Corporate Restructuring: Myths and Realities." *Financial Management* 19 1: 13, and "Leveraged Employee Stock Ownership Plans: Strategies For The Nineties" (New York: Morgan Stanley Inc., 1990, private circulation), Section II. Regarding the use of ESOP interest expense to free up foreign tax-credit limitations, Scholes and Wolfson say in footnote 2: "The 1986 Act [Tax Reform Act of 1986]

made foreign credit limitations a significantly greater concern than they had been previously. The U.S. restricts foreign tax credits to an amount equal to foreign taxable income divided by worldwide taxable income, multiplied by U.S. tax on worldwide taxable income. One way to mitigate this problem is to make foreign source income, as a fraction of worldwide income, as large as possible. Under Code [Internal Revenue] Section 861, interest generated on domestic debt typically must be allocated partially to foreign activities, thereby reducing foreign source income. It appears possible to allocate 100% of the interest on certain ESOP debt to domestic income, thereby increasing the allowable foreign tax credits." (p. 13).

21. This section is largely based on the National Center for Employee Owner-ships guidebook (Steiner), 1990: 25–32.

22. Although Section 4123 of the Internal Revenue Code is entitled Employee Stock Purchase Plans, it actually deals with stock options.

23. The Internal Revenue Code Section 4975 defines an *ESOP* as a stock-bonus plan or as a combination of a stock-bonus plan and a money-purchase pension plan, in which case the annual contribution limit goes up to 25 percent of W-2 compensation.

24. Based completely on Steiner, 1990: 17–19.

1

Corporate Finance

Merrill Lynch & Co.'s (NYSE) present and former employees own 28% of the brokerage and financial services firm. The company has a market value exceeding $2.2 billion, revenue exceeding $10 billion, and over 30,000 employees. In the late eighties, commission revenue began to lag and the company embarked on a program to clean up its balance sheet, support its stock price, cut staff and benefits, tie pay to performance, and perhaps inoculate itself against a takeover. The company decided to buy its shares after the crash in several transactions. In October 1988, the company terminated its defined-benefit pension plan and used $220 million of excess assets to purchase 9 million newly issued shares for its Employee Stock Ownership Plan to raise employee holdings from 19 to 25%. To control retirement costs, the company will contribute a set amount annually to a new stock plan, and employees are encouraged to invest new contributions in company stock. In December 1988 and September 1989, the ESOP bought additional shares. Employees have been concerned about tying up so much of their retirement security in company stock.[1]

In 1983, U.S. Sugar Company (formerly NYSE), the country's largest sugar processor, was 70% owned by the Mott family and affiliates. In a complex transaction, the company and a new ESOP—with an $80 million loan from the company—made a cash tender offer of a majority of the company's shares. The Mott family wanted to cash out half of their investment but retain control of the company. This transaction allowed the Mott Children's Health Center in Flint, Michigan to get cash for its shares. The company retired many of the shares it bought back. Finally, the company was taken private, and the Motts ended up controlling 53% of the company while 47% was employee held. A class-action suit alleging company officers and the ESOP violated fiduciary responsibility to shareholders was rejected by the Delaware Chancery Court.[2]

Weirton Steel Corporation, a flat-rolled steel division of National Intergroup of Pittsburgh, was sold to a new corporation using an Employee Stock Ownership Plan in 1983. National got out of substantial shutdown costs and removed itself from an industry that it concluded could not remain profitable, given the high-wage rates. Eighty-four percent of Weirton's workers voted to reduce their take-home pay by 20% and to reorganize the company, which began a string of profitable quarters. Quality circles, management training, Statistical Process Control, employee representatives on the board, and closed-circuit TV's throughout the plant have been used to encourage more communication and joint problem solving. The company distributed 33% and later 50% of net income to employees in cash during these years. In 1989, the 8000 employee-owners decided on two major changes, so that the company could execute an ambitious $740-million capital improvement program. The corporation went public on the New York Stock Exchange, and active employees sold close to 35% of their shares. Unionized and salaried employees also voted to reduce their cash profit sharing. Weirton is today 73% employee held and well on its way to retaining its competitive position.[3]

The ESOP of Old Stone Bank (OTC) owns 37.4% of its outstanding common stock. In the mideighties the bank's Employee Stock Ownership Plan purchased newly issued shares several times. In 1987, the ESOP purchased additional newly issued shares, increasing employee voting power to 28% from 23%. Old Stone reported that earnings per share increased in 1984 despite a 33.4% increase in average common shares outstanding resulting from issuance of shares to the ESOP. In 1988, Old Stone redeemed all of its outstanding Series C preferred stock, which paid high dividends for $45 million. The point of this new employee ownership was to replace the high-cost burden of this Series C preferred, which was issued in 1981, when the prime rate was in the 20% range with much lower capital costs. In November of 1989, the Wall Street Journal *reported that the price of Old Stone's shares was falling for the second straight session, amid rumors that the company would cut its dividends. The stock did fall 11% but Old Stone announced dividends are very important because it is 37% employee held. Employee ownership did, however, become a central retirement benefit at the bank to offset the pension plan. The current ESOP balance is used as an offset in computing the projected benefit obligation of the company.[4]*

United Postal Bancorp expects to raise between $32.7 million and $50.9 million from an initial offering of its common stock as part of a conversion from a chartered mutual association to a stock corporation. "The additional equity capital raised in the conversion will enable us to further expand our lending and investment activities, to diversify our operations, to consider future merger *and acquisition opportunities and to better access the capital markets for future equity or debt offerings," said Robert Gorman, president and CEO. The thrift anticipates offering almost 4 million shares of its common. No individual or group will be allowed to purchase more than 2.5% of the total, with the exception of the thrift's ESOP, which may purchase up to 10%.*[5]

Introduction: A Revolution in Ownership Structure

In the public mind, the large- or medium-sized public corporation in America has traditionally been identified with its rich founders, its major core shareholders, its top managers, or the hoards of shareholders spread across the country, who were its silent majority and quiet investors. For several reasons, the old ownership structure has been radically transformed.

Look at Table 1.1. Households still own a good chunk of these companies, but their holdings are declining significantly. Many of these shareholders do not vote their shares. Pension funds and employee holdings are visibly increasing. The bottom line from the Employee Ownership 1000 and these observations is that the new key owners of public corporations are institutions and employee groups. Their ownership is substantial and neatly organized into one bloc, often the dominant bloc, but in most companies, these new owners have not yet begun to express their ownership interests in any coordinated way.

Why have the sources of capital for public companies changed so radically? One reason is that the average citizen is simply not going to use his or her core income or modest extra savings to play the market in any big way. Another reason involves the structure of retirement security in the United States. The U.S. Government does not take responsibility for peoples' retirement, and Social Security is just a supplement. U.S. policy says the real job belongs to the private sector, so that company contributions to retirement benefits are both deductible expenses and attractive to employees, who realize that their retirement is not going to be like socialized medicine, namely, everything is taken care of completely. Since the stock market has delivered 12-percent returns on average per year for long-term investors, the stock market tends to soak up a large proportion of retirement funds' capital.

Employee benefit plans, which do not invest in the employer's own stock and are managed by investment managers, have gained substantial legitimacy in capital markets. They have quietly blessed the role of employee capital funds, of which employee-ownership funds are a newer example. Then, as both the necessity of hefty benefits and the annual expense to maintain them grew, companies looked for ways to make them cheaper, more versatile, and more compatible with corporate interests and the concerns of all the shareholders. Simply put, a dollar in any Smith Corp.'s retirement plan can be invested in AT&T, but

TABLE 1.1 *Stock Ownership Patterns*

	1960	1965	1970	1975	1980	1981	1982	1983	1990
Total Stock Outstanding[a][b]	$451.0	$740.0	$906.2	$892.5	$1,635.6	$1,568.5	$1,810.5	$2,151.5	$4,339.8
Held by									
Households	87.7	84.9	80.4	72.5	72.6	72.3	70.4	68.1	58.5
Private Pension funds[d] (self-administered)	3.7	5.4	7.4	11.4	12.8	12.5	13.7	14.2	16.9
State and local government retirement funds	0.1	0.3	1.1	2.7	2.7	3.0	3.3	4.2	6.8
Mutual Funds	3.3	4.1	4.4	3.8	2.6	2.4	2.7	3.4	5.8
Brokers and Dealers	0.1	0.2	0.2	0.4	0.2	0.4	0.2	0.1	0.3
Life insurance companies[d]	1.1	1.2	1.7	3.1	2.9	3.0	3.1	3.0	3.3
Other Insurance	1.7	1.6	1.5	1.6	2.0	2.1	2.1	2.2	2.2
Commercial Banking[c]	0.0	0.0	0.0	0.0	0.0	0.0	0.0	0.0	0.0
Mutual savings banks	0.3	0.3	0.3	0.5	0.3	0.2	0.2	0.2	0.2
Foreign owners	2.1	1.9	3.0	4.0	3.9	4.1	4.2	4.5	5.7

[a] Totals may not balance due to rounding
[b] Current dollars in billions. Includes publicly traded and closely held stock.
[c] Less Than 0.05 percent
[d] Includes holdings of mutual fund shares

Source: U.S. General Accounting Office, *Employee Stock Ownership Plans: Interim Report on a Survey and Related Economic Trends* (Washington, D.C.: U.S. General Accounting Office, February 1986), p. 39; U.S. Federal Reserve includes publicly traded and closely held corporate stock.

it immediately goes out the company door. Or a dollar in any Smith Corp.'s retirement plan can be invested in Smith Corp.'s stock, and it's used by the company until Joe or Jane Worker retires. This transformation is being rapidly accelerated by the rise of employee-ownership corporate finance.

Dilution, a Major Problem: Is Employee Ownership Good for Public Shareholders?

This book reviews many ways employees can own companies, but the hard question to answer is not how often it happens but whether it is really worth it for shareholders. The common stockholders are the owners of the corporation, and they have a general right to value in the company as well as ultimate control over the affairs of the company. If employee ownership has a viable future in public companies, it must demonstrate that its social, political, and personal benefits to workers translate into financial benefits for *all* public shareholders or, at the least, do not injure the financial interests of all shareholders.

The main potential problem public shareholders and investors can have with employee ownership is *dilution,* or a decline in value of the interests of public shareholders in the company. It will surface continually throughout the book. Our goal here is to introduce the main trends and themes, since the actual dilution of a specific company in the real world of the market will depend on a variety of issues unique to that company and the stock market at any point in time.

Types of Dilution

There are three types of dilution that involve a decrease in value for public shareholders.

Dilution in earnings per share is the consequence of a company's increasing the number of shares it has outstanding without increasing its earnings. Earnings in a corporation are what is left over from sales revenue when operating expenses, depreciation, interest, and taxes are subtracted. For example, a company with 10 million shares and $15 million in earnings has earnings per share of $1.50. If 2 million newly issued shares are added through a leveraged ESOP, those earnings must now be divided among 12 million shares, or $1.25 cents a share. To the extent the ESOP increases operating expenses and interest expenses, it will additionally depress earnings. But there would also be earnings-per-share dilution if the same company established a leveraged ESOP and bought 2 million shares on the open market without increasing the total number of shares. In this case, lower earnings, which have probably been depressed by interest expenses on the ESOP debt and the cost of the new benefit as an operating expense, are distributed among the same number of shares, causing a dilution in earnings per share. One reason earnings-per-share dilution is so critical to public companies is that it is linked to investors' judgments about how much companies are worth. While the price-earnings ratio (P-E ratio) is typically used to express this relationship, in fact the relationship between stock price and *cash flow* is considered more relevant by financial scholars.

Dilution in the market value of the stock results when the actual market stock price declines significantly after an ESOP transaction. Many factors cause market prices of stocks to fluctuate, and it's generally difficult to separate out the causes because changes in securities prices are fundamentally unpredictable. But if investors believe that an ESOP transaction has materially contributed to a decline in the value of the company, this perception will likely impact on the stock price for many reasons. The sale of newly issued shares to an ESOP noted in the preceding paragraph can depress earnings per share and influence earnings. Or the purchase of stock on the open market by an ESOP may be viewed as frivolous, because the compensation of employees with company stock through the ESOP adds an operating expense and interest expense when the company already has given raises for the year and has a competitive benefit package. It may be viewed as a strategic maneuver by management to put a block of voting stock in employees' hands and entrench themselves. Or if the company increases its debt substantially to establish an ESOP, this move may concern investors. Later in the book we will examine studies of what actually happens to the stock price of public corporations after major employee-ownership transactions.

Dilution in voting power occurs when an investor who owns 30 percent or 3 million shares of a company's 10 million shares, wakes up one morning to discover that the company has taken out a huge loan, so that the company-sponsored ESOP could purchase 5 million shares. Now the firm has 15 million shares. Overnight, the employees own 33.3 percent of the firm while this investor now owns only 20 percent of the company. The investors' voting power and influence has now been diluted.

Working with Some Examples

But let's take a general example to illustrate dilution. Throughout this book we will discuss two basic types of leveraged employee-ownership transactions. The first involves ownership replacement, or cashing out public shareholders and replacing them with employee-shareholders. No new capital formation occurs in this transaction. The second involves selling newly issued shares to an employee-ownership plan and increasing the total number of shares. In this transaction new capital formation does occur. Let's now examine how the types of dilution play out in each case and then look at how the dilution may be offset.

Ownership Replacement: ESOP Buybacks, or Newly Issued Shares with Share Repurchases. In an employee-ownership buyback, the company sets up an ESOP, borrows funds and relends them to the ESOP, which buys shares on the open market. The transaction reduces company earnings by the interest expense costs of the ESOP and contributions to the ESOP used to repay the ESOP loan, which are the company's new operating expenses. But this operating expense may be offset by ESOP tax incentives, which would not normally offset more than 30 percent of the expense. This transaction reduces company earnings. If the establishment of the ESOP is not offset by some other reduction in employee compensation, then indeed the compensation expenses for employees are being increased and this dilution will not go away. What will happen to the company's stock price, or market value per share? Frankly, no one knows because a variety of factors unique or external to this company and its industry can affect stock price. But cash did in fact go out the door to pay public shareholders, and one would expect the market value of the company to drop, all other things being equal. There would be no dilution in voting power, although clearly employees would now control 10 percent of the company. How they exercise this power could affect different sets of shareholders, for example, in a hostile takeover.

Ownership replacement can also be accomplished by implementing an ESOP with newly issued shares and a related-share repurchase. In this case, Company X borrows funds and relends them to an ESOP that purchases newly issued shares. The company uses the proceeds from the transaction to repurchase an equivalent amount of stock on the open market. The net result is that the company continues to have the same number of shares outstanding. The impact of this transaction is identical to the one just described in an ESOP purchase of common stock.

If, however, the ESOP uses convertible preferred stock, it is possible to further reduce the dilution from this transaction, since convertible preferred shares typically convert into a smaller number of common shares because they offer employees fixed dividends but less capital appreciation. By converting into a smaller amount of common, this transaction minimizes dilution in earnings per share, as there are fewer common shares outstanding dividing the earnings. Convertible preferred securities were also adopted by companies such as Mobil Oil Corp. because they were viewed as less risky for employees. Firms even guaranteed a floor price for the stock. Before 1990, when accounting rules changed, the convertible preferred shares were not treated as their common-stock equivalent for accounting purposes when computing the earnings per share of the company. Since convertible preferred shares were not treated as outstanding, such transactions could actually result in an earnings-per-share increase. Although the Emerging Issues Task Force of the accounting profession has changed this feature for ESOPs after 1990, convertible preferred shares still have the first advantage in helping to offset dilution.

Selling Newly Issued Shares to an ESOP.   When newly issued shares are sold to an ESOP, the same Company X borrows funds and relends them to the ESOP, which purchases newly issued shares of common stock. The result is that the company now has more shares of stock. It has additional capital and a liability to the lender for the same amount.

Earnings per share are diluted because now earnings must be distributed over more shares. Add to this the additional dilution in earnings themselves, as shown in the preceding section on ownership-replacement ESOPs. But this operating expense may be reduced by ESOP tax incentives. In any event the transaction has reduced company earnings. If the establishment of the ESOP is not offset by some other reduction in employee compensation, then indeed the compensation expenses for employees are being increased and this dilution will not go away.

What will happen to the share price of the company or the market value per share? In reality we do not know because the market is unpredictable, but without anything else changing in a perfect market, we would expect a decline in share price because the company now has more new shares and may not have created added value. Think of the problem in the following way. Market equity is a claim on the company's assets after other claims—such as those of bond-holders, workers, and suppliers—are paid off. The value of a share of stock is related to what a shareholder thinks would be left over after all these other claims were paid. Anything that would cause shareholders to think that there would be fewer assets after other claims are paid would likely trigger a share-price decline. In brief, there are now more shares, and each share has a claim to the value of the company. But nothing has been done financially to increase the value of the company, and since more new shares have been created, the value per share could therefore be expected to go down. This decline in value would come from added compensation expenses and added interest expenses attributable to the ESOP. To the extent that the ESOP represents a new compensation expense for the company, beyond what workers would normally be expected to receive, it would mark a drop in value, because shareholders may view it as a frivolous compensation expense. Given the ESOP tax advantages, most companies should be able to earn enough on this new capital to defray the interests costs, less the tax savings. For the company to add value as a result of this transaction, it would have to project or actually prove that it employed the new capital to make more money than it cost in interest and compensation expenses for the ESOP, less tax savings.

Moreover, there is clearly dilution in voting power: the ESOP now owns shares while a shareholder who previously owned 30 percent of the company now finds that he or she controls less of the company. This dilution may be worrisome to investors in hostile takeovers or in proxy fights or to shareholders who have acquired a certain amount of voting power for a specific reason.

If this ESOP uses convertible preferred stock, it may be possible to reduce the dilution as previously noted. Again, it is important to recognize that this was partly the result of an accounting mechanism. The impact of market value per share, or stock price, cannot be firmly predicted; however, the general principle just established still holds that increasing employee compensation expenses through an ESOP will dilute existing shareholders, regardless of the technical structure of the stock that the ESOP buys.

The Bottom Line

In general, dilution in earnings per share is likely, and dilution in market value per share is probable—all things being equal—whenever a public corporation implements an Employee Stock Ownership Plan. The major exception is that earnings-per-share dilution did not occur in a transaction used by many public corporations in 1988–90, where the ESOP purchased convertible preferred stock.

Nevertheless, this general conclusion does not mean that all forms of employee ownership cause dilution in public companies. For example, if employees as individuals purchase stock with cash, or their employee benefit plans purchase company stock with cash, the cash purchase clearly will not dilute earnings per share, since no new shares are being offered or retired: one shareholder is simply being exchanged for another shareholder. Such transactions are not likely to cause a dilution in market value per share or a decline in stock price, although this cannot be said with certainty. One possibility is that employees and/or employee benefit plans could purchase enough stock to become a factor in a hostile tender offer or a proxy battle, where expectations about how these shares may be voted would affect the stock price of the company.

Is Offsetting Dilution Possible?

The reality of dilution must be embraced, not hidden from view, so that the facts of employee ownership for public companies can be confronted. But dilution is still not a foregone conclusion. *Employee-ownership transactions can be structured and coordinated with other corporate actions with potential positive financial or other benefits to companies, which can offset some or all of these forms of dilution.* Public corporations can look to four possible actions to offset the types of dilution just discussed. Whether a particular employee-ownership program in a specific company causes dilution overall will depend on carefully evaluating these issues, checking computations, and, in the case of dilution in market value per share (share price), simply observing and trying to understand how the share price of the company behaved after it adopted the employee-ownership plan.

Tax Savings.   First, ESOPs have various tax advantages that can help reduce the company's tax bill. Earnings in a corporation are the sums left over from its sales revenues minus its operating expenses, depreciation, interest, and taxes. If taxes are reduced, then the company's earnings are increased and can help offset earnings-per-share dilution. As a rule of thumb, however, these tax advantages alone would not meaningfully offset dilution. The reason is that all ESOP tax incentives are deductions from corporate income on which taxes are then paid, not tax credits. In other words, companies may deduct only *a portion* of the monies used to fund an ESOP. Typically, these tax savings would not exceed 30 to 40 percent of the cost of an ESOP. While the *entire amount* is deducted from corporate income before taxes are paid, only a portion of the amount is actually saved because of the tax incentive.

Restructuring Wages and Benefits.   Second, corporations can offset the cost of employee ownership primarily by considering the corporate expenses for the employee ownership as reasonable and justified deferred compensation to employees for services rendered. Initially, a company can evaluate its wage and benefit package vis-à-vis comparable companies and discern whether increases make sense, given its needs to remain competitive with other companies and to motivate and retain employees. Indeed, some companies *are* paying under market wages and benefits for a variety of reasons. A corporation can decide to pay employees more than market wages as part of a program to alter significantly employee incentives and corporate culture in a way designed to increase productivity and/or profitability or to attain other corporate goals beneficial to shareholders. This strategy is feasible in ESOPs that represent a substantial proportion of the workers' pay and with workers informed enough to see a link between their activities and the success of the entire firm. Clearly, these conditions will be hard to attain and maintain in most firms.

The company may restructure its wages and benefits by replacing these with employee-held stock. Since the stock is a form of deferred compensation, it will have the effect of increasing the cash flow of the company. In addition, a company may actually reduce its wage and/or benefit expenses by providing workers with less stock than the cost of the benefits it replaces. For example, a corporation may replace an expensive defined-benefit pension plan, whose cost to the company is unpredictable, with an ESOP that has a lower yet fixed-upfront cost to the company. Sometimes, as when companies combine funds, their 401(k) matches with ESOP stock, they can actually reduce their benefit bill yet increase benefits because of the tax savings. Either way, the company can argue that wage and benefit cuts or replacements "paid for" the employee-ownership program. Since these costs are part of operating expenses, they reduced the impact of the ESOP on earnings and therefore reduced the earnings-per-share dilution. Investors may respond more positively to an employee-ownership program that employees essentially "bought" with restructured compensation, and this response may be reflected in the market price of the stock. A number of public companies go out of their way to announce wage and benefit restructuring actions when implementing employee ownership. Because of the clear impact of wage and benefit restructuring on the company's operating expenses, this represents an explicit and potentially powerful way to address the issue of dilution.

Promoting Employee Involvement.   Third, a company can argue that increased productivity and/or profitability might result from employee ownership. In this case, a corporation will claim that reorganizing the company and/or implementing employee involvement has allowed them either to decrease operating expenses and thus increase earnings and/or to increase revenue without increasing labor compensation or both. Some companies claim that merely adopting employee ownership will lead to increased value, but they base their claims on flimsy reasoning. In the book, *Employee Ownership: Revolution or Ripoff?*, Blasi conclusively reviews the evidence that improvements in economic performance from employee ownership will probably not be automatic without practical employee involvement in specific problem-solving activities to improve company operations that impact productivity and profitability. However, companies can get one-time improvements in productivity or profitability by making explicit cuts in the workforce or levels of management or by reorganizing the company, so that the same, or more, sales are produced by fewer persons. Some companies, such as Polaroid, have argued that they adopted reorganization as a way of paying for employee ownership. To the extent that any of these improvements cut operating expenses, or have a realistic possibility of doing so, they may increase earnings and reduce earnings-per-share dilution. Such increased earnings can directly offset the interest expenses and the compensation expenses that pay for employee ownership.

Share Repurchases.   Fourth, a corporation may decide to coordinate the sale of newly issued shares to an ESOP with an additional transaction, whereby they use the capital that the ESOP loan brings into the company to repurchase an equivalent number of shares on the open market. As we have noted, the share repurchase could help reduce dilution in earnings per share because it would keep the number of outstanding shares the same. But some corporations suggest that a share repurchase addresses a large part of the dilution problem. That is false. The crucial cause of dilution is still that employees may be getting added compensation for which they are not paying. Whether a corporation coordinates an ESOP transaction with buying back its own shares does not affect this dilution. Sure, this share repurchase eliminates the dilution in voting power, since investors who have not sold their shares generally own the same amount of the company before and *after* the employee-ownership transaction.

Who Pays for Employee Ownership?

The fundamental conclusion of this corporate finance analysis is that someone must pay for the employee ownership provided to employees through leveraged ESOPs or value is being stripped from public shareholders. Finally, the "cost" of employee ownership not borne by these "payments" is borne by shareholders themselves, and a legal issue can be raised as to whether the employee ownership is a gift to employees. On the other hand, if employees really *are* paying for their employee ownership out of compensation and tax incentives granted to them and the corporation by the federal government, it is wrong and misleading for corporations—as many do—to suggest that they are "giving stock to employees." In fact, employees are paying for their stock. If they are paying for their stock, they deserve the strongest possible voting rights and at least an opportunity to discuss board representation proportional to their ownership stake.

In the following pages, the reader will hear of hundreds of employee-ownership transactions in public companies. We have not computed who paid for employee ownership in each company, but we suggest that many public corporations seem to ignore the problem of dilution and consciously or unconsciously engage in behaviors or make announcements that cloud the issue.

Corporate Finance Uses

From an article, "United Postal Going Public," written by Joe Dwyer III in the *St. Louis Business Journal,* January 28, 1990, Donald Davis of Bank of America, makes the following observations:

> Leveraged ESOPs for public companies have been driven by economics, ac-
> counting, takeover defense concerns, and overall employee benefit issues. In most
> of these, a critical factor has been the ability to deduct dividends on ESOP shares.
> Because this provision was left intact, after 1989 Congressional changes in ESOP
> laws, these deals have continued in volume since the change in the law.

The corporate finance uses of employee ownership include buying back stock, cashing out large shareholders, issuing new shares, going private and going public, including public start-ups, spinning off units, recapitalizations, and other types of restructurings. Employee Stock Ownership Plans (ESOPs) serve as the primary vehicle for most of the transactions that will be discussed although we will refer to other kinds of employee stock ownership formats.

Employee-Ownership Buybacks

A widespread use of employee ownership by public companies is for share re-purchases, or stock buybacks, in which a firm's employee-ownership plan buys back its company's shares from the public market, thereby replacing public-shareholder ownership with employee-shareholder ownership. In an employee-ownership share repurchase, a company's ESOP or employee benefit plan typ-ically purchases the shares of other stockholders and thus converts public-shareholder ownership into employee ownership. Companies usually borrow money for the company-sponsored ESOP to repurchase these shares.

Figure 1.1 summarizes the evidence of ESOP stock buybacks from 1980 to 1990. While this and other charts of ESOP growth show a falling off in

FIGURE 1.1 *Employee-Ownership Buybacks and Takeover Environment*

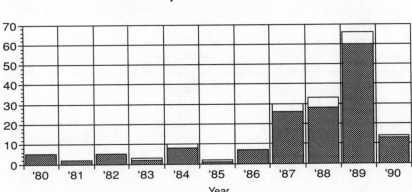

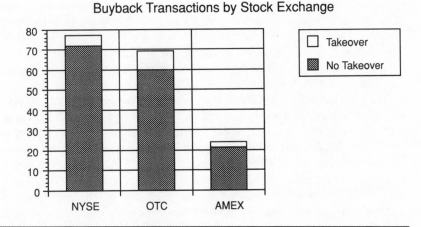

Source: Public Company Employee Ownership Database, 1990. Chart by Lawrence R. Greenberg

1990, the reader should be aware that 1989 was a year of unusual growth and that our charts include only transactions from the first half of 1990. Most of these transactions involve a significant amount of the company's stock, that is, over 5 percent. Appendix B.1 lists the transactions. What are the major trends?

Employee-ownership stock buybacks have grown steadily since 1980 and have appeared mainly in New York Stock Exchange and Over-the-Counter corporations. Several factors explain why corporations are converting their public shareholdings into employee shareholdings in this way. As the takeover threats of the late eighties created crises in many corporations, some companies, who determined they viewed their employees as "friendly" investors, were, perhaps, predisposed to consider employee-ownership stock buybacks. Company benefit plans contribute to the cash flow of the corporation by investing in company stock, so this can be viewed as a way to make the funding of benefits less taxing on corporate monies. Also, hundreds of companies decided to buy their own shares after share prices plunged in the 1987 crash. And tax incentives certainly played a part. But despite the takeover-eighties impact on these trends, we have discovered little relationship between employee-ownership stock buybacks and an announced takeover environment for that company, no matter the company's Stock Exchange listing.[6] One might think that the exception would be 1989, when public companies were feverishly setting up ESOP buybacks and replacing public shareholders with employee-shareholders. (We will call this *ownership replacement* throughout the book.) But even in that year, 90 percent of the companies that established ESOP buybacks were *not* in an announced takeover environment.

The growth of leveraged-ESOP stock buybacks reflects tax law changes. In 1984, Congress passed two tax incentives, which allowed banks to deduct 50 percent of their interest income on loans to ESOPs and pass along the savings to corporations as lower interest rates permitted corporations to deduct from corporate income dividends paid directly to workers on the employee-owned stock. Buybacks escalated after these laws were passed and almost tripled after 1986, when Congress allowed corporations to deduct dividends from corporate income paid on employee-held stock—even when they were used to repay the loan financing the stock rather than being paid directly to workers.

The eighties saw an explosion of varied corporate buybacks to establish employee ownership. In 1986, Honeywell Inc. (NYSE) repurchased 5 million of its 45.5 million shares for its ESOP and adopted a series of antitakeover measures. But Central Bancshares of the South Inc. (OTC) opted out of the Delaware "antitakeover law" in 1990 and announced an array of stock repurchases for its employee benefit plans, amounting to sizable employee holdings. The Farr Co. announced an ESOP buyback, which would operate in conjunction with two profit-sharing plans to establish employee ownership.

Sometimes large transactions take place without any immediate takeover threat. Ameritech (NYSE) did a $700 million open-market repurchase of over

4 percent of its stock in 1990. Many companies make a habit out of regular employee-ownership repurchases. Butler Manufacturing Co. (OTC) undertook two repurchases in 1985 and one each for the years 1987, 1988, and 1989. Its president, announcing in his annual report to shareholders said:

> The cornerstone of our programs to build better career-oriented employee commitment is our ESOP, which was established for all salaried and non-union hourly employees in 1983. Surplus pension funds have now all been transferred to the ESOP, and the value of that Plan for the future will depend entirely on the level of corporate earnings that will support ESOP contributions and dividends, and on the market value of Butler stock.

Financial services companies, as we saw in the last chapter, are intensely active. Frequently, these transactions place a tenth of the stock in employee's hands overnight! Capitol Federal Savings and Loan Association of Colorado (OTC) managed to do this in 1988. Commfed Bancorp Inc. (AMEX) bought its shares as it acquired other thrifts. Cayuga Savings Bank (OTC) bought almost 10 percent of its common, as President Robert J. Steigerwald announced: "This action supports our goal to be a community-owned-and-operated bank. The total ownership by staff, officers and directors now exceeds 30% of the total shares outstanding. An additional 35% of Cayuga stock is held within the communities we serve."[7] A surprising number of smaller OTC banks bought back sizeable holdings of their stock for their employees: Commerce Bancorp, Indiana Federal Corp., Integra Financial Corp., Polifly Financial Corp., Peoples Federal Savings of Dekalb City, the Boston Bancorp, and Cape Cod Bank and Trust.

There is an astonishing number of employee-ownership stock buybacks in non-ESOP benefit plans that did not use leverage. We have discovered examples too numerous to list here. Many of these are company employee benefit plans that gradually repurchased stock on the open market over the years. We have tracked such announcements in the *Wall Street Journal* for the last 11 years and discovered that benefit plans typically announce purchases up to 1 to 3 percent of the corporation's stock. It is not clear how many of the Employee Ownership 1000 companies became employee held through these gradual purchases. Some corporations will adopt regular buyback strategies as a form of low-key advance preparation for a takeover environment, while others may be motivated by corporate cultural concerns. When the price of a company's stock is low, there will also be an incentive to purchase for employee plans.

One shocking finding reveals there's little evidence that companies publicly discuss the expected or actual dilution caused by ESOP stock buybacks. Companies that do ESOP stock buybacks need to detail what combination of "payment" methods they are using to offset possible dilution. We will review later the data on what has actually happened to the share prices of companies that have implemented "ownership-replacement" ESOPs.

Cashing Out Large Holders

James O. Wright, Chairman of Badger Meter Co. (AMEX) reaffirms his company's goals in a June 21, 1984 press release:

> Our principal objectives are to: establish opportunities for employees to become shareholders and experience the benefits of ownership; provide an environment of continuity in which the company's production, marketing, research and management skills can be concentrated on serving customer needs; retain control of ownership to avoid acquisitions or takeovers unfavorable to shareholders; and strengthen the company's commitment to its present headquarters location and assure continued community support from both the company and the Badger Meter Foundation.

In 1990, Rohm & Haas Co.'s ESOP (NYSE) purchased 9.5 percent of the company from the William Penn Foundation for $185 million in the largest use ever of employee ownership to cash out a major holder. Recently, the Gannett Foundation began discussing a similar transaction for its holdings of Gannett Co. (NYSE) and Salomon Brothers was hired to explore this transaction. In 1984, David Butler resigned as a senior manager of the Bell National Corporation (OTC), and an ESOP bought a large number of his shares. The Las Vegas Casino, Circus Circus Enterprises Inc. (NYSE) used an ESOP in a similar way. In 1988, Adams-Russell Electronics (AMEX) purchased almost a million shares from GAMCO Investors (an affiliate of Gabelli & Co.), who agreed to refrain from purchasing more shares in the company, which regarded GAMCO's holdings as unwelcome. Mobile Telecommunications Technologies Inc. (OTC) entered into a similar arrangement with Shamrock Holdings.[8]

It is difficult for a public company to purchase a large block of its own stock without disrupting the share price on the market. As these examples illustrate, however, the firm can arrange a private transaction in which a leveraged employee-ownership plan buys the shares of a core shareholder who is a founder or a member of a founding family, a senior manager or director, a raider, another corporation, or a nonprofit foundation. It is also possible for the investment manager of the company's employee benefit plans to use plan assets to buy out such a holder, although there are few public announcements of this type of transaction.[9]

The employee-ownership option has been used in a variety of special scenarios. In 1987, the ESOP of a subsidiary of Frozen Food Express Industries Inc. (NYSE) bought out an institutional investor. The Comptroller of New York State's pension plans, Edward V. Regan, is one of 29 men who controls the major national public pension funds in the United States. Because these holdings are so extensive, he believes that most institutional investors are loathe to sell huge blocks and have thus become patient investors. But if such holders are searching for a way out, the Frozen Food Express model may point the way toward many future transactions.[10]

Such transactions have been controversial. In 1989, the *OTC Review* criticized the lavish lifestyle of the CEO of The Flight International Group, including his selling of 100,000 shares of his stock to the company's ESOP for the year's high of $14.25 when the company was strapped for cash. Subsequently, an announcement that the company's financial statements contained errors and the company was having trouble maintaining liquidity, led to a broad inquiry into the manager's actions. But there have also been deft solutions. In late 1988, Continental Bank Corp. (formerly Continental Illinois Corp. [NYSE]) had begun to recover from its near demise and federal bailout. An ESOP was established to purchase 1.3 million shares that were offered by the U.S. Federal Deposit Insurance Corporation in an initial public offering.

Figure 1.2 summarizes how this has developed as a regular corporate transaction, which occurs among companies on all stock exchanges. OTC companies have a definite interest in this type of transaction, probably because it is used as a method to cash out family founders or core investors that helped raise equity to start the firm. The threat of a takeover explains only 9.5 percent of these transactions and is not the major reason why such ESOP transactions took place. A complete list of all companies that cashed out large holders with employee-ownership plans is found in Appendix C.1.

Despite the obvious advantages to the shareholders who wish to be cashed out, we again found little evidence that companies confronted the problem of dilution. In smaller OTC companies, there actually may be a conflict of interest, because the senior officer, family member, or core shareholder who actually benefits from the cashing-out transaction, may have considerable influence over the board of directors, which makes the decision. All the more reason, the methods of offsetting dilution should be clearly confronted and explicitly explained. So far, no one has studied the actual performance of the share prices of companies after employee-ownership cashing-out transactions.

Issuing New Shares to Employees

In the *Wall Street Journal,* May 3, 1989, Boise Cascade said the ESOP will "directly increase shareholder value by reducing the company's cost of providing certain employee benefits." The company said it expects the ESOP to have over time "a significantly positive effect" on after-tax cash flow, a "modestly positive effect" on diluted per-share earnings, and cause very little change in its debt-coverage ratios. It is interesting to note as well the President of Northern Trust Inc.'s letter in a December 1989 SEC filing:

> For many years Northern [Trust Inc.] people had the opportunity to acquire NT common shares through a Thrift Incentive Plan (TIP) and a high percentage of our employees own Northern shares through this savings plan. Since there is a practical limit to how many Northern shares can be held in the TIP, we established the ESOP, which provides Northern people with the incentive and continued opportunity to acquire Northern shares and provide the corporation with certain tax advantages.

FIGURE 1.2   *Cash-outs of Large Shareholders by Employee Ownership*

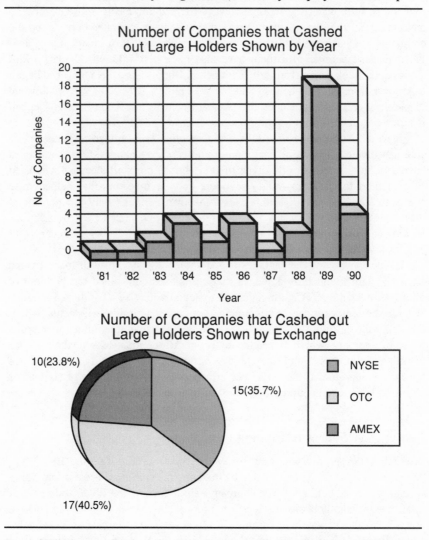

Number of Companies that Cashed
out Large Holders Shown by Year

Number of Companies that Cashed out
Large Holders Shown by Exchange

Source: Public Company Employee Ownership Database, 1990. Chart by Lawrence R. Greenberg

Many public companies establish employee ownership by selling newly issued shares to their employees. Because this type of transaction has been so
prevalent in, and central to, establishing employee ownership in public companies, we shall take a very close look at it. Typically, the corporation establishes
a leveraged Employee Stock Ownership Plan (LESOP) and borrows the capital

from a lending source to purchase either common or convertible preferred shares. This transaction results in an immediate formation of a large block of employee ownership in the corporation. Unlike the use of an ESOP or other benefit plan to buy back stock in the open market, a company can typically sell a huge block of newly issued shares to an ESOP in one single quick transaction—no trifling matter in a takeover environment, when a public company may wish to transfer a substantial number of shares to employees' hands.

As the Boise Cascade and Northern Trust quotes illustrate, corporations want to persuade shareholders to believe that these transactions are good for the corporation and its shareholders as a whole *and* good for employee relations, incentives, and corporate culture.

The Growth of Employee Ownership Using Newly Issued Shares. The sale of newly issued shares to employees has undergone dramatic growth in the last decade. Let's examine the key trends and discern how sensitive corporations have been to the issue of dilution. Appendix D.1 provides a complete list of companies based on these criteria: their use of common or preferred stock, their participation in a coordinated share repurchase or wage and benefit restructuring, and their status in a takeover environment. (The broader implications of dilution for takeovers will be dealt with in Chapter 3.)

Figure 1.3 indicates that the use of newly issued shares with employee ownership has been growing steadily since the early eighties, mainly in NYSE and OTC companies, both in number of transactions and dollar value. Common stock has been dominant until 1989, which suggests that companies may not have been adequately confronting the problem of dilution in earnings per share before then. The predominance of preferred stock in NYSE companies points to the increased usage of the convertible preferred shares to offset dilution, which became a model for such transactions after 1988. When looked at as a group, a firm's involvement in an announced takeover environment is clearly not the main determinant of newly issued shares in transactions of this type. The number of transactions, dollar value of transactions, and instances where the firms were in a takeover environment—all grew enormously in 1989. This is probably due to three factors: first, many companies, wrongly fearing that ESOP tax incentives might be cut back, implemented plans before such an anticipated event; second, corporations, observing the growing number of ESOPs, began to feel more comfortable with the idea and to copy each other; and third, this year marked the turning point in the "takeover era" of the eighties, and some firms may have been influenced by takeover threats to encourage employee holdings.

With this background, let's continue to sort out exactly what public companies did and some trends in how they confronted the tough problem of dilution. Every company could argue that ESOP tax advantages helped increase company earnings and reduce dilution, but because this would not generally eliminate the problem of dilution, the important question is which companies coordinated

FIGURE 1.3 *Selling Newly Issued Shares to Employee-Holders*

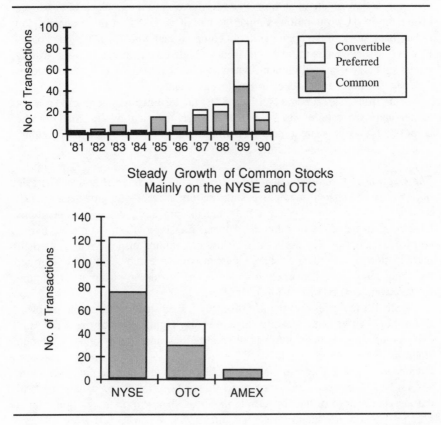

Steady Growth of Common Stocks
Mainly on the NYSE and OTC

(continued)

their employee-ownership plans with announcements of share repurchases to counteract dilution in earnings per share and wage and benefit restructuring and employee involvement programs or reorganizations to improve economic performance to help pay for the employee-ownership plans.

Our study shows that during the decade, 1980 through 1990, almost 75 percent of companies using newly issued common shares and almost 50 percent of companies using newly issued convertible preferred shares did not announce that they coordinated the employee-ownership plan with a share repurchase. These numbers suggest that considerable dilution in earnings per share may have occurred. This same group of firms are the ones that used the ESOP for new capital formation rather than ownership replacement. This was the original purpose for which ESOP inventor Louis Kelso intended the ESOP. Thus, it would follow that about 25 percent of the company transactions were using common shares and about 50 percent of the companies were using convertible

FIGURE 1.3 *(Continued)*

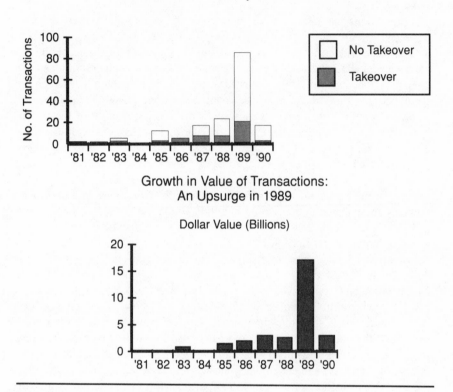

Takeovers not a Key Factor in General

Growth in Value of Transactions:
An Upsurge in 1989

Dollar Value (Billions)

Source: Public Company Employee Ownership Database, 1990. Chart by Lawrence R. Greenberg

preferred shares. In the end, these ESOPs were used for ownership replacement. While "newly issued shares" were purchased, the net effect of combining this issue with a share repurchase was the same as if an ESOP-stock buyback were completed.

A look at Figure 1.3 shows how the use of convertible preferred shares versus common shares was distributed by stock exchange. The larger New York Stock Exchange companies tended to use convertible preferred shares more than firms in other stock exchanges—a fact that suggests dilution received less attention in the AMEX and OTC markets than in the NYSE. We found that share repurchases to counteract dilution in earnings per share did not really become prominent until 1988, although some companies used share repurchases in the early eighties. In Chapter 3, Takeovers, we will argue that the threat of shareholder lawsuits increased company awareness on this issue. NYSE companies were clearly in the forefront on establishing ESOPs in 1989, and they used share repurchases to attempt to address earnings-per-share dilution during this boom period for ESOPs. But, remember, earnings-per-share dilution is not the entire dilution story.

Corporations that use both common stock and convertible preferred ignore wage and benefit restructuring more than they use it. Over 60 percent of public companies adopting newly issued shares ESOPs have made no public announcements about the ways they're managing the added compensation expense of employee ownership. These companies may simply be hoping that shareholders mistakenly think that ESOP tax savings, share repurchases, and presumed automatic productivity increases as a result of "owning a piece of the action" will wipe out the dilution. Because of the startling neglect of this issue in the public record, we suspect that many of these companies have simply ignored the issue, because it is better left undiscussed and unanalyzed.

Orchestrating Financial, Strategic, and Benefits Objectives in one ESOP.
Probably the pioneering transaction in public companies—the J.C. Penney Inc. ESOP, announced in August 1988—was among the first to illustrate clearly to public corporations that they could integrate financial, strategic, and benefits objectives in the same transaction. The investment bank of First Boston designed an ESOP that bought a new issue of convertible preferred stock (corporate finance objective), yet included a large buyback while putting a hefty 24 percent in employee hands (strategic objective), and replaced existing contributions to profit sharing and savings plans with employee stock ownership (benefits objective). This final action ensured that employees paid for the employee ownership out of existing compensation arrangements. This one innovation led to many similar plans in the three years that followed and is largely responsible for the growth of the convertible preferred employee-ownership option shown in the preceding graphs. The restructuring of the wages and benefits was a crucial part of the formula for offsetting dilution. Indeed, the most cautious companies during this period would use convertible preferred, set in motion a share repurchase of common, and restructure wages and benefits.

Large and small companies adopted the J.C. Penney approach. In 1989, A. P. Green Industries (OTC) sold 268,456 newly issued shares or 9.2 percent of its common stock to its ESOP and announced it would initiate a buyback of 300,000 shares. One common approach is called a *treasury stock transfer,* in which the company initiates a stock buyback and retires outstanding stock, but then turns around and issues new shares to the ESOP. Colgate Palmolive Co. (NYSE) increased its employee ownership from 5 percent to 11 percent in a similar transaction. CEO Reuben Mark reported in the *Wall Street Journal,* June 18, 1989, that "shareholders will benefit over the long term from the strengthened linkage between employee and shareholder interests, as well as improved cash flow that emanates from the transaction."

The Barry Wright Corporation (NYSE) issued new shares to an ESOP in the context of an extensive reorganization. In 1988, the company sold its Wright Line trucking business and combined the proceeds with funds from a new leveraged ESOP to make a special cash distribution to shareholders. Its public recapitalization and restructuring led to reduced holding in the company for non-management holders and an increased holding of 39 percent for management, directors, and employees through the ESOP, which bought newly issued shares on several occasions. Later, the company restructured compensation by terminating its defined-benefit pension plan and both reduced its debt from its loans to its ESOP and its cash distributions with the proceeds of this termination and used some excess assets to buy more stock for employees. These moves clearly were designed to address the issue of shareholder neutrality. In November 1988, a state court lawsuit charged that the ESOP was an unlawful gift and a waste of corporate assets, but the company survived this suit. Harcourt Brace Jovanovich Inc.'s (NYSE) similar transaction led to a bitter war and lawsuit with British raider Robert Maxwell, resulting in a Pyrrhic victory for the company, which was saddled with debt.

It is not easy to generalize about these situations. Travelers Corp. (NYSE) saw its newly issued ESOP preferred stock as an economical way of raising capital to finance insurance operations while Turner Corp. used the proceeds of its new issue 20-percent ESOP to refinance real estate debt. Champion Parts Rebuilders Inc. (OTC) ESOP, which borrowed $3.6 million at a fixed interest rate of 8.5 percent in 1988 to purchase 400,000 newly issued common shares, used the proceeds to retire its 13.25 percent subordinated debentures at a discount from face value. The company used funds that it would normally direct to its profit-sharing plan to repay the ESOP loan. There were differing views. On one hand, management announced in the *Wall Street Journal,* June 22, 1989, that "this is projected to save the company a significant amount of cash . . . because the contributions to the leveraged ESOP will be less than the sum the company had projected to contribute to the profit-sharing plan and pay interest on the bonds that were retired." But General Refractories, which was making an unsolicited proposal to buy the company, said the plan diluted all shareholders!

Dahlberg Inc. (OTC) reported that its sale of 250,000 newly issued shares to its ESOP was its principal source of working capital in 1988, and Freedom Savings and Loan Association (OTC) simply cut its ESOP in on a sale of new capital to investors. On the other hand, Exxon's 1990 sale of $1 billion of convertible preferred stock to its ESOP, while only equal to about 1.4 percent of equity, was a transaction that got barely any press attention. A number of investment bankers have said that as a rule of thumb a company can institute a 2-percent ESOP and not risk much dilution in earnings per share. Lowe's Companies (NYSE), the operator of hardware stores and lumber yards, reflects the approach of Merrill Lynch featured at the beginning of this chapter, and probably indicates the direction in which many firms are heading. Since 1981, this company has used both employee-ownership stock buybacks and new issues of stock to its ESOP and replaced defined benefits with employee stock benefits to regularly update and change its structure. It may well be the public corporation with the longest running continuous list of employee-ownership transactions. [11]

Companies are using either newly issued common or newly issued convertible preferred shares. Selecting which one to use depends mainly on how a corporation wishes to structure the ESOP financing and what kind of stock will be more appealing to employees. Some common stocks declare no dividend or the dividend fluctuates considerably. A public company can issue as much common stock as is authorized by its shareholders, up to certain limits. [12] Companies that use the dividends on the common stock to repay the ESOP loan will find that unpredictable or possibly low dividends make planning its repayment more complicated. From the employee's point of view, the price of a share of common stock is crystal clear: it is in the newspaper every day. But it is also risky, since the share price and the dividends can suddenly go up or down.

Newly issued convertible preferred stock used in an ESOP is a stock whose value is not usually listed on the Stock Exchange. But it can be converted to common stock. As a "preferred" stock, employee-holders would get preference in receiving the assets of the company in the event of bankruptcy. Paul Mazzilli of Morgan Stanley & Co. points out four key aspects of a preferred stock: first, its dividend rate, typically a lower dividend than common stock because the security is less risky; second, the conversion ratio, expressing the number of underlying shares of common into which it converts. Convertible preferred shares will usually convert into fewer common shares; third, it may have a special feature called a *par put,* which simply means that a share of preferred always has a minimum floor value beyond which it cannot sink; and fourth, the preferred has the same voting power as the underlying common. From an employee's point of view, this type of convertible preferred stock is designed to reduce market risk and to be easy for employees to understand. Simply stated, the employee-ownership convertible preferred is always equal to one share of common stock, but it has a minimum guaranteed floor value and offers employees a set dividend and an opportunity to share in the equity upside while controlling downside risk. [13]

Remember that we have examined mainly the issuance of new shares to ESOPs because these are typically material transactions over 2 percent that merit a public announcement. We expect that many public companies on the Employee Ownership 1000 list have sold or given newly issued shares to their employee benefit plans or ESOPs in small or large numbers under 2 percent without public announcements. The primary reason we say this is that insufficient public announcements explain what is behind the enormous amount of employee ownership in the Employee Ownership 1000, other than knowing the type of employee-ownership plan and the percentage of employee ownership. We have information on less than half of these companies. [14] There is little stopping a company from accumulating considerable worker stake by doing this year after year.

Going Private and Going Public

Employee ownership surfaces as a way for public companies to go private and as a way for private companies or entrepreneurs with new business ideas to seek financing in the public market and involve the company's employees at the same time. Sometimes, as the Weirton Steel example at the beginning of this chapter illustrates, privately owned firms with employee ownership go public to enable workers to sell their shares more easily when they retire or leave the firm. While the stories vary, in general, employee ownership has become an option for corporations that must transform their structure in order to adapt to change. This need to adapt supports our emerging conclusion that the corporate finance uses of employee ownership cannot be explained only by takeover threats but are part of a more fundamental change in employee participation in American companies. Takeover environments explain about 40 percent of companies' going private with ESOPs.

When a public company goes private using an ESOP, usually the employees and a small group of management and/or outside investors borrow money to purchase all of the firm's stock from public shareholders. Appendix E.1 reviews all announced transactions. In the early eighties at the height of the takeover boom when large amounts of debt could be easily and quickly raised through junk bonds, some companies saw "going private" as their last-ditch effort to remain independent of a looming raider. Frequently, management did not have enough equity to purchase the company themselves. Thus, employees became possible partners. The story of taking companies private through employee ownership plays an important part in the development of employee ownership, because it was the first time that large public companies demonstrated that a sale to employees could take place smoothly and efficiently.

Among the first companies to move in this direction were the National Spinning Co. of New York and the Pamida Company (formerly NYSE) of Nebraska. National Spinning went private and became owned by the Leff family and a salaried employees' ESOP. Pamida operates 196 discount centers in the Midwest and had some employee ownership as a public company. In 1981, shareholders approved a proposal to sell its assets to a new corporation, majority owned by an ESOP.

In 1982, the investment banking firm, Kelso & Company, put together a unique transaction to take the engineering consulting firm, Raymond International (formerly NYSE) private, using an ESOP. The company became majority employee held but raised controversy: the employees were sold one class of shares at a much higher price than were a group of managers, and another class of shares were bought by a Kelso affiliate, so that employees ended up paying more for a proportionally smaller segment of the company while getting reduced voting rights on their stock and a lower level of return than did managers and investors. This type of transaction is known as a *multi-investor buyout*: investment bankers and managers simply decide that a permanent price differential and significant power differences between their shares and those of employees should prevail. In Raymond, this differential was not abandoned, even though $41 million of accrued assets from employee benefit plans was used in the transaction while managers put up little money of their own.[15]

The taking private of Wranglers' maker Blue Bell Inc. (formerly NYSE), engineering consulting firm Parsons Inc. (formerly NYSE), sugar processor U.S. Sugar (formerly NYSE) were similar, while the issue, the workers' return on investments equity versus that of managers and investors, played a crucial role in the ESOP privatization of Amsted Industries Inc. (formerly NYSE), Dan River Textiles (formerly NYSE), Northwestern Steel & Wire (formerly NYSE), Lyons Metal Products (formerly NYSE), and Kroy Inc. Under Labor Department pressure, the equity distribution between the workers and investor-manager groups at Amsted was later refigured in favor of the employees. In 1984, another Kelso & Co. proposal to take *Encyclopedia Brittanica* and Kirby vacuum cleaner manufacturer Scott & Fetzer Inc. (formerly NYSE) private fell apart because of delays and disagreements over these issues. These companies were facing hostile takeovers by the who's who of senior and junior investors of the eighties: Ivan Boesky, Carl Icahn, the Bass Brothers, Irwin Jacobs, Charles Hurwitz, and Bennett LeBow. Another type of transaction likely to be repeated was the management–Kelso & Company buyout of American Standard Inc. (formerly NYSE) in 1988. Black & Decker mounted a fierce attempt to take over the company. Management terminated the company's pension plans and used excess assets to fund a $50-million nonleveraged ESOP, which participated in the transaction and acquired 20 percent of the company.

But takeovers were not the only given reason. It will likely become more common that public companies with small- or medium-sized ESOPs will find themselves becoming more employee held through this route. In 1988, Arthur D. Little Inc. (formerly NYSE) went private when an ESOP acquired the 30 percent of the firm not already owned by employees. Security American Financial Enterprises was 12 percent employee held when the trustees of the ESOP took the company private in 1989 by bringing its holdings up to 50 percent while inviting some existing shareholders to continue ownership in the private company.

Another unique situation was in 1988, when S. David Norris, the Chairman and CEO of Commonwealth Savings Association (formerly OTC), said the company would become the subsidiary of a new holding company owned by an ESOP and management in order to recognize its market value and glean a positive net worth by taking advantage of an accounting rule that allows buyers to value assets and liabilities of newly purchased companies at their market value. While the company had a negative net worth of $172 million on March 31, 1988, it believed that this transaction would allow it to show a higher value for its Commonwealth Mortgage Company subsidiary. The bank has $1.8 billion in assets. Charter Medical Corp. (formerly NYSE) went private, partly because they were concerned over depressed stock prices. This transaction consolidated family control over the company but also raised issues with the Department of Labor. Carl Icahn, usually the loser of his takeover battles against ESOPs, took TWA (formerly NYSE) private in 1987, with the ESOP ending up owning 10 percent because of prior wage concessions. The trends are shown in Figure 1.4.

FIGURE 1.4 *Going Private with Employee Ownership*

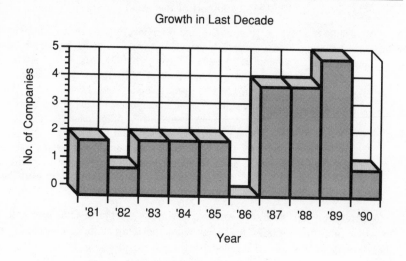

Growth in Last Decade

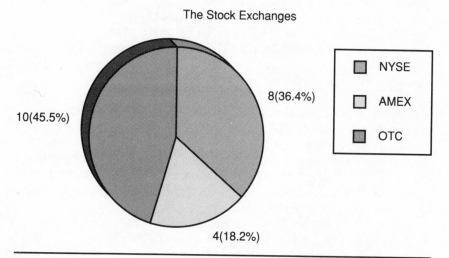

The Stock Exchanges

Source: Public Company Employee Ownership Database, 1990. Chart by Lawrence R. Greenberg

Playing out Three Scenarios.   Public offerings involving employee ownership usually play out three different scenarios, which give an employee-ownership firm a market for its stock and an opportunity to raise capital, encourage new public start-ups and participation in public offerings, or allow the conversion of mutually owned thrifts to public stock corporations. The Oregon Steel ESOP was one of the first to take a closely held ESOP public. The company was near collapse in 1984 from Pacific-rim imports. After a bitter strike the union was decertified, and the owners sold nearly all of the company to an ESOP, which used the public market as a source of capital for growth. The *Wall Street Journal,* December 12, 1988, told part of the story:

> Kohlberg Kravis Roberts & Co. and other investment bankers aren't the only ones profiting from leveraged buyouts. The game is being invaded by a new player—the working stiff. Meet Judy Lyons. In 1984, Ms. Lyons and her co-workers bought their company, Oregon Steel Mills Inc., through an employee stock ownership plan—an ESOP—financed almost entirely with debt. And last spring, the company went public, establishing a market value of nearly $400,000 for her stake. The 49-year-old employee-benefits office manager now has sold $95,000 of her stock, fixed up her kitchen, and paid for her son's senior year at college and her daughter's wedding. Fun isn't what employees usually have when their companies are taken private or taken over. Often, they are laid off or told to work harder for less pay. Meanwhile, the big guys make millions of dollars by paying back takeover debt, then going public again.

A different perspective sees workers as victims. As the LBO firms that bought up America in the eighties finish repaying the debt of these companies, it is likely that combinations of employee ownership and going public will become popular. The *American Banker,* September 13, 1987, notes, "LBO firms will sell companies in their portfolios to stock-ownership plans because that's how they will get the highest price. They may not have much of an alternative. Some investment bankers say the stock market is wary of companies that are going public again after a recent buyout. And in this age of deconglomeration, it may be hard to find a large corporation that wants to diversify."

The public offering served as a mechanism for workers to cash out a proportion of their shares, raise capital, and establish a market value for the stock. It was not bad news: the ESOP bought most of the company for $22.8 million, and its market value in 1988 stood at $138.5 million! This play is similar to what Weirton Steel implemented when it went public. As privately held employee ownership spreads throughout the economy, creating a public market for the stock will be a way for those companies to avoid the cash drain of having to repurchase the stock of departing or retiring workers. American Financial Corp. is a privately held company, but it generated a publicly traded Series E preferred stock for its ESOP, which can be used to ease the company's repurchase liability to its worker-owners.[16]

The National Center for Employee Ownership reports on the case of Copper Range Inc., in which the United Steelworkers of America engineered an employee buyout in 1985 following a two-year shutdown. The newly formed ESOP borrowed enough money to buy 70 percent of the company. In 1987, the company filed an initial public offering of about 3 million shares, hoping to use the proceeds for capital expenditures, working capital, and repayment of long-term debt. In this case, the ESOP did not tender any of its shares and planned to retain a majority interest. In 1989, however, Metall Mining Corporation of the Federal Republic of Germany acquired 100 percent of all common shares. The result: the company's stock rose in value from $9 a share to $84 a share in three years since the buyout, and the average employee sold his or her stock to Metall for $69,000. The unique structure of Oregon Metallurgical Corp. (OREMET), was developed by Steven Hester of Arnold & Porter in Washington, D.C., so that the company was kept as a public corporation. The deal was financed by the investment banking firm, Keilin and Bloom.

The establishment of new publicly traded corporations using employee ownership has been a tough project to manage. The reason for this goes back to Louis Kelso's, the father of ESOPs, initial observation: workers do not have enough liquid capital to buy a significant number of shares in corporations without access to credit markets and therefore must depend on the leveraged ESOP. Slowly, however, some corporate finance innovation is showing up in this arena. People Express Airlines was initially founded as a public company with substantial investments by the core group of employees. As the company grew, new employees were asked to buy modest amounts of stock, and employee ownership was integrated into the employees' compensation package. People Express failed because it grew too fast, was poorly managed, and had thin profits in its fare war with established airlines—not because of employee ownership, which amounted to over a third of its stock. The more successful America West Airlines (OTC, 30 percent employee held) requires all its employees to buy stock but also uses leveraged ESOPs to buy large blocks of stock for employees. American Steel & Wire (OTC) of Ohio is a company 51 percent owned by Chicago West Pullman Corp., which is scooping up rust-belt companies, hiring fewer workers, and paying them less than previous owners had paid. A recent *Wall Street Journal* story says that the company requires employee ownership, with every employee expected to buy $100 worth of the stock.

There are also examples of Employee Stock Ownership Plans participating modestly in public offerings, as was the case in 1987, with Industrial Training Systems (OTC) and Met-Coil Systems Corp. (OTC), using a leveraged ESOP. In 1987, Shearson Lehman Hutton made an initial public offering of 18 percent of its stock. It reserved 8.5 percent for executives and other employees under a program known as Camelot, where 200 executives would own a stake in the units' profits and this stake would be translated into shares in the public offering.

The employees would be buying some shares directly and receiving shares in return for giving up other benefits. Also, 1 million shares were placed in a newly created ESOP. Forum Re Group Bermuda Limited, however, ended up 30 percent employee held after closely held Forum Reinsurance of Hamilton, Bermuda, filed with the Securities and Exchange Commission to offer its entire 72 percent stake in the company in a public offering in which an ESOP also acquired 1.8 million shares. Employee ownership has also played a crucial role in the conversion of thrifts from mutual to stock corporations. The typical scenario is for the savings and loan undergoing the conversion to offer stock to officers, directors, certain depositors, and an ESOP, with any unsubscribed shares being offered publicly. This approach has been almost exclusively used by OTC banks, including Pioneer Federal Savings Bank (Lynnwood, Wash.), Regional Bancorp, Inc. (Medford, Mass.), VanFed Bancorp (Vancouver, Wash.), FMS Corp. (Burlington, N.J.), Portsmouth Bank Shares Inc. (Portsmouth, N.H.), Northbay Financial Corp. (AMEX-Calif.), New York Bancorp. (Douglaston, N.Y.) and NFS Financial Corp. (Nashua, N.H.).

Over the last decade, the announced use of ESOPs in public offerings has been spotty, with less than 35 transactions. OTC firms are predominant among the Exchanges in using ESOPs in public offerings, probably because their stock is usually thinly traded. Also an employee-ownership plan can be a faithful customer in such an offering and can help support the entire venture. But there are many reasons to believe that more and more public corporations and mutual savings banks will settle on the corporate objectives described by our examples and consider employee ownership.[17]

Spinning Off Units: The Employee Buyout

In the first quarter of 1990, leveraged buyouts totaled $117 million, down 98 percent from the first quarter of 1989.[18] This decline has been reflected in ESOPs as well, the National Center for Employee Ownership, 1990, discloses.[19] Only two ESOP LBOs over $10 million have occurred in the first six months, Textileather ($10 million) and AECOM (an estimated $50 million).

An employee buyout of a unit of a publicly traded corporation is a purchase of more than 51 percent of that unit by a broad-based group of nonmanagement and management employees, as a divestiture or spin-off of that unit. Sometimes, the employees get a smaller stake as part of a spin-off in a management buyout involving outside investors.[20] The employee buyout emerged on the American scene from 1975 to 1980, as firms in mature or highly competitive industries faced closure for various reasons: Sometimes the firm was simply losing money, and could in fact be run profitably with work-force cuts, task reorganization, and compensation cuts; sometimes it was owned by a larger firm and was profitable, but its profits were inadequate; occasionally, the owners wished to sell to employees to avoid the shutdown costs associated with an existing collective bargaining agreement; and often, the line of business simply conflicted with the strategy of the parent company or the original owner-investors. The bottom line was that corporations and investors were weeding out the companies that could not give them a competitive advantage. While the employee buyout does not create employee ownership in a publicly traded corporation, it provided the financial staffs of many such companies with their first knowledge of, and experience in, the techniques and possibilities of sizable employee ownership and prepared the way for its further applications in their companies.

Some of the first cases involved privately held businesses that were unionized, such as the buyout of Vermont Asbestos Group, but Sperry Rand Corp. (then NYSE), LTV (NYSE), Amsted Industries Inc. (then NYSE), and W. R. Grace and Company also sponsored several employee buyouts in this early period. Two of the earliest cases to achieve national prominence involving units of public corporations were the proposed buyout at Youngstown Sheet & Tube in Youngstown, Ohio in the 1970s and Rath Packing Company in Waterloo, Iowa in 1979. Youngstown was an aging steel mill in an industry rife with overcapacity, where the parent corporation used profits only to buy other businesses rather than to invest in steel-making technology. Rath, then trading on the New York Stock Exchange, dealt in pork products and had an inefficiently organized plant in an industry with increasing competitiveness and highly cyclical prices. The Youngstown buyout never materialized and Rath went into bankruptcy in 1983. A buyout established it as an employee-owned company.[21]

These early cases publicized the employee-buyout option throughout the country and proved that with proper financial planning and restructuring, units of public corporations could continue business after an employee buyout. During this period, many communities were being adversely affected by the tremendous loss of employment, tax revenue, and social stability when a core industry shut down. Congress repeatedly underscored its support of responsible employee buyouts as a private-sector alternative. By 1980, the movement to unwind the conglomerates of the sixties and seventies was in full swing, and the employee buyout became an institution. Appendix F.1 chronologically lists these cases, most of which are employee buyouts.

Large public corporations encourage employee buyouts for very different reasons. AMPCO Pittsburgh Corporation (NYSE) sold Pittsburgh Forgings to the employees in 1988, because it made a strategic decision to divest itself of metalworking businesses. National Health Corp. (AMEX) proposed the sale of eight health-care centers in order to use the proceeds to retire debt, yet it planned to hold second mortgages for the centers and continued to manage them under contract. Ogden Corp. (NYSE) spun off its Avondale Shipbuilding unit as it restructured itself into a service-oriented company in 1985. Control Data Corp. (NYSE) wanted to shed its Burke Marketing Services unit and thought that employee ownership made sense in a professional services company. Sears (NYSE) was reported to be selling its Coldwell Banker Commercial real estate unit as part of its antitakeover measures.

Employee buyouts have witnessed a rare entrepreneurial partnership between management of the parent firm and employees in attempting to structure win-win situations. LTV Corp. was eager to sell its steel bar unit as part of its Chapter 11 bankruptcy reorganization, but it was the United Steelworkers of America that energetically pursued the offer once they realized that the only likely purchasers were leveraged-buyout firms who might not be interested in running the company as an ongoing concern and in mounting the massive capital investment program that it needed. Indeed, as part of a strategy both to maximize job security and promote highly competitive operations with new capital investment, the Steelworkers' union has become the national leader in employee buyouts, such as Northwestern Steel & Wire, OREMET, Columbia Aluminum, Republic Container, Republic Storage, White Pine Copper, and Pittsburgh Forgings.[22]

Marked by diversity, the employee-buyout arena does not exclusively involve buyouts of failing companies. Hospital Corporation of America sold 100 of its 180 general hospitals to an employee-owned firm, HealthTrust in 1987. Although the parent company retained the more lucrative general and psychiatric hospitals, HealthTrust has maintained its profitability. Many buyouts involving unionized workforces actually restructure the companies by reducing the workforce, eliminating some levels of management, changing work rules and work organization, and reducing wages and benefits. Employees are asked to consider these reductions as investments, for which they receive stock in the company and greater control over their own destiny. In effect, the employee buyout is a way to restructure the firm's contractual commitments to unions, because workers are willing to give concessions to themselves if they are actually investments. Malon Wilkus, an ESOP buyout expert of American Capital Strategies who has worked with the Steelworkers, puts it this way: "Investment bankers do not simply help workers buy the company. Rather, we analyze the whole business operation and help labor and management restructure the company, buy it, and get the working capital to make it profitable." This effort accounts for the National Center for Employee Ownership's estimates that 80 percent of the buyouts that have occurred since 1974 are still in business, although some are struggling financially.[23]

Figure 1.5 shows that employee buyouts and spin-offs involving some employee ownership have definitely grown and are continuing to show aggressive growth. New York Stock Exchange companies comprise 97 percent of the affected parent companies. Our analysis indicates that the buyouts, or spin-offs, are concentrated usually in the Northeast or Midwest in mature manufacturing industries and in only a few service industries.

One reason that New York Stock Exchange companies are so disproportionately represented is that they participated more in the conglomerate phenomenon

FIGURE 1.5 *Annual Growth of Employee Buyouts*

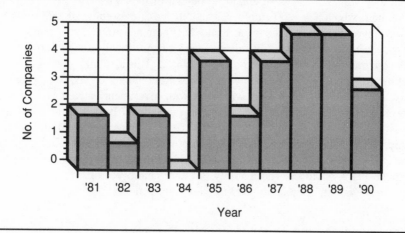

Source: Public Company Employee Ownership Database, 1990. Chart by Shane Williams and Lawrence R. Greenberg

than did AMEX and OTC companies and employee buyouts and spin-offs represent the undoing of that fiasco. A closer look at a complete list of the transactions in Appendix F.1 shows that the units are concentrated in industries that have suffered from exports, such as steel, textiles, and automobiles, or cyclical industries that rely largely on basic resources, such as pork, wood pulp, oil, and chemicals, or those that have been impacted by deregulation, such as health care and airlines.

It is likely that employee buyouts and spin-offs involving employee ownership will substantially increase. As global and national competition intensifies and as recessions strike, companies will be more inclined to prune their operations. Unit managers will recognize that rigid union contracts can be traded for employee ownership, and they will press for spin-offs, some of which involve the parent's ongoing holding in the new unit in partnership with employees. Such partnerships benefit both parties, since the parent gains stock warrants and payments for financing the employee acquisition along with a continuing interest in the business, while employees get to own a portion of a company. Unions have learned one lesson from employee buyouts: if the buyout is structured properly, it makes more financial sense to offer concessions to your own company as stock investments than to present them as a gift to an often ungrateful corporation. This will probably lead to more union rigidity in bargaining, since they may realize that an employee buyout is always lurking in the background.

Management of public corporations, who now view the track record of employee buyouts and spin-offs as generally successful, will be more likely to provide the spark by announcing as Cigna Corporation did on January 6, 1989, that they would consider an employee buyout of their Financial Services Division unit, which has 2200 employees nationwide and revenues of $800 million. Some investment bankers, such as Keilin & Bloom and American Capital Strategies, are now experienced in this area and can justifiably assure corporations that the transaction will most probably be closed. This assurance creates the possibility of forming employee-buyout groups in nonunion companies, where ad hoc associations of employees will work with investment bankers and lawyers to orchestrate transactions. The sale of Sears Coldwell Banker commercial unit was not an employee buyout but a spin-off with 40-percent employee ownership, which indicates that a nonunion employee transaction is feasible. In this case, the employees teamed up with outside investors led by former government official Frank Carlucci. The inability of either employees or investors alone to mount buyouts will probably lead to more joint action.[24]

Restructurings and Other Corporate Purposes

Employee ownership has frequently been used to restructure companies that stay public, recapitalizing them for various corporate purposes. The common thread in these cases is the company's need to accomplish a corporate objective and a decision to make employees a partner in this endeavor. The motives differ from case to case. Some of the transactions are routine, but some raise important questions about the integrity of the employee-ownership decision, which we'll examine later. All of them raise the issue of dilution. In most of these cases, there is little published evidence that shows how the corporations conceived of the relationship between the new employee-ownership plan and their current wage and benefit expenses.

In the arena of restructuring, Dune's Hotels and Casinos' ESOP gives new meaning to the notion that employee ownership can be a gamble. In 1983, the company confronted a daunting restructuring: it began converting the debts it owed to various creditors into preferred stock. In addition, it would establish an ESOP that would pay 20 percent of employees' salaries in shares of common stock for two years.

Emery Air Freight used employee ownership in a host of corporate transactions since 1987. At that time, the company decided to acquire Purolator Courier Corp. and assumed enormous debt to complete this transaction. Part of the plan to make this possible involved terminating defined-benefit pension plans and creating an ESOP retirement program, which used the excess pension assets to buy company stock and give it a cash infusion. But the company ran into trouble when it was unable to pay interest on the debt used in the acquisition. At that point, the company's ESOP more than doubled its voting stake from 12.7 percent to 26 percent. The situation became complicated by the presence of Towers Financial Corp., which reportedly was interested in a takeover. Shortly thereafter,

8.2 percent of the company's common moved on the markets in a block trade, and it was rumored that the ESOP had made this purchase. Finally, in 1989, Emery and its major air-freight competitor, Consolidated Freightways, merged to create Emery Worldwide. Consolidated purchased all of the ESOP's common and preferred stock. The Emery situation illustrates that no matter how hard we try, we cannot separate different employee-ownership scenarios. This case had many facets: an acquisition, a benefit-plan change, an employee-ownership transformation, a takeover defense, a sale, and an unclear return on employees' investment. We find it puzzling that we were unable to find a news report that analyzed the return on the employees' investment in nearly a quarter of the company!

To some extent, these stories sound as if management may be adopting the adage, "If anything goes wrong, set up an ESOP." These extreme cases, however, are the exceptions. Most of the examples are pedestrian. American Express Inc. owned all of the Fireman's Fund insurance company before 1988, which suffered as a result of an insurers' price war. In early 1988, the company bought back 15 percent of its common stock from American Express and decided to place the repurchased shares in its treasury in order to allot them equally to management and an ESOP and make the company 23 percent employee held. Kinnard Investments Inc. of Minneapolis (OTC), a brokerage firm operating 30 branches in seven states under the name John G. Kinnard & Co., sold close to $800,000 in shares to an ESOP in 1990, and 27 key employees bought 435,000 shares and warrants for $1.2 million. Several executives and members of the board resigned, and the result of these transactions is that the company's ownership was restructured, with employees now owning 75 percent.

One complex transaction corporations face is recapitalization. Firms typically reshape their capital ownership structure as a response to difficulty or threat. In 1988, Optical Coating Laboratories Inc. (OTC) approved such a plan in which the nonmanagement holders received a $13 per-share cash payment and a reduction in their equity stake from 85 percent to 60 percent of the company while management holders of the stock got 3.6 million shares and no cash. Management invited an Employee Stock Ownership Plan to participate, so that its stake would increase from 6 to 17 percent of the company. This complex reshuffling was part of a defense against a possible takeover by the Alpine Group, whose shares were ultimately bought out. Similar transactions were attempted by Entertainment Publications Inc. (AMEX) and Barry Wright Corp., Harcourt Brace Jovanovich, Kroger, and Macmillan—all NYSE companies—in 1987 and 1988. These transactions leave companies with a tremendous amount of debt, but can, if successfully managed, repel a takeover raider.

Some companies have turned to employee ownership to confront unique financial problems and seek short-term financial advantage. On October 28, 1983, Financial Corporation of America's stock price dropped 27 percent in just 14 trading days, and the stock rose only one trading day since October 6 when it had a high of $46.50. The company went through dazzling growth in the eighties, but by the mideighties problem loans were 2.5 percent of its assets and 19 percent of its 1980 loans ran into problems by 1983. The company initiated an ESOP ostensibly to support the stock price. The ESOP bought 219,500 shares for $34.25. Once the price dropped below $16 a share, the company began repurchasing it. In April 1984 its ESOP repurchased 2.3 million shares, increasing its holding to 4.3 million shares. The company's shares were buffeted in May to June of 1984 by rising interest rates and its inability to get speedy approval of a debt for equity exchange. In fact, in April one third of the trading volume for the company was in ESOP trades!

Employee ownership has also played a role in bankruptcy reorganization as employees come to the table both to reorganize their relationship to the company and to help the company deal with its obligations. When Consolidated Capital Equities Corp. (OTC) filed Chapter 11 in 1989, the company had been one of the nation's largest syndicators of real estate limited partnerships, but it was battered by changes in tax laws that made tax shelters unattractive. The reorganization plan gave general unsecured creditors 49 percent of the stock in the reorganized companies, plus the proceeds of a $3.5 million-note issued to an Employee Stock Ownership Plan, which will now own 51 percent of the new company.

Employee ownership has also played a role in internal corporate struggles. In 1983, the Sarah Getty Trust, controlled by Gordon Getty, Jr. and the Paul Getty Museum, teamed up with their 52 percent stake to force bylaw changes in the Getty Oil Company (NYSE). They planned to use a section of the Delaware law that allowed shareholders to make such changes by written consent. The changes would give the trusts broad veto power over management in an intensifying dispute for control of the company. Earlier the board and management had challenged Gordon Getty, Jr.'s control of the Sarah Getty Trust. The two trusts then learned the board had authorized that an additional 9 million newly issued shares be placed in an Employee Stock Ownership Trust to be controlled by management, which would reduce the trusts' joint control below 50 percent through dilution.[25]

It is now clear that employee ownership is begetting employees as transaction partners in a wide range of corporate financial developments. The wage relationship is not the sole relationship between a company and an employee. Although corporate takeovers are part of this story, they do not explain the bulk of the developments.

Some Important Issues

The growth of employee ownership in public corporations has led to knotty issues in employee-ownership accounting and in creating an employee-ownership capital market, which loans Employee Stock Ownership Plans the money to purchase company stock.

Employee-Ownership Accounting

"Unfortunately, a lot of public corporations will make the decision on employee ownership based on economics and accounting. I've seen accounting kill some deals this year," commented a prominent ESOP investment banker.

Public companies are required to disclose considerable financial information to the public and to their shareholders. For this reason, the impact of the employee ownership on the company's financial statements and their financial statement reporting may play a role in the employee-ownership decision. All employee ownership does not have the same accounting impact on a public company. It really depends on whether there's dilution and whether there's debt.

If a company's employee benefit plan—a stock-bonus trust, a deferred-profit-sharing plan, a savings, thrift, or 401(k) plan, or a defined-benefit pension plan—purchases the corporation's stock with its assets, there is no debt involved. Since no new shares are created, no dilution occurs to shrink the value per share, the earnings per share, or the voting power of current shareholders. This simple fact, illustrated in Figure 2 in the Introduction, is that nonleveraged non-ESOP employee-ownership plans hold 47 percent of the employee ownership estates. The implications are clear: a large proportion of Employee Ownership 1000 companies have never reported using debt to achieve employee ownership. There is little public evidence that the ways in which these companies accumulated employee holdings radically altered the firms' accounting. Thus, half the employee-ownership purchases have been somewhat insulated from accounting-related problems. Public companies with large holdings in employee benefit plans can look at this result and use the assets of those plans to purchase stock, rather than publicly announced transactions involving leverage.

If leveraged Employee Stock Ownership Plans borrow funds to purchase stock, there *are* clear accounting effects. First, the ESOP is borrowing money and is thus increasing the company's debt. This loan is recorded on the company's balance sheet as debt. Second, company contributions to an ESOP are a reported expense. Contributions used to pay interest are an interest expense, and contributions used to pay principal on an ESOP loan are a compensation expense. This compensation expense is deferred-employee compensation, or benefits. Third, the equity is placed in a holding, or suspense account, until it is allocated to employees, since this equity is being purchased with borrowed money or debt. This debt becomes equity "on the company's books" as the debt is repaid and shares are allocated as benefits to employees' accounts. So, in leveraged ESOPs, while the stock is "owned by the employees," it is actually allocated to employees' individual accounts as the debt is paid off. Fourth, all shares in the ESOP, both allocated and unallocated, are outstanding for earnings per-share purposes.

Fifth, to the extent employee ownership creates tax deductions, it increases a company's earnings. To the extent that other wage and benefit reductions are traded for employee stock holdings, the company can rightfully say that the compensation expense of the ESOP is offset by some compensation reductions, as Polaroid does below.[26]

Each corporation should evaluate the effects of accounting issues on its employee-ownership structure before the transaction, but the real impact on the corporation and its shareholders is exhibited when credit rating agencies pronounce their public judgments on a public corporation's ESOP. These judgments are regularly made available by Standard & Poors and Moody's Investor Services for large New York Stock Exchange companies and usually appear in the *Wall Street Journal*.[27]

Morgan Stanley & Co. says that "the rating agencies understand the temporary nature of the increase in leverage and focus more on changes in cash flow and interest coverage" and "may also give credit for reduced 'event-risk' in cases where there is significant employee ownership." Indeed, one investment banker, noting that the debt in an Employee Stock Ownership Plan is viewed more kindly than the debt in a share repurchase program, says that creditors view the two scenarios as not comparable.

ESOP tax incentives also influence credit-rating agencies and companies. One investment banker is quite blunt: "I would venture to say that you would see next to no public corporation Employee Stock Ownership Plan deals without the ability to deduct dividends used to pay down the debt. This is absolutely critical. Without this, ESOPs would be used only for takeover defense."[28]

We reviewed some recent comments by credit agencies on major leveraged employee ownership transactions over the last few years. Ratings agencies are assessing several aspects of employee ownership: the debt-to-equity ratio created, the time needed to repay the debt, the use of employee stock ownership to replace benefits, and the tax and cash-flow advantages. Morgan Stanley & Co. studied 80 major companies with investment-grade credit that created leveraged ESOPs in 1989 and discovered only two cases where both Moody's and Standard & Poors downgraded the credit following implementation. In both cases, this was primarily related to non-ESOP issues, such as additional share repurchases and corporate restructuring. The investment bank found that leveraged ESOPs in which employee ownership replaces existing employee benefits, such as savings and profit-sharing plans, are seen as ratings-neutral if the company repurchases less than 15 to 20 percent of the common shares outstanding. Conversely, when the proceeds are used to refinance debt or fund acquisitions, the transaction is viewed as an equity offering and can be a positive rating consideration.[29]

Weighed together, these accounting and credit-rating observations suggest that the general financial environment is positive for employee-ownership if it is positive for the corporation adopting employee-ownership. Beyond that, depending on how a company structures its employee-ownership plan, it can possibly improve its position vis-à-vis credit agencies. On the other hand, it would seem that a 20 percent stake emerges as a practical limit to single-transaction employee ownership in public corporations when leverage is involved. This does not mean, however, that most publicly traded corporations will not attain more than 20-percent employee ownership. Many of the examples in this chapter illustrate that companies are beginning to consider multiple employee ownership transactions. Science Application International CEO Robert Beyster recommends that companies seeking to remain partly employee held must develop an "employee-ownership strategic plan," which takes account of financial, strategic, and benefit concerns, including credit ratings, shareholder relations, and their employee-ownership objective, if one exists. He believes an important component of this strategy will be integrating opportunities for developing ongoing employee ownership through nonleveraged employee benefit plans. Indeed, when credit is expensive and tight at times of high interest rates or when the credit position of a corporation is restricted, modest employee ownership can be attained gradually within legal limits, year to year by investing the assets of such plans in employer securities. The comprehensive planning of an employee-ownership strategy, which adroitly manages debt year after year in leveraged ESOPs and assets in nonleveraged plans, is likely to be an essential investment banking service for public companies. Understanding the employee-ownership capital markets will be another requirement.

Employee-Ownership Capital Market

Employee benefit plans and Employee Stock Ownership Plans of corporations have many sources of funds to purchase stock for employees. As noted earlier, any firm with an employee benefit plan *de facto* has its own source of funds for employee stock ownership, its own "bank," whether the firm recognizes it or not. This is reality. To the extent these employee-ownership plans are governed by ERISA, this reality raises, and continues to raise, profound questions for employees about their risk and their responsibility as shareholders and investors.

Many employees are probably completely unaware that their pension funds are the major investors in their own companies and, we expect, will learn of this for the first time from this book. Private pension funds own about 17 percent of all corporate stock, and we estimate that *direct employee ownership* accounts for another 3 percent of all corporate stock. We estimate that all private pension funds invest on average less than 3 percent of their assets in stock in employees' own companies. If employee benefit funds invested the full 10 percent of their assets in direct employee ownership, this would amount to 3 percent of the total stock market. While an extensive move toward employee ownership could not be funded through this nonleveraged method, it does illustrate the potential of employee benefit funds, which constitute an internal capital market for employee ownership in companies.[30]

Nonleveraged Employee Ownership Financing: Straight Employee Investments

Employees' savings and wage or benefit investments are another source of non-leveraged employee ownership financing. In general, employees have little cash available to invest directly in company stock. The New York Stock Exchange's study of employee share-purchase programs found that very few companies attained more than 5 percent of employee ownership through employee share-purchase programs, and we estimate that less than 1 percent of all corporate stock is held as a result of such programs. But, if a firm has employee ownership as a goal, such a "small" stake can be an important part of an employee-ownership strategy.

A more substantial source of employees' wage and benefit investments are their own contributions to 401(k) and savings plans. More and more companies, for example, Merrill Lynch mentioned at the beginning of this chapter, set up such savings plans, which depend on employee contributions and either encourage or require that a portion of the assets be invested in company stock. In industries under competitive pressure from global markets, deregulation, or the entry of smaller more nimble firms into the national or regional markets, we expect to see more companies offer compensation packages that constitute combinations of reasonable set wages and stock ownership that depends on company performance. A new perception and consciousness will be required so that companies and employees can see such arrangements, not as wage arrangements but as investor arrangements. This will be examined in detail in the next chapter. Let's examine one back-of-the-envelope estimate of these sources. We have estimated that the compensation costs of the Public Employee Ownership Companies is $250 billion, and we know that the total market value of these corporations is $965 billion. If these companies as a group implemented employee share-purchase programs constituting 5 percent of pay in one year, they would as a group attain 1.3-percent additional employee ownership per year, based on their current market value. If all these companies implemented separate annual wage and benefit and work organization investments of 2.33 percent each, constituting 7 percent of pay in total per year in exchange for company stock, they would as a group attain 1.8-percent additional employee ownership per year, based on their current market value. Thus, even a modest widespread exchange of stock for other forms of compensation would have major repercussions. Employees would become the top shareholder in most of these firms in just a few years.

The employee-ownership capital market has gone through several stages in the last decade. Let's briefly examine the development of the bank loan, private placement, and public financing market for employee-ownership transactions by drawing on a few interviews with employee-ownership investment bankers.

Leveraged Employee-Ownership Financing: Bank Loans

In reviewing the development of leveraged ESOP capital markets, we see that most pre-1985 leveraged financing for ESOPs was from bank loans, mainly through commercial money-center banks that made direct floating-rate loans to ESOPs.[31] As part of the Deficit Reduction Act of 1984, President Reagan signed a law allowing banks, insurance companies, and other commercial lenders to deduct 50 percent of their interest income on loans to ESOPs used to purchase employee stock ownership (called the Section 133 incentive). This typically resulted in the lenders passing on some of their savings in lower-than-prime interest rates to leveraged ESOP borrowers. These rates generally were 80 to 90 percent of the prime lending rate.

Commercial lenders realized that they were gaining tax deductions every time they made an ESOP loan, and large money-center banks, such as Manufacturers Hanover Trust Company of New York, Chemical Bank of New York, and Citicorp, took out national ads touting their availability for employee-ownership financing. A small number of experienced lenders dominated the market. This clearly became a factor in the upsurge in leveraged ESOP transactions after 1985, as shown in a chronological picture of buyback, newly issued shares, and cashing out major-holder ESOPs (Figures 1.1, 1.2, 1.3). At this time, money-center banks seemed destined to dominate the employee-ownership capital market. But employee ownership rapidly expanded in the mideighties, and companies were trying to figure out ways to gain access to the capital more cheaply.

Leveraged Employee-Ownership Financing: Private Placements

In a private placement, a lender packages a lending instrument that does not require extensive public disclosure. These loans are then sold to large investors through a private network that also does not require extensive public disclosure. Higher interest rates are usually charged, and large sums of capital can often be arranged very quickly. Congress's extension of this key tax incentive to insurance companies and other commercial lenders rapidly increased the private placement of employee-ownership debt.

The private placement market in general grew threefold from 1983 to 1988, when it was a $150 billion a-year market. Insurance companies and pension funds poured their assets into this market. When Procter & Gamble tried to raise $1 billion for its leveraged ESOP through a private placement, it was hastily oversubscribed! A section of the private placement market was junk bonds, where small companies or risky deals raised funds at higher interest rates with more restrictive debt covenants with the borrower, but most ESOP private placements were less risky and did not involve junk bonds. Indeed, none of the fabled Drexel junk-bond failures have been companies with major ESOP transactions. Public corporations usually avoided the private placement market because of its identification with risk and high capital costs. But in the mideighties they began raising capital for leveraged ESOPs through this market because the pent-up demand for private placements significantly reduced the cost advantage of raising debt publicly.

The private placement market for employee ownership capital had a distinct advantage. Money-center banks were unwilling to arrange a leveraged ESOP loan for more than seven years, while private placement lenders were able to deal with such time periods.

Another innovation was the securitized ESOP note, a long-term security that is re-priced every thirty days and re-issued. Investors have the right to return the securities to the issuer after each re-pricing. Securitized notes became lower-cost offerings of ESOP debt. A small cottage industry in refinancing ESOP debt grew up as banks helped corporations exchange high for lower ESOP debt. This was facilitated by the 1986 tax act, which permitted corporations to refinance their ESOP debt for the first time. Bankers Trust used securitized ESOP debt to refinance a $105 million loan for Enron Corp.'s (NYSE) ESOP. The new issue was expected to save the company 70 to 100 basis points in capital costs, replacing a conventional bank loan to the ESOP priced at 85 percent of prime, with a much lower cost in the 65 percent prime range. Bankers Trust aimed this product at corporations with single-A, or better, credit ratings. They named the product, FRESOP Notes, or Floating Rate Employee Stock Ownership Plan Notes.

The flexibility that was developing in employee-ownership capital markets led to greater flexibility in establishing employee ownership in public companies. Remember, public corporations are concerned about the accounting impact of showing ESOP debt on their books. They are also worried about establishing a leveraged ESOP that, for example, buys 1 million shares of stock today at $1.00 a share, using a ten-year loan of $1 million, which next year could fall below $1.00. This can happen, and it communicates to employees that their employee-ownership benefit is declining in value. It also displeases a company that hoped to provide employees with a full $1.00 worth of benefits for each of those remaining nine years.

As a response to this concern, Chase Manhattan Bank developed their trade-mark DIAL (Direct Immediate Allocation Loan) ESOP loan. With a DIAL loan, a public corporation does not purchase at one time all of the stock that it intends its ESOP to allocate to employees over many years. Rather, the company only borrows enough to fund one year's contribution to the ESOP, and the stock is allocated immediately. This reduces the leverage the company must carry on its books and avoids the risk of allocating to employees stock in any year, using our example, that cost $1.00 a share but is worth only $.75 a share today. In 1987, Chase Manhattan securitized the first DIAL loan for Allied Signal Inc. (NYSE).

Nevertheless, the private-placement ESOP market was dominated by larger institutions, because the process of analyzing, negotiating, and documenting private-placement financing individually was cumbersome for smaller institutions. They could not compete with larger lenders that had personnel dedicated to this market. Also, smaller institutions had portfolio constraints, which determined investments in specific types of securities or market sectors based on legal limitations or credit or investment parameters established internally. The minimum participation requirements in a private placement were often too large for smaller institutions and private placements were less liquid.[32]

To change this, in March of 1988, Salomon Brothers asked the Internal Revenue Service to clarify the Section 133 tax incentive, so that the path would be open to develop a public market for ESOP notes. In Revenue Ruling 89–76 in June 1989, the IRS encouraged the sale of ESOP debt instruments both from lenders who sell their loans to other lenders who qualify for the Section 133 tax deduction and from corporations to institutions directly in the form of bonds that companies issue.[33]

In 1989, Congress withdrew the 50-percent interest income deduction for lenders to ESOPs (Internal Revenue Code Section 133), unless the employees owned a majority stake in the company. The public trading of ESOP securities that Salomon Brothers envisioned would have allowed institutions to trade ESOP securities based on their tax appetite. This collapsed. The expectation of this action and further cutbacks in ESOP tax benefits partially explains why ESOP transactions jumped enormously in 1989, as the reader notes on most of our bar charts. Companies and lenders raced to conclude transactions before the lenders lost the tax incentive and the corporations lost a lower cost of capital. In retrospect, Congress's removal of this tax incentive was a foolish mistake. For the first time in the United States, a capital market for financing broader capital ownership was developing, and Congress destroyed it for a relatively small savings in deficit reduction. The decision on Section 133 should be reevaluated in light of a comprehensive employee-ownership policy for the country.

Some securitized ESOP debt is still being developed and traded among institutions, but it is "grandfathered ESOP debt," namely, debt from capital before the law changed or the refinancing of old ESOP loans. Given the number of expensive ESOP loans outstanding, this may still be a lucrative market for banks. Also, private placements of ESOP debt continue to be made. Recently, the Securities and Exchange Commission adopted a new rule, Rule 144a, which is designed to ease the trading of privately placed securities among institutions by exempting billions of dollars in new offerings from disclosure rules. This will allow large U.S. institutions to sell and trade private placement securities without having to fill out long financial disclosure forms. The new rule is also designed to draw foreign companies and sovereign governments into the U.S. capital market. While institutions may no longer trade securitized-ESOP debt to exchange tax incentives, Rule 144a will make a secondary market in ESOP debt somewhat more flexible. But the focus has shifted to publicly traded ESOP debt as public companies search for other ways to access cheaper capital to finance employee purchases of their stock.[34]

Leveraged Employee-Ownership Financing: Public Capital Market

The elimination of the 50-percent interest exclusion deduction for ESOP lenders has generated a public capital market for ESOP debt. This illustrates just how much the creation of employee ownership cannot be separated from innovations in capital markets or the role of Wall Street investment bankers, who have been the midwives of most of these financial innovations. In 1989, three significant transactions of this type were announced. Unisys Corp. (NYSE) announced that Shearson Lehman Hutton Inc. would raise $250 million in medium-term publicly issued notes in order to complete a leveraged ESOP that would secure 5.8 percent of the corporation in the hands of employees. Shearson planned to offer the notes on a continuous basis. At the same time, Brunswick Corp. (NYSE) filed with the Securities and Exchange Commission to raise $100 million to pay a bridge loan that financed the purchase of 5.9 percent of the firm's stock by its ESOP. This offering was managed by Shearson Lehman Hutton and Merrill Lynch Capital Markets. In December 1989, CPC International (NYSE) filed with the SEC to raise $200 million in notes bearing a 7.78-percent interest rate, so that its ESOP could purchase 5.1 percent of the company's stock.[35]

The employee-ownership public capital market took off in 1990. The leaders in this employee ownership capital market as calculated by Morgan Stanley & Company, along with examples of specific deals, are listed in Table 1.2. This market is expected to expand even further.

The notion that an employee stock ownership capital market of this sophistication even exists in the United States will probably surprise many. It attests to the interplay between the evolution of credit markets for employee ownership and the adoption of employee ownership as a corporate strategy by major corporations. There is now no doubt that the two are intimately tied.

Because of the variety of funding sources that have developed for employee ownership, public corporations will now begin to examine many alternative scenarios, including the full range of nonleveraged and leveraged sources of capital.

TABLE 1.2 The Public Market for Employee-Ownership Debt: Underwriters and Volume Share—Fully Taxable ESOP Financing in the Public Market

Selected Transactions of $25MM and Greater

| Underwriter | January 1, 1990–March 1, 1990 | | |
	Volume (in millions)	Percent of Total	Number of Deals
Morgan Stanley	$891.7	49.2	1.8
Merrill Lynch	$591.7	32.7	0.8
Goldman Sachs	$191.7	10.6	0.3
Morgan Guaranty	$137.0	7.6	1.0
Total	$1,812.1	100	4.0

1990 Public Market Financings

Specific Financings

Issuer	Size (in millions)	Issue (Average Life)	Lead Manager
BellSouth ESOP Trust	$275	13.5 Yr/8.5-Amortizing MTNs	Morgan Stanley
BellSouth ESOP Trust	$300	13.5 Yr/8.5-Amortizing MTNs	Morgan Stanley
Mobil ESOP Trust	$800	10 Yr/6.5-Sinking-Fund Debentures	Morgan Stanley
Upjohn Co. ESOP Trust	$275	14 Yr/11.4-Amortizing Notes	Morgan Stanley
Dow ESOP Trust	$138	14 Yr/8.4-Amortizing Notes	J.P. Morgan
NYNEX Corp.	$450	20 Yr/11.2-Debentures	First Boston
Columbia Gas ESOP Trust	$ 92	11.6 Yr/7.8-Amortizing Debentures	Morgan Stanley
Rohm & Haas Holdings Ltd.	$150	30 Yr/20.5-Amortizing Debentures	Goldman Sachs

Source: Data from the Morgan Stanley Group Inc., 1990

77

Conclusion

In an address to the Young Americans for Freedom, July 1974, Ronald Reagan comments on expanding the ownership of productive capital:

> Over one hundred years ago Abraham Lincoln signed the Homestead Act. There was a wide distribution of land and they didn't confiscate anyone's already owned land. They did not take from those who owned and give to those who did not own. We need an Industrial Homestead Act. It is time to accelerate economic growth and production and at the same time broaden the ownership of productive capital. The American dream has always been to have a piece of the action.

Public corporations, which control the American economy, are energetically exploring the emerging new model of employee-ownership corporate financing. Contrary to popular views it is not only, or mainly, fueled by takeover environments but by a wide variety of corporate motives. Employee ownership has grown steadily throughout the eighties in almost every major area where corporations engage in financing decisions.[36] One source of financing is *stockholders' equity,* which is raised by new stock issues or retained earnings, and *preferred stock,* which, like debt, has a fixed dividend payment. Richard A. Brealey and Stewart C. Myers in their *Principles of Corporate Finance* point out that the most striking aspect of the relative sources of capital for U.S. corporations is the dominance of internally generated cash, defined as *cash flow from operations less cash dividends paid to stockholders.* In fact, during the eighties internally generated cash covered more than 60 percent of the total requirements of corporations, while external financing has covered more than 30 percent, mostly long-term and short-term debt.

Corporations employ capital to build value and then share their profits with the shareholders. Typically, the use of internally generated cash and debt has created what employee-ownership thinkers, Louis Kelso, Jeffrey Gates, and Norman Kurland, call a closed system of credit in American public corporations. The reasoning is simple: individuals who are a significant part of the existing shareholder club are reaping the benefits of using internally generated cash, debt, capital appreciation, and earnings growth. Employees cannot buy their way to sizable capital ownership in these corporations with their savings, and their lack of access to big-item credit sentences them to serfdom. Their reasoning is central to understanding what has taken place in employee-ownership corporate finance in the last decade.[37]

Excluding the holdings of pension trusts, 90 percent of the stock is owned by just 10 percent of the households. The bottom line: too many citizens are shut out of the ground floor of the public corporation finance machine. In fact, only 5 percent of families with incomes under $10,000 and 13 percent of families with incomes under $20,000 hold corporate stock, while families in all income groups under $30,000 average less than $10,000 in total financial assets. And less than 50 percent of the families with so-called middle-class incomes between $50,000 and $99,000 own any publicly traded stock. This is *not* an argument for rank-and-file ownership and against manager ownership. Indeed, G. Bennett Stewart of the financial advisory firm Stern Stewart & Co. has stressed that few executive groups—no matter what their annual salary and bonus—can afford to accumulate enough financial resources to purchase more than a fraction of their company's outstanding shares.[38] How did it get and stay that way?

Typically, when corporations use retained earnings to invest in new projects, the new projects are owned by the current owners. So too, when corporations use external credit, the corporation, in the name of current shareholders, as it were, borrows the funds. After the initial cost of the investment is paid, the equity resides wholly in the *current owners* and is expected to turn additional profits for them indefinitely. This is called self-liquidating credit. *Those with money typically get rich, not by using their own money, but by using self-liquidating financing methods to acquire ownership of capital instruments before they have saved the funds to buy and pay for them.* Corporations are simply social tools to produce wealth. The key insight of the broadened capital ownership analysis is that the rich really do get richer with traditional methods of corporate finance, and most employees of corporations remain propertyless, simply because they have no initial foothold in the public corporate wealth-creation machine nor access to substantial credit. With over 90 percent of American households having no significant economic stake in public corporations, corporate finance has indeed become a closed system that recycles credit until wealth grows bigger and bigger and rewards existing owners. In fact, as Brealey and Myers so persuasively show, during the eighties most public corporations bought more new stock than they issued because of mergers and acquisitions. That's just more of the closed system. The net new stock issues was negative for this entire period. It's really a gigantic myth to think that many average-income people are stashing their savings in the stock market and gaining capital estates. The broadened ownership analysis strongly suggests that corporate credit be expanded so that our economy will become a broad-based system of capital ownership and the control of credit will be more democratic. As long as dilution is addressed, corporations now have the tools and the precedents to do this. They must only choose.

In just ten years, the revolution that has taken place in ownership structure in the United States means that a large portion of the capital in the economy is in pension and retirement funds. But unfortunately most of this capital—deferred compensation of employees invested for their retirement—has been used mainly to provide credit to existing owners of corporations. While the growth of institutional investors is transforming corporate control, it has not altered the nature of wealth creation for most Americans.

First and foremost, public corporations have used the tax incentives for contributions and loans to Employee Stock Ownership Plans to invite employees into the closed system of corporate finance. These developments prove definitively that if the federal government is determined and serious, a combination of government incentives for credit availability to working citizens and innovative corporate financing techniques can truly change this country's economic structure and democratize the process of wealth creation. The leveraged ESOP has been, as we have pointed out in previous books, a resounding social, political, and economic success. Despite the recent fear of leverage, most public corporations engage in borrowing, and average debt ratios have increased during the postwar period, although they're lower than in the first third of this century. Brealey and Myers indicate that successful companies in many other countries, such as Germany, operate with much higher debt ratios than U.S. companies would think prudent.

Public corporations have gone beyond Louis Kelso's ideas in a unique and original way. They have simply recognized that a new alternative source of capital exists right under their noses, which does not require borrowing nor using retained earnings: their employee benefit plans. These plans are serving as banks and investors in employer companies within existing Congressional guidelines. Employee-ownership capital markets have matured significantly, and the investment banking creativity in this area is finally serving to pool capital from insurance and pension funds to finance broadened ownership.

But this is not where the story ends. We have also demonstrated that in public companies employee-ownership plans involving the repurchase of shares on the open market (ownership replacement ESOPs) or new capital formation through the selling of newly issued shares to an ESOP creates dilution, which is not reversed by ESOP tax incentives. Giving employees the access to credit, which employee ownership enthusiasts staunchly defend, can create a problem for shareholders: Who pays for employee ownership if the government does not foot the bill? The main solution seems to be to plan and restructure wages and benefits, so that employees are in fact purchasing the employee ownership with their own deferred compensation. This can be supplemented with contributions attributable to company reorganizations and employee participation programs. One implication will be that employees who pay for their stock will want to be treated like core shareholders.

What are the implications for senior managers, boards of directors, and employees? Every corporate officer can now clearly choose between being a "feudal concentrator of wealth" and a "democratic capitalist" in at least some dealings of his or her corporation. These developments give corporate leaders the first decisive opportunity in a long time to sculpt the ownership structure of the companies they manage. Should shareholder interests and employee interests be aligned? Is it better for the company to have employees as core shareholders and patient investors? Can employee-shareholders serve as a balancing force for other kinds of investors? Thus, employee ownership is not something corporate leaders are doing for employees; it can also be a venture for the corporation as it confronts uncertain changes in the twenty-first century.

Employees need to decide if they care about employee ownership enough to actively suggest/plan/push for—*work* for it. Finally, employees in the flagship companies of the society also have a real choice. Would they like to own 10 to 20 percent of a major corporation where they work, without putting their savings at risk? Or not? Does this fit into their retirement planning or personal goals? How will nonunion and union employees respond to the restructuring of wages and benefits to pay for employee ownership? It may be safer and easier for some corporations to avoid restructuring existing wages and benefits but to grant further wage and cost-of-living increases in company stock. What kinds of expectation will this generate among employees? Employees have spent so much time being cynical—rightly or wrongly—about ESOP transactions that seem to plummet from the corporate sky that they have lost sight of one key fact: the financial stake in ESOPs is quite real, and their possibilities are startling. Companies will have to borrow money anyway; why not encourage them to consider employee ownership, if all things are equal? Moreover, shareholders and employees—often the antagonists in most public companies—will enter into a symbiotic relationship. Depending on how employee-ownership transactions are structured, they can be competitors for value or partners in building value. Shareholders will be outrageously threatened by frivolous employee ownership in some firms, while they will be enamored of its contribution to building their investment in others.

The next chapter goes beyond employee ownership as a "tool" and asks how it's affecting the structure of wages and benefits, the assumptions of the fixed wage system, and the bread-and-butter "is-it-getting-better-or-worse" money issues of workers and their families. Mastering the philosophy and the options of wage and benefits restructuring will be crucial to creating employee ownership.

Notes

1. *The Wall Street Journal*, October 14, 31, 1988, December 6, 1988, January 24, 1989, September 22, 1989; SEC filing December 1989.
2. *The Wall Street Journal*, September 15, 20, 1983, October 3, 18, 1983.
3. *The Wall Street Journal*, August 23, 1983, June 23, 1988, January 26, 1989, March 7, 1989, October 6, 1989; SEC filing December 1989; Blasi, 1988: 212–219, and company press releases.
4. Old Stone Bank: SEC filing 1986; July, 1987, December, 1989; *The Wall Street Journal*, April 5, 1988, July 2, 1988.
5. Quoted and excerpted completely from "United Postal Going Public," by Joe Dwyer III. *St. Louis Business Journal*, January 28, 1990.
6. Our data report announced only employee ownership stock buybacks and announced takeover environments. Throughout this book the criteria for determining *a takeover environment* (when that specific term is used) is as follows. Using public and private data sources listed in Appendix A.1, we

built a database with all reported information about employee-ownership transactions for each firm. If a journalist, a company press release, or SEC filing, or an analyst reported on a takeover fact (Company X has made a tender offer for Company Y.) or a takeover rumor (It is rumored that Company Y is a potential takeover target.), that we considered to be firm in a takeover environment. Also, we had access to the databases of several other researchers who evaluated public information on takeovers related to these firms.

7. Honeywell: *The Wall Street Journal*, February 19, 1986; Boston: *The Wall Street Journal*, September 1, 1987; PR Newswire May 23, 1990; High: *The Wall Street Journal*, November 16, 1987, December 8, 1987; SEC filing July 1987; Bowater: *The Wall Street Journal*, May 5, 1985; Central: PR Newswire January 2, 1990; Farr: PR Newswire September 1, 1989; Leggett: PR Newswire August 15, 1980; Butler: *The Wall Street Journal*, March 1, 1983, January 16, 1985, November 20, 1985, January 5, 1988; SEC filings 1986, December 1989; Avon: PR Newswire June 20, 1984; Capitol: *The Wall Street Journal*, May 27, 88; Comfed: *The Wall Street Journal*, July 23, 1986, September 24, 1987; PR Newswire September 23, 1987; Cayuga: PR Newswire August 30, 1988; Commerce: *The Wall Street Journal*, August 17, 1989; Indiana: *The Wall Street Journal*, April 26, 1989; Integra: *The Wall Street Journal*, January 27, 1989; Polifly: PR Newswire March 22, 1989, July 14, 1989. Bank merged with Fellowship Savings and Loan; Peoples: SEC filing December 1989; Pacific: *The Wall Street Journal*, April 27, 1989; Cape: *The Wall Street Journal*, November 17, 1988; Boston: April 19, 1989.

8. Rohm: *The Wall Street Journal*, June 18, 1990; Gannett: *The Wall Street Journal*, May 14, 1990; Bell: *The Wall Street Journal*, May 17, 1984; Circus: *The Wall Street Journal*, January 25, 1989; Adams: *The Wall Street Journal*, February 16, 1988; Mobile: April 18, 1984.

9. It is highly probable that this type of transaction happens regularly. If the investment of employee benefit plan assets is a prudent investment and is done primarily for the exclusive benefit of the employees in compliance with ERISA, it is feasible for a corporation who wishes to cash out a large holder to have a nonleveraged employee benefit plan slowly buy out the holder. The secondary purpose of serving corporate interests are certainly allowable if the firm complies with ERISA. Such a transaction might, however, raise labor-management issues with employees.

10. Synergen: *The Wall Street Journal*, October 21, 1988; American Western: *The Wall Street Journal*, March 29, 1989; Integrity: *The Wall Street Journal*, January 7, 1983; Frozen: PR Newswire November 30/ 1987. Personal communication from Edward Regan, 1990.

11. For references, see Penney: August 30, 1988; Green: *The Wall Street Journal*, November 7, 1989; Ameritrust: *The Wall Street Journal*, May 18, 1989; AT&T: *The Wall Street Journal*, September 13, 1989; Colgate: *The*

Wall Street Journal, June 18, 1989; Barry Wright: *The Wall Street Journal*, January 6, 1988, May 3, 10, 18, 1988, November 25, 1988; PR Newswire May 10, 1988 SEC filing December 1989; Harcourt: *The Wall Street Journal*, May 27, 29, 1987, June 1, 1987, September 23, 1987, April 1, 1988, SEC filing December 1989; Financial Footnotes; Travelers: *The Wall Street Journal*, June 22, 1989; Turner: *The Wall Street Journal*, July 1, 1989; Champion: *The Wall Street Journal*, February 16, 22, 1988, April 14, 1988, SEC filing December 1989; President's Letter as source for quote; Dahlberg: SEC filing December 1989; Management Discussion; Exxon: *The Wall Street Journal*, June 1, 4, 1990; Federal Express: PR Newswire July 16, 1985; Freedom Savings and Loan Association: *The Wall Street Journal*, June 15, 1985; Lowe's: PR Newswire July 31, 1981, March 1, 1982, July 23, 1985, August 22, 1988; *The Wall Street Journal*, September 22, 1981, January 25, 1982, July 24, 1985, October 21, 1987, November 16, 1987, September 13, 1988, March 3, 1989; SEC filing July 1987, December 1989.

12. Stock exchange rules and the fact that many ESOPs are not put to a shareholder vote encourage dilutive ESOPs.

13. Personal communication, Paul Mazzili, Morgan Stanley & Co. See also, Morgan Stanley & Co., 1990, Section II and *Leveraged Employee Stock Ownership Plans: Strategies for the 1990s*, by Morgan Stanley & Co. (New York: Morgan Stanley & Co., Section V, 1990).

14. Also, there is no public record of transactions for the public corporations that are 1 to 4 percent employee held.

15. Briefly put, the question is whether a dollar from employees and a dollar from managers or investors should both buy a dollar of stock or whether managers and/or investors should get more stock for less money, more voting rights, and more dividends and return, and if such differences are structured into a transaction, what is their objective basis in financial analysis. This and similar transactions led to a bitter fight between agents of ESOP transactions, such as investment bankers, managers, lawyers, and valuation consultants and the U.S. Department of Labor. The correspondence between the Labor Department and proponents of various deals is contained in *ESOPs and ESOP Transactions*, by William Kravitz and Charles Smith (New York: Practicing Law Institute, 1985) and some of the controversy is reviewed in Blasi, 1988: 132–142.

16. Employee ownership is a relatively young phenomenon. In the next decade, privately held firms that become employee owned from 1975 to 1990 will see large numbers of employees retiring. The law requires the companies to repurchase the workers' shares. Going-public transactions will become common among these firms. For a discussion of repurchase liability, see Blasi, 1988: 52–55.

17. Oregon: *The Wall Street Journal*, March 3, 1988, April 14, 1988, October 24, 1988, December 2, 1988; *American Banker*, September 13, 1987;

American Financial: *The Wall Street Journal*, January 7, 1986; Copper Range: National Center for Employee Ownership, *Employee Ownership: A Handbook for Unions* (Oakland, Calif.: NCEO, 1989): 17; *The Wall Street Journal*, October 13, 1987, February 6, 1989; OREMET: *The Wall Street Journal*, August 7, 1987, November 18, 1987, December 15, 1987, August 8, 1989, October 10, 1989; America West: *The Wall Street Journal*, August 2, 1986, June 16, 1987; American Steel: *The Wall Street Journal*, August 21, 1990; Industrial: SEC filing January 1987; Met-Coil: SEC filing January 1987; Shearson: *The Wall Street Journal*, March 24, 1987; Forum Re: *The Wall Street Journal*, October 21, 1988; Pioneer: *The Wall Street Journal*, July 12, 1989; Regional: *The Wall Street Journal*, February 10, 1986, October 20, 1986, January 5, 1989; VanFed: *The Wall Street Journal*, January 27, 1989; FMS: *The Wall Street Journal*, November 7, 1988, PR Newswire December 14, 1988; Portsmouth: *The Wall Street Journal*, February 9, 1988; Northbay: SEC filing December 1989; NFS: *The Wall Street Journal*, January 23, 1990, SEC filing July 7, 1987.

18. For an excellent review, see, "Employee Takeovers," by Alan Hyde and Craig Livingston, *Rutgers Law Review* 41 (Summer 1989): 1131–95. See also, *Job Saving Strategies: Worker Buyouts and QWL,* by Art Hochner, Cherlyn Granrose, et. al. (Kalamazoo, MI: W. E. Upjohn Institute, 1989).

19. "Leveraged Buyout Market Collapsed in 1990," *Employee Ownership Report* 10, no. 4 (July-August 1990):8.

20. This use of the term, based on an evaluation of the common usage, has evolved in the research and journalistic literature, which has been carefully monitored and reviewed since 1980. Generally, the exhaustive search of databases conducted for this book has found this to be the accepted formulation. By *employees* we mean a broad-based group of the firm's full-time employees. In an employee buyout, employees as a group are somehow involved in developing the transaction either through initiative, agreement, consultation, planning, or outright execution, or all these stages. Managers usually play a key role in "managing" the transaction. But an "employee buyout" is in contrast to a "management buyout," which means that managers are leading all developmental phases of the transaction in which employees as a broad-based group and employee ownership play a modest role. Both an employee buyout and a management buyout are types of leveraged buyouts. This definition is also generally followed by the National Center for Employee Ownership (NCEO) whose database, constructed independently of our own, shows a similar formulation. See NCEO, *Employee Ownership: A Handbook for Unions,* 1989, for a review of material on employee buyouts. While the common usage of the definition has been evolving, the major aspects of it were already being used by Blasi and Corey Rosen (currently Executive Director, NCEO) in preparing legislation to encourage government loans to employee groups in the late seventies,

which was introduced into the House and the Senate. Excellent research on the early employee buyouts is contained in William Foote Whyte, Charles Craypo, et. al. *Evaluation Research on Federally-Assisted Worker Buyouts* (Washington, D.C.: U.S. Department of Commerce, Economic Development Administration Research and Policy Unit, 1987). Blasi, 1988: 275–286 summarizes research on employee buyouts and their impact of labor-management relations and economic performance of firms.

21. On Rath, see NCEO, 1989: 7–8

22. Hospital: *The Wall Street Journal,* June 13, 1989; GM: *The Wall Street Journal,* September 10, 1986, NCEO, 1989: 9–10; AMPCO: NCEO, 1989: 17; National: *The Wall Street Journal,* December 2, 1987; Ogden: PR Newswire July 18, 1985, October 1, 1985, *The Wall Street Journal,* April 29, 1986, SEC filing, 1986; Control: PR Newswire February 17, 1989; Sears: *The Wall Street Journal,* March 14, 1989, October 16, 1989; LTV: *The Wall Street Journal,* May 31, 1989;

23. Hospital: *The Wall Street Journal,* May 18, 1987; Malon Wilkus, American Capital Strategies, Bethesda, Maryland, personal communication, 1990. NCEO, 1989: 14. The three major failures are discussed on pp. 7–14. The steelworker policy on employee ownership is discussed on pp. 18–20 and is available in full from the research department of the union in Pittsburgh, Pa.

24. Cigna: PR Newswire January 6, 1989; Sears: *The Wall Street Journal,* March 14, 1989, October 16, 1989

25. Dune: *The Wall Street Journal,* October 11, 1983, November 8, 1983; Emery: *The Wall Street Journal,* August 27, 1987, February 4, 11, 1988, June 17, 1988, February 13, 1989; Firemans: *The Wall Street Journal,* September 12, 1985, March 8, 1988; Kinnard: PR Newswire February 18, 1990; Dominion: *The Wall Street Journal,* SEC filing 1986; Freedom: *The Wall Street Journal,* June 25, 1985; Public: SEC filing January 1987; Optical: *The Wall Street Journal,* January 6, 1988, February 1, 1988, August 19, 1988; Entertainment: *The Wall Street Journal,* August 26, 1988; Financial: *The Wall Street Journal,* October 28, 1983, March 22, 1984, April 24, 1984; Moncor: *The Wall Street Journal,* August 7, 1985; AM: *The Wall Street Journal,* September 29, 1983; Consolidated: *The Wall Street Journal,* October 3, 1989; Getty: *The Wall Street Journal,* December 6, 1983.

26. We are grateful to Morgan Stanley, 1990, Section II for our discussion on these issues. The Morgan Stanley material also makes the following additional observations. *Income Statement Impact:* Regarding dividends, dividends used to service the ESOP loan reduce required company contributions to the ESOP, effectively lowering reported compensation expense and although the dividends are not expenses, the Company still gets a tax deduction for the employee benefit provided by the dividends. The effect is to increase cash flow and reduce reported expense because dividends which would otherwise be paid to outside shareholders are used to finance

employee benefits. *Balance Sheet Impact:* New issuance of stock to an ESOP thus results in no initial change in reported shareholders' equity. The common or preferred stock account increases by the amount of the ESOP stock issuance. Unallocated ESOP shares are treated as a prepaid benefit expense (liability) and are recorded as a "contra-equity" account, reducing total equity, but as shares are allocated, the "contra-equity" account is reduced, increasing equity. Finally, an open-market purchase of stock for the ESOP initially reduces reported shareholder's equity. Stock issued to the ESOP is offset by the stock purchased in the market, however, total equity is reduced by the contra-equity account until shares are allocated. See also, American Institute of Certified Public Accountants (AICPA) Statement of Position 76-3, "Accounting Practices for Certain Employee Stock Ownership Plans." Kevin B. Reilly in "Accounting Aspects of ESOPs" notes that AICPA says that the dividends paid on shares held by an ESOP should be charged against the employer's retained earnings account and not included at any time in compensation expense, but since the AICPA position the 1984 Deficit Reduction Act has expanded dividend deductibility to the extent those dividends are used to reduce the principal or pay interest on a loan used to buy stock. Some accountants have argued that dividends used by a plan to reduce indebtedness should be reflected as a compensation expense, but this is presently at odds with the AICPA. The Financial Accounting Standard Board's Emerging Issues Task Force (EITR, Issue 86-4) said tax benefits realized on dividends paid to an ESOP should be reported as a direct credit to retained earnings and not a reduction in the company's income tax expense. A new accounting standard for income taxes (SFAS No. 96) reversed this position and had to be implemented by calendar year 1989. See Robert W. Smiley, Jr., and Ronald J. Gilbert, *Employee Stock Ownership Plans.* (New York: Prentice Hall/Rosenfeld Launer Publications, 1989): 12–21. In December 1989, FASB issued new accounting standards that reduce the usefulness of convertible preferred shares in ESOPs, noting that convertible preferred stock subject to a "par put" will require additional fully diluted shares treated as outstanding if the par put exceeds the underlying value of the common shares.

27. Readers may obtain these ratings in full by calling Standard & Poors or Moody's in New York City.

28. Morgan Stanley, 1990: Section II. Another Wall Street ESOP Investment banker, personal communication, 1990. This banker criticizes academics who say that there is no difference between a company setting up a leveraged ESOP and borrowing money and then contributing treasury shares to a nonleveraged ESOP, because "in the real world people view the two very differently." This may explain why this academic view mentioned by Scholes and Wolfson, 1990, has de-emphasized the leveraged ESOP.

29. See Morgan Stanley & Co., 1990, Section VII. Some other findings are "A company on the edge of a rating category would be downgraded by this

transaction (15–20% ESOP replacing benefits). A company with a rating below 'A' category would face a more negative impact than a better-rated company. Company with repurchases over 20% of its outstanding common stock in conjunction with an ESOP would lose some of its financial flexibility and consequently suffer a downgrade. [The agencies] focus more heavily on the net cash-flow impact of a leveraged ESOP than on debt/capital or pre-tax interest coverage. Agencies are concerned with how quickly debt is repaid. Those companies with an 'A' rating or better are seen as more capable of 'repairing' their balance sheets than companies with lower ratings."

30. Total private pension fund assets are $1221.8 billion from the Flow of Funds Section of the Federal Reserve Board for first quarter 1990. Ten percent or $122 billion would constitute 2.8 percent of total stock outstanding.

31. Jennifer Hourihan in "The Public Market for ESOP Notes," *Journal of Employee Ownership Law and Finance* 1, no. 1 (Fall 1989): 140, also adds that "as the need for funding grew, lenders expanded capacity using "put bonds," which have floating interest rates and were marketed primarily to an expanded universe of banks in unregistered formats."

32. Abridged and drawn completely from Hourihan, 1990: 141–142.

33. Discussed in detail in Hourihan, 1990.

34. This section draws liberally from several excellent articles on the subject in the *American Banker:* September 2, 4, 8, 18, 23, 1987, December 10, 29, 1987. See also, *The Wall Street Journal,* February 10, 1989, October 2, 1989, March 31, 1990.

35. Unisys: *The Wall Street Journal,* April 18, 1989; Brunswick: PR Newswire April 20, 1989; CPC: *The Wall Street Journal,* December 21, 1989.

36. We have drawn from Richard A. Brealey and Stewart C. Myers, *Principles of Corporate Finance,* (New York: McGraw Hill, 1988), Chap. 14 for this conclusion.

37. Taken from The Industrial Homestead Act: National Infrastructural Reforms To Make Every Citizen A Shareowner by Norman Kurland. (Washington, D.C.: Center for Economic and Social Justice, 1990). Readers are also referred to Kelso's seminal work, *The Capitalist Manifesto* with Mortimer Adler (New York: Random House, 1958). Gates is a well-known lecturer on these subjects and is a partner at the Washington, D.C. law firm of Powell, Goldstein, Frazer & Murphy and is the author of many essays.

38. A complete analysis of stock ownership and wealthholding is contained in Blasi, 1988: 106–119 and Kevin Philips *The Politics of Rich and Poor: Wealth and The American Electorate in the Reagan Aftermath* (New York: Random House, 1990): 4–31. See G. Bennett Stewart, "Remaking the Public Corporation from Within" *Harvard Business Review* (July-August 1990): 128.

2

Restructuring Wages and Benefits

From a Letter to Procter & Gamble (NYSE) employees, from CEO John G. Smale: I am pleased to announce that the Company intends to make some changes in our Profit-Sharing Plans, effective July 1, 1989. The annual allocation to your Profit-Sharing account will be just as large as it would have been prior to these changes. The Board of Directors believes that increasing the employees share ownership and voice in the conduct of the Company's business enhances commitment and the performance of its employees. We think this benefits all P&G shareholders. Presently, P&G employees, through our Profit-Sharing Plans own 14% of the company's stock. An additional approximately 2% is owned outright by active employees. An important benefit of these changes will be to further increase, by an additional 6%, the amount of Company stock in our Profit-Sharing Plans. So, in total, our employees and benefit plans will own approximately 22% of Procter & Gamble. . . . [The plan will] . . . purchase a large number of shares of newly issued P&G Convertible Preferred Stock . . . . Convertible Preferred Stock offers some attractive features, including a higher current dividend rate than the common, and protection against downward movement in the common stock price . . . . You will be able to vote all of the P&G shares, both common and preferred, you hold in the Profit-Sharing Plans on all corporate issues.[1]

In 1989 Salomon Inc. (NYSE), the parent of the investment banking firm Salomon Brothers, approved an employee stock purchase program that enables employees to buy common stock through payroll deductions at 85% of fair market value. The firm decided that 3 million shares of common stock will be made available. In May 1990 the firm announced new compensation plans that will require employees to plow more of their salaries into their firm's stock or into other incentives tied to the firm's performance. This marks a return to payment practices during Wall Street's old private partnership days. The plan, called an equity partnership plan, was outlined by Chairman John Gutfreund at the firm's managing director's weekend in Orlando, Florida. It was reported that employees would receive anywhere from 5–33% of their compensation in publicly traded stock. The higher their salary the bigger the percentage employees would receive in stock. The Wall Street Journal *reported that it is expected the board will approve this in 60 days. The plan will significantly increase employee ownership above the current level, which is below 5%.*[2]

Conrail (NYSE) is today 11% employee held and is one of the first examples of a currently publicly held corporation trading stock for compensation concessions. In 1978, Congress required that the company establish a 15% ESOP as a condition for receiving Congressional funds and operating as a government corporation. The 15% stake compensated employees for $600 million in concessions but also gave them influence. In 1981, Congress decided to sell the railroad to the private sector. Bidders such as Norfolk Southern and a group led by Morgan Stanley wooed the unions, who staunchly opposed a government plan to sell to Norfolk Southern as financially unfair to them and to the taxpayer. Norfolk planned to buy out the employees, while Morgan Stanley wished to preserve the ESOP and give employees seats on the board. Former Treasury official and ESOP investment banker Brian Freeman, who helped the unions develop an activistic bargaining strategy toward the future of the company, including a proposal to buy it, notes, "Management did not like the idea of employees' running a transaction themselves. The employees became a player at the table and this produced an auction process in which their support and potential concessions were things bidders sought. Ultimately, this was a game of strategy and tactics." In 1987, the government sold its entire 85% stake in the largest initial public stock offering in U.S. history. The Conrail Privatization Act said the new corporation must distribute the ESOP stock to employees within 3 months, and 10.4 million shares were distributed to 92,000 employees. In 1989, Conrail started a new ESOP for its union and nonunion employees subject to some changes in benefits.[3]

In 1990, Whitman Corporation, the maker of Whitman chocolates and other consumer products, carried out one of the most radical benefit substitutions using employee ownership. It was speculated to be a takeover target of Zeus, a partnership of the Belzberg and Pattison Canadian investors in 1989. The company sold $500 million in convertible preferred stock to its ESOP, raising employee ownership to 15%. The employee-held stock replaced the company's pension plan, its match to the 401(k) plan and its commitment to pay for postretirement health benefits for 5300 salaried employees. Here's what the company said: "Our retirement program encourages you to assume more responsibility for your own financial security. The ESOP represents a substantial change in the way retirement benefits are provided. It requires you to do a great deal of advance budgeting and planning. In the future, we will provide materials designed to help you do that job. If you are a salaried employee, you will be eligible to participate in the ESOP. Each share carries a minimum value of

$457.50. You can supplement your ESOP account and your personal savings by contributing to the SRS (a savings plan). The Company will match your savings—dollar for dollar—with additional ESOP shares. You can save 2% to 6% of your total compensation on a before-tax basis. You can invest your savings in any combination of three funds in multiples of 25%. Your fund choices are: The Fixed Income Fund, a series of Guaranteed Investment Contracts, The Diversified Fund, primarily common stocks, and The Whitman Common Stock Fund, where dividends are used to purchase additional stock.[4]

Long a mark of executive privilege at big companies, stock options have gone democratic at PepsiCo. Inc. which includes Pepsi-Cola, Pizza Hut, Taco Bell, Kentucky Fried Chicken, and Frito Lay. In the past few days, the restaurant, cola, and snack-food giant has begun rolling out a stock-option plan for all 100,000 employees who average at least 30 hours a week. It includes everyone from Frito Lay truck drivers in California to bottling engineers in Cyprus. "It's been part of our whole culture to say 'you are important' to every employee," says D. Wayne Calloway, Pepsi chairman and chief executive officer. "This says that in spades." Pepsi hopes that its Share Power program, along with other efforts to spread decision-making and build team spirit, will make employees identify more with the company and their work, encourage them to stay longer, and increase productivity. Under the Share Power plan, each July 1 employees will be granted options totaling 10% of their compensation, including bonuses, overtime and other extras, for the previous calendar year. The options give the employee the right to buy the company's stock at the July 1 price any time within the next 10 years. The employee can exercise each annual grant at the rate of 20% a year. And employees don't have to have cash in hand to make purchases; they may use the appreciation in the stock value over time to buy stock. A company brochure draws a best-case scenario: An employee now making $30,000 a year would accumulate $387,000 after taxes in a 30-year career, assuming the stock price rises 10% annually. Pepsi will acquire stock for the program on the open market with borrowed funds. Pepsi's program may be all the more persuasive because of the rising stock price in recent years; it closed yesterday at $56.625, up from the equivalent of $14.04 five years ago.[5]

Introduction

In "Issues for the 1990s," Michael I. Lew of Coopers and Lybrand examines the dynamics of employee benefits, productivity, and corporate structure.

> There are several major trends that will affect compensation in the 90s . . . [and] how employers face these challenges . . . may well affect their profitability and their ability to attract and retain a high-quality, productive workforce.

Flattening of the corporate pyramid: Companies are reducing and simplifying their organizational structures [rather than] determining pay based primarily upon worker's level in the corporate pyramid.

Quest for lower fixed costs: [Companies] are reducing pension benefits and medical benefits for active and retired employees . . . and seeking ways to reduce the basic salary structure, which is an important contributor to high fixed costs.

Uncertainty over the long-term future: "Shareholder value" principles require the company to focus on maximizing and accelerating present cash flows . . . . In this environment it is difficult for an employee at any level to develop a life-long commitment to the company.

Changing relationship between companies and workers: Well before [the year 2010] there should be shortages in workers at every level . . . . Employers will be required to develop flexible compensation and reward systems that will attract and retain these persons, particularly in light of the projected shortfall in workers.

As a result of the issues discussed above, we predict the following trends:

leaner corporate structure with fewer employees . . . [who] will be relatively higher paid

salary systems more responsive to current market and [reduced] emphasis on negative elements

incentives provided to more employees at all levels and based on measurable standards

employee stock ownership plans to replace pension plans because they often serve corporate purposes in addition to providing an employee benefit[6]

A fundamental transformation in the compensation system in the United States is underway. The central features of this context are the following: fixed wage and benefit increases have become a habit in the American economy for union and nonunion workers; although wages and benefits have risen rapidly, ironically, inflation-adjusted wages have not substantially increased (see Figure 2.1); lagging productivity makes any wage increase more expensive in terms of remaining competitive; and the risk to the retirement benefits of workers will increase. One note before we proceed. When we use the term *workers* or *employees,* we mean all persons in a company below the senior management level. We believe this group has more commonalities with each other than differences, and we do not believe that class distinctions help this discussion.

The major concept under an uncoordinated and disorganized attack in our economy is no less than the notion of a fixed wage and benefit obligation made by the company to the worker, regardless of the company's performance. Since World War II, both companies and workers—rank-and-file and management, union and nonunion alike—have been seriously attached to the paternalistic idea that the company will increase wages to keep up with inflation, despite the short-term performance of the company. Part of this expectation has been that nonwage benefits, such as current and postretirement health and life insurance, and a cafeteria of benefits will also regularly increase in their variety and their

FIGURE 2.1   *Changes in Wages and Benefits*

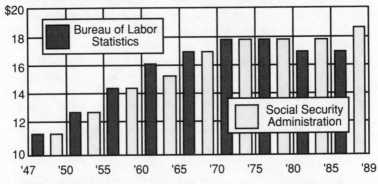

Average Annual Wages Adjusted for Inflation Grew until the Mid-1970s

Average annual wages in thousands of 1987 dollars, according to the Bureau of Labor Statistics and the Social Security Administration.

Source: Bureau of Labor Statistics and Social Security Administration, 1990; Robert J. Myers, "Real Wages Went Up In The 1980s," *The Wall Street Journal,* August 21, 1990. Chart by Lawrence R. Greenberg

size. As the postwar boom got underway, unions won agreements that gave workers clearly deserved annual wage increases, which both kept pace with inflation and provided regular annual increases. The notions that one would never pay for health costs and would retire with 70 percent of one's current pay provided through an employer-paid retirement program, plus family-wide postretirement health care, became the expected and desirable norm for most citizens. Benefits increased almost 80 percent between 1979 and 1990. It is generally accepted that many leading nonunion companies and firms who wished to prevent unionization in their other units tried to meet these expectations both to keep unions out and to attract and retain good workers.

This system initially worked and created prosperity for workers before this decade, because the United States was the dominant economic power in the world after World War II. All our competitors' economies were largely destroyed or seriously disabled, and we dominated the markets for goods and services. In this wonderland where there was little serious competition for a quarter of a century, management took an easy attitude toward wages and benefits, because such increases could be passed along to the consumer in increased prices. It was okay for nonunion firms to mimic union wages to some extent. The costs could be absorbed. Also, as the technological leaders, companies continually came up with ideas that allowed them to surpass themselves in improving productivity, which offset increased labor costs. A parallel organization of companies' management and human resources reflected this "absorb-the-fat" approach to compensation. Many companies had multiple levels of management, who planned everything that workers did and constituted the "brains" of the company. There was little emphasis or need, it seems, to involve employees deeply in examining company information, managing quality, or solving productivity problems. All this came from the top.

This all changed in the midseventies. A coincidence of factors weakened U.S. superiority. Energy costs jumped. Competitors from Europe and Asia blasted on the scene with an array of methods to cut and control fixed costs and increase their products' appeal: newer technologies, lower labor costs, more involvement of workers in managing productivity, leaner management structures, and greater focus on design quality and customer satisfaction. For the first time, the United States had to compete worldwide. It had the added obligation of having to support a military-industrial complex, which drained more resources and creativity from its private sector than in any of these other countries.[7] The United States also became used to living beyond its means, as large government deficits turned it into a debtor nation. In this new environment, management and union or nonunion workers simply could not continue to think about constant increases in wages and benefits without close attention to the profits and productivity of the enterprise. The first reaction was to cut labor costs quickly and reduce the size of annual wage cost increases.

The widespread decline of unions in the United States to less than 13 percent of the private sector workforce has not led to the "solution" many people who blamed unions for the lack of competitiveness expected. It has not increased productivity. Obviously, one reason is that both union and nonunion workers and managers and both companies and employees have all been deeply embedded in the fixed wage and benefit system as a cultural value.

Despite the decline of unions, when labor costs rise, productivity gains are not enough to offset this added compensation. Just because the portion of business costs that are labor costs are rising does not mean *real* wages can be expected to go up—a cruel irony for employees and for companies. Also, the Department of Labor noted that benefit costs have continued to increase more rapidly than wages. From 1966 to 1989 benefit costs rose 5.1 percent versus 4.1 percent for wages. For 1990, however, wages and salaries increased 4.5 percent while benefit costs rose 6.9 percent. And the trend is up. Just as industry reduced the momentum of wage increases temporarily in the late seventies and eighties, the Labor Department believes that employers undertook several cost-containment measures such as self-funding insurance plans, increasing the availability of health-plan alternatives, increasing defined contribution plans and cost sharing by employees. But the slowdown in benefit advances, which took place from 1981 to 1985, was short-lived, and benefit costs are continuing to rise rapidly, primarily because of rapidly growing health insurance costs and the increased Social Security tax rate.[8] There is a controversy about how to measure inflation-adjusted wages. But Figure 2.1 is crystal clear: real wages have gone down miserably or up negligibly in the last decade and a half. Specifically, average earnings went from a peak of about $18,150 in 1972 to $15,970 in 1989 (according to the Labor Department) or $18,778 in 1989 (according to the Social Security Administration). These figures underscore the necessity for two-earner families.

With this erosion or very small increase of workers' real spending power during their working years, even those workers with defined-benefit pension plans are not able to look forward confidently to retirement. As a rule, the employer-funded defined-benefit pension plan, in which one can rely on approximately 70 percent of one's last three years in salary, is declining with fewer and fewer workers being covered each year. Seventy percent of workers were covered in 1979, while 49 percent are covered in 1990. In addition, those workers with defined-benefit pension plans are finding that most employers do not add cost-of-living increases (COLAs) to the pension over the years. Thus, these plans may be "defined" but they may not be enough. A number of compensation consultants echoed this: "Most pension plans don't have COLAs built in. The real problem is that pension plans themselves are not moving forward. Companies are looking for an alternative to pensions. Only a minority of plans have COLAs and in most it is done on an ad hoc basis at the discretion of the company."

It may not be surprising that workers were evenly split when asked in a recent Gallup Poll, sponsored by the Employee Benefits Research Institute, whether they would be willing to trade their next pay increase at a job for a share in the ownership of the company that could be cashed out at retirement.

What does all this add up to? No matter which interpretation one chooses, the reality is that the advantage of the fixed wage and benefit system has been that it is "fixed," but the result for many employees has not been a significant uptrend in real wages nor widening coverage for comfortable pensions. Ironically, low productivity and higher wage and benefit costs recently put workers in an anomalous situation, where they're getting little, or less, yet costing their employers more! Over the same 1970-to-1990 period, the shocker is that the real value of stocks has risen more than the real value of wages. In retrospect, employee involvement in stock ownership may have made more sense.

The Role of Employee Ownership

I believe you will see employee ownership implemented as a supplemental benefit and not as a primary form of retirement income. I think you will see a growth in employers seeking to combine ESOPs with other benefit plans, like the attractiveness of 401(k) plans with employee ownership features. Clearly, employee ownership is not as certain a benefit as what many sponsors would have had before with the employer-supported defined benefit plan. From a practical standpoint, I see a lot of employers that are backing away from the retirement security promise all together, at least with regard to future retirees. While employee ownership is not certain or secure, at least when you are offering this benefit it could be in lieu of nothing.

—The senior pension expert at a major accounting and consulting firm

Let's begin to examine in detail how employee ownership is changing the structure of wages and benefits as shown in Figure 2.2. This application of employee ownership has grown rapidly since 1980. According to the number of companies, it is most prevalent in New York Stock Exchange companies—a finding that supports the preceding prediction by our anonymous benefits expert, since most of these companies have not eliminated their defined-benefit plans. Rather, they simply have not provided for cost-of-living increases with their defined-benefit plans or extended them to other employees but have somehow moved to restructure their benefits. Employee ownership often fills this new function. Over-the-Counter corporations have the next most extensive use of employee ownership. But, it is important to recognize a crucial difference vis-à-vis NYSE companies. OTC companies as a rule are much smaller than NYSE companies and generally do not have employer-paid defined-benefit plans. In these companies employee ownership or ESOPs are, as our benefit expert notes, "in lieu of nothing."

At the beginning of this chapter, Michael I. Lew of Coopers and Lybrand said that companies may be restructuring wages and benefits as part of a plan to maximize shareholder value and avoid takeovers. He is partly correct. We found that the restructuring of benefits and wages in firms without an announced takeover environment outnumber those in a takeover environment in every year, but the firms operating in takeover environments are a substantial fraction in every year except 1990, when the takeover market temporarily collapsed. Finally, more New York Stock Exchange firms restructured wages and benefits in a takeover environment compared with the other exchanges. In Appendix G.1 we have provided a company-by-company list of all documented uses of employee ownership to restructure wages and benefits from 1980 to 1990 in public corporations which also notes the role of takeovers in each case.

The major approaches to wage and benefit restructuring are trading stock for wages, replacing and restructuring defined-benefit plans, restructuring profit-sharing plans, funding postretirement health benefits with employee stock holdings, using leveraged ESOPs to prefund the company match in a savings or 401(k) plan, and some special applications.

One benefits expert described how employee ownership is now being widely used in defined-benefit pension plans that are not terminated or replaced:

Companies are increasing the amount of pension assets invested in their own companies because it conserves cash flow and it is a means to obtain some of the benefit of the surplus assets of an over-funded defined-benefit plan without paying tax on it and without violating ERISA. And if you are a utility, you are

FIGURE 2.2   *Wage and Benefit Restructuring and Employee Ownership: Some Trends*

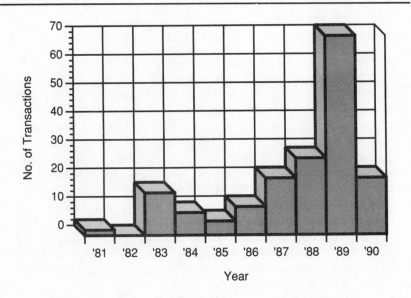

Rapid Growth

. . . But NYSE and OTC Dominate

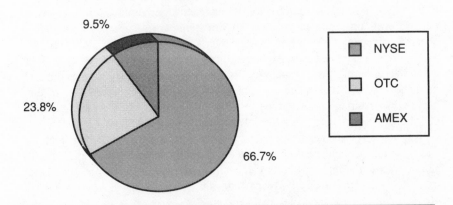

Source: Public Company Employee Ownership Database, 1990. Chart by Lawrence R. Greenberg

not going to get most of that money back because the consumer is going to be required to give that money back or the government is going to come after it. A lot of companies are investing up to 10% of the plan's assets in their own stock. If that is newly issued stock, then the corporation will also get new capital. But you do not get employee ownership in a real sense, because in the case of the defined-benefit plan, the trustee ends up voting most of these shares.

Trading Stock for Wages

The employees of the New Continental will be significant partners in the company. This plan provides employees with an immediate share in the airline's profitability. It is also part of Continental's commitment to long-term planning and growth, and its commitment to employees sharing very directly the returns that are possible from a company properly structured to take advantage of the opportunities afforded by deregulation. Employees are being presented with a plan that makes a very sharp change in their compensation and productivity levels. Therefore, we believe those employees should share significantly in the ownership of the company in order to participate with other investors in the rewards that come with a competitive cost structure.... While the plan would sharply reduce Texas Air's ownership of the company, it would result in a much stronger and more stable company and substantially benefit Texas Air's public shareholders. Employee ownership is particularly important in a high service business such as Continental's. We would become the largest employee-owned airline in the world.

—Frank Lorenzo

What I would recommend and predict, due to the threat of takeovers and to competitive pressures, is that you are going to see corporations substituting stock for salary increases and bonuses and other things. This will happen despite the fact that leverage has lost a lot of its attractiveness. As a neo-classical economist, I believe anything that makes wages more flexible in fact makes wages higher.

—A benefits consultant who wishes to remain anonymous

Until 1986, the major way employee ownership was used in restructuring wages and benefits was trading stock for wage and benefit investments and commitments to reorganize work or improve productivity. Indeed, employee ownership in general and ESOPs in specific, became mistakenly identified in the mid-eighties with "rescuing a failing firm." But our complete list of wage and benefit restructuring employee-ownership plans clearly establishes that trading stock for wages make up less than 17 percent of all wage and benefit restructuring between 1980 and 1990. (See Appendix G.1 for a complete list.) Most of the public companies using this approach were unionized companies in industries that had come under severe competition or had been deregulated: steel, airlines, auto, trucking, meatpacking, and railroads. These comprise nine of the ten cases. Both labor and management initiated concession bargaining: frequently management asked for concessions without offering stock, while unions quickly figured out that this request gave them the opportunity of assuming the role, "investor," rather than employee. Most of the public corporations that used concessionary ESOPs were locked into fixed wage and benefit costs, rigid work rules in collective bargaining agreements, patterns of mismanagement—and bloated management—and a cycle of underinvesting in new technology in their own facilities. Their development is shown in Figure 2.3. There has been steady appearance but not real growth, mainly in New York Stock Exchange companies.

In retrospect, it's noteworthy that less than 25 cases in a decade received extensive print, TV, and radio coverage—both regional and national—probably because these were the first high-visibility corporations to seriously consider employee ownership and the prospect of unions and management becoming partners piqued media interest. The first widely publicized case involved Rath Packing Co. (formerly NYSE), whose story was also monitored by the National Center for Employee Ownership.

Rath was the largest meat packing plant in the world for many years. Failure to modernize its facilities and market its products to supermarkets in the 1950s and 1960s, combined with rising hog costs, falling consumer demand for pork products, and increased competition from lower wage nonunion packers got Rath into serious trouble by the late 1970s. The company also had large unfunded pension obligations, long-term debts, and an expensive benefit package for older and retired workers. In May 1978, management asked for a wage concession. United Food & Commercial Workers Local 46 rejected these demands. Under the union's plan (presented in March 1979), the employees purchased 60 percent of the company by buying authorized but unissued treasury stock with a federal Urban Development Action Grant (UDAG) loaned through the city of Waterloo, Iowa. All employees chose to join the ESOP except for members of a small union in one of Rath's branch plants. Each employee received 10 shares of stock in exchange for $20 a week in deferred wages. Vacation, sick pay, and pension increases were put into an escrow account; the union could veto any disbursements from this account. The plan was approved in June 1980.

The union negotiated a very democratic structure. Workers elected 3 worker and 10 outside directors out of a board of 16 and voted for 3 of the 5 ESOP trustees, giving them control of stockholders' meetings, and negotiated for the establishment of shopfloor problem-solving groups to get their ideas to management. But the company continued to lose money, which led to termination of the defined-benefit pension plan and a three-year freeze on wage increases and COLAs. But the company declared bankruptcy in November 1983 for a number of reasons unrelated to the ESOP, which sharply reduced labor-management tensions and helped improve productivity. A number of factors caused the decline: the death of two CEO candidates at a critical point in time, falling prices for pork products, rising costs for raw materials, 20-percent interest rates on some loans, more nonunion competition, allegations of collusion by certain industry entities in the firm's demise, all leading to a series of desperate actions, which shattered labor-management peace. Under the circumstances, researchers say it is surprising the company held out this long.[9]

FIGURE 2.3 *Trading Stock for Wages: Growth by Year and Stock Exchange of Company*

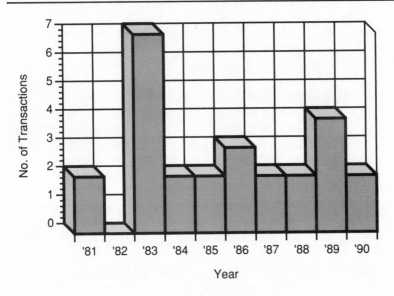

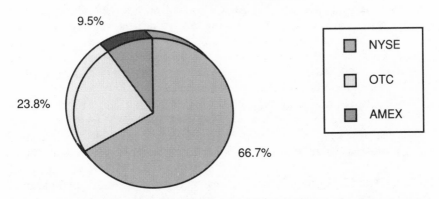

No Steady Growth

Mainly NYSE Companies

Source: Public Company Employee Ownership Database, 1990. Chart by Lawrence R. Greenberg

In the summer and fall of 1979, the problems of Chrysler Corporation transfixed the United States and evoked enormous public debate about whether to allow it to fail or to have it undergo a government rescue. Late in the fall, Congress approved the Chrysler Loan Guarantee Act of 1979, through which the government guaranteed the company's loans until it regained its health. As part of that package, United Auto Workers and other nonunion employees traded wage and benefit concessions for $162.5 million of newly issued Chrysler stock, or about 25-percent of the company plus a seat on the board of directors for the UAW president Douglas Fraser.

If Rath illustrates proaction and initiative by union and management, Chrysler illustrates foolish and narrow-minded behavior. Despite taking credit for the employee-ownership idea, Lee Iacocca and senior officials of the company fought it tooth and nail. The United Auto Workers leadership was no better. They never had a coherent plan to use their status as a 25-percent holder in a major public corporation to empower themselves and contribute to share-holder decisions, board decisions, or labor-management cooperation. Designed by Congress and the administration, the Chrysler ESOP was grudgingly ac-cepted by both parties. In 1985, the company and the union decided to end the ESOP. The company bought back the entire worker stake for $442.9 million, and 60,000 out of the 80,000 employees indicated they preferred to cash out their shares rather than hold onto them—a clear financial success for the workers given their investment. In the winter of 1990, however, Chrysler management decided it needed more concessions and floated the idea of employee ownership, which the union roundly rejected.[10]

The steelworkers' union unsuccessfully discussed buying out the current shareholders of Kaiser Steel Corp. as part of a stock-for-wages trade in 1981. In April of the same year, the employees of Continental Airlines unsuccessfully initiated a plan to pledge one half of all their salary increases to repay a loan needed to purchase 51 percent of the corporation and prevent a hostile takeover by Frank Lorenzo, whose Texas Air Corporation then owned 48.5 percent of the company. Later, employees offered to take 15 percent wage cuts and lined up $185 million in loans from nine banks, but the plan failed on a series of technicalities and led to a bitter behind-the-scenes fight between the company and Texas Air. It assumed a tragic overtone when Continental Chairman Alvin Feldman took his own life. The takeover succeeded.

Ironically, because of his reputation as unfriendly to labor, Lorenzo became the *first chief executive* to propose a wide-ranging program of profit sharing and employee ownership in a major American corporation. In 1983, he proposed a plan to permanently restructure Continental's labor costs with a reduction in the range of 25 percent and implement a 35-percent ESOP. He also proposed to contribute 15 percent of the airlines earnings before taxes to a profit-sharing program with return on revenues of 2 percent and 25 percent of earnings if return went above 15 percent. The unionized pilots and flight attendants refused to agree, although 60 percent of the workforce did agree. A bitter strike began. Some observers might be inclined to trace Lorenzo's deep bitterness toward la-bor to this particular event. His approach to employee ownership was never the same. In 1984, he declared bankruptcy to break the unions and the Bankruptcy Court approved the first phase of *his* ESOP plan, giving "founding" employees (mainly those who crossed picket lines) 5 percent of the company, an additional stock plan, plus the original profit-sharing plan. Approval of the stock plans was delayed because of opposition from the Airline Pilots Association.[11] Continental then hobbled along until late 1990, when it declared bankruptcy.

Concessionary ESOPs amounting to 10 to 25 percent of several airlines then followed rapidly. In airlines, Pan Am (NYSE 1981), Eastern[12] (then NYSE 1983), Republic (then NYSE 1983), Western[13] (then NYSE 1983), and Frontier (then AMEX 1984) confronted this challenge. Table 2.1 provides more detail. The lessons are clear. Airlines such as Western and Republic, which adopted plans early and engendered cooperation among the work groups, successfully used employee ownership to restructure. Those, such as Continental, Eastern, Frontier, and Pan Am—which waited until the carrier was weakened, prolonged the negotiations and struggles, did not resolve interunion difficulties, and allowed a poisoned labor-management atmosphere to contaminate the employee ownership—either failed miserably or achieved too little, too slowly.[14]

The next major industry to restructure with employee ownership was trucking where nonunion truckers and the 1977 deregulation created havoc with cost structures. In January of 1984, Branch Industries instituted a 15 percent wage cut in place of stock to reduce debt, increase its borrowing power, and continue fleet modernization. But it went out of business in 1986. Interstate Motor Freight Systems offered its employees 48 percent of the company for a 15-percent wage cut, which would create $75 million in capital over five years, but the company was bought in 1985. The Ryder/ P-I-E unit of IU International Corporation (NYSE) made a similar arrangement with its 11,000 employees, although IU planned to shed the troubled unit by distributing its shares to company shareholders. And Smith Transfer with 133 terminals in 33 states entered a more complex situation when it made another similar arrangement with employees as it confronted a takeover from American Carriers Corp., which caused the company to terminate the ESOP. Halls Motor Transit tried a similar plan and failed.

By early 1983, Transcon, then the tenth largest trucking company, decided it had to compete with thousands of small fleet or single-trucker carriers, and it initiated a marketing effort that increased business, although it was unable to obtain capital because of considerable past losses. Employees, who already owned 8 percent of the company's stock, chose to take a five-year 12-percent wage cut for 49 percent of the company and 3 seats on a board of 13 members. The plan caused stockholders to reassess the situation, and the stock rose from about $8 to about $14 a share; it caused lenders to commit a $30-million-line of credit, and the company has been profitable since the second quarter of 1983. But the union preferred cash without stock risk, and the company wanted less employee ownership and more control, so the ESOP was terminated under an agreement in June 1988, which distributed shares to employees. But the firm continued to lose money in 1987–1989 after it replaced the ESOP with a profit-sharing plan tied to continued wage concessions. In April 1990, it was sold to Growth Finance Corp., a private Miami firm.

TABLE 2.1 *Concessionary ESOPs in the Airline Industry*

Pan Am[a] ● On October 8, 1981, eighteen-thousand employees accepted a 10% immediate wage cut and wage freeze through 1982, saving the company $200 million. The five unions agreed to rotate one seat on the board and received about 13% of the company. In 1987 the unions hired Skadden, Arps, Meagher & Flom to represent its interests in case of a merger and proposed a restructuring of the company with substantial employee ownership in return for further concessions. Unions and the company have disagreed on the size of the holding the employees would get. Four unions hired Drexel Burnham Lambert to aid their bid and also held discussions with takeover investor Sir James Goldsmith about joining with them as a "white knight." Unions have sought to unseat several senior managers. The carrier continued to be very weak and no agreement was ever reached until it declared bankruptcy in early 1991.

Eastern Air Lines[b] ● The company's financial difficulties preceded the 1978 deregulation, and management initiated a number of profit-sharing and variable pay schemes. The unions refused further concessions in 1983, and Frank Borman threatened bankruptcy "à la Continental" unless he got 20–25% pay cuts. But the International Association of Machinists (IAM) forced Borman's hand and got a 32% three-year wage increase. A few months later, their financial analysts became convinced the situation was bad, and the IAM and other unions working with consultants Brian Freeman and Randy Barber traded 18% pay reductions, 5% productivity improvements and work rule changes for 25% of the airline plus 3 million shares of newly issued noncumulating preferred stock. In return, the company provided four board seats, access to its books, a promise of union input on corporate planning, and the development of an extensive employee involvement program. In 1984, substantial wage savings and extensive productivity improvements worked wonders. The company did turn around and labor-management relations changed dramatically, although substantial distrust existed. Tension between the unions, always a problem at Eastern, continued partly because the IAM took its wage cut off of its earlier 32% raise! While employee involvement made progress with the IAM and nonunion employees, it moved slowly with pilots and flight attendants. But the company had an enormous debt load from a poor strategic decision to buy fuel-efficient airplanes just before fuel prices fell. On December 31, 1984, Chairman Frank Borman ignored his own promise of joint problem solving and unilaterally extended the wage concessions for another year in a surprise message in his New Year's Letter. The employee-involvement program and labor-management cooperation collapsed. Unions and management fought all year. Under threat of bankruptcy, the pilots and the flight attendants offered 20% wage cuts, but machinist leader Charlie Bryan would agree only to 15% cuts if Borman was fired, because the IAM saw poor management as a key problem. Borman meanwhile had opened secret negotiations with Frank Lorenzo, and when the board refused to fire him and Bryan refused to give an additional 5% in wage concessions, the airline was sold to Lorenzo's Texas Air on November 25, 1986. Disagreements continued as Lorenzo began transferring assets from Eastern to his other airlines in a variety of ways, and employees used their status as preferred stockholders to fight these moves. Lorenzo sought deep concessions, which finally led to a strike during which employee groups attempted several failed buyout attempts, one led by former Baseball Commissioner Peter Ueberroth. Finally, Eastern filed bankruptcy and in 1990 the judge provided for a

(continued)

TABLE 2.1 *(Continued)*

court-appointed executive to run the company. While the interests of labor and management did diverge at points, the destruction brought upon Eastern for all parties, including Lorenzo, has led many observers to conclude that the Eastern situation might have been salvaged were it not for the particularly poisoned atmosphere between the headstrong individuals. The company was liquidated in 1991.

Western Airlines ● Several years of losses were the result of bad management, bad labor-management relations, and airline deregulation. A new CEO, Lawrence H. Lee, worked with the unions and created the Western Partnership, which was ratified by the Air Transit Employees, ALPA, the Transport Workers Union, Flight Attendants, Teamsters, and nonunion employees. The plan was much like a plan the Air Transit Employees had proposed to the former management, which had been unreceptive. Western employees received 32% of the airline, with full voting rights and 4 of the 15 board seats in exchange for one year of 10% wage reductions for most employees (12.5% for management and 18% for the pilots). Previously scheduled cost-of-living increases were deferred. While the wage reductions amounted to $42 million, actual savings were small because the Partnership was created as a replacement for previous wage concessions. It provided for a profit-sharing plan, which would allocate to workers 15% of the first $25 million in pretax profits and 20% of any profits above that amount during 1984–1986. Western expanded its route system to remain one of the major carriers in the West, and the company turned around with further concessions and a moderately successful labor-management problem-solving program. In 1985, Western was bought by Delta Airlines and employees received a fair return on their investment.

Republic Airlines[c] ● In 1983, nearly 8300 of the company's 14,500 employees were shareholders but six unions proposed to receive 25% of the stock. Previously, Republic completed a major program for a 15% wage cut that saved $65 million through May 1984. The company presented employees with a Partnership Plan to improve financial conditions over three years. Employees already held close to 20% of the airline and this could increase it to over 30%. The plan included profit-sharing provisions, several cost reduction measures, plus an extension through 1986 of 15% wage reduction and pay freeze, and lower pay and benefit scales for new employees. A Coalition of Unions of Republic Employees (CURE) met to explore solutions. The IAM was not a member of CURE. While labor and management struggled, the IAM in 1984 took the lead among the unions and ratified a stock for concessions agreement, which Republic President Stephen Wolf said would return the company to profitability. Other unions followed and in August 1986, Republic was sold to Northwest Airlines, with employees receiving an adequate return.

Frontier[d] ● In 1984, Frontier was actively traded, up 1 ⅜ to 13 ¼, as unions said they were considering making a bid. The unions agreed to 17% pay cuts for an annual savings of $30 million—in addition to cuts they had already accepted. The pilots took 30% cuts while Transport Workers Union representing 20 dispatchers took only 4%. Los Angeles investor Travis Reed met with unions to see if they would work with him. The company gave the unions a six-month option to purchase it for $220.4 million in

(continued)

TABLE 2.1   *(Continued)*

---

return for wage concessions. The wage concessions would support a $19 per-share offer in competition with an offer by Travis Reed for $17 a share, but wages would return to current levels if the ESOP was not completed or the option was canceled. The company's losses widened significantly in 1984, and the two parties began to disagree on the value of the concession package. The company placed further conditions that unions must agree to cover a certain portion of losses the carrier might expect during the winter months. In July 1985, all parties agreed and the four unions tentatively agreed to labor contracts. Both sets of agreements were to be submitted to union memberships for ratification in August. But then the company was purchased by People Express, which was then bought by Texas Air.

TWA • In 1987, TWA employees were seeking ways to block the proposed takeover by Texas Air Corp. because they feared that Frank Lorenzo would use Chapter 11 bankruptcy to eliminate union representation as he did in Continental Airlines. The unions created an alliance with Carl Icahn. They provided wage concessions and received 10% of the airline and a board seat. With this agreement in hand, Icahn was able to make a more attractive offer for the airline and Texas Air withdrew. Since the transaction, however, Icahn and the unions have been at a stand-off. Icahn took the airline private in 1988. What began as an Icahn-union partnership has turned sour for many reasons. Originally, the flight attendants did not support Icahn, who fought them in a bitter strike. Then, another group of unions—led by the machinists and flight attendants—tried to line up financing to do another buyout and avoid working with Icahn. Finally, the unions have been unhappy that Icahn is using the airline as an investment vehicle for possible takeovers. The company is weak; it does not have domestic routes to feed its international service and is saddled with debt of over $2 billion. Icahn wants more concessions to support capital investment in the company, whereas the unions are unwilling to give him concessions. The unions had been studying the possibility of a buyout with advisor Brian Freeman, but they too would inherit the staggering $490 million in annual debt service as of May 1990.

---

[a] *The Wall Street Journal,* October 8, 1981, April 11, 1985, February 2, 1987, July 23, 1987, August 3, 1987; PR Newswire July 7, 1982.

[b] *The Wall Street Journal,* January 2, 23, 1985, May 9, 1986, June 12, 1986, November 20, 1986; PR Newswire January 19, 1984, January 4, 1985, August 3, 1987.

[c] *The Wall Street Journal,* December 22, 1983; PR Newswire October 13, 1983, December 20, 1983.

[d] *The Wall Street Journal,* December 19, 26, 1984, January 10, 16, 1985, February 5, 7, 1985; PR Newswire December 23, 24, 1984, July 22, 1985; NCEO, 1989: 23–26.

Source: National Center for Employee Ownership *Newsletters,* 1981–1985: 219, 229, 236.

Although the Teamsters (IBT) did not endorse these experiments, they did not object to the carriers' conducting employee votes to create and approve voluntary employee-ownership plans as long as the National Master Freight Agreement Standards were bargained through such a plan and wages returned to this agreement at the end of the concession-for-investment agreement. It is believed they informally coordinated the ESOPs, which are comparable among the carriers. Some positive features of the trucking experiment were the carriers' promise to use the savings for capital investments and to give workers proportional board representation and full voting rights. But the NCEO January 1989 *Newsletter* concluded that, "of the nineteen or so ESOPS established at major, unionized carriers between 1983 and 1988, only one survived through 1989: PIE. The other firms either closed or were bought out.... The Management of PIE is planning to terminate its plan."

The lesson from trucking is that last-minute employee-ownership wage restructuring is just a BandAid over a hemorrhage. Management and unions lived in a fantasy-land blind to the economic realities of their industry that would ultimately bring them down. When they initiated plans, they focused mainly on cutting pay and investing in equipment rather than on reducing labor-management conflict and reorganizing work to improve productivity.

The next industry to try its hand was steel. It was hard going, because labor and management never entertained such cooperation before. As one steelworker put it, "There's about as much commonality between Bethlehem and us as there is between Quadafi and Reagan. We're so far apart we can't even agree on concepts, let alone contract language." Nevertheless, the 1980 master wage agreement between the industry and the United Steelworkers of America specifically authorized employee ownership "in addition to, or in substitution of, other provisions." Generally, concessions were exchanged for preferred stock. The first such agreements were Continental Steel and Chemical (NYSE) and Wheeling-Pittsburgh Steel (NYSE) in 1982. In 1986, Bethlehem Steel (NYSE) traded 10-percent wage reductions, which were repayable in cash from a pool of profit-sharing funds comprising 10 percent of its earnings up to $100 million and 20 percent of any earnings that exceed that sum. Employees were to receive preferred stock, convertible into common if the firm was not profitable or if the profit-sharing plan did not equal the level of givebacks. LTV Steel (NYSE) reached a similar agreement, which could amount to as much as 15 percent of its common stock.

CF&I Steel Corp. in Pueblo, Colorado (OTC), had to go far beyond this, taking significant wage and benefit reductions for almost 40 percent of the company and a board seat, but the company was forced to file for bankruptcy in 1990. Continental Steel tried the same but ended up in bankruptcy. The Steelworkers also exchanged profit sharing for wage and work-rule concessions at Northwestern Steel & Wire (formerly NYSE) several years before they bought 51 percent of the company. They also accepted 20-percent wage cuts at the Oregon Metallurgical Corporation (OTC), where they bought Corning-Fiberglass's 80 percent stake, and restructured the company to remain publicly traded but majority employee held. McLouth Steel was reorganized twice using employee ownership.

Steel has had the best track record of any unionized industry, because the United Steelworkers of America took a serious management attitude toward its industry and carefully put together a plan. Using respected consultants—

such as Eugene Keilin and Ronald Bloom of the ESOP investment banking firm of Keilin & Bloom and Steven Hester of the Washington law firm of Arnold & Porter—key union leaders, such as Lynn Williams, the President and his top aide, James Smith, painstakingly reviewed the financial situation of each firm and worked with management on a plan suitable to its special circumstances. Labor-management participation teams were introduced into many plants and changes in work organization were begun to improve productivity. The most troubled companies were thoroughly restructured. Even LTV Steel and Wheeling-Pittsburgh, which went into bankruptcy, have emerged with significantly more efficient steel operations, some of which are setting a standard in productivity improvements and labor-management cooperation. [15]

Recently, a form of "concession bargaining" has emerged in nonunion companies. We refer to this as "bargaining," because management seems to have decided that it must trade something for the reductions it feels the firm requires. In 1983, Dune's Hotel and Casino established an ESOP, so that 20 percent of employees' salaries would be paid for two years in shares of common stock as part of an extensive restructuring with its creditors. This plan specified that all employees would have to voluntarily agree. In 1987, Moseley Holding Corp. (OTC), which operates brokerages, approved an employee stock incentive program that provided for the following: 6 million common shares granted to employees in exchange for reductions in broker commission levels and salaried-employee compensation; an award of stock at year end as restricted stock grants to 325 commissioned salespersons and key managers; and a contribution to the ESOP for 300 clerical and sales support staff.

Bargaining is just what it was at Polaroid. Before adopting its 19-percent ESOP in 1988, the company initiated extensive meetings with representatives of its nonunionized workforce to explore what cuts could be used to fund a restructuring of compensation through employee ownership. The company decided to restructure and fund the ESOP with several elements of its fixed wage system. They eliminated a five-year seniority increase, which had been a company tradition, company contributions to the matching 401(k) program and the profit-sharing program, plus a budgeted pay-scale increase for 1989 and 1990 and then successfully argued to shareholders and before the Delaware Chancery Court that the employee ownership was largely shareholder neutral. The reasoning: we are aligning employees to shareholders and connecting them to the performance of the company, rather than just "laying" money on them as we did in the past. With cases such as that of Polaroid, Salomon Brothers, and the restructuring at Merrill Lynch discussed at the beginning of the next chapter, a new era of nonunion concession developments has begun. In the eighties, many of the employee-ownership plans in stock-for-wages trades in union industries did not raise serious questions about dilution because employees were in fact buying the employee ownership, and companies were skirting so close to disaster that shareholders saw the increased cash flow generated by concession bargaining as a benefit rather than an attack on their interests. We expect that stock-for-wages trades will grow enormously between now and the year 2000, as tougher national and global competition force wage and benefit restructuring in businesses, both union and nonunion, where unilateral decreases in wages and benefits by management would be impossible from an organizational and morale point of view, if the company gives nothing in return. Many management and employee groups see wage restructuring as a zero-sum game: I win/you lose or you win/I lose. As in the case of the Greyhound Bus Lines and New York *Daily News*, both sides let unproductive and destructive conflicts wreck the companies rather than explore this solution. We believe that compensation consultants, investment bankers, and outside shareholders themselves will be more likely to recommend the stock-for-wages trade as a way to avert the destructive effects of such rigid thinking.

Replacing Defined-Benefit Plans

In a recent *Los Angeles Times* article, Howard Weitzmann, executive director of the Association for Private Pension and Welfare Plans, said that about 15,856 defined-benefit pension plans were terminated in 1989, a 37-percent increase from 1988, while only 5461 plans were created, a 67-percent drop. Weitzmann believes that many companies now consider the costs of running a pension plan too high to justify them and expects a continued erosion of defined-benefit plans under which employees know how much benefit they are entitled to receive, based on their salaries and years of service.[16]

How does employee ownership fit into this? The bottom line is that while defined benefits are in decline, their *complete* replacement by employee ownership is happening only in a relatively small number of cases that affect mainly nonunion workers. Figure 2.4 shows the trend has been generally on the upswing but—charts can lie—this documents less than 50 cases over a decade in publicly held firms. The growth can be directly tied to federal law: from 1986 to 1988, precisely when we see the emergence of this trend, Congress allowed companies to terminate defined-benefit plans, to buy annuities for workers with their accumulated assets, and to use the excess assets—called a rollover—to purchase stock on behalf of employees in an ESOP. Before this temporary window of opportunity for companies, they had to pay a 10-percent excise tax on the rollover. Some very large companies were able to use employee ownership to transfer enormous amounts of capital to their corporate coffers. Thus, it was most prevalent in New York Stock Exchange companies.[17] Appendix G reviews all the cases.

There are two sides to this issue. On one hand, few employees would prefer an uncertain pension plan tied to the company's stock in place of an assured benefit. While employees do not *lose* their pension when the plan is terminated, because they do get annuities for the assets accumulated to that date, they can

FIGURE 2.4   *Replacing Defined-Benefit Plans with Employee Ownership*

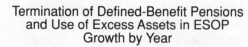

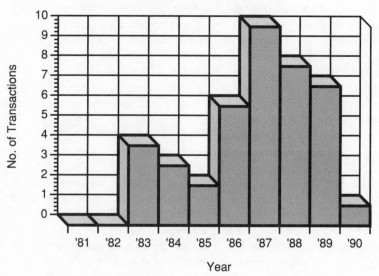

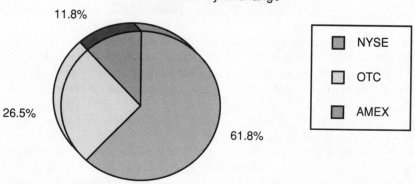

Source: A Public Company Employee Ownership Database, 1990. Chart by Shane Williams and Lawrence R. Greenberg

no longer rely on a promise that is changed midstream. A young employee, who worked 15 years for a company and was motivated by a generous pension commitment, suddenly finds himself or herself with an annuity whose value is far below what his or her ultimate pension would be because the company will stop contributing to the pension plan, say, 15 years before his or her retirement. One cannot tell for certain in each case whether the employee-held stock the worker receives over the years will or will not raise the total retirement plan to the level it would have been without the termination. William D. Partridge, a benefits consultant at the Wyatt Company, has this to say about the problem: "If a final average-pay, defined-benefit plan is to be curtailed or terminated and replaced with an ESOP, the company will be transferring to employees the investment risk and a portion of the inflation risk . . . . The allocation of the ESOP contribution may have to be skewed in favor of the older or longer-service employees to reduce this risk. Since the value of the pension accrual in a defined-benefit plan is more significant at the older ages, the ESOP may not be an effective replacement plan for veteran employees.[18]

On the other hand, most corporations that terminate their defined-benefit plans probably do not offer employees anything in return. Compared to the thousands of terminations, the documented number of ESOP replacements is miniscule! So it is *inaccurate* to see ESOPs as the reason for defined-benefit terminations. Many companies simply try to pocket the excess assets that they accumulated in these tax-free pension trusts over the years. While employees surely cannot be happy to hear that their pension plan is terminated, relatively speaking, the companies that attempt to restructure these assets in the form of employee-held stock may be more responsive to their employees' interests. Replacing defined-benefit plans with ESOPs and other defined-contribution plans, which load risk onto workers, is a fundamental fear of employee ownership by union officials, according to a recent poll, but there are few documented examples of an existing publicly traded company terminating its pension plan for its unionized employees and replacing it with an ESOP. The most prominent case is Dan River textiles. Termination would be difficult to effect, because such plans are determined by collective bargaining contracts. Employee benefits expert Steven Hester suggests that a number of unionized companies have agreed to replace defined-benefit with defined-contribution plans. Later, the workers may find that a significant portion of the assets of these plans are in company stock. In public companies, such plans are terminated for union workforces mainly for bankruptcy, as in the case of LTV Corp. and Wheeling Pittsburgh Steel (formerly NYSE), but employee ownership did not replace the plans. Both companies had earlier tried to trade stock for wages to forestall their demise. If the steelworkers had known what they now know, they could have ended up taking a bigger cut but owning most of those firms and avoiding bankruptcy. Wheeling Pittsburgh Steel Corp. has emerged from bankruptcy as a NYSE corporation with 11-percent employee ownership, which was negotiated with the United Steelworkers during the reorganization. In fact, in an era when nonunion wage increases on average exceed union wage increases, the defined-benefit pension plan seems to be a major economic benefit of being a union worker.

Monarch Capital Corp. (NYSE) saw the replacement as "an important step toward a goal of a more entrepreneurial workforce. Employees will be able to share in the results of their efforts and will be able to see first-hand how new sales, improved productivity, and cost savings impact the corporations earnings." Equimark Corp., the NYSE holding company for Equibank, said that the move would increase its capital by $8 million and create the largest employee ownership of any major U.S. bank. Another financial services firm to move in this direction was Primark Corp. (AMEX) in 1988. Indeed, the financial services sector's nonunion employees seem mostly affected, as this idea has been used by Poughkeepsie Savings Bank (OTC) of New York, Merchants Bancorp. (OTC) of Connecticut, Indiana Federal Corp. (OTC) of Indiana, Pacific Western Bancshares (OTC) of California, and Banks of Mid-America (OTC) of Oklahoma among others. Two prominent NYSE nonfinancial companies that used this idea were the Roper Corporation and the H. H. Robertson Company.[19]

Many terminations take place in the context of a takeover or acquisition, where the company is trying to restructure or raise large amounts of capital quickly. The best-known case is Harcourt Brace Jovanovich's (NYSE) fight against Robert Maxwell. In 1983, Michael Baker Corp. (NYSE) restructured its ownership using benefit-plan terminations as one funding source to avoid accepting another company's offer and to resolve a yearlong internal battle with a group of directors for control of the firm. In 1986, Ashland Oil Company (NYSE) used excess assets from a salaried-employees plan to fund most of its $225 million-ESOP. The idea was used by the Bank of New York and Enron Corp. (NYSE) in 1986, the Barry Wright Corporation and Universal Foods Corp. (NYSE) in 1988. Emery Air Freight terminated its plan to aid its restructuring to avoid a takeover and facilitate its acquisition of Purolator, while Figgie International and Allied Group Inc. (OTC) used the assets to facilitate new acquisitions. After the Imperial and Holly Sugar corporations merged in 1987, the company restructured its pensions, became significantly employee-held, and used the proceeds to repay long-term debt.

This new use of employee ownership raises serious issues for unorganized salaried-employee groups. Defined-benefit pensions represent one of the few crucial conditions that many nonunion employees accept as tantamount to a company commitment to them. Indeed, given the prevalence of such plans in union workforces, it is probable that many public corporations with defined-benefit pensions enhance the antiunion motivation of their salaried and nonunion workforces by offering to secure precisely this economic benefit, which distinguishes the union workforce.

In 1984, the salaried employees of Lyons Metal Products (formerly NYSE) charged that management's use of the excess assets to take the firm private in the face of a tender offer by Irwin Jacobs violated a commitment the company made to them. That case led to a settlement where the firm did go private in a leveraged buyout (LBO), but the salaried employees restructured that LBO to attain majority ownership of the firm and control of its board. These cases suggest that a new form of nonunion employee activism over employee ownership may be emerging.[20]

What does the future hold? Possibly many more transactions of this type exist in public companies than we have documented because they may have had no reason to announce the transaction. Congress no longer excuses companies from paying an excise tax on rolling over excess assets to an employee-ownership plan, but these transactions persist. It is also likely that more and more companies planning to simply terminate their defined-benefit plans may entertain the employee-ownership concept as employee ownership becomes more widespread and acceptable among public corporations. At least, companies will continue to supplement modest defined-benefit plans with employee-ownership plans. Ken Weinberger of William M. Mercer Inc. comments that employers will examine their defined-benefit plan and their employee-ownership plans in terms of producing a combined retirement income that exceeds the typical 70 percent of final average pay, which most employers target for retirement income.[21]

More activism can be expected among salaried-employee groups, which will probably try to get written commitments from companies to use the excess assets for the employees' benefit. In any event, the trends we are documenting in this chapter point toward increased employer-employee tension over the structure of benefits, the existence of benefits, the final economic value of benefits in retirement, and the role of employee ownership in benefits. The need of boards of directors and management teams to use defined-benefit plans to pay for employee ownership in order to avoid dilution will rise as shareholders become more vocal and activistic about the impacts of dilution on employee-ownership plans. But if a company decides to terminate a defined-benefit plan, it is better to get employee ownership instead of zero in return.

Replacing Profit-Sharing Plans

In our discussion of replacing profit-sharing plans,[22] we turn first to a letter written to employees of the Quaker Oats Company by the chairman and CEO, William D. Smithburg, and the president and COO, Frank Morgan.

> The Quaker ESOP will provide employees with an audible voice in determining the future direction of the Company. What's more, as each owner-employee's stake increases, the strength of his or her voice will grow. Your management's desire that employees have such a voice is reflected in last year's amendment to the Profit-Sharing and Investment Plan and the Stocksharing Plan, which affords employee participants, rather than a bank trustee, the right to vote their Quaker shares. We value your ownership in Quaker and your voice in the Company's future.[23]

Many public companies never adopted defined-benefit pension plans, or they adopted them only for their unionized workforces. Several of these companies created deferred profit-sharing plans for all employees or just for salaried employees. A large percentage of the Fortune 100 companies have such plans, and deferred profit-sharing plans are a preferred retirement vehicle among many smaller and OTC companies. While a profit-sharing plan puts the risk of the size of the ultimate pension payout on the employee, liberal profit-sharing plans in many public companies are viewed by workers as a company obligation and an important part of the company's culture. The expense of such a plan increases the more: (1) employees come to expect a set amount of profit sharing each year as a fixed part of their compensation; and (2) the profit-sharing trust invests its assets in the securities of other companies, leaving the firm without the use of that capital.

Recently, however, public companies have been moving aggressively to restructure profit-sharing plans with employee ownership in order to cut costs and increase employee identification with the firm. Figure 2.5 shows steady growth, with NYSE and OTC companies being the leaders.

Quaker Oats is a case in point. The corporation had a tradition of encouraging employees to own its shares. In 1985, the company established an ESOP and notified employees that 20 percent of their annual profit-sharing award would be provided to them in company stock. The company argued in its literature to employees that "because the ESOP can purchase shares with borrowed funds, it can acquire a relatively large number of shares at 1985 prices for future allocation" and that employees "will enjoy any and all appreciation in share price of this initial block of shares, even though the stock is allocated to them over time." The company has encouraged employees to invest capital in their profit-sharing accounts, over which they have sole control in Quaker stock. Since 1984, employees transferred $5 million into the Quaker Stock Fund. They were directing 45 percent of another benefit fund, called the Convertible Compensation Fund—the company's 401(k) plan—for investment in Quaker stock.

In 1988, the company announced a further extension of employee holdings. Half of the annual profit-sharing award would be in the form of an Employee Stock Ownership Plan. A blue-chip company such as Quaker could be very persuasive since, "In the initial modest ESOP program, we have seen that the ESOP award value can be significantly greater than the portion of profit sharing it replaced." Indeed, the restructuring caused the award to go up from 7.5 percent of pay under profit sharing alone to 8.1 percent of pay. ESOP tax advantages allowed the company to contribute more on behalf of participants without increasing their after-tax costs beyond historic levels. In 1989, the company decided to move yet again. It ended profit sharing altogether and replaced it with an ESOP. To reduce the risk of investment loss, the company's ESOP used convertible preferred stock, which would be less vulnerable to market swings than common stock and have a higher dividend rate.

FIGURE 2.5 *Restructuring Profit-Sharing Plans with Employee Ownership*

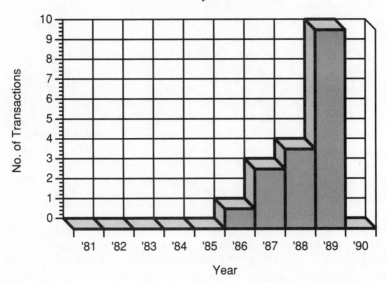

Profit-Sharing Contributions to Fund Employee Ownership Growth by Year

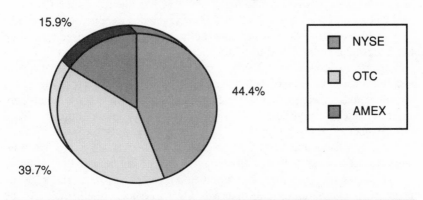

Profit-Sharing Contributions to Fund Employee Ownership Shown by Exchange

Source: Public Company Employee Ownership Database, 1990. Chart by Shane Williams

Quaker eased its employees into a complete restructuring of a fixed-benefit program, which resulted in "a closer linkage between employee and shareholder interests and increased value to both." But the company pointed out repeatedly that the value of the ESOP depends primarily on the investment performance of Quaker stock over time. The risk passed to employees.[24]

Companies have used various ways to transform their profit-sharing commitment into an employee-ownership stake. The dominant factor is that companies can often reduce the after-tax cost of their profit-sharing benefit because of the ESOP tax advantages and gain use of the capital until employees retire. Faced with many corporate challenges, Sears, Roebuck & Company (NYSE) set up an $800 million ESOP in 1989 and will use the shares to fund its contributions to its profit-sharing plan over the next 15 years. The Sears move was closely watched, since the company began profit sharing in 1916 and is considered a bellwether for the concept. Some companies, such as Lydall Corp. (AMEX) make their full profit-sharing contribution in employer stock. The firm is now 19 percent employee held. Many firms, such as Radiation Systems Inc. (OTC), Team Inc. (AMEX), have moved in this direction by completely replacing their profit-sharing plans with ESOPs.

Some firms have been more conservative. The Hach Co. (OTC) decided in 1989 that its ESOP would receive just 25 percent of the company's profit-sharing contribution, while McCrae Industries (AMEX) has made the determination flexible from year to year. Other firms are seeking to use the conversion of profit-sharing contributions into employee-held stock as a way to firm up employees' perception of the link between profits and profit sharing. Thus, Greiner Engineering (AMEX) came up with a sliding formula that will determine the amount of profits that go into the firm's new ESOP, while the Chubb Corp. decided that its profit-sharing payout would be triggered at a lighter level of profit. Many of the companies that restructure profit sharing with employee ownership have had a long commitment to both concepts.

Many people confuse the term *profit sharing* with cash profit sharing. In fact, less than 1 percent of U.S. firms have cash profit sharing. Since most companies make their profit-sharing contributions to defined-contribution pension trusts and invest the assets over many years, there is in fact little difference between many "profit-sharing plans" and "employee stock-ownership plans." Recently this distinction has further broken down because Congress has concluded that contributions to a profit-sharing plan need not be based on profit, so that companies with such plans can turn them into employee-ownership plans by making stock contributions to them at will. Over 15 percent of all employees are currently members of deferred-profit sharing plans. We estimate that well over one third of all publicly traded corporations maintain such plans and expect that the restructuring of such plans with employee ownership and the investment of their assets in more employer securities will grow briskly. Because profit sharing occurs in many firms without any other form of pension, we do believe that this trend will raise profound questions of risk for employees.[25] We do expect the flush profit-sharing plans in many public companies that are invested in securities outside the company to be both a major source of financing for employee ownership and a critical way of restructuring wages and benefits to prevent the aftermath of dilution from employee ownership.

Restructuring Postretirement Medical Benefits

There are a few problems with using ESOPs for postretirement health benefits. The lack of diversification represents a substantial risk. Moreover, in specific industries it would clearly be disastrous. When an ESOP is used to fund postretirement health benefits, it loses some of its attractiveness because you must pay taxes on monies withdrawn and then you must buy the medical coverage.

—Doug Edwards, Foster Higgins, a benefits consulting firm

Postretirement health benefits are one of the main directions ESOPs are going. Particularly with leveraged ESOPs, in the past the driving force has been strategic, a corporate end for a defense against a hostile takeover. With the demise of the junk-bond market and takeovers, there's been a downturn in the ESOP market. Unless there's some other major motivating factor for causing employers to adopt ESOPs, other than tax advantages, then they will really die down. Retirement health benefits is a cutting edge issue and a new purpose for ESOPs. Employers will have to do something like set up a floor value of the stock to make this use of employee ownership palatable to employees, and that's the negative from the employer's point of view.

—Ken Weinberger, William M. Mercer Co.

Many companies have made written commitments or voluntarily offered to pay the health costs of their employees and immediate families when the employee retires. When these assurances were originally provided to employees, the liability was thought to be immaterial. While employers have been aware of the increasing costs of these promises, companies now account for retiree health costs as they are paid to employees. Some companies, like Whitman featured at the beginning of this chapter, have phased out their retiree insurance program and have introduced an employee stock ownership program. Instead of the company paying medical bills, employees get convertible preferred stock during their working years. After they retire, they can use the value of the shares to buy company-arranged group health insurance.

The retiree benefits issue has intensified into a crisis because the Financial Accounting Standards Board (FASB), the rule-making body of the accounting profession, has proposed to change the accounting rules for this liability:

Currently, premiums paid for retiree medical insurance and other benefits are accounted for on a cash basis, with costs expensed as paid. Cash-basis accounting has been acceptable because the liability was originally thought to be immaterial and because the benefits were viewed as revocable. However, the liabilities are now known to be significant and the courts have limited management's ability to reduce or revoke promised benefits. The FASB has concluded that retiree health care and life insurance benefits are a form of deferred compensation and that the cost should be accrued during the years an employee provides service rather than when the benefits are paid. The [FASB] Exposure Draft requires that the employer estimate the future cost of postretirement benefits and recognize that cost over the period the benefits are earned in 1992, although that date may slip to 1993 or 1994. It also requires the employer to book the accrued postretirement benefit expense as an accrued balance sheet liability beginning in 1997. Industry experts estimate the total liability for all U.S. corporations to be as high as $1 trillion while one major corporation estimates that its annual cost under FASB will be as much as 2.5 to 3.0 times the pay-as-you-go expense and that total liability accrued will be 14.5 times the annual pass-as-you-go expense.[26]

Indeed, on June 28, 1990, the FASB's latest decision will let the date that corporations must recognize these costs slip into 1993. The Board will probably issue a final rule by the beginning of 1991. The group tentatively agreed to allow companies to take a one-time charge to income for benefits the companies are already committed to pay, although other companies could account for the accumulated costs over a 20-year period. Despite this flexibility, this rule will present huge difficulties for many companies, especially firms that have a large number of retirees.

In 1988, 1989, and 1990, fourteen publicly traded corporations decided to establish leveraged Employee Stock Ownership Plans to fund this benefit as shown in Table 2.2. In all cases the change covered only salaried or nonunion employees. It is reported that both Armstrong and Boise Cascade are trying to negotiate such a plan with their unions. Eighty-five percent of the cases are NYSE companies, and the larger established companies that are most worried about the financial impact are now entertaining this idea. About 40 percent of the companies were in a takeover environment, which suggests they decided to create a large ESOP and make it as shareholder neutral as possible by replacing significant benefits with employee-held stock. This strategy indicates that takeovers are likely to play a role directly or indirectly in the future of employee-ownership restructuring of retiree medical benefits.

Obviously, no employee would prefer employer stock as an uncertain funding source for health benefits over a fixed all-inclusive commitment. Nevertheless, all such plans are not equal. Four factors that can help distinguish plans benefiting employers from plans maximizing benefits to employees:

1. *The Kind of Plan Replacement.* An employee ownership plan, which replaces a corporation's revocable assurance not enforceable in court, is more appealing than one in which the employer simply dissolves the benefit altogether. If a plan is meant to replace a clear enforceable commitment from a corporation to its employees, the same mechanisms below help reduce risk to employees. Some companies plan to use employee ownership to fund health

TABLE 2.2   *Funding Retiree Health Plans with Employee-Held Company Stock*

Date	Company	Stock Exchange	Size of ESOP(%)	Takeover Environment
11/7/88	Ralston Purina	NYSE	9.1	No
1/23/89	Whitman	NYSE	15.0	Yes
4/4/89	Lockheed	NYSE	16.0	Yes
4/28/89	Sara Lee	NYSE	11.0	No
5/3/89	Boise Cascade	NYSE	15.0	No
5/26/89	Ball	NYSE	10.6	No
6/20/89	Armstrong World Industries	NYSE	12.0	Yes
6/22/89	Travelers	NYSE	5.0	No
9/9/89	SPS Technologies	NYSE	10.0	No
9/21/89	Lincoln Telecommunications	OTC	N/A	N/A
11/22/89	Builders Transport	OTC	15.0	Yes
1/17/90	Conrail	NYSE	11.0	No
1/17/90	Gillette	NYSE	2.0	No
11/14/90	Procter & Gamble[a]	NYSE	5.1	No

[a] This is in addition to a 19.4% ESOP created in March 1989.
Source: Public Company Employee Ownership Database, 1990.

benefits into the future. Ralston Purina decided to use employee ownership to fund health benefits for those who retire over the next five years, and thereafter it will no longer provide the benefit.

2. *Guaranteed Floor Value of the Stock and Size of Dividend.* Both Ralston and Boise Cascade structured their shares with a floor value, which cannot sink below a specified price. This provides some risk protection and predictability of the total benefit for employees yet preserves the corporation's ability to predict its own costs. The size of the dividend will determine how fast the "nest egg" grows.

3. *Treatment of Employees Unable to Fully Use the ESOP.* There are three groups: currently retired employees, employees who would not accumulate benefits, and employees close to retirement. Boise Cascade has said that currently retired employees will not be affected by its plan and has established special features for employees who cannot take advantage of the ESOP. On the other hand, Ralston Purina funded its employee ownership by doubling the company's match from 50 percent to 100 percent of the employee contribution to its 401(k) plan. But since many lower-paid employees may not have enough funds to save under this plan, they might not receive any benefits.

Some plans provide for workers over age 55 and close to retirement full benefits paid by the company. Armstrong World Industries, for example, eliminated future retiree medical coverage for employees over 47 years old.

4. *The Quality of the Group Insurance Plan and Related Health Care.* Companies that invest considerable time and energy in finding a high-quality but reasonable group insurance plan increase the chances that employees will get good health care. Also, companies whose current plans focus on preventative health care can minimize future problems. Some companies have also restricted current health plans. Armstrong, for example, redesigned its current plan to combat rising medical costs and also increased out-of-pocket premiums for current employees.[27]

5. *The Soundness of the Program and Employee Involvement.* The assumptions underlying this method of funding future health insurance will greatly determine its success. Companies make assumptions mainly about medical inflation, the cost of health insurance, and stock appreciation. Companies can spring the program on employees or invest time in involving them in the planning and communication. This is yet another employee-ownership issue that may lead to some form of coordinated approach to companies by their nonunion employees.

6. *Considerations of the Tax Impact on Employees.* When the employer pays health benefits after retirement, the employee pays no income taxes, but when the employee buys healthcare with the assets from employee ownership, he or she must pay income taxes on the stock distribution. Exempting employees from this tax payment used in such circumstances may require federal legislation. Also, perhaps such legislation should require that the ESOP trustee have independent legal, benefits, and financial counsel to evaluate the risk for employees if the ESOP is presented as a retiree health fund.

7. *The Quality of the Company.* No matter how liberally the plan is otherwise structured an employee holding in a solid company, such as Ralston Purina listed on the NYSE, will have a vastly different risk than an employee holding in Hocus Pocus Inc., an OTC firm highly leveraged with junk bonds! Some fundamental measures of the current financial integrity of the company and past performance of its stock and its industry's stock will allow an educated guess about the level of risk.

Salaried and union employee groups and government policymakers need to beware of cutting off their noses to spite their faces. If a certain group of corporations must choose between adopting the employee-ownership alternative and simply abandoning the benefits, then attacking this alternative will probably result in fewer retiree health benefits for tens of thousands of workers. Very few of the public companies that terminated defined-benefit plans replaced them with ESOPs because many companies replaced them with savings plans, which put most of the risk completely on the employee. At least this approach still involves a corporate commitment to the benefit. It is entirely possible that corporations will adopt employee-ownership vehicles other than leveraged ESOPs to resolve this problem.

The combination of the huge liabilities for shareholders represented by these benefit obligations *and* the need for public companies to offset the dilution in further major employee-ownership transactions as awareness of dilution grows will spur this type of transaction. On December 13, 1990, the *Wall Street Journal* reported that the IRS has raised questions about allowing these transactions.

Prefund Company Match to Savings and 401(k) Plans

> *The easiest place to integrate an Employee Stock Ownership Plan into a public corporation is to establish a leveraged ESOP and use the stock to prefund an existing benefit plan. Many public companies have 401(k) or savings plans in which they match employee contributions to the plan. In many the match is already in company stock. The leveraged ESOP accelerates the acquisition of that stock. When this happens, the company is making a long-term commitment to maintain the program and provide minimum funding. Companies do not always do that. In many instances corporations increase the match and enhance the benefit. It is often a no-lose situation for the employees.*
>
> —*Deborah Baker, ESOP Group, Chemical Bank, New York*

Public corporations have fully digested these facts. The most common benefit that is restructured using employee ownership is the company savings, thrift, or 401(k) plan (called a KSOP). Two thirds of the matching contributions in larger public companies are already in the form of company stock. In these firms, the ESOP is simply used to prefund the company's contribution by buying all the stock up front.[28] Almost half the wage and benefit restructuring employee ownership cases are KSOPs (Appendix G.1), which is the fastest growing type of employee ownership. That may be surprising to some, since the instances of trading-stock-for-wages employee ownership attract so much more publicity. This approach represents a large proportion of all public company ESOP transactions in 1989. In many companies, the savings plan is a supplement to a defined-benefit pension plan. In some companies 401(k) plans are the only retirement benefit plan. No matter which it is, introducing employee ownership is a way for the company to reduce its benefit costs or control increase in those costs.

By utilizing company stock through an ESOP, the company can use the potential savings to increase the benefit at nominal cost. Employees typically have some choice over how the assets they contribute to the plan are invested. As in the Whitman Corporation example at the beginning of this chapter, many companies encourage employees to invest their contribution in a company stock fund. In fact, some companies provide few investment choices, so that employees are required to put larger amounts of their contributions in company stock.

But the common approach in KSOPs is to invest the employees' contributions in assets other than company stock.[29] Figure 2.6 summarizes the growth, some trends, and the potential.

Our data prove the enormous popularity of this approach, which has grown rapidly since the early eighties. This growth really started in 1988, when it became clear that it was legal to graft an ESOP onto a 401(k) plan. With the assistance of the investment bank First Boston, J.C. Penney Inc. figured out a way of doing this that simply replaces the usual employer match with stock from a leveraged ESOP. That one innovation inspired a trend. The overwhelming number of companies are NYSE firms, although a sizable proportion are in the OTC sector. Before the J. C. Penney transaction, many public company ESOPs were largely defensive, but the use of ESOPs as a benefit substitution has not completely changed this. Note that NYSE companies establishing KSOPs are more likely to be in a takeover environment than are companies on other stock exchanges, and about a third of NYSE companies set up KSOPs in a takeover environment.

The typical scenario: a company generates a new issue of convertible preferred stock and then buys back a similar amount of common stock. The convertible preferred shares are used to prefund matches to the 401(k) plan. The net effect replaces nonemployee-shareholders with employee-shareholders, what we have called an ownership-replacement ESOP. In this transaction, dilution is addressed mainly by the use of employer stock to restructure the 401(k) match, while the share repurchase functions to reduce earnings-per-share dilution by keeping the number of shares outstanding lower. The potential for this form of employee ownership is enormous, because 401(k) plans are increasing more rapidly than any other type of retirement plan.

Some of the most well known companies in America have initiated KSOPs, and companies have done this for a variety of secondary reasons. KSOPs account for most of the dollar value of all major ESOP transactions in the 1988–90 period. Because companies are prefunding existing benefit programs, they are often able to undertake enormous leveraged ESOPs. Since many of these companies are highly creditworthy, they are able to borrow the funds to purchase employee stock ownership at reasonable rates, even in tight credit markets, as noted in the section on capital markets in the last chapter. AT&T and five of the seven Bell operating companies and GTE have aggressively set up extensive employee-ownership plans. AT&T included both salaried and nonsalaried employees. Bell Atlantic leveraged $1 billion of company stock to fund its 401(k) plan, Ameritech's ESOP amounted to $700 million, and BellSouth's amounted to $500 million, all in 1989–90. Whitman Corporation, Boise Cascade Corp., Lockheed, Conrail, and Lincoln Telecommunications decided to fund postretiree health insurance with employee ownership, but they boosted their 401(k) matching contribution and used that as the mechanism to establish a large amount of employee ownership. All these are NYSE companies.

FIGURE 2.6 *Prefunding Company Match to Savings Plans with ESOPs*

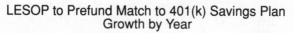

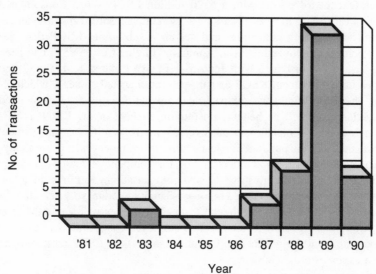

LESOP to Prefund Match to 401(k) Savings Plan
Growth by Year

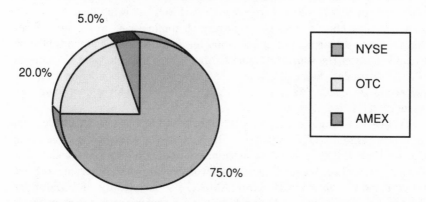

LESOP to Prefund Match to 401(k) Savings Plan
Shown by Exchange

Source: Public Company Employee Ownership Database, 1990. Chart by Shane Williams

Takeover jitters were reported as a motivation in some cases. But Appendix G.1 shows this is true only in a few cases. Delta Air Lines's (NYSE) stock went up 13 percent in the summer of 1989 amid takeover speculation in that industry. The company amended Delta's Family-Care Savings Plan for its nonunion workforce (except for pilots) with a $500 million ESOP. When Consolidated Freightways (NYSE) purchased Emery Air Freight, it resolved much takeover speculation among both companies and set up a substantial KSOP that created a 19-percent employee-held firm. Cummins Engine Co. (NYSE) had been involved in a takeover dance with Industrial Equity Limited in 1989–90 and established an 11.4-percent KSOP as part of a multifaceted strategy, which restructured the ownership of the company with several other parties, yet avoided this particular investor. The benefit substitution element of the KSOP is particularly relevant to companies in takeover environments. As one investment banker we interviewed put it, "You can't just throw money at your employees out of deference to shareholders. Also, for competitive reasons in some companies there is no need to just add new compensation. You must maintain a reasonable cost structure." Thus, because shareholders are very sensitive to uses of company resources that entrench management, they will sue at the drop of a hat. Cummins argued that "since future employee contributions to existing benefit programs will be matched in Cummins shares, the ESOP represents no additional expense to the company."

Indeed, many companies find that after benefiting from the tax incentives and the internal use of the capital because the match is invested in their own stock, they can often increase the size of the matching contribution. ITT Corp. noted that it paid $215 million a year in taxes and would get dividend tax deductions of $16.7 million per year with its KSOP, allowing them to increase their matching contribution for employees at nominal cost to the firm. Firms that enhanced their matching contribution for employees include the following: Conrail, Dayton Hudson, McDonald's, May, Mobil, Texaco, and Upjohn—all NYSE companies. Some firms are very aggressive in encouraging employee ownership and saving: Tandycrafts (NYSE) matches employee contributions at a rate of 200 percent!

This benefit-substitution approach has offered flexibility to smaller companies. Dahlberg Inc. (OTC) reported to the Securities and Exchange Commission that its 1988 KSOP represented its principal source of working capital. This example crystallizes the notion that employee benefit plans are serving as banks for corporations! Guardian Bancorp (AMEX) also adopted the "KSOP for performance model" by tying additional company contributions to company performance. The Rochester Community Savings Bank (OTC) is 6.8-percent employee held and relies on its KSOP as a major retirement benefit. Syncor International Corp. (OTC) needed to purchase 10 percent of its outstanding common stock from the foreign firm, Compagnie Oris Industry. Its board approved the addition of an ESOP to its 401(k) plan, which accomplished the purchase. INB Financial (OTC) also used its KSOP for an open-market purchase of its own stock.[30]

KSOPs raise some difficult planning issues, which usually require the assistance of an experienced investment banker or compensation consultant. These problems arise from the advantages of this form of employee ownership for both companies and employees. A clear advantage for employees is that in the best possible arrangement they can receive convertible preferred stock that has a guaranteed floor value and a high dividend and is matched to their employee contributions at a higher rate than when the company provided a cash matching. A clear advantage for the company is that if the shares purchased by the ESOP go up in value, that appreciation means the benefit costs less for the company. To illustrate, Company X establishes a KSOP in 1990 for ten years with 10 shares of stock costing $1 each or $10 total, which is raised through public issue of debt. It agrees to match every employee contribution to the savings plan of $1 with $1 of stock. But from 1990–2000 the company's stock price is $2 a share. The company can now match employee savings half as cheaply as during those years! An ESOP can become misused: shares grow more quickly than expected, or the firm undergoes a major acquisition or divestiture. Morgan Stanley & Company notes that if more shares or value is allocated per year than is desired, the company can extend or refinance its loan, credit excess value to future years, offset other benefits, intentionally "undersize" the ESOP, or give the excess to employees. If, however, the shares decline in value, the company may have to contribute additional cash or stock or prepay the loan.[31]

Employee ownership savings plans, or KSOPs, will continue to play a major role in the development of employee ownership in the United States. We also predict that new corporations emerging in Eastern Europe and around the world in the nineties may adopt this hybrid form of employee ownership-retirement security as a simple way to increase employee involvement in their firms and deal with inadequate state retirement systems. KSOPs will present a significant challenge to unions in the coming years, as unions with defined-benefit plans are offered KSOPs instead, at a time when firms come under competitive pressure and unions in companies without defined-benefit plans discover that KSOPs are the only benefit the employer is offering. So far, BellSouth and AT&T are two of the only large companies to integrate successfully their union and salaried employees into the KSOP program. How will adversarial unions confront a benefit that is likely to make them the major owner of the firm? We'll return to this question in Chapter 4, Corporate Culture and Governance.

Other Approaches

I am seeing a number of plans similar to Pepsi's SharePower, particularly in large service and retail companies. For example, Federal Express and UPS have spread stock ownership very far down the hierarchy. Stock options that work to build commitment are a growing trend.

—Al Candrilli, William M. Mercer Company

I know of two major Fortune 500 companies that are considering a Pepsi-type stock-option program. The accounting for stock options is a fabulous way to give people money from a Profit and Loss perspective. Stock options are not a charge to reported earnings, which is one of the reasons Pepsi may have done it in my opinion.

—Senior partner of a major compensation consulting firm

Clients are interested in and talking about the Pepsi plan. Upper-level management makes a lot of money from stock-option plans and the dollars that are driving their high salaries are from stock options. Lower-level employees may not be willing to make a trade for part of their salary.

—Doug Tormey, Towers Perrin

I have seen little evidence that proves to me that stock options or management incentives accomplish a great deal. What these things seem to be motivated by is business looking over its shoulder and seeing what everybody else is doing. No one ever stops to say hold it a minute. It's what I call the country club thing. You're sitting around the bar after the 19th hole, comparing everyone's benefits and what they got. Once in a while you encounter a board director who says, we pay this guy $850,000 a year to run the company; why does he have to have the opportunity to make twice his salary in options every year? It's hard to come up with an answer. The guy is paid enough to do his job and run the company. Options have just become part and parcel of the compensation package, but it's all very seat of the pants.

—Bernie Schaeffer, Hay Higgins

Compensation consultants see increasing interest in more broad-based stock options and some of them have begun to question the value to corporations of narrow stock options that aggressively benefit senior executives. There is scant evidence that stock options improve the performance of executives. Also, since many executives and managers cash in their stock options quickly, the "stock option" functions more as an immediate cash profit-taking than as an ongoing form of stock ownership in the corporation. The trend seems to be toward considering the usefulness of the Pepsi challenge: spread the stock options throughout the organization, so that they visibly impact on everybody's wages and encourage ongoing stock ownership by a broad number of employees.

Presently, the use of stock options is firmly in a state of feudal bliss. Several recent surveys show the following:

- Stock options are the most popular long-term incentive grant and are used by 90 percent of the 200 largest industrial and service companies.

- Eligibility for participation is $60,000.

- One survey of large companies found that only .01 percent of U.S. exempt employees participate in long-term incentive plans while another suggests that less than 1% of employees participate.[32]

Three trends are capturing the interest and experimentation taking place around the country. First, companies are integrating many types of employee ownership and employee holdings into a coherent ownership program. Second, companies are designing programs that fit their unique situation rather than depending on prepackaged ideas. Science Application International is an SEC-filing company that is not public, but its 10,000 professional employees have multiple opportunities to gain ownership of the company. Its chairman, Robert Beyster has designed an employee-ownership program that integrates stock options, stock awards, leveraged ESOPs, and benefit-plan ownership. International Minerals & Chemical Corporation has adopted a company-wide stock-option program.

Experimentation with broad-based stock-option and stock-grant programs is in its infancy. At some point, it will be useful to analyze more systematically the impact of stock option versus other forms of employee ownership. What is the future likely to hold? The Science Application International model is about a decade ahead of its time. Its chairman, Robert Beyster, cautions: "As employee ownership of various types continues to become an integral part of the ownership structure *and* the compensation program of many public corporations, companies will need to figure out a way to coherently meld the various programs, so that the overall 'employee-ownership culture' makes sense to employees and makes sense for the company's long-term corporate and short-term financial objectives." Second, as broad-based stock-option programs become more prevalent, Congress will need to examine and update the whole array of employee-ownership incentives in a way consistent with national economic objectives.

Making the Employee-Ownership Decision

The National Center for Employee Ownership revealed that in a survey of large public companies by the *Institutional Investor* in November 1989, 36 percent of the firms reported having an ESOP, and 33 percent of those without a plan indicated they'll probably create one. Seventy percent of the respondents with plans developed their plans mostly to restructure benefits inexpensively; only 11 percent said they implemented them to prevent a takeover.[33]

How does a typical public corporation make the employee-ownership decision? Many major employee-ownership transactions have used the services of investment bankers. In fact, investment bankers, compensation consultants, and outside legal counsel are serving as the high priests of employee ownership. What financial criteria do these advisors use in helping corporations make the decision? We interviewed a selection of the top employee-ownership investment bankers on this question. Their key role is not odd, since most companies will undertake only one significant employee-ownership transaction a decade while these professionals can give their clients the benefit of many transactions and the experiences of many companies. Investment bankers play a pivotal role in spreading employee ownership. Let's examine the typical scenario and then look at the financial criteria.

Frequently, senior managers in the financial or human resource department of a corporation will seek information from their counterparts at other companies that have experience with employee ownership. It is more typical for investment bankers to be approaching the financial managers, the chief executive officer, or the chairman. They may be reviewing opportunities for employee ownership in general or attempting to address a particular corporate event, such as a takeover environment, the spinning off of a unit, a public offering, the need for a stock buyback or new equity, the need for an increase or reduction of benefits or benefit costs, a company's desire to go private, the acquisition of another firm, restructuring of benefits to maximize employee holdings of company stock, or simply a company decision to improve its tax deductions, cash flow, or working capital.

Most investment bankers were especially critical of the role of the human resource and benefits staff. One banker said that "we get the financial staff interested and they get the human resource staff uninterested and it may die right there." Some bankers portrayed the human resource or benefits staffs as frequently narrow minded and short-sighted in their inability to see employee ownership in the large picture of the company's relationship with its employees and its overall corporate finance objectives. They were often worried about the technical complications of designing a new program, changing the status quo, and communicating a new benefits package to employees. Other investment bankers noted a growing interest among the human resource and benefits people in the last two years. These corporate staffers are now the initiators of the employee-ownership idea in a few companies. Sometimes the idea is planted with the benefits staffs by compensation consulting firms.

At this point the investment bankers discuss thoroughly with the financial and benefits staffs a series of options to the company. Many bankers agree that if the chair of the board of directors or the chief executive officer is genuinely interested in employee ownership and pushes it, then in most cases this involvement alone will determine that the corporate staff comes up with a plan. Otherwise, the proposal may die as a result of interdepartmental turf battles and the slowness of corporate bureaucracies. One effective approach has been to create a task force with representatives from the various departments—tax, legal, accounting, human resources, and treasury—one that examines the employee-ownership decision for several months and then makes a recommendation to the Chair or CEO.

Some corporations may undertake what is called a "bakeoff," in which several investment bankers are invited to show their wares and make proposals regarding possible transactions and their fees. Sometimes different banks are used to design the employee-ownership transaction, which is called *structuring* rather than *finding the financing,* which includes designing the securities and approaching lenders through private placements or the public market owing to the varying strengths of the different banks. A takeover environment, however, usually casts a distinct shadow on this process. A law firm experienced in takeover defenses and litigation counsels the company and works with its other advisors on all aspects of the employee-ownership transaction. Otherwise, in a more stable environment the final employee-ownership proposals go to the legal department or outside counsel for review. This is the point at which various fairness standards of the Employee Retirement Income Security Act of 1974 are tested against the employee benefit plan, which will be used as the vehicle for employee ownership.

The final stage involves agreement on the one employee-ownership transaction the company wishes to complete. Some companies have advisory committees of their salaried or nonunion employees or unions and will conduct discussions with them during this stage. Very few companies have attempted to involve employees at an earlier stage. Such was the case with Polaroid, which consulted its nonunion Employees Committee years before it adopted its ESOP. Management then thoroughly reviews it and brings it to the board for approval. Sometimes shareholder approval is also required. At this point, bankers suggest that the employee-ownership initiative be announced to employees and the public on a preliminary basis. After that, a legal trust is established (in the case of an ESOP).

The role of employee voice in the decision is presently confused. If union members are to be involved in the employee-ownership program, the union may have initiated the proposal in the case of an employee buyout or a stock-for-wages trade. Many corporations with unions simply assume that the union will not be interested and will establish the employee-ownership program for nonunion employees without ever consulting the union. Nonunion employees without an advisory committee or an employees committee are usually in a situation of having an employee-ownership program—whether it is in their interests or not—"done to them." For both legal and organizational reasons, some observers recommend that during this phase of the transaction the trustee of the Employee Stock Ownership Trust retain an independent legal and financial advisor(s), who would examine the entire transaction to insure that it is financially fair and prudent for employees. This scrutiny is in addition to valuation firms, such as Houlihan, Lokey, Howard, & Zukin, Inc. who analyze the value of nontradeable convertible preferred shares in public company transactions. Finally, the employee trust is funded internally or externally. If funded internally, a corporation may simply loan the capital to purchase the shares to the Employee Stock Ownership Trust. If funded externally, the funds will be loaned through a commercial bank, a private placement, or a public offering of securities. Then, the transaction is completed. Since many companies do not publicly announce employee-ownership transactions in much detail at this point, our research suggests, it is impossible for us to track how several companies on the Public Corporations with Employee Ownership list came to be significantly employee held. This will be discussed in the next chapter.

Some key employee-ownership investment bankers listed the criteria they use to advise public companies.

1. They compute the impact of the additional leverage on the corporation's balance sheet and the expected credit rating the company will receive from Standard & Poor's and Moody's Investor Services. One view is that an ESOP under 15 percent will usually not downgrade a firm's credit. Will the company foresee needing equity in the future, and is this the best use of the company's debt capacity? One banker said that "we do not look at balance sheet type ratios or leverage ratios because the rating agencies have been very reasonable. They are much more concerned about the effect of an ESOP on compensation structure and cash flow. They recognize that often employee ownership is neutral or even favorable in that respect."

2. They evaluate the company's current benefits program and the retirement benefits the company feels it needs to offer employees to remain competitive. All bankers agree that most companies will need to replace some stream of benefits with employee ownership, since shareholders might object to an imprudent use of their resources increasing benefits without clear reasons. The company must decide if its goal is to cut costs, maintain existing benefits, or enhance benefits. The company's current nonemployee-ownership benefits costs are closely examined, and any savings and advantages to the corporation from using various levels of employee ownership are computed. Typically, replacing the benefit costs of most companies will not result in more than a 20-percent employee ownership program. All agree that the prefunding of the company's matching contribution with employee-held stock for its savings/investment/401(k) plans is the top priority. Extensive computer models are developed to examine these possibilities. In addition, they evaluate whether employees are likely to be comfortable and willing to have their benefits restructured in this way. Finally, what savings, if any, on current benefits costs will accrue to the company?

3. They compute the impact on earnings per share on a primary and fully diluted basis. Most bankers agree that it can sometimes be helpful to the company to deal with this problem by selling newly issued shares to an ESOP and then repurchasing shares on the open market to keep the number of outstanding shares the same. If the company is already planning to buy-back shares or conduct a major financing or refinancing then one banker says, "The ESOP is the perfect program." Bankers say that they will caution management about ESOPs that cause significant dilution.

4. They assess the outlook for the company's stock price. One banker notes that "I have yet to talk to a CEO who thinks the company's stock is going

down." But they caution that they form their own opinion based on the work of outside analysts. As one banker puts it, "People overlook this and look to the tax and defensive incentives, but forget that you're really incurring debt to buy your own equity. It is the biggest economic risk." Companies may consider buying their own stocks when they are low or using convertible preferred shares to protect employees and the firm against risk.

5. They examine the company's profitability and compute the level of tax benefits, if any. Tax benefits generally are computed by "assuming that the present value of compensation received by employees through an ESOP . . . would have been contributed to another defined-contribution pension plan."[34] The net new tax advantages of an ESOP are derived by using dividends to repay the ESOP loan or to pay employees directly. These are completely tax deductible. In figuring financial benefits, companies should be aware that profitability and tax deductions are not always crucial factors, because some benefit and wage substitutions ESOPs can enhance companies in other ways.

6. They evaluate strategic and defensive concerns, that is, the impact of employee ownership on a takeover. Bankers maintain that the defensive function of employee ownership is unpredictable.

7. Most bankers consider employee ownership counterproductive for a management wholly antagonistic to the idea of expanding employee holdings. Apart from financial issues, some managers were "scared of an ESOP. " One banker observed that management should at least be neutral. Some bankers argue that significant employee ownership may not be healthy in some industries in which the employees' cash compensation is already variable and based on profits. In this case, retirement benefits based largely on stock would give those employees a volatile compensation package. One put it this way: "We would think twice about whether a stock-oriented benefits package made sense there."

8. Some bankers examine whether the employees have indicated a desire to be shareholders. There are some signs that both union and nonunion employees are both fighting for employee ownership and "beating management to the punch and asking to be involved."

9. They perform a sensitivity analysis in which they plot the best case and worst case scenarios of the employee-ownership decision for the financial benefits to the employees, the company, and shareholders. One banker said that "we do a discounted cash-flow analysis of doing the ESOP, as opposed to doing nothing."

10. They consider the company's corporate financial transactions for the near future and whether employee ownership fits with them. Now that an employee-ownership sector exists, bankers report that companies are examining ways to extend their employee-ownership programs in time and space by expanding them into the future and to overseas units. Also, they look at special

considerations and problems. For example, in commercial banks ESOPs have the effect of reducing regulatory capital. U.S. subsidiaries of foreign parents find it difficult to get the ESOP dividend deduction. In utilities, the accounting effect of an ESOP is to reduce equity and add debt, a result that can hurt them regarding their reimbursability for costs.

Conclusion

We have examined the different ways public companies have restructured benefits but have been unable to say definitively whether total compensation was actually increased or decreased. As a result of a recent survey by two University of Michigan financial researchers, it is now possible to look inside a selection of 83 public companies in order to see exactly what happened. Obviously, more intensive investigation will be necessary in the future. Figure 2.7 shows the results: About 48 percent of the companies report that their employee-ownership

FIGURE 2.7   *How Companies Restructured Wages and Benefits*

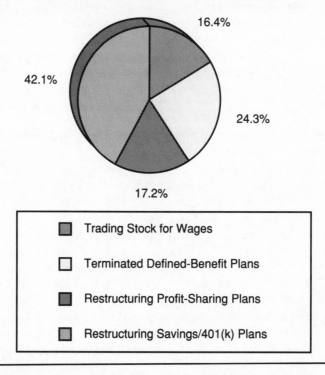

Source: Public Company Employee Ownership Database, 1990. Chart by Lawrence R. Greenberg

plans increased their overall compensation; 40 percent report no change; 6 percent report a decline; and 6 percent did not respond. The bottom line is that current wages and benefits are being exchanged for stock ownership in many cases while in 48 percent of the cases employee compensation was increased. This last statistic may support our deepening contention that many public companies are ignoring the issue of dilution and the question of who pays for the employee ownership.

Now, let's summarize the ways that public companies restructured wages and benefits to get to these results.

Workers are not getting ripped off by any stretch of the imagination, yet companies are replacing fixed wages and benefits with variable deferred compensation. From the point of view of employees and employee advocates, this means that employees are not having compensation taken from them and being given *at the time of ESOP adoption* less value in deferred compensation, since almost nine out of ten times the worker's compensation is not reduced! The actual outcome depends on the stock's performance. If the stock exceeds the level at which it was bought and allocated, employees may get more. If the stock falls below the level at which it was bought and allocated, employees lose benefits and retirement benefits are at risk. The risk for workers in all cases cannot be clearly defined, since this will depend on how the stock performs in the future, whether the company guaranteed a floor level of the stock for the employee, how the stock is structured, since convertible preferred carries lower risk and higher dividends, whether dividends are paid directly to employees, and whether the benefits of share appreciation and tax benefits are passed onto employees or retained by the company. All these considerations would have to go into a detailed analysis of the impact of a public company's ESOP on the employees.[35] Unfortunately, this low impact on employees is probably short-lived, as the awareness of who pays for employee ownership and how dilution is addressed continues to grow.

The University of Michigan analysts argue that public companies may be overstating the purported benefits of ESOPs to their shareholders when they construct employee-ownership programs that do not reduce other forms of compensation but maximize dividend tax benefits.[36] We'll look at the shareholder-employee controversy more in the next chapter. But let's return to the big picture.

The two pillars of the American compensation system are collapsing: the pure fixed wage system and the pure fixed retirement system. Regardless of comfort, it *is* taking place. The fixed wage system is collapsing because it does not serve the interests of *either* American workers *or* American corporations in a time of stiff national and global competition. Toward the year 2000, this ideology of labor-management relations is a recipe for disaster. Homage to the overpaid and unaccountable top of the organization and quiet uninvolved wardship at the bottom are not the stuff of which twenty-first century entrepreneurial businesses will be made.

Unions share the guilt with corporate leaders for buying into the fixed wage system and systematically, often fanatically, avoiding the concepts of profit sharing and employee ownership since World War II. The American workforce can look at the last twenty years as a couple would, who moved into town twenty years ago, convinced that they could have more security by paying rent rather than by investing equity in their house. Their rent has gone up but not the amount of their assets or their control. Every five years someone tried to persuade them to switch to buying into the economic system, but they answered that they were comfortable. Only now as they look back do they see that the underlying motive of their action was stupid. One reason unions opposed the ideas of employee ownership and profit sharing is they wrongly feared that if "pay" was no longer determined by a collective-bargaining contract, the union organization would have no reason to exist. As competition becomes fierce, it is ironic that except for a few unions, senior managers in public corporations, investment bankers, and lawyers, not unions, are in the forefront of restructuring enterprises, so that middle managers to machine tool operators can own a piece of the manor estate and share in its future earnings.

The pure fixed wage system has boiled down to feudalism for the American rank-and-file and salaried employee. Real wages have dropped or grown slowly. Much of the aggressive wage increases and COLAs of unions and their nonunion mimics have been eaten away by inflation, and it takes a two-earner family to earn the standard of living a one-earner family used to supply. Home ownership, the one central equity goal of this "feudal social contract," has declined over the last decade as housing costs have risen dramatically. Republican political analyst Kevin Phillips has analyzed what happened during the Reagan years and concludes that "the eighties will be known as the decade of the fat cats." In retrospect, the promise of the *certainty* of the fixed wage system turned out to be—in the inflation-adjusted sense—essentially a method to secure the serflike service of cheap labor and to award the earnings generated by this labor to the lords and ladies of the American feudal economic system.

The pure fixed retirement system has shriveled to an empty promise. A growing number of people have told the government that their company pensions have shrunk to less than a fifth of their retirement income.[37] The growth in defined-benefit pension plans has reversed. The inflation protection of defined-benefit pensions has disappeared. The one clear economic advantage that unions can offer workers—a negotiated defined-benefit pension—has eluded many workers as unions decline to 12 percent of the private-sector workforce. Retirement plans invested in company stock are not insured by the U.S. government. They are risky, yet they are the direction of the future.

The initial reaction of many who have read this chapter may be to blame employee ownership as the cause of greater risk and less certainty to the working people of America. That is wrong. A common example of this analysis is the false claim by many union leaders that employee-ownership plans replace many defined-benefit pension plans and therefore employee ownership is bad. Yes, this is true in a few cases, but most companies that are either terminating defined-benefit pension plans or choosing not to set them up offer employees very little in return.

The restructuring of wages and benefits with employee ownership will not be a welcome event for many senior managers and many employees. For managers, it is a realization that ironically cheap labor costs are not easier to secure in a nonunion workforce because workers without unions still have attitudes and beliefs and needs. For employees, this all adds up to one word: risk. But risk does not necessarily mean loss. Employees are being transformed from receivers-serfs-tenants to members-investors-owners. Whether a flexible wage and benefit plan for an individual worker consisting of some fixed wages and benefits and a measure of employee ownership is good or bad will depend on several factors:

- general riskiness of the company
- employee trade-offs to secure equity
- management's dependence on the employee's active or passive consent to initiate the program
- the performance of the stock
- size of employee-ownership estate
- the employee's ability to contribute to, and participate in, the company's success and reduce the possibility of serious failures.

The restructuring of wages and benefits with employee ownership is not untried in the United States. Perhaps, the discomfort of some managers and employees and aggressive support by unions is related to the memory of what happened before. In the early part of this century after World War I, Harvard Professor Paul Lawrence tells us that unions made a big push to organize labor in the steel, automobile, rubber, machinery, chemical, and electrical industries. Management launched a two-pronged attack: one was a well-publicized Red-scare, often backed by state militias. In the other prong, several prominent industrialists and social do-gooders launched many new company "programs," including nonleveraged employee stock ownership plans, profit sharing, medical insurance, pension plans, accident compensation, and the beginnings of unemployment insurance. In the twenties for the first time an economic boom did not trigger an increase in union membership, which dropped from 20 percent to 10 percent of all employees. Companies moved rapidly to structure employee representation or company unions to increase labor-management cooperation, which covered 1.5 million workers by the end of the 1920s. Expectations of a new nonconfrontational system of relations were high among both labor and management. The Stock Market Crash and Great Depression wiped out the value of many stock ownership plans and companies were forced to cut wages. Within a few years, unions swiftly organized all the major industries.[38]

Many believe the stock market is safer now. Also, the defined-benefit plan pension system was created to eliminate risk for workers, but increased employee ownership does raise the root issue: If workers are invited into t.ᴜ feudal manor as shareholders, how do they exercise the judgment of investors to protect themselves from undue risk? Throughout the seventies and early eighties, corporate managers in public companies talked about "giving" employee ownership to their employees. It was a grant, a bestowal, a gift, a favor. They also worked hard at ignoring the corporate governance—full voting rights and board representation—implications of significant employee ownership. The concept of gift was, we think, intricately connected to the act of ignoring. "If it was a favor we are doing for you, then why do you really deserve any say or responsibility." Now, that is all changing. Employees are now paying for their employee ownership with wage and benefit restructuring in a large number of public corporations. Corporations must make them pay for stock ownership to avoid dilution, but workers then become real shareholders.

Notes

1. Letter of January 10, 1989. See also, press release by the Proctor & Gamble Company, Cincinnati, Ohio, January 11, 1989. We are grateful to the company for providing copies of this material.
2. *The Wall Street Journal,* May 8, 1989, May 24, 1990.
3. Interview with Brian Freeman, 1990; Joseph R. Blasi, *Employment Ownership: Revolution or Ripoff?* (New York: Harper & Row, 1988): 33–35; *The Wall Street Journal,* September 9, 1982, June 20, 1984, July 5, 17, 31, 1985, October 1, 1985, March 26, 1987, July 29, 1987, July 31, 1989; PR Newswire May 5, 18, 1985, October 15, 1985, September 29, 1987, December 21, 1987, January 17, 1990, March 26, 1990; SEC filing July 1987, December 1989. Hardin quote from PR Newswire November 9, 1982.
4. We are grateful to the Whitman Corporation for providing copies of this material, which is abridged and quoted directly. See also "ESOPs As A Benefit Substitution," Susan Glass DePadron, First National Bank of Chicago, in *ESOPs: Building Equity and Growth for America's Future* (Washington, D.C.: The ESOP Association, 1990): 161.
5. Quoted in entirety from "Workplace: Pepsi Offers Stock Options to All, Not Just Honchos," by Jolie Solomon, *The Wall Street Journal,* June 28, 1989. See also, "PepsiCo's Sharepower Plan," *Employee Ownership Report* 9, no. 5 (September-October 1989): 6.
6. Adapted and shortened for "Issues for the 1990s: Solutions for Your Employee Benefit Concerns of Tomorrow" (Chicago, Ill. Coopers & Lybrand, 1990): 10–11.
7. For an excellent analysis of this issue, see the books of Seymour Melman.

8. Department of Labor, Bureau of Labor Statistics, 1989: 3. Social Security tax increased 5 percent in 1988. Figures for 1990 from *News* (Washington, D.C.: U.S. Department of Labor, Bureau of Labor Statistics, USDL 90–379): 1.

9. NCEO, 1989: 7–9. Significant research on Rath was done by William Foote Whyte and his associates at Cornell. The Cornell University group studies are summarized in Blasi, 1988: 275–286.

10. The Chrysler Loan Guarantee Act of 1979 is Public Law 96–185. See Blasi, 1988: 21, 34; *The Wall Street Journal,* November 8, 1985, December 17, 1985, September 5, 1986, July 20, 1990, August 27, 1990; PR Newswire December 16, 1985; Letter of December 21, 1979, from Senator Donald W. Stewart, Senator Russel B. Long, and Congressman Stanley N. Lundine to Douglas Fraser and Letter of January 17, 1980, from Lee Iacocca to these senators.

11. Continental: *The Wall Street Journal,* April 8, 1981, May 7, 1981, June 8, 12, 1981, August 10, 1981, September 24, 1983, March 23, 1984, April 24, 1984; PR Newswire April 1, 1981, October 6, 1983, September 14, 1983, December 5, 1983, July 31, 1984. The technicality was this. Although the New York Stock Exchange had originally decided that qualification of their shares by the California Corporate Commissioner was not necessary, it reversed its decision. The banks then felt they had to withdraw financing. Issuing the new shares would dilute the Texas Air shares in half, and the employees and the company were trying to avoid a shareholder vote for fear Texas Air would block the move in a proxy fight. Mr. Feldman said he provided the NYSE with documents proving no real change in control was taking place because "the (ESOP) plan's stock will be voted by 11,000 widely dispersed employees. Just as no stockholder controls Continental today, no stockholder will control Continental if shares are issued to the plan." Nevertheless, the Civil Aeronautics Board approved the Lorenzo bid.

12. The first author was involved in an extensive study of this case for the U.S. Department of Labor. See Labor-Management Cooperation at Eastern Air Lines (Washington, D.C.: U.S. Department of Labor, BMLR 118, 1988).

13. *The Wall Street Journal,* September 20, 1983; PR Newswire December 23, 1981.

14. Since these events ALPA, the IAM, and various flight attendant unions have become more knowledgeable about ESOPs.

15. I am indebted to Steven Hester for his assistance. See, "Concessionary ESOPs," by Steven Hester (Washington, D.C.: Arnold & Porter, 1988). See also *Interest and Equity: Uses of Employee Ownership and Participation in the Restructuring of the U.S. Steel Industry* by Adam Matthew Blumenthal (Cambridge, Mass.: Harvard University Social Studies, 1986). Kaiser: *The Wall Street Journal,* December 8, 1981; Bethlehem: *The Wall Street*

Journal, April 7, 1986, May 28, 1986; LTV: *The Wall Street Journal,* March 17, 1986, April 7, 1986; CF&T: *The Wall Street Journal,* October 9, 1986; Northwestern: Shareholder Proxy Statement-Prospectus, June 30, 1988; Oregon: *The Wall Street Journal,* August 7, 1987, December 15, 1987; Prospectus: Oregon Metallurgical ESOP, December 9, 1987; McClouth: Detroit Free Press: March 12, 1990.

16. "Beware: Pensions Are an Endangered Species," by Linda Stern (Reuters), *Los Angeles Times,* July 30, 1990.

17. The exclusion from paying the excise tax was allowed in the Tax Reform Act of 1986 but expired on December 31, 1988.

18. "The Benefit Side of Employee Stock Ownership Plans," by William D. Partridge, The Wyatt Company, in *ESOPs: Building Growth and Equity for America's Future* (Washington, D.C.: The ESOP Association, 1990): 162–167.

19. Monarch: *The Wall Street Journal,* October 4, 1988; Equimark: November 9, 1984; Primark: July 26, 1988; Poughkeepsie: *The Wall Street Journal,* July 22, 1987; Indiana: April 26, 1989; Mid-America: *The Wall Street Journal,* January 29, 1986; Merchants: SEC filing July 1987; Pacific: *The Wall Street Journal,* May 30, 1990; Roper: *The Wall Street Journal,* May 18, 1987; Robertson: SEC filing December 1989.

20. Harcourt: SEC filing December 1989; Michael: *The Wall Street Journal,* November 14, 1983, December 13, 1983; Ashland: *The Wall Street Journal,* April 3, 1986, March 17, 1987, April 24, 1987, November 16, 1987; SEC filing March 1988; Bank: *The Wall Street Journal,* January 10, 1986, July 13, 1989; Barry: *The Wall Street Journal,* January 6, 1988, PR Newswire February 13, 1989; Enron: *The Wall Street Journal,* October 20, 1986, SEC filing July 1987; Imperial: *The Wall Street Journal,* October 13, 1987, SEC filing December 1989; Allied: *The Wall Street Journal,* October 24, 1989; Figgie: *The Wall Street Journal,* September 21, 1988; Universal: *The Wall Street Journal,* November 14, 1988; Emery: *The Wall Street Journal,* August 27, 1987; Graniteville: SEC filing December 1989; Lyons: *The Wall Street Journal,* April 18, 1984, February 27, 1985, March 21, 1985, March 26, 1985, May 1, 1985, May 14, 1985, August 30, 1985; PR Newswire April 12, 25, 30, 1985.

21. Interview, August 1990.

22. On the legal issues in such a conversion, see Gregory Brown and Jared Kaplan, "Tax, ERISA, and Securities Issues," in Robert Smiley and Ronald Gilbert, Employee Stock Ownership Plans (New York: Prentice Hall, Rosenfield Laumer Publications, 1989): 13–64.

23. May 17, 1985. The author wishes to thank the company for this material.

24. The Quaker Oats literature is particularly impressive. Sources for these quotes on Quaker's ESOP include August 25, 1985, letter to employees,

December 16, 1988 letter to employees, January 17, 1989, company press release, May 23, 1989, letter to employees, and two brochures, *The Quaker Shareholder* and *Quaker Benefits: Quaker Capital-Building Plans*.

25. Blasi, 1988: 12; U.S. Department of Labor, *Employee Benefits in Medium and Large Firms 1989* (Washington, D.C., U.S. Department of Labor, 1989).

26. DePadron, 1990: 160.

27. For this section we have drawn liberally from DePadron, 1990; Partridge, 1990; *The Wall Street Journal,* October 13, 1989, June 28, 1990; "Post Retirement Medical Benefits: Planning For The Future," in Coopers & Lybrand, 1990: 8–9.

28. According to surveys by Buck Consulting and Hewitt Associates quoted in, "New Research Sheds Light on Public Company ESOPs," *Employee Ownership Report* 9, no. 4 (July-August 1989): 6.

29. This section based partly on Luis Granados, "Combining ESOPs with 401(k) Plans," *Employee Ownership Report* 9, no. 1 (January-February 1990): 4. Granados reviews various legal issues.

30. Bell Atlantic: *The Wall Street Journal,* May 26, 1989; BellSouth Corp.: *The Wall Street Journal,* June 26, 1989; Delta: *The Wall Street Journal,* July 11, 1989; Consolidated: *The Wall Street Journal,* May 19, 1989; Cummins: *The Wall Street Journal,* July 1, 1989, PR Newswire February 15, 1990; Rohm & Haas: *The Wall Street Journal,* February 16, 1990; Federal-Mogul: PR Newswire January 10, 1989; Hartmarx: SEC filing February 1989; Scholes and Wolfson, 1990: 19; Olin: *The Wall Street Journal,* May 26, 1989; Square D; PR Newswire, May 1989; ITT: *The Wall Street Journal,* May 10, 1989; PR Newswire May 9, 1989; Tandycrafts: SEC filing December 1989; PR Newswire June 13, 1990; Dahlberg: SEC filing December 1989: PR Newswire April 25, 1988; Guardian: SEC filing December 1988; Rochester: PR Newswire November 30, 1987, *The Wall Street Journal,* January 5, 1990; Syncor: November 22, 1989; INB: *The Wall Street Journal,* February 22, 1990.

31. Morgan Stanley & Co., 1990: Sections III and IV. For further discussion on structuring problems, see "Combining ESOP and 401(k) Plans," by Kenneth Lindberg, Hewitt Associates. *Journal of Employee Ownership Law and Finance* 1, no.1 (Fall 1989): 23–48; "401(k) Plan Conversion," by Kim Mende, Chemical Bank. ESOP Association, 1990: 343–358.

32. "Long-term Incentives for Management, Part 4, Performance Plans," Jeffrey M. Kanter and Matthew P. Ward. *Compensation & Benefits Review* (January-February 1990): 36–48; "Long-term Incentives for Management: An Overview," George B. Paulin, *Compensation & Benefits Review* (January 1989): 36–46; *Executive Compensation Strategies and Trends—The Factual Base* (Scottsdale, AZ: American Compensation Association, 1989). The survey was done by ACA and Peat Marwick.

33. NCEO, "ESOPs Popular in Estate Planning, Public Companies," *Employee Ownership Report* 10, no. 1 (January-February 1990): 7.

34. Susan Chaplinsky and Gregory Niehaus, "The Tax Distributional Effects of Leveraged ESOPs," *Financial Management* 19, no. 1 (1990): 29–38. Financial analysts should read this entire article, which provides an excellent analysis.

35. We are generally defining the issues here while simplifying a bit. Certainly, the present value of the capital and the tax considerations for the employers and employees will have a bearing on this computation because "immediately paying out dividends on ESOP stock increases the personal tax burden of ESOP compensation, because employees must pay tax on the dividends when they are received. In addition, employees forego the opportunity to earn the before-tax rate of return on the dividends." (Chaplinsky and Niehaus, 1990: 37). From the company's point of view when ESOP stock is used as a matching contribution in a savings plan, remember that if the stock price rises too slowly to match employees' contributions over the life of the program, the company may have have to "top off" their contributions with cash.

36. Chaplinsky and Niehaus, 1990: 37–38.

37. Louis Uchitelle, "Company-Financed Pensions Are Failing to Fulfill Promise," *New York Times,* May 29, 1990.

38. "The History of Human Resource Management in American Industry," by Paul R. Lawrence. *HRM: Trends and Challenges.* (Boston, Mass.: Harvard Business School Press, 1985): 25–27.

3

Takeovers

Harcourt Brace Jovanovich (NYSE) became the target of Robert Maxwell's British Printing Company in 1987. The board rejected Maxwell's offer of $44 per share or $1.73 billion and approved a recapitalization plan that would pay out to shareholders significant special dividends of $40 a share in cash, plus a fraction of newly issued preferred stock intended to have a market value of $10 per share. The company issued about $1 billion in junk bonds and took on $3 billion in debt. The company also sold First Boston newly issued preferred stock, carrying 8.1 million votes and sold 4.7 million shares of convertible preferred stock to its Employee Stock Ownership Plan. Earlier the company converted the assets of two of its pension plans into an ESOP, which held about a third of the company's stock. Excess assets from one terminated pension plan netted $56 million for stock purchases. Later the ESOP bought more company shares with its special dividend. Bitter exchanges took place in the press between Jovanovich and Maxwell. Maxwell and other shareholders sued the company, but the court ruled that neither the recapitalization plan nor the ESOP "locked up" the company against future takeovers. One reason was that the ESOP allowed for the independent voting of shares by the employees. A court settlement established the procedure that the unallocated shares of the ESOP would be voted in proportion to how employees vote the allocated shares. The takeover failed and the company won this scuffle but has been struggling under the heavy debt load imposed by its "victory." At the time, the company contended that the value of its common shares could escalate rapidly in the coming years, if it can meet share projections. In 1991, the company was sold.[1]

In 1988, A&P launched a $30 per share $210-million hostile tender offer for Delchamps Inc. (OTC), an operator of supermarkets in Louisiana, Alabama, Florida, and Mississippi. A&P had tried unsuccessfully to buy the company several times and had accumulated less than 5% of the shares but the company *insisted on remaining independent. An ESOP owned 25% of the company and an additional 30% was held by parties who had agreed not to sell their holdings until a certain cutoff date. In 1985, the Food and Allied Services Trade Department of the AFL-CIO tried to use a proxy solicitation of shareholders to get the names of employee holders and create a favorable environment for establishing a union. The company beat back the union's attempt to get the names and remained nonunion. In 1988, Alfred Delchamps, Jr., the President and Chairman said: "We believe A&P started this fight with two possible goals in mind. Either it would pick up this company at a cheap price and proceed with its plan to achieve dominance in the Gulf coast retail stores market; or, even if A&P were unsuccessful in achieving control of Delchamps, the result of its disruptive effort would be to cause internal dissension and uncertainty, force a much smaller company to incur the high expenses associated with fending off a hostile takeover, or perhaps induce us to undergo a massive leveraging of some kind, thereby, weakening us as a competitor. A&P has not been able to compete with us effectively in the marketplace, so it has obviously decided, 'If you can't beat them, buy them or bury them with investment bankers and lawyers.' We don't intend to be beaten, bought, or buried." The company adopted a share-purchase rights plan and amended its ESOP to give employees the right to control all voting of shares by having unallocated shares voted in proportion to allocated shares. The takeover failed.[2]*

Polaroid Corporation (NYSE) began to consider an ESOP as far back as 1985 as part of a "change process" to improve company performance. Under consideration were work redesign, compensation, job security, and staffing decisions. The huge damage settlement it expected in a court case against Kodak made it the subject of takeover rumors in 1988. Senior managers agreed any ESOP would be paid for by the employees in 1987. Since the 1930s, the nonunion company has had a democratically elected employees' committee that discusses company policies with management, which was involved in planning the ESOP until the board approved a small ESOP in March 1988 and again on June 14, 1988. On June 17, Roy Disney of Shamrock Corporation notified I. MacAllister Booth, Polaroid's CEO, that Shamrock had a substantial investment. On July 12, the board decided to fund the ESOP with a 5% pay cut, the company's 401(k) matching contribution, the company's profit-sharing contribution, and the delay of pay-scale increases. Most of these had been discussed with the employees' committee earlier. It also adopted a massive restructuring plan to produce conventional film, cut the U.S. workforce 8%, and repurchase its own shares. On July 13, Shamrock filed suit against the ESOP and launched a $40 per-share hostile tender offer, which it kept renewing until it reached $47 a share. In early 1989, Chancellor Carolyn Berger of the Delaware Chancery Court ruled: "The fact that the ESOP was partly defensive does not make it unfair. This is *a defensive device [assuming it is one] that is designed and appears likely to add value to the company and all its shareholders." Later that month, Polaroid sold $300 million in preferred stock to white knight Corporate Partners L. P., and Shamrock challenged this action. The ESOP provided for confidential and "mirrored" voting of all shares by employees. The judge said that "there was no direct evidence that the Polaroid ESOP is likely to do anything but improve productivity." The company had been respected for years for its emphasis on employee communications and participation, profit sharing, and a well-regarded program for handling employee grievances. This is exactly the kind of situation in which employee ownership is likely to raise productivity. The Court found that the ESOP was "fundamentally fair," not a "lock-up," and did not give management a leg up in a takeover situation and that "a minimal reduction in earnings per share is fair where, as here, it is necessary in order to promptly implement a large ESOP that is intended to increase corporate earnings." On March 17, 1989, the Delaware Supreme Court upheld this decision. Shamrock later withdrew its bid.[3]*

Dear United Pilot,

There is no question that the 3½ year struggle toward achieving an employee-owned United Airlines has been fatiguing to everyone. When Iraq invaded Kuwait, United Employee Acquisition Corp. (UEAC) was within days—in some cases hours—of securing the commitments needed to complete the transaction. The invasion changed all that. . . . There is ample evidence that outside investors may still be in a position to cause irrevocable damage to the company by forcing "an extraordinary transaction to enhance shareholder value." This phrase usually translates into some form of debilitating financial restructuring. Of immediate threat is the potential for some of the company's large shareholders, such as Coniston Partners, to force action to recover the current paper losses of their stock. The financial press has reported that Coniston's losses could approximate $150 million. . . . Employee ownership will forever end the threat of raiders at United. Faced with these stark realities, the Association of Flight Attendants, the International Association of Machinists, and recently the noncontract employees through the System Roundtable, reached the same conclusion as we; employee ownership continues to offer the best long-term protection for our company and our collective futures. . . . Current management has won contracts with the three major unions on the property. . . . While we pursued employee ownership, labor costs at United, including our own, are now well below those at comparable carriers. . . . If we are unable to achieve employee ownership this time around, we will attempt to bridge this gap and recover the full [amount] retroactively. Rest assured, Mr. Wolf has other ideas in mind. Like Mr. Ferris, he believes you to be "overpaid and underworked." In the event we abandon the Employee

Ownership Initiative, we, as your leaders, are confident in our ability to confront senior management pursuant to the provisions of the Railway Labor Act—up to and including a strike.

Fraternally,

Frederick C. Dubinsky, Chairman, UAL Master Executive Committee Air Line Pilots Association[4]

In the Wall Street Journal, *September 25, 1990, Rick Wartzman writes that Lockheed Corp. says it wants to "address concerns expressed by some of our shareholders" and soften its poison-pill plan to allow for a specific type of "qualifying offer" that wouldn't be subject to any of the plan's antitakeover measures. The company would suspend those provisions as long as these conditions are met: (1) the bid is a fully financed cash offer; (2) owners of a majority of the shares (excluding the offer's) accept the bid; (3) the offer provides a . . . written fairness opinion; (4) the offeror commits to a second-step transaction, providing equal treatment of all shareholders on the same terms and price; and (5) the offer remains open for at least 60 days. The California Public Employees' Retirement System, a major institutional holder that has encouraged Lockheed to amend its poison pill, said yesterday that it was encouraged by the new action. . . . But at the same time, the defense contractor's board spurned proposals from financier Harold Simmons to amend or redeem the pill in a way that would permit one of his companies, NL Industries Inc., to buy 10 million additional shares of Lockheed common stock from the employee stock ownership plan or on the open market. . . . J. Landis Martin, NL's CEO, attacked the decision about the 10 million shares as confirming "to me that [management] is afraid to death of losing the ESOP vote." NL has sued Lockheed in federal court in Los Angeles, claiming that the ESOP, while it's supposed to be administered by an outside trustee, is really executing "a creeping management-led, employee buyout of the company." Lockheed counters that the employee stock ownership plan is run independently and provides motivational incentives to a broad base" of employees and takes advantage of "significant tax and economic benefits."*[5] *In November 1990, Simmons made another offer for the company.*

Introduction: The Impact of Employee Ownership on Takeovers

In 1896, the Supreme Court of New York state considered a complaint for an injunction by Henry W. T. Steinway, a stockholder, against Steinway & Sons, a manufacturer of pianos and other musical instruments. Mr. Steinway, the stockholder, claimed that the corporation was engaged in wasteful, extravagant, and unnecessary expenditures for the benefit of its employees, which had no proper relation to the specific business of the corporation. We summarize the story and quote from the final opinion of Judge J. Beekman, who wrote the Supreme Court's decision. Mr. Steinway wanted the court to interfere in the decision making and activities of the corporation and to stop the actions in question. The corporation's manufacturing facilities were within New York City, but it owned 400 acres of land in Astoria, to which it planned to transfer its manufacturing operations. The reason was that the expansion of the business required larger accommodations. The company also planned to gather together a large number of its employees on this land under exceptional conditions in order to influence them to provide "better and more permanent service." The company built houses for the employees and sold some of them to the employees. "At a very moderate expenditure" the company contributed property and money toward establishing a church, a school, a free library, and a free bath.

Judge Beekman said that these actions were "all agencies, the usefulness of which in the development of the best in industrial results of a community is fully recognized." He affirmed that the employees were skilled operatives who were loyal to the company and had been in its service for many years with harmonious relations and practically without strikes or suspension of business for any cause. Judge Beekman called the policy toward the new employee benefits "a wise one, and apart from its moral aspects, has materially contributed to the resources of the corporation." Obviously, Mr. Steinway claimed that these actions were without authority in the law. Judge Beekman said that if a corporate act "is one which is lawful in itself and not otherwise prohibited and is done for the purpose of serving corporate ends in a substantial, and not in a remote and fanciful sense, it may be fairly considered within corporate powers."

The judge said that the field of corporate action in respect to the exercise of incidental powers is an expanding one, because "as industrial conditions change, business methods must change with them and acts become permissible, which at an earlier period would not have been considered to be within corporate power." The judge cautioned that in the absence of a more specific guide there will be ample room for difference of opinion. But his conclusion was firm that Steinway & Co.'s actions for the benefit of its employees' "physical, intellectual, and spiritual wants" was not illegal and was a reasonable exercise of discretionary power, which he could not question or criticize. He said that a relationship between the employee benefits and the purposes of the corporation existed for these reasons: moving employees without providing for their wider needs was not enough to secure corporate purposes; the company was trying to influence employees to minimize unreasonable strikes and agitations; and evidence since the case was brought showed that many employees really did provide fruitful and uninterrupted service, while the company made some money on rentals and sales of property.

Finally, the judge said that the plan was carried out with fairness and frankness with the shareholder whose permission was sought and who even participated in some of the meetings where the decisions were made. In a few instances, acts may have been debatable, but the corporate officers acted in good faith. He concludes that the board did not display an excess of corporate power nor violate their duty. The judge dismissed Mr. Steinway's complaint on its merits and said he should pay court costs.[6]

The Steinway case about the limits of corporate benefits for employees raises momentous questions, which are also at the root of employee ownership in takeovers. Is employee ownership of stock in a publicly traded corporation good or bad for the shareholders? What are the limits on management's and the board's authority in implementing employee benefits, such as employee ownership? What is the relationship between employee ownership and the company's bottom line? Is it reasonable for a board of directors or management or even a judge in a court of law to consider the broader social and moral implications of employee ownership in evaluating its relationship to the purposes of the corporation? What importance is to be attached to the role of employee ownership in the changing nature of business and industrial methods? And finally, an issue beneath the surface of the Steinway case, are there disadvantages for corporations and employees when the corporation becomes too much like a "company town"?

All these issues come to a head when we consider the impact of employee ownership on corporate takeovers and takeover defenses. The Steinway case pinpoints shareholders' concerns that their value in the corporation will be diluted by cozy relationships and gift-giving between management and employees. On the other hand, it also clarifies that courts can give management wide latitude in figuring out exactly how it will structure wage and benefit compensation and what philosophy it will use as a basis for this structure. Briefly, ESOPs and other employee benefit plans can potentially help or prevent an acquirer from taking over a company or can play a decisive role in a proxy battle between different groups of shareholders in a corporation, if the shares are voted for or against the takeover investor or a particular slate of directors. The power of any particular employee benefit plan with employee ownership depends mainly on five factors: (1) how many shares the plan owns; (2) who controls the voting of those shares; (3) what the rules for the voting contest are in a tender battle or proxy battle in that state; (4) how other shareholders are likely to line up vis-à-vis the employee stake; (5) what the facts are of that particular case. Remember, each company is different, and each state has different takeover provisions, although 57 percent of Fortune 500 companies are incorporated in Delaware, and unique factors will influence each situation. The following two scenarios are constructed to provide the reader with a feel for the disparate possibilities.

Scenario One involves a successful "plain-vanilla" takeover defense with employee ownership. Target Corporation is incorporated in Delaware, like most public corporations. (See Table 3.3, which demonstrates that some states have takeover laws similar to those of Delaware.) Delaware law since 1988 prohibits a takeover between a Delaware corporation and a potential acquirer for three years, unless he or she gains ownership of 85 percent or more of the target's stock not owned by officers who are directors of the corporation or by employee stock plans that do not give employees the right to confidentially vote on the tender offer. Thus, an employee benefit plan with confidential voting by individual employees owning more than 15 percent of a Delaware corporation can potentially block a takeover. So, One Tough Investor launches a hostile tender offer for Target, which has a 16 percent ESOP with confidential voting by individual employees. Unallocated shares are voted in proportion to allocated shares. Let's assume management and officers hold no shareownership in the company. If 84 percent of the shareholders vote to sell to One Tough Investor, and 16 percent of the employee-controlled stock votes against selling, One Tough Investor cannot buy and take over the company, all things being equal. That's an enormous amount of power in employees' hands. But Scenario One can turn around.[7]

Scenario Two also involves an unsuccessful takeover defense involving employee ownership. In this case, Target Corporation is also incorporated in Delaware. The company's 401(k) and profit-sharing plans own 20 percent of the outstanding stock and employees are allowed to confidentially vote these shares. But this time it turns out differently. Employees have been distressed with management's leadership. Most of their retirement future is based on the value of their stock. Nonunion or union, they also object to a corporate culture that is clearly hostile to employees. They agree with One Tough Investor that the company is mismanaged. He or she has also assured them that a takeover will not mean the dismemberment of the company, but a more effective reorganization of the company. The employees vote to tender their shares; One Tough Investor takes over the company; and management and the board are fired.

All the possibilities we will discuss fall between these polar scenarios. Although the amount of employee ownership is important, since more than 15-percent employee ownership can potentially stop a takeover in Delaware, it may be insufficient in a state that has a different set of rules. Some states do not even have takeover laws. And how other shareholders feel is important, because in many takeover contests a certain coalition of employees *plus* other shareholders may be necessary to support or defeat a tender offer or a proxy battle. And finally, the facts of any particular case are crucial because these can influence the situation in unforeseeable ways. These facts are often critical in lawsuits.

Describing the relationship between employee ownership and takeovers is more complex than making a list of ESOPs used in takeovers, or summarizing a few recent court cases, or reviewing a study about whether the share price of a public company rises or declines within 48 hours of implementing an ESOP. At the end of the chapter, we also consider the hundreds of corporations that are the "employee-ownership-takeover-defense silent majority": they have not been approached by a takeover investor; they are not even in a general takeover environment; they have not announced plans to set up an employee-ownership plan. *However, our research shows that they have significant employee ownership, which could play an important role in a future takeover environment.* While the battles in the newspapers and the courts are more exciting and adventurous, these other cases are more numerous and perhaps just as meaningful.

Management and Shareholders: A Tense Relationship?

The guts and the subtleties on employee ownership and takeovers will simply not be clear to a reader without an appreciation of how the public corporation and some of its basic legal concepts developed. Economic historian William Lazonick observes that corporations in the nineteenth century were characterized by the integration of asset ownership and managerial control.[8] He notes that owners of firms made the strategic investment decisions, relying on their own capital and that of friends, family, and former business associates to launch new ventures. They then relied primarily on retained earnings to transform new ventures into going concerns. Without developed stock markets at that time, these owner-managers mobilized capital by founding banks from which they could have privileged access to loan capital. In either case, owners remained managers, and the tension between shareholder and manager was not a serious problem. Owners were patient investors.

The Split Between Ownership and Control

Railroads, Lazonick points out, initiated the separation between ownership and managerial control. Local businesspeople contributed the initial capital and the rest was raised through the flotation of bonds that gave rise to the Wall Street investment banks. As the railroads expanded, they created huge hierarchies of salaried managers. Because they were permanent concerns that enabled original investors to sell their shares and because many bonds were converted into shares of railroad stock, a secondary market in railroad stock was created, so that owners could come and go and a career managerial organization would always remain.

Nevertheless, a wider market for securities did not exist in the United States, and entrepreneurs had to rely on their reputations and connections to raise capital. Carnegie drew on connections he made as a railroad executive to finance his steel-making operations, and Alexander Graham Bell secured financial backing from the parents of two deaf children he was teaching. Successful businesses would finance their expansion through retained earnings. Carnegie had an "iron-clad agreement" with his financial partners to plow back earnings into steel-making rather than submit to their persistent demands for dividends. The firms that came to dominate the new markets weaved together an investment in highly trained, motivated managerial staffs and plant and equipment, continuous improvement in products and technology, and energetic use of workers. These firms had high fixed costs, but the most successful ones translated them into low unit-costs for high-quality products.

In the 1890s and early 1900s, a merger and takeover movement began with dominant firms attempting to eliminate competition and consolidate their market share. With J. P. Morgan taking the lead, Wall Street financed these mergers by selling to the wealthholding public the ownership stakes of the entrepreneurs who had built up these companies. The result was to transfer the assets of the original owner-managers to a widely distributed set of shareholders. Shareholding did not require further commitments of time, effort, or finance for "their" firms. Finally, ownership and managerial control became separated in the American corporate system in the public corporate sector.

Lazonick notes that this separation of ownership from control enhanced the stable commitment of finances to these firms. The Great Merger Movement made the higher risk of common stock more acceptable to portfolio investors who were willing to hold common stock despite their lack of power to ensure the distribution of earnings. According to Lazonick the new owners of American corporations were a multitude of removed and passive shareholders, with the managers left firmly in financial control. These managers had cautious dividend policies, which gave them privileged access to the earnings of the firm. This allowed these firms to boost their bond ratings with Standard & Poors and Moody's as Wall Street moved into a corporate bond business of raising their new capital for expansion. Indeed, since the 1920s, new share issues have been only a small proportion of capital raised by U.S. corporations.

The Declining Loyalty of Shareholders

Despite the shock of the Great Depression, public companies were, until recently, characterized by loyal shareholders who lacked direct power to influence the distribution of surplus revenues and did not challenge managerial control over the firm's financial policy and did not make their shares available on the market to those who might. Lazonick notes companies would pay some dividends, try to maintain the initial dividend expectations they established, but set the dividends high enough to secure the shareholder loyalty but low enough to permit "a strong bias toward the reinvestment of earnings," in the words of economist Gordon Donaldson. Nevertheless, during the 1920s large manufacturing corporations were paying out over 60 percent of their net income as dividends. In Lazonick's view, the rise of the market for corporate control is the rise of the disloyal shareholder.

The struggle for corporate control in public companies is a direct outgrowth of the way power is distributed among shareholders and boards/senior managers in corporate law. This section quotes and summarizes parts of Robert W. Hamilton's book, *The Law of Corporations* (1987), to provide a general appreciation of the important concepts. A corporation is an artificial entity that is liable for the debts and obligations of its business, but shareholders as individuals risk only what capital they have invested, namely, they have limited liability. Corporations spread rapidly in the early nineteenth century, because they made it easier to raise large amounts of capital from investors and carry out intensive economic development, such as the building of railroads, canals, and large manufacturing businesses.

The Distribution of Power in Corporations Through Corporate Law

Despite the popular perception that corporate management has tremendous power, under law, power in the corporation is distributed between boards, management, and shareholders. This distribution, called the statutory scheme of corporations, is what the law demands. Although the shareholders are the ultimate owners of the corporation, they have only limited powers to participate in management and control, that is, compared with the board and management. Their main channels of power are to elect and remove directors, approve or disapprove of corporate actions, amendments to the articles of incorporation or bylaws, or fundamental changes not in the course of regular business, such as mergers or dissolution. Corporations must have an annual meeting so that the shareholders can elect a board of directors. In many corporations shareholders actually ratify "the selection of directors by management," a group of persons who control the corporate destiny but often have a small financial investment in the corporation. One significant source of the tension between board/senior managers and shareholders *is* that members of the board and senior management are generally not large or significant shareholders in public companies.

In large corporations all corporate power is exercised under the authority or direction of the board, whose main task is to select and fire management and delegate details of actual daily operation to them. The board must formulate the policy of the corporation and retain some responsibility for general supervision of management. One source of tension is that "the power of directors in a sense flows from statute rather than from the shareholders who elected them." This is, however, subject to the ultimate power of the shareholders to elect different directors next time, but this does not usually happen as a practical matter. Also, it is not consistent with the view of shareholder democracy in publicly held companies.

Nevertheless, directors have a duty of care and a duty of loyalty to the corporation, even if this conflicts with the wishes of a majority of shareholders. *Duty of care* means they must act in good faith, in a manner he or she reasonably believes to be in the interests of the corporation and with the care of an ordinarily prudent person in similar circumstances. *Duty of loyalty* means that the director generally cannot engage in transactions involving self-dealing or a conflict of interest, in which the corporation may be treated unfairly, but as a result the director may benefit. A director must give the corporation the benefit of his or her uncorrupted business judgment and not appropriate profitable business opportunities that belong to the corporation. These duties are often referred to as fiduciary duties, and directors, as fiduciaries. But it would be wrong to see directors as simply "trustees" of shareholders' assets because they "are expected and indeed encouraged to commit the enterprise to risky ventures in order to maximize the return to shareholders." And directors owe duties to the corporation as a whole, rather than to individual shareholders or to individual classes of shareholders.

Management as Agents of Shareholders

While corporate management or officers have broad practical power in public companies, under the law, they are seen strictly "as agents carrying out the policies established by the board of directors." Shareholders have a limited role on business matters.[9] These ideas, pulled together by what is called a law and economics analysis of the public corporation, are associated with scholars at the University of Chicago and are called the "Chicago School." Robert Hamilton describes this point of view as one that sees the corporation as a "nexus of contracts" in which shareholders are considered contributors of capital rather than the ultimate owners of the business. Because management usually owns a small, or insignificant, portion of the common stock, the interest of management in maximizing its own interests conflicts to some extent with the interest of providers of capital, particularly the common shareholders. The providers of capital must incur costs to monitor the performance of management and minimize the diversion of assets to them. These costs are usually referred to as "agency costs" and may include the cost of external public auditors, bonding, and similar activities. These costs may also be reduced by establishing compensation schemes that tend to align management with the maximization of value to the holders of common shares—hence, the widespread popularity of stock option plans, stock purchase plans, and similar arrangements.[10]

This is often referred to as the *principal-agent problem,* meaning that the shareholders, who are the principals, have a problem ensuring that the board and management act strictly as their agents in maximizing the return on their capital. Thus, proponents of the Chicago School see an inherent tension in the shareholder/board-management relationship. They are concerned that their limited power to be involved in the management and control of the corporation—sometimes combined with the lack of an ownership interest of management and directors—can lead to an abuse of power on the part of the board and management. Their main concern is not political, but the fact that this "management entrenchment" results in policies that are inefficient for the success of the company and prevent them from getting the value out of the corporation that they as investors deserve.

Electing Agents in Proxy Contests and Testing Them in Tender Battles

Shareholders' concern about corporate power is reflected in the election of directors. Since the chief executive officer or a committee of management or the board often selects the slate of directors, these shareholders consider that selection as the beginning of the "principal-agent" problem and their own role as merely ratifiers. Indeed, "most shareholders routinely vote for management," and shareholders rarely hear competing points of view from management. Managers also control the proxy machinery, whereby shareholders are notified about annual meetings, are provided information, and are sent a proxy, or document, which grants authority to a person who will be present at the meeting to vote their shares. Persons seeking to challenge incumbent management are unlikely to get a list of shareholders without a court proceeding. Finally, by a process of self-elimination, shareholders unhappy with management often tend to disappear, "rather than to fight city hall."

What actions are open to these shareholders? To be effective, they must be informed. State corporate and federal securities laws require that certain kinds of information and material disclosures be available to shareholders.[11] Shareholders have six options. First, they can simply sell their shares and invest elsewhere. This strategy can result in dissatisfied shareholders leaving in dribs and drabs. But it can also mobilize enough shareholder selling because of poor performance by management to produce "depressed share prices" and "may lead indirectly to the ouster of management." Second, they can seek to represent their point of view informally to the board and management. Third, they can initiate a "proxy contest," in which they "compete with management in an effort to obtain sufficient proxy appointments to elect a majority of the board of directors and thereby obtain control."[12] Fourth, a hostile tender offer could be mounted, an outside proposal from a person or persons—either former or new shareholders—who believe they "can provide more to the shareholders from the same assets than the incumbent management." The tender offer is a public invitation for shareholders to tender their shares usually at 25 to 50 percent in excess of the current market price. Typically, an "aggressor" offers a package of cash and securities for the outstanding stock of the firm. Fifth, they can file a lawsuit alleging that directors/senior management are abusing their power regarding a certain decision, such as refusing to accept a merger offer (a state corporate claim) or charging that directors/senior management somehow violated securities laws (a federal claim). Typically, however, once disagreement brews, lawsuits are filed by both sides—the aggrieved shareholder and the directors/senior management acting as "the corporation"—as a proxy battle or a hostile tender offer is underway. Sixth, they can seek board representation. It is essential to remember these six possibilities, for they will be crucial to understanding the role of employee ownership in corporate takeovers. Employee-shareholders will be turning to these six options in the future.

Arguments over the Market for Corporate Control

A principal thinker dealing with the relationship between corporate boards/management and shareholders is Harvard Business School Professor Michael C. Jensen. He focuses sharply on the fact that, as Hamilton says, "management control is not limitless," and the securities market is a disciplining device. Jensen sees the public stock market as a market for corporate control. Shareholders can use their ultimate power to freely buy and sell stock and vote those shares as a way to pressure or even force corporate management to act strictly as shareholders' agents in maximizing the return on their investment. The ability to unseat a board and select new management through a proxy battle, or to sell their shares to a hostile tender offer, or to threaten both actions and force the firm to change management or strategy becomes a tool of corporate governance for shareholders. Jensen says that

> alternative management teams compete for the right to manage corporate resources. . . . Managers often have trouble abandoning strategies they have spent years devising and implementing, even when these strategies no longer contribute to a corporation's survival. Such changes can require abandonment of major projects, relocation of facilities, changes in managerial assignments, and closure or sale of facilities or divisions. . . . Restructurings usually involve . . . increased use of debt and a flurry of recontracting with managers, employees, suppliers, and customers. . . . Takeovers generally occur because changing technology or market conditions require a major restructuring of corporate assets, and it is easier for new top-level managers with a fresh view of the business and no ties with current employees or communities to make such changes.[13]

While there are many forces that drive takeover activity, such as "deregulation, synergies, economies of scale and scope, taxes, the level of managerial competence, and increasing globalization of U.S. markets," Jensen believes more attention should be paid to the core principal-agent problem: managers and shareholders have a basic conflict over the payout of free cash flow, namely, any cash left over after a firm funds all of its good investment projects. He is blunt in his views:

> Such free cash flow must be paid out to shareholders if the firm is to be efficient and to maximize value for shareholders. However, payment of cash to shareholders reduces the resources controlled by managers, thereby reducing the power of managers and potentially subjecting them to the monitoring of capital markets that occurs when a firm must obtain new capital.[14]

Jensen believes that many managers are trying to expand the size of the firm in order to maximize corporate wealth and increase their own power and even compensation since "changes in management compensation are positively related to growth." The conflict becomes sharpened when a corporation generates substantial free cash flow. The problem is "how to motivate managers to disgorge the cash rather than invest it at below the cost of capital or waste it through organizational inefficiencies."[15]

Jensen and his colleagues have been accumulating evidence for their point of view. It is important to note that while the tension between shareholders and boards/senior management, to which the principal-agent notion refers is a concern of corporate law, Jensen's response to this problem is not *the law* but one point of view.

This is the case because the law does not impose the corporation's distribution of earnings—"free cash flow"—on the board, and the courts generally do not interfere in the business judgment of boards and senior management. The legal reason for this is that, as Hamilton points out, "The decision whether or not to pay dividends rests in the hands of the board of directors of the corporation." He goes on to say that the profits of a business corporation may be accumulated by the corporation or paid out in whole or in part. Surely, as he says, in large publicly held corporations dividends are paid periodically, because many investors identify stable dividends with financial health and an attractive reason to buy the company's shares. Corporations will distribute dividends in cash—in-kind or property—in other shares, in rights, or in warrants, which are options to purchase additional shares usually at below the current market price. Mostly, these dividends are regular—quarterly or semiannual—and sometimes, "special" or "extra." Corporations will occasionally make distributions of their capital and can also repurchase their own shares, resulting in the equivalent of a dividend, since the corporation's total worth is now divided up among a smaller number of shares (that is, each share is theoretically worth more).[16]

The Courts' Opposition to Second-Guessing Management

The other reason limiting the Jensen point of view is the *business judgment rule* or *business judgment doctrine,* a fundamental principle applied by judges in cases of corporate governance, which Hamilton summarizes in the following way: Directors are granted discretion with regard to the management of the corporation, and the exercise of that discretion is generally not subject to judicial review. Courts have held that they cannot run businesses and often have little knowledge or familiarity of the specific business before them. Thus decisions made by boards "upon reasonable information and with some rationality do not give rise to directorial liability, even if they turn out badly or disastrously from the standpoint of the corporation . . . and such decisions are valid and binding upon the corporation and cannot be enjoined, set aside, or attacked by shareholders."[17] The bottom line is that a strong showing of fraud, bad faith, abuse of discretion, abuse of power, clear failure to exercise power honestly, a disabling conflict of interest, or self-dealing is necessary for a court to overturn a board's decision.

The business judgment rule has been central to takeovers because it's the interpretation of business judgment that has led to disagreements between shareholders and boards/senior management and has often determined the outcome of a battle between a corporation or a person attempting a hostile tender offer and a board/senior management pronouncing the takeover contrary to the corporation's interest.

Jensen rejects this rule noting, "The altruistic model of the board that is the implicit foundation of the business judgment rule is obviously incorrect as a description of human behavior. But in spite of its falsity, the altruistic model has been sufficiently robust to yield good law for a wide range of cases for many years. Alternative agency models of the corporation that incorporate conflicts of interest between board members and shareholders are much more complicated."[18] Jensen's concern is that directors/senior management will cease to be agents of shareholders and exploit their power to obtain ultimate control themselves.

. Other observers of the corporate scene see things very differently. William Lazonick views the corporate raiders of the 1980s as the source of declining competitiveness, not the solution. He claims that at an extreme Jensen's desire to see retained earnings distributed to shareholders can undermine the corporation's commitment to long-term investment projects that would make it competitive, and force corporations to borrow at a high rate of interest on corporate debt—a rate, he notes, which has increased in real interest terms from .39 percent in 1950–1954 to 6.45 percent in 1985–1989.

Jensen and Lazonick form two extremes on how to discipline managers in public companies. Jensen's approach sees managers kept in tow by the power of shareholders to throw them out, or threaten to do so, through the stock market—a hostile tender offer—or in a proxy contest. He regards debt as beneficial, because it reduces the cash flow available for spending at the managers' discretion and bonds their promise to make principal and interest payments out of future cash flows. It motivates managers and their organizations to be efficient.

One Viewpoint: The Importance of Organizational Commitment and Patient Investors for Management Success. Lazonick's approach suggests managers ought to be disciplined, "not by portfolio investors, but by participants in the enterprise who really contribute to the process of value creation—the organization's employees." Japan is his example, where there are patient investors, no significant market for corporate control, few stock options for management, and an emphasis on the corporation's internal organizational capabilities, which can develop its capacity to invest heavily in innovation and reduce unit costs. From his point of view, patient investors profit over the long term and do not seek quarter-to-quarter results. They allow the firm to use retained earnings for investment. He sees the market for corporate control as forcing some firms to burden themselves with high-interest capital either to pay off shareholders or fend off raiders by ill-advised acquisitions, thereby losing focus. He stresses the long-term competitive advantage of the product and the organization while Jensen focuses on the immediate competitive advantage of the investor. Lazonick believes that the Jensen worldview has contributed to the decline of American business. Other critics of Jensen have suggested that a takeover does not necessarily lead to improved efficiency in a firm. Others worry that potential takeover investors may offer a high price to purchase control of a company and then attempt to buy the remaining shares at a lower price, thus disadvantaging some shareholders. This suggests that manipulation and strategems of unfairness are possible on both sides of the takeover battlefield.[19]

Real differences of opinions arise between certain sets of shareholders and the directors/senior management of corporations over precisely these issues when a corporation is in a takeover environment or a set of shareholders is concerned about management's performance in a particular corporation. If a shareholder decides not to keep quiet or sell his or her shares, he or she may file suit, or mount a proxy battle or a hostile tender offer, or all three. Then, either a court—in the case of a lawsuit—or the other shareholders—by casting their votes in a proxy battle or selling their shares in a tender offer—will decide. Management's judgment goes on trial.

The takeovers and mergers of the 1980s have differed from the creation of massive trusts in the early 1900s or the conglomerate movement of the 1960s, where firms were seeking to grow mainly by acquiring a variety of often unrelated businesses. The eighties and nineties have seen more of these direct challenges against the board/senior management's vision of the firm and its strategy. These challenges are often more environmental than direct. Jensen points out that high-visibility hostile tender offers made up only 40 (an all-time record) out of 3300 takeover transactions in 1986. There were 110 voluntary or negotiated tender offers unopposed by management, and the remaining 3100 deals were also voluntary transactions, although "many of the voluntary transactions would not occur absent the threat of a hostile takeover."[20] As both tender offers and proxy contests succeeded in the eighties and nineties, corporations "paid a great deal of attention to defensive tactics to make takeovers more difficult." Also, in a new development, employee groups themselves have initiated employee-ownership proposals, which, in effect, have prevented the corporation from being taken over for a period of time (see the United Air Lines case at the beginning of this chapter), even though the employee-ownership plan was not sponsored by management or the board of that company.

Shareholder Defense or Management Entrenchment?

It is not our goal to thoroughly review takeover defense tactics. These tactics, commonly called poison pills, alter a company and make it difficult for an acquirer to swallow. In general, courts have struck down some tactics they have judged as clearly unfair to shareholders and evident of management entrenchment, while they have used the business judgment rule to support a variety of poison-pill mechanisms.[21]

Michael Jensen believes that takeover defense tactics adopted without shareholder approval and that court allowance of such tactics under the business judgment rule give "the agents [managers and the board] the right to change unilaterally critical control aspects of the contract [the corporate rules that govern the relationship between shareholders, managers, and the board of directors], in particular, the right to prevent the firing of the agents."[22]

Whatever point of view one accepts, the facts go in only one direction: a broad-based trend of shareholder activism has been slowly growing in the United States since World War II that has been pushing to replace domination of shareholders by boards and managers. This effort is reflected in the growth of acquisitions, tender offers, and proxy battles. The numbers are small, but tender offers and proxy battles influence corporate management far in excess of their actual numbers. They send a message to corporate management in other companies, highlighting that market discipline and shareholder democracy can express their power in dramatic ways!

Some General Trends and Patterns: How Employee Ownership Evolved in a Takeover Environment

Unlike poison pills or golden parachutes, ESOPs serve a number of legitimate non-control-oriented corporate purposes.

—*Judge in the Buckhorn ESOP case, citing the judge in the Norlin ESOP case*

It is instructive that both judges in two cases where the court was most critical of senior management and the boards' abuse of employee ownership distinguish between employee ownership and straightforward poison pills and shark repellents.[23] *However, employee-held stock can be voted against a takeover investor or other shareholders in a tender offer contest or a proxy battle. Whatever the reason for establishing employee ownership, its effect can be defensive.*

The rise of the large employee holding in the public company is occurring at the same time that institutional investors are becoming more prominent as the controlling shareholders in many public companies while the number of passive individual shareholders has declined, giving core-employee benefit plan holders higher standing.

For different companies, certain tactics of corporate takeover defense have become too complicated, too expensive, too risky, too obvious, or too difficult to get approved by shareholders. Corporate managers are exploring the implications of their company structure for takeovers that might benefit or hurt shareholder value. All takeover investors may not have the best interests of all the shareholders and the corporation in mind. Shareholders are frequently divided among themselves over supporting management or takeover investors on an issue-by-issue basis.[24]

These factors do not mean, however, that the motivation for every significant employee holding can be reduced to simply an unequivocal takeover defense. We have discovered an explicitly named takeover investor in less than 10 percent of public corporations that have more than 4-percent employee ownership. On the contrary, we have demonstrated in previous chapters that a range of other motives and circumstances exist, which can also explain the rise of employee ownership in public companies. Taken together, all the cases where employee ownership is part of a corporate takeover environment are actually a small proportion of situations where employee ownership was used.

Let's start with a review of a core issue: are employee-ownership plans in takeovers bad for shareholders? We mentioned that management can argue that dilution can be offset by a combination of tax savings, wage and benefit restructuring, productivity increases, and other methods to repurchase common shares or structure the securities to minimize only earnings-per-share dilution.[25] Appendix H.1 chronologically lists all the cases, including whether the employee ownership was proposed or adopted, whether newly issued shares were used, whether a share repurchase took place to reduce outstanding common, and if wage and benefit restructuring was used. We also note whether there is a public record of a lawsuit, and if the use of employee ownership resulted in a takeover.

Figure 3.1 shows steady growth for employee-ownership plans in takeover environments, with the NYSE being the dominant exchange. Only about a third of the companies restructured wages and benefits to deal with shareholder dilution. This is quite alarming.

> *I have yet to see an ESOP that will stop a fully financed hostile deal. It will impede a transaction that is not fully financed or is not all cash. My view is that an ESOP gives the sponsoring company significant present value savings but is not a screen against a full and fair offer, so institutional investor groups have not been deprived of a full and fair offer. An ESOP helps insure that if and when a company is sold, it is sold for fair value and no one can come in to steal the company from shareholders. Long-term, that is truly a benefit, not a detriment.*
>
> *—Senior investment banker at a major Wall Street firm*

To date, there has never been an attempt to walk through the evolution of employee ownership in takeover environments over the last decade and a half.[26] There are three main periods: 1973–1984 indicates a good deal of confusion

FIGURE 3.1 *Employee Ownership Adopted or Proposed in Takeover Environments*

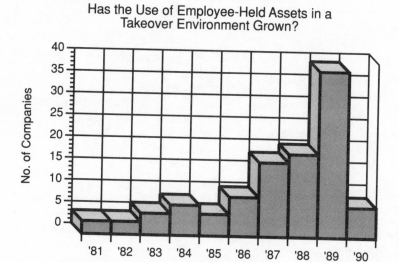

Has the Use of Employee-Held Assets in a
Takeover Environment Grown?

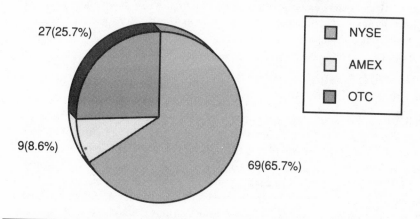

Is the Use of Employee-Held Assets in a Takeover
Environment Related to its Stock Exchange?

27(25.7%)

9(8.6%)

69(65.7%)

NYSE

AMEX

OTC

(continued)

FIGURE 3.1   *(Continued)*

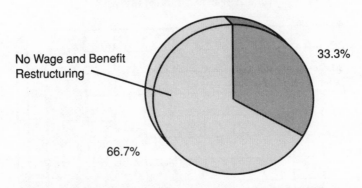

Do Companies in a Takeover Environment Restructure Wages and Benefits?

No Wage and Benefit Restructuring

33.3%

66.7%

Source: Public Company Employee Ownership Database, 1990. Chart by Lawrence R. Greenberg and Shane Williams

about the role of the "employee" in employee ownership; 1985–1987 points to several innovative defensive approaches to employee ownership; and 1988–1990 marks the high point of its development, providing more clarity about the appropriate format of employee ownership, increased sensitivity to shareholder neutrality and management's manipulation of employees' shareholder rights. The following analysis will show how the preceding trends for the past 15 years or so make sense through these three periods.

1973–1984: Confusion About the "Employee" in Employee Ownership

In this period some management groups cynically used "employee ownership" to defend the company against takeovers by manipulating the structure of employee ownership. Technically, all allocated shares in ESOPs in public companies must be voted by employees. But in leveraged ESOPs, shares are allocated proportionately over the term of the loan, so that in fact the trustee ends up controlling the vote on a majority of the unallocated shares until they are allocated to employees during the years of the loan's term. Various methods were designed by managers and their advisors to control the employee ownership and voting in ESOPs and other benefit plans. Despite years of confusion, by the late eighties it became widely accepted for employee-shareholders to confidentially vote the holdings of their employee benefit plans, including voting unallocated shares in ESOPs in proportion to allocated shares ("mirror voting").[27] Phillips Petroleum discovered how to deliver value to shareholders who demanded it, yet gird itself for future battles by establishing significant employee ownership in a way they felt was viable for shareholders. Also, the salaried employees of Lyons Metal Products Inc. used a prior management commitment about their excess benefits to prevent what they felt may have amounted to a hijacking of their ESOP.

Early Cases.   The earliest relevant situation we have identified happened in April 1973, when an investor named Klaus began trying to acquire Hi-Shear Corporation in California.[28] The company bought back 660,000 of its own shares and sold them to a wholly owned subsidiary called Caribe. In August 1974, Klaus acquired 45 percent of Hi-Shear. If it had not been for the Caribe share, he would have controlled over 50 percent of the company when his tender offer closed in October 1974. At that point, Hi-Shear management approved several new stock issuances, which further diluted Klaus's holdings. Klaus brought suit in federal court, alleging a breach of fiduciary duty under state law, and he sought relief regarding the ESOP. The district court granted several orders, including an injunction against the ESOP and an order denying Hi-Shear's motion to modify the ESOP, which allowed the employees to vote, rather than an ESOP committee under the influence of Hi-Shear's management. The court found that management's conduct in establishing and transferring shares to the employee-ownership plan violated California law. On appeal, a higher court agreed with these findings but reversed the injunction. This begins a judicial tradition of courts limiting management's and the board's authority in implementing employee-ownership plans.[29]

The question of limits on management's authority rose again when an ESOP was used to oppose a takeover at Calumet Industries. In March 1978, when Calumet Industries (OTC) put 50,000 shares in a trust for the benefit of its employees, a shareholder named Podesta, formerly on the board of directors, brought suit charging that a senior manager undertook this as a scheme to dilute the voting strength of shareholders who supported a Shareholder Protective Committee. The Committee was trying to remove officers of the company for mismanagement through a proxy contest. The shares contained some unusual provisions that assured they would be voted at the next annual meeting on May 3, 1978, and would give corporate officers control of 22.3 percent of the ESOP votes. The court found that the ESOP was created as an "eager, if not desperate, attempt by Fair [a senior manager] and his colleagues to manipulate almost every resource available in order to defeat a challenge to their control." The court also found that Fair and other managers failed to disclose the ESOP in a proxy statement in violation of the Securities and Exchange Act and that "the deliberations which led to the final adoption of the Calumet ESOP demonstrated that the goal of entrenching incumbent management was foremost in the minds of Fair and his colleagues."[30] The court prevented the employee holdings from voting on the takeover. This lesson about having only wrong motives for employee ownership and not having any right motives would take a decade for management to digest. The role of employee ownership in proxy battles, rather than tender offers to discipline management, would lay in abeyance for another decade as most disgruntled shareholders and investors simply used the free and easy credit and leverage of the eighties to go in and buy the whole company!

In 1980, Texas International Air Lines began open-market purchases of Continental Air Lines, Inc. stock. As part of a takeover attempt, Continental tried to issue $185 million in new shares, representing more than half the corporation's total equity, to an ESOP through an agreement with employees who would defer pay concessions to pay for the ESOP. The employees would acquire one half of the airline, and the company would acquire new equity capital. Texas accumulated 9.5 percent of the shares and launched a hostile tender offer, which netted it 48.5 percent of the shares. In May 1981, it proposed a resolution at the stockholder's meeting, prohibiting the board from implementing an ESOP without prior shareholder approval but was ruled out of order, infringing on the board of directors' authority to act in the best interests of the company. Texas Air later sought an injunction against the ESOP, contending that it would lower earnings per share and that directors breached their fiduciary duty and were just trying to entrench themselves. But Continental succeeded in convincing the court that the ESOP would lead to increased equity financing and increased employee production by virtue of their significant equity participation in the company. The court ruled against Texas Air, although subsequent events outside of court negated its decision and the company was taken over.[31] Shortly thereafter, a 1981 offer for United Cos. Financial Corporation (OTC) took place, and the board approved a significant employee-ownership plan. The company is still independent.

In 1981 and 1982, LTV Corporation (NYSE) tried to take over Grumman Aerospace Corp. (NYSE) with a tender offer for 70 percent of its shares at $45 per share. Grumman's defined-benefit pension plan owned just over half a million shares, and not only declined to sell its shares to LTV, but it went out and purchased about 1.1 million more shares of Grumman for $38.27! Senior managers of Grumman were trustees of the employee pension plan. The Secretary of Labor, in the first action of its kind against a large corporate pension plan, persuaded the court to remove the trustees and appoint independent trustees, who would make all share-ownership decisions strictly for the benefit of employees who were the beneficiaries of the pension plan. The court felt that the management trustees were acting to protect their interests, not those of the employees. They had dual and divided loyalty. While the manager's lack of objectivity is clear in the court record, it is also clear that the Department of Labor and the court itself refused to allow employees to decide for themselves: an affidavit to the court noted that 17,000 of the 22,000 employees in the pension plan signed a petition supporting the trustees' actions, but this had no effect on the judgment. The issue of whether employees or trustees would control employee holdings continued to intensify.[32]

The most publicized case, however, involved a full-scale war between Martin Marietta Corp. (NYSE) and the Bendix Corporation (formerly NYSE), which started in August 1982. Bendix tried to raid Martin Marietta, which countered by launching a tender offer for Bendix. At the time the Bendix employee savings plan was the largest Bendix stockholder, owning approximately 23 percent of the shares, with Citibank acting as the trustee. But under provisions of the plan, Citibank was prohibited from tendering the Bendix stock in the plan. Citibank voted the shares for the takeover, but Bendix amended its savings plan to require Citibank to withdraw the tendered shares unless otherwise instructed by the employees involved in the savings plan. Ninety-nine percent of the employees directed that 94 percent of the tendered shares be withdrawn. But the situation ended badly for Bendix when Allied Corporation offered to merge with Bendix, which it subsequently controlled. Later Martin Marietta bought 44 percent of Bendix's stock and William Agee resigned as chairman of Bendix. This case showed corporations that they could not simply set up employee benefit plans as shareholders and control their trustees like ventriloquists![33]

Again in 1982, Burlington Northern Inc. (NYSE) launched a hostile tender offer for the El Paso Company. El Paso's ESOP and Savings Plan held about 8 percent of its stock. After the offer, El Paso amended its benefit plans to allow the employees to vote how the stock should be tendered. While El Paso mounted an extensive campaign to inform employees about their right to give instructions, they claimed to have avoided pressure or coercion. An independent CPA firm opened the votes. On the last day that shares could be tendered, Burlington tried to have the court prevent the company from implementing these changes and order the trustee to tender all the shares to them. The court denied Burlington's request without written explanation or opinion. Although El Paso was subsequently bought out, this proceeding foretells the attitude courts would have toward less manipulatively structured employee holdings.[34]

The Growth of Employee Ownerships in Takeover Environments.   In 1983, Michael Baker Corporation (AMEX) was offered a merger by Century Engineering. An ESOP committee was formed, notifying the board that it would purchase noninsider shares, using the company's pension plans and individual employee payroll deductions. Ultimately, the company terminated its defined-benefit plans and used the excess assets and employee deductions, which surpassed the amount needed—because of broad-based employee support—to buy 39 percent of the shares. Most of these shares were purchased from the Baker family members. In the same year, the board of Odetics Inc. (AMEX) said they instituted an ESOP to make an unfriendly takeover more difficult. The company now has a small amount of employee ownership but has not been taken over.

Employee ownership did not prevent a takeover of the Graniteville Corporation in 1983. Victor Posner's Southeastern Public Service Company tried to block the establishment of an ESOP, alleging it would dilute shareholders interests, waste assets, and prevent suiters from making bids. The Federal District Court in South Carolina would not grant an injunction, and management went ahead and sold almost 15 percent of the company in newly issued shares for $14 a share. This was funded with assets from the termination of two pension plans. The board then rejected a $15-a-share offer by Posner as unfair, because of a concern that he was willing to buy out only a minority of shareholders. Southeastern took over the company, but the Department of Labor sued again on behalf of the employees in an interesting twist: they claimed the company made a commitment to use excess pension assets for the employees' benefit. Employees were not going to be passive observers in a corporation's use of their benefit plan assets. But Cone Mills Corp. escaped a takeover by Western Pacific Industries by using an ESOP to take the company private. This plan succeeded partly because it was supported by institutional investors, who this time clearly formed a coalition with the employee holdings. Finally, Scotty's Inc. (NYSE) announced the issuance of stock to a number of employee plans, an ESOP right of first refusal if largest shareholders decided to sell their shares, and a package of antitakeover measures.

The year 1984 marked the time in which the role of employees in employee ownership came to a head. By January 1984, Rooney Pace, an investment corporation employed by Piezo Electric Products Corp., and Piezo had accumulated shares of the Norlin Corp. (NYSE), representing a stake of 32 percent. Norlin immediately took defensive action and transferred stock to a subsidiary in exchange for voiding a promissory note. The board also created an ESOP and retained voting rights over the stock involved in both transfers. All together, this gave the board control of over 49 percent of the corporation's outstanding stock. The CEO wrote a letter to shareholders asserting the transfers were defensive measures. In a court battle, the court ruled that the timing of the ESOPs formation, the financial impact on the company, the trustee's identity, and the voting control of the ESOP shares meant that the "ESOP was created solely as a tool of management self-perpetuation." The New York Stock Exchange even warned management that without shareholder approval, the stock transactions violated its rules and ended up delisting Norlin's stock. Norlin marked one of the first systematic judicial analyses of the misuse of an employee-ownership plan. Norlin was taken over.

But, later that year, the war between The Limited and Carter Hawley Hale was to turn out completely differently. Leslie Wexner, chairman of The Limited began a 2 and one-half year pitched battle, as *Barron's* called it, to take over Carter Hawley Hale Stores (NYSE), where Philip Hawley had been a director of the bank for almost ten years. The magazine reports on the employee-ownership passion play that ensued. Carter Hawley's 56,000 employees had the right to receive a small amount of profit each year in a deferred-profit-sharing trust administered by the Bank of America trust department. The bank agreed to be the agent for a $900-million line of credit to help Carter Hawley resist the takeover and stipulated that if control of the company changed hands, all its loans from the bank would be in default. The bank was also receiving $500,000 as a fee for assembling this credit, even if it were not loaned. Bank of America was required by ERISA to act solely in the employee participants' interest in the profit-sharing plan. Under Carter Hawley's management, the share price had reached $20, yet The Limited was offering $30 a share. Thus, Bank of America as trustee for the profit-sharing plan could add 50 percent to the total assets of the plan if it voted for the takeover. To deal with such a potential conflict of interest, the plan had a "pass-through voting provision," allowing employees to confidentially vote the shares in a tender offer, but immediately after the Limited's offer, which was drastically revised, as *Barron's* reported on May 4, 1987.

> The following bizarre procedure was to be followed: Employees would request information about the tender. After evaluating that information, they could either do nothing, which would be a vote for management, or they could ask the trustee for their share certificates. In fact, of course, the records of share ownership were kept at Carter Hawley Hale headquarters. This meant that every store manager would have a printout every morning of any employee who had asked for shares and might be about to show disloyalty to Phil Hawley. Even if an employee were determined to tender, the rules of Bank of America, as the trustee, said that six to eight weeks would be required to obtain share certificates. Then it was each employee's responsibility to tender on his own. The offer had been made in late November. Its stated expiration date was five weeks later on December 31. By simple arithmetic, the trustees' plans made it impossible for CHH employees to tender their shares, effectively removing voting or tendering as one of the facets of share ownership under the CHH profit-sharing plan.

The U.S. Department of Labor, which twice wrote the company, questioning B of A's stewardship of the profit-sharing plans, planned to file suit but later dropped its plans. A lawsuit was filed by one lone employee questioning this stewardship. Wexner never did succeed in taking over Carter Hawley.

Later the same year, dissident shareholders of CPT Corporation (OTC) were unhappy with the stock's performance and pressed the board to remove the chairman, threatening to call a special meeting and elect a new board. The chairman was the largest holder. In the ensuing month, the chairman increased the ESOP's holdings in a number of transactions and was the sole trustee of the ESOP. Later the company settled a class-action suit with employee participants in the ESOP. Again, internal conflict broke out in the company over the role of employee ownership.

Employees Challenge Management. The tide continued to turn, however, as employees began to assert their rights in these situations. In April 1984, Lyon

Metal Products was the target of a hostile bid first by Florida investor D. D. Rhoads and then by Irwin Jacobs, whose Minstar Corp. increased its stake to 42.9 percent. A group of Lyon officers proposed using an ESOP to take the company private by using $12 million in excess pension assets, but salaried employees filed a class-action suit, charging that management had promised to use these excess assets for their benefit. They felt that management was assigning too much stock ownership to themselves in an LBO transaction that used mainly the excess benefit funds of the broader employee group. Active in their own defense, these nonunion employees obtained consents of a majority of shareholders to expand the board from 10 to 13 members for the purpose of moving forward with the ESOP. The salaried employees gained control of the board, settled the suit out of court, and used the excess assets as leverage to get a sizable bank loan to take over the company. The settlement provided for an LBO transaction in which the salaried employee group won considerably more employee ownership in the resultant LBO than management had originally allotted to them and linked management's rewards to specific performance goals in increasing the value of the company. The employee-dominated board then ousted the chairman.

In the case of Phillips Petroleum Co. (NYSE), management itself changed the structure of the ESOP to make it fairer. T. Boone Pickens Mesa Partners mounted a hostile bid. In a new twist, the takeover investor himself publicly promised to consider maintaining sizable employee ownership in the company if his bid succeeded! Management countered by saying that employees would also control voting of the unallocated shares of the ESOP, which would have a democratic structure. Indeed, one financial analyst commented that the tax advantages of an ESOP would help the takeover with its debt load. Pickens' attempt ended with an agreement for a major, complicated financial restructuring, which would put value in the shareholders' pockets and involve the creation of a large ESOP, whose stake would rise to 40 percent over the year. Shareholders sold off shares and some accused Pickens of "greenmail." Management lost a shareholder vote on the plan and faced a Delaware lawsuit alleging entrenchment. Carl Icahn, another shareholder, did not feel the plan was fair and pressed for a sweetened recapitalization plan and a termination of the ESOP idea. In the end, the company's current benefit plans, which owned a sizable percentage of company stock anyway, took their "dividends" in the recapitalization in stock and later expanded their employee holdings in a major 1988 employee-ownership transaction. Icahn said he dropped his bid for the company because the company dropped the ESOP idea in the initial recapitalization. The Phillips' case vividly demonstrates some of the arguments against the Jensen viewpoint: the company did not attempt a fly-by-night ESOP to hoodwink shareholders, but it paid them value, discerning that substantial employee ownership was a necessary part of a future without constant raids on its treasury by impatient investors.

1985–1987: Some Innovative Defenses

"This is probably one of the most beneficial ways to pay greenmail I have ever seen. They are increasing the value of their stock, but they aren't just paying one party. They are benefitting all shareholders," observed Robert Morris III of Prudential-Bache Securities Inc. in the *Wall Street Journal,* November 7, 1986, on the GTE Corp. plan to increase shareholder value and expand employee ownership. This period was marked by management and boards developing a wide variety of ways to establish employee ownership in takeover environments. Courts began to define more sharply exactly what constitutes management entrenchment under employee ownership, while corporations with and without shareholder approval became more original at weaving employee ownership into companies in takeover environments.

Carl Icahn walked away from Phillips Petroleum with enormous profits and $30 million in takeover expenses. The man who so hated ESOPs in 1984 became their friend in 1985. In June 1985, he joined with an employee group at TWA (NYSE) to help defend it against a hostile takeover by Texas Air's Frank Lorenzo. Wage concessions were traded for a sizable employee stake in the newly organized company. Later in 1985, New Jersey Resources Corp. (NYSE) used an ESOP to buy out a holder who had been accumulating its shares, thus ending all litigation between the two parties.

Recapitalizing and Giving Something to Shareholders. In 1986, FMC Corp. (NYSE), concerned about an unfriendly suitor, approved a recapitalization plan to shrink public ownership of shares. The novel plan paid out value to shareholders with $70 in cash per share plus one share but gave management and employee benefit plans approximately 4 to 6 shares for each share they held, leaving employee holdings to over 25 percent of the firm. Although Rexnord Corporation (NYSE) tried a restructuring and recapitalization to avoid a takeover, it was subsequently sold. Holly Corp.'s (AMEX) shareholders approved a 20-percent ESOP, with a recapitalization that distributed $50 million to shareholders, but the company put itself on the auction block in 1989. Greiner Engineering (AMEX) also began a series of wide-ranging employee-ownership transactions. Management and the ESOP made a joint bid, which the board chose over a hostile raider's bid, but the management-ESOP bid did not get financing, and the company's ESOP partly bought out another major holder, later expanding its size significantly. In the same vein, Honeywell Inc. (NYSE) and Apogee Enterprises Inc. (OTC) adopted antitakeover measures and expanded ESOPs at the same time. A Honeywell spokesman insisted no connection existed between the two. From the other end of the spectrum, labor tried its muscle with an unsuccessful attempt by the union-led Eastern Air Lines Acquisition Corp. to snatch Texas Air's Eastern subsidiary from Lorenzo.

Controversy was not far behind. Texas American Energy Corp. (OTC) was sued by two holders who formed a stockholder's committee to elect a slate of six directors in order to invalidate an ESOP. A Resorts International (then AMEX) ESOP was widely rumored as a way to buy out a founder's estate and avoid a takeover by an outside suitor. GTE Corp. (NYSE) moved adroitly to boost value to shareholders in a number of moves and to increase employee ownership in response to a rumored accumulation of their shares by the Belzberg family. The $750 million of cash on hand and an overfunded pension plan made the company an attractive target. One analyst called it "a beneficial way to pay greenmail."

Troubled Petro-Lewis Corporation (AMEX) had set up an ESOP as a takeover defense in 1985, after reducing other employee benefits against Jakonson Kass Partners. The company was the largest marketer of oil income funds and had sold $2.5 billion of interest in the funds, leveraging itself to the hilt in a gamble that oil prices would climb for years. Investors lost more than $1 billion by the time the firm was acquired by Freeport-McMoRan Inc, closing the books on "a colossal investor catastrophe in corporate history." In this case, the ESOP might have forestalled a takeover, but the ultimate sale and restructuring of the firm was a necessity. However, one result was different for management and employees: they ended up owning 18 percent of the newly acquired company.

In 1987, Bank Building & Equipment Corp. of America (AMEX) requested an offer from Amcat Corp. but then countered with a joint tender by its ESOP and management when the offer proved disappointing. Its 40 percent ESOP successfully repelled several takeovers. The president echoed Michael Jensen's ideas when he said in a 1988 SEC filing, "The primary purposes of the transaction were to permit our stockholders to receive a significant distribution of assets, which we believed we did not need to retain in our business, while at the same time to provide our employees with an ownership interest in the company through an ESOP." But the discipline of the debt market was more than the company could handle, and it ran into difficulty in 1990. Crazy Eddie Inc.'s (OTC) board's flirtation with an ESOP could not undo the difficulties that firm was experiencing and the pressure of a Committee to Restore Shareholder Value, set up by major stockholders.

Experimentation.   In quick succession several companies used employee ownership to deal with takeovers. Both Imperial and Holly Sugar Corps. merged to avoid a takeover of Holly, with the combined company being more than 20-percent employee held. Integrity Entertainment Corp.'s (AMEX) ESOP bought out its founder's estate at the time that Shamrock Holdings was launching a subsequently unsuccessful takeover bid. Swank (NYSE), announcing a recapitalization under threat of a hostile takeover, declined to disclose to the *Wall Street Journal* how many shares were held by employee benefit plans. Sooner Federal Savings & Loan Association (OTC) approved an ESOP after an investor group notified the Federal Home Loan Bank Board that they intended to raise their stake from 9.9 percent to 50 percent of the bank. Sometimes suitors and corporations seem to be playing with employee ownership as a way to signal each other's intentions and, perhaps, to scare a raider into offering a higher price. JWT Corp. (J. Walter Thompson Inc.) announced that they were considering an ESOP or other LBO to counter a proposed acquisition by a British company. First Fulton Bancshares Inc. set up an ESOP but held back on selling it stock, as acquiror Barnett Banks moved to take it over. Trailways flirted with an ESOP before its sale to Greyhound. Another approach was using an ESOP to "cash out the suitor." Thus, Resdel Industries entered into a complicated transaction, which involved its ESOP cashing out Saul Steinberg's Reliance Electric's stake.

Courts Draw a Line in the Sand. The limit of management's power to use employee ownership became the focus of five important lawsuits, and in response, the courts drew some very clear lines. In 1985, Frantz Manufacturing was a takeover target by Philadelphia investment firm SMC. When negotiations between target and acquirer failed, the Frantz board approved an ESOP without shareholder approval as another acquirer, EAC entered the picture. The acquirer succeeded in buying some of the shares Frantz wished to purchase for its ESOP and took control of the board on April 18 with 51 percent of shareholder consents. But the original members of Frantz's board enacted the ESOP on April 24, diluting the EAC holding to less than 51 percent. EAC attempted to nullify the ESOP, and the court agreed that the creation of the ESOP, both before and after the meeting on April 24, was unauthorized. It upheld a Chancery Court finding that the original purpose of the ESOP was to perpetuate the present management's control by taking the firm private.

In 1987, Ropak Corporation sought an injunction against an ESOP plan adopted as a poison pill by the Buckhorn Corp. Buckhorn lacked the timing advantage of Chicago Pneumatic Tool (which is discussed below). Since its ESOP was adopted during the takeover, the court gave it "heightened scrutiny."[35] The court decided that the ESOP failed the test, since it was adopted conceptually without the board's examining drafts of the plan or specific operational details of the ESOP. The company purchased the shares below the raider's price despite Buckhorn's claim that Ropak's offer was inadequate! The court ruled there was no evidence in the record to indicate that the ESOP would benefit shareholders or how Ropak's offer would hurt employees. The ESOP was invalidated and the court permanently enjoined the voting of its shares.

Nevertheless, courts continued to focus on what they viewed as fair structuring and fair timing of ESOPs, criteria supporting their merit for normal business purposes. The challenge to the ESOP at Anderson Clayton Corp. (then NYSE) thus differed from the previous cases. Anderson Clayton, a major processer and marketer of foods and feeds, including Gaines dog food, Chiffon margarine, and Seven Seas salad dressings, grew concerned that some family trusts owning 27 percent of the stock were about to expire. First Boston presented a recapitalization plan that would involve 25 percent of the firm being employee held, and the board called a meeting for shareholder approval on June 3. Shareholders sought an injunction against this meeting but the court denied them twice—once after Bear Stearns offered to purchase the company. Finally, three shareholder groups jointly sued the company, but the court ruled that the ESOP did not constitute illegal management entrenchment for these reasons: the ESOP trustee was a bank, enjoying no significant relationship with the company; voting of the shares would be directed by the employees; and officers would control only 1.3 percent of outstanding stock after the recapitalization. The court said that the ESOP was neither a fraud, nor a waste, nor a giveaway because an appropriate price, approved by a disinterested board, was paid for the stock, and it really represented a "form of future compensation."[36]

The case of *Danaher* v. *Chicago Pneumatic Tool* illustrates that all elements of an employee-ownership plan do not necessarily earn a court's support when it is challenged. At the time of Danaher's tender offer, Chicago's ESOP held a large block of stock, 99 percent of which was not allocated. The company's CEO, serving as trustee of the benefit plan with full authority over the shares, strongly opposed the tender offer and publicly stated he would not tender the shares. The court did not find that management violated its fiduciary duties in setting up the ESOP, because it was established before Danaher began to buy the stock. The Department of Labor also argued that the CEO had a conflict of interest in serving as the trustee. Both parties engaged in extensive discussions and negotiations about the appointment of a new trustee. The CEO resigned as the trustee, and the court accepted the appointment of two independent successor trustees, who decided not to tender the shares also. But later, Danaher was able to line up financing, obtain shareholder support to purchase the company, and win several procedural fights, which eased the success of its tender offer.

Finally, Harcourt Brace Jovanovich's ESOP, as noted at the beginning of this chapter, got support of the court, who stated its ESOP did not a priori *prevent* a company takeover, although as events turned out, the ESOP helped the company withstand a takeover just the same. The court focused especially on the structure of the ESOP, which allowed independent voting of the shares by the employees.[37]

A Scorecard for 1973–1987

What was the scorecard for employee ownership in takeover environments as 1988 started? It's startling indeed. Where a specific raider was identified, the presence of employee ownership in their defensive line-up resulted in no takeover almost 70 percent of the times. But 28 percent of the times, the company was taken over, and in 70 percent of the cases, a lawsuit was filed against senior management and the board of directors. In every takeover but one— *Continental Air Lines* v. *Texas Air*—the shareholders who sued prevailed, and in all cases the court found some "abuse" of power in structuring the employee

TABLE 3.1 *Scorecard: Presence of Employee Ownership in Takeover Environments: 1973–1987*

	Number	Percent
Companies with a Specific Takeover Investor Identified	40	100
Taken over by Takeover Investor Despite ESOP	11	28
Not Taken over by Takeover Investor	27	67
No Information	2	5
Of Those Not Taken Over: (27)		
No Material Change in Company at the Time	13	48
(Presumption of No Immediate Increased Value to Holders)		
Recapitalization Used to Pay Shareholders	7	26
Company Went Private	6	22
Rescued by Unions with White Knight	1	3
(Presumption of Some Increased Value to Holders)		
Of Those Taken Over: (11)		
A Lawsuit Was Filed against Senior Management/Board	8	73
A Lawsuit Was Not Filed	3	27
Of Lawsuits Filed: (8)		
Senior Management/Board Found to Have "Abused" Power	8	87
Court Found No Abuse of Power by Senior Management/Board	1	13
Companies Without a Specific Raider Identified	9	100
Taken over by Takeover Investor despite ESOP	0	0
Not Taken over	9	100

Source: Public Company Employee Ownership Database, 1990[38]

ownership. This is the clearest evidence to date that management's extreme manipulation of the structure of employee ownership makes both legal sanction and failure at any potential takeover defense fairly certain. It also suggests that the supposition of Michael Jensen that business judgment can serve as a cover for management to seize power from shareholders is not completely borne out in the employee-ownership cases. The alleged journalistic accounts of the Carter Hawley Hale scenario do, however, show that Jensen's fears may be real.[39]

But shareholders and takeover investors are not merely standing around, trying to make sure employee-ownership plans are structured and voted fairly. They might not view principle as a victory for them. They are out to make money or, at least, not have their investment in the corporation materially weakened by a defensive environment. Of the companies that were not taken over, there is some evidence on both sides pointing to how shareholders make money. Employee ownership was part of a transaction, either a recapitalization, a going private, or a white-knight union spin-off, which allowed a sale of the company, presumably with some increased value for shareholders in half of the cases. But in the other half of the cases, employee ownership was clearly part of a defensive environment, with little published evidence of a major change in the company: an indication that Jensen's fears may possibly be coming true in some of these cases.[40] One conclusion is clear: companies and courts generally ignored questions of shareholder dilution during this period.

1988–1990: High Point of Development, More Clarity About Appropriate Format of Employee Ownership

> *It reduces the takeover prospects that all retailers are worried about these days.*
>
> —*Walter F. Loeb of Morgan Stanley & Co. on the J.C. Penney ESOP*

> *It's death by a thousand cuts. Texaco's strategy is to create a substantial disincentive to takeover by putting in place a number of small anti-takeover provisions, which in aggregate, become significant.*
>
> —*Dennis O'Dea, counsel to a Committee of Equity Holders*

Without a doubt this period has the largest concentration of employee-ownership plans used in a takeover environment. This might suggest that some boards were responding to increasing threats; thus a larger number of ESOPs emerged as part of a defensive environment. Another possible explanation is that employee ownership in public companies was growing rapidly during this period anyway, in effect many corporations were interested in employee ownership when they found themselves swept up in a real-life takeover environment. Combinations of the two are probable, and it is reasonable to assume that some lawyers and company officials were trying to learn from the general trends how courts judged the fairness or unfairness of employee-ownership plans in the previous years and apply those lessons to their own plans. While many courts had not explicitly focused on this issue, one pattern that emerged in this period is that many companies began to exchange employee holdings for other wage and benefit costs and could therefore assert that the employee-ownership plan was shareholder neutral, that is, did not cost the shareholders anything or had limited costs.

Many companies set up employee-ownership plans where there were general rumors of takeovers, such as Acme Steel (OTC), which replaced some other benefits with employee holdings and FirstCorp. Inc. (AMEX), which terminated the defined-benefit plan of First Federal Bank of Durham. Cabot Corp. (NYSE) did the same under a takeover threat from GAF Corp., as did the Jefferies

Group Inc. (OTC). The replacement of other employee benefits, which may have been mainly a cost-cutting measure in many of these smaller companies, would become a critical factor in changing the character of takeover environment employee ownership.

Buying out the Takeover Investor. A common development, frequently not controversial, was one in which the employee-ownership plan bought shares on the open market and simply replaced public ownership with employee holdings. Thus, Medtronic Inc. (NYSE) bought a modest stake of 2.2 percent and announced it considered the move a potential antitakeover measure, even though it was not aware of takeovers. This trend would grow as firms became less apologetic and more forthright about having employee-holders if they felt confident about the fairness of their actions. Horn & Hardart Co. (NYSE) purchased 6.9 percent from an investor group, the Riese Organization, which had earlier said it might seek control. Fairchild Industries (NYSE) agreed to repurchase the stake of George Soros mostly for its ESOP, but takeover investor Carlyle Group successfully petitioned the Department of Labor to investigate whether the ESOP paid too much for the stock. Others were responding to clear-cut situations.[41] Kansas City Southern Industries (NYSE) sold a large block of shares to its already established ESOP before New York real estate developer Howard Kaskel's group made an offer.

The situations of some others cannot be clearly determined. Perhaps, KMS Industries Inc.'s (OTC) sale of a large issue of new shares to its ESOP and repurchase of shares from Burmah Oil Public Limited Co. was an attempt to buy out a possible takeover investor. Some firms raised the ESOP idea but were never able to implement it. Thus, Farmers Group Inc. talked about employee ownership, but apparently, at the last minute.[42]

Some companies did not learn the lessons of previous court cases. In January 1988, Charter-Crellin Inc. (OTC) replaced its profit-sharing plan with employee ownership of about 23 percent of its shares to fight a tender offer from the Atlantis Group. The company was alleged to have set up the ESOP quickly and structured voting to assure management control. A suit was filed but the case ended with a settlement, whereby the company bought out the takeover investor's stake and promised not to buy shares for five years. Here an alleged "abusive" employee-ownership plan still served as a successful defense, although that outcome may be related to the unwillingness of the takeover investor to press the case.

A Record for Management Manipulation. But the takeover battle at Macmillan Inc. (formerly NYSE), which carried on throughout 1987 and 1988, set a record for management manipulation of employee ownership. The company realized it was a likely target of an unsolicited takeover bid in May 1987 and started considering a recapitalization with an ESOP the day after Harcourt Brace

Jovanovich defeated Maxwell. In October 1987, the board authorized the sale of newly issued shares to the ESOP, thrift, and retirement plan of the company. In June, the board authorized the recapitalization, which included having the ESOP purchase a large block of shares with borrowed funds, bringing total employee ownership to 26 percent. The board granted restricted shares to more than 35 key managers, representing 7 percent of the company, for which the managers paid nothing. The existing independent trustee of the employee-ownership plan was replaced by management personnel who would have control over unallocated shares. The company was also authorized to issue up to 50 million new blank-check preferred shares, with disproportionate voting rights to be set by its board. It also adopted a mammoth golden parachute program for 21 executives funded by a $60-million letter of credit and a shareholder rights plan. Shareholders voted to approve the ESOP, unaware of an offer by the Robert M. Bass Group.

The company responded with a plan to split itself into two public companies, named Macmillan Publishing and Macmillan Information, and offer a special cash dividend to shareholders, which would increase company debt from $260 million to $1.77 billion. The ESOP and insiders would control 36 percent of the publishing company. Managers, who a year earlier controlled 1.2 percent of the company, could now trade their restricted shares and stock options for 39 percent of the information services business! Bass continued to up its bid and filed suit to halt Macmillan's restructuring, charging it defrauds shareholders. The restructuring did not require a vote by shareholders, who heard about it the day after it was adopted. Bass included employee ownership in its proposal and offered to let employees and management continue to own 36 percent of publishing. Then the situation got more complicated.

Mills Acquisitions, an affiliate of Robert Maxwell's Maxwell Communications, topped the Bass bid. Management tried to reach agreement with Kohlberg Kravis and Roberts to buy the company without giving Bass or Maxwell a chance to top that offer. The Delaware Chancery Court stopped the restructuring and said the agreement with KKR was invalid and that the board did not act in the best interest of the company in rejecting the Maxwell offer. The board declared that the restructuring would give the top executives "excessive" ownership and had "an offending quality." Ultimately, the company was taken over.

The employee-ownership plan played a small part in the complex legal proceedings, but the court found "conduct that fails all basic standards of fairness." The trustee replacement for the ESOP was used as an example of the beginning of unfair, illegal dealings by the Macmillan board. Subsequently, the Securities and Exchange Commission filed a complaint against the management "trustees" of the ESOP, charging they did not fully disclose the purposes of the employee-ownership plan. The Macmillan scenario focused attention on the abuse of management power in employee ownership.[43]

Enduring Themes in Court Rulings.   During this period similar themes about what courts saw as fair and unfair persisted. A shareholder of the Standard Brands Paint Company (NYSE) sued to prevent a restructuring that would provide two ESOPs 15 percent of the stock and increase shareholder value and company debt, but the court ruled that in spite of its definite takeover defense effects, the primary purpose of adopting the ESOP was not for management entrenchment, because most of the board were outside directors, no acquisition proposal was pending at the time of adoption, and the plans had pass-through of voting rights to the employees, thereby eliminating management control of these shares. Providing voting rights directly to workers became widespread from 1988–1990. Thus, while many opponents of ESOPs in corporations attacked management for "Macmillan-type" voting arrangements, Kaufmann Alsberg & Co. attacked Kysor Industrial Corp. (NYSE) because it had mirror voting. He charged that the trustee, not the employees, must vote the employee holdings in the way that affords the greatest gain. His suit filed in Wexford County Circuit Court was not successful. Although Kysor became over 20-percent employee held, it took actions to reduce dilution through share repurchases.[44]

But companies that actually implemented ESOPs continued to raise the ire of shareholders who may have come to one realization confirmed by the facts just presented: before 1988, ESOPs were simply not perfect takeover defenses and companies with ESOPs did get taken over. Surely, employee ownership is least effective as a defense when companies stupidly institute "abusive" ESOPs that are a sham for employee-shareholders and are likely to be invalidated by a court of law. But, the record before 1988 did provide evidence that companies could initiate employee ownership in a takeover environment without announcing any actions to provide further value to shareholders or confront the problem of dilution. Thus, in 1988 and after two new trends started to manifest themselves, shareholders became more concerned about the cost of employee ownership, and companies became more concerned about implementing employee ownership in the context of a restructuring that would deliver a positive message to their shareholders. These included recapitalizations, restructuring wages and benefits, repurchasing shares to reduce dilution in earnings per share when newly issued shares were sold to ESOPs, and making employee ownership part of a progressive corporate culture.

One of the most direct responses to the shareholder value issue was to continue to use employee ownership as part of a plan to give greater value to shareholders rather than simply as an approach either to stonewall shareholder dissension or to press for increased value from a takeover investor. Optical Coating Laboratories (OTC) invited its ESOP to participate in a recapitalization that returned value to shareholders, reduced public shareholders, and bought out a large holding from the Alpine Group with preferred stock. Interlake Corp. (NYSE) tried a similar approach by reducing costs, issuing a special dividend, attempting to refocus on its core businesses, and adopting a 9.9-percent ESOP in its fight with Mark IV Industries.[45]

Restructuring Wages and Benefits: Shareholder Concerns. A phenomenon, beginning in early 1988 and becoming a trend toward the end of that year, was to implement wage and benefit restructuring employee-ownership plans that would replace company matching contributions to employee 401(k) thrift plans or replace profit-sharing plans or defined-benefit plans, or postretiree health benefits. (See Figures 2.4–2.5.) From 1981 to 1987, very few companies reported restructuring wages and benefits in implementing an ESOP in a takeover environment, yet 20 companies reported doing this from 1988–1990. The concept of using such approaches to make employee ownership more shareholder neutral took off in all public companies—not just those in takeover environments. It became a way that companies concerned about takeovers could coherently defend a large ESOP to shareholders. The earliest example of this strategy can be seen when Champion Parts Rebuilders Inc. (OTC), who was in a takeover environment, decided to fund its ESOP in February 1988 with tax deductible funds formerly directed to its profit-sharing plan and become almost 15 percent employee held. General Refractories, in its bid to buy the company on April 14, said that the ESOP diluted all shareholders, but management was able to counter in its President's Letter by saying that "the company will annually save a significant amount of cash because the contributions to the Leveraged Employee Stock Ownership Plan will be less than the sum the company had projected to contribute to the profit-sharing plan and pay interest on the bonds that were retired." In 1988 to 1990, companies restructuring their profit-sharing plans to establish employee ownership included Advest Group Inc. (NYSE) and Chevron Corp. (NYSE). A company terminating its defined-benefit plans to establish employee ownership was Applied Power Inc. (OTC). Texaco Inc. (NYSE) entered these waters in December 1988 with a $500 million ESOP tied to its savings plan. Its denials said a lot: " 'Texaco didn't divulge many details about the ESOP.' A spokesman asserted, however, that while the preferred issue contains a change-in-control provision, the move was intended solely as an employee benefit." This approach became extremely popular and was used by Citizens and Southern Corp. (NYSE) confronting NCNB Corp., Colgate Palmolive Inc. (NYSE), Delta Air Lines Inc. (NYSE), Greyhound Corp. (NYSE), and ITT Corp. (NYSE).

Finally, many companies, threatened with specific takeover investors, restructured several kinds of benefits. Armstrong World Industries (NYSE) confronting the Belzbergs, Lockheed Corp. (NYSE) confronting Harold Simmons, and Whitman Corp. confronting a related group called Zeus Partners replaced postretirement health benefits and 401(k) matching contributions with employee-held stock. A similar program with an associated share repurchase led to a class-action suit against SPX Corp. (NYSE), which has not been successful. The sensitivity to shareholder relations led one firm, Bel Fuse Inc. (OTC), to cancel its ESOP after a takeover investor objected, even though it would have been funded with reductions in employee compensation. (For a complete list, see Appendix G.1).[46]

There is even more evidence that shareholder concerns about employee ownership continued to grow in the judgments of boards and senior managers, as companies began to exhibit concern for possible dilution caused to shareholders by selling newly issued shares to ESOPs as shown in Table 3.2. To offset this problem, a significant minority of companies started in 1988 to buy back stock on the open market. Remember, these share repurchases do not really address potentially more serious dilution in market value per share and the book value per share, nor do they address the question, who pays for the employee own-

TABLE 3.2 *Attempts to Make Employee Ownership Shareholder Neutral, Before and After 1988*

| | Announced | | | |
| | Restructured Wages/Benefits | | Associated Share Repurchase | |
	Before 1988 (%)	After 1988 (%)	Before 1988 (%)	After 1988 (%)
Takeover Environment				
Using Newly Issued Shares	0	55	0	48
Specific Takeover Investor		34		31
General Takeover Environment		25		20
Companies Using Newly Issued Shares with a Specific Takeover Investor		61		55
Companies both Restructuring Wages/Benefits and Announcing an Associated Share Repurchase		44		
Companies Using Newly Issued Shares in a General Takeover Environment		57		42
Companies both Restructuring Wages/Benefits and Announcing an Associated Share Repurchase		22		

Source: Public Company Employee Ownership Database, 1990[47]

ership. The high points of this evidence on wage and benefit restructuring and share repurchases are as follows:

- Before 1988, *none* of the corporations in takeover environments using newly issued shares in ESOPs reported implementing wage and benefit restructuring or associated share repurchases, whereas a large proportion of the companies using newly issued shares in takeover environments after 1988 did. *In fact, 34 percent of all companies in takeover environments in this period issuing new shares to their ESOP did both.*

- Of all companies using newly issued shares in takeover environments after 1988, 34 percent had a specific takeover investor and restructured wages and benefits; 25 percent were in a general takeover environment and restructured wages and benefits; 31 percent had a specific takeover investor and established an associated share repurchase; and 20 percent were in a general takeover environment and set up an associated share repurchase.

- In companies with specific takeover investors as a group, 61 percent of those restructured wages and benefits, 55 percent initiated an associated stock repurchase, and 44 percent did both.

- Of the companies in a general takeover environment as a group, 57 percent of those restructured wages and benefits, 42 percent initiated an associated share repurchase, and 22 percent did both.

- Twice as many companies with a specific raider turned to both methods, presumably to address issues of shareholder neutrality, than did companies in a general takeover environment.

- There were very few instances of using corporate culture arguments to claim that actual changes in motivation, work organization, or staffing would likely increase productivity.

Associated share repurchases of common stock may help reduce dilution in earnings per share, but they can contribute to other forms of dilution, which must be addressed by wage and benefit restructuring and/or reorganization and employee involvement to improve economic performance. Companies not under threat of a takeover began associated share repurchases in 1988, with J.C. Penney being the most prominent. Polaroid Inc. (NYSE) was the first corporation faced with a specific raider to announce a share-repurchase program in 1988. Shortly thereafter, Cabot Corporation (NYSE) and Texaco Inc. (NYSE) followed. A small OTC company, A.P. Green Industries, announced that it would sell newly issued shares amounting to 9.2 percent of the company to its ESOP while buying back slightly more in common stock "in an anti-dilutive move." The U.S. District Court denied East Rock Partners' request for a temporary injunction against the ESOP, and a takeover never took place. But note that no evidence exists on how many companies that announce share repurchases actually implement them. The announcements may be a way to ignore the problem. In fact, it is entirely possible that *announcing* a share repurchase might affect the company's stock price positively, because investors *think* dilution is being addressed, even if the repurchase never materializes.

Just as Macmillan Inc. evidently chose to ignore some developing standards for fair play in structuring ESOPs, many companies chose not to emphasize the issue of shareholder neutrality. Clearly, the textbook case of management shooting from the hip was Emery Air Freight (formerly NYSE). Emery threw employee ownership around like a multipurpose piece of garden equipment: In 1987, it overextended itself with debt in its purchase of Purolator Corp.; terminated pension plans for excess assets in an ESOP to finance the sale; restructured itself in a raft of lease-back transactions to get more cash; doubled its ESOP's voting stake to 26 percent as it ran into more trouble and Towers Financial Corp. began circling; continued to sell newly issued shares to its ESOP; frantically tried to amend its credit accords; and was rumored to have bought another large block of stock on the open market for its ESOP. Finally Emery gave up and sold out to Consolidated Freightways, one of its large competitors. Consolidated purchased all of Emery's ESOP shares. While it is unclear how shareholders and employees fared among these ins and outs, there is little evidence that employee ownership was viewed as an important organizational concern of the company. Shareholders became restless in other companies. At Anchor Class Container Corp. (NYSE) after the company rejected a $20-per share offer from Vitro Sociedad Anoima, shareholders filed a class-action suit to "block a poison pill or any other plan including an ESOP."[48]

Make Corporate Culture Your Defense. In their report, "ESOPs and Corporate Control," Lilli Gordon and John Pound of The Analysis Group observed that

> the effect of an ESOP-caused ownership structure shift will be positive if the ESOP leads to increased monitoring of management behavior by motivated employee-owners or their designated fiduciary representative.[49]

Some companies with employee ownership already in place fought hard and gave their employees the choice, such as Delchamps mentioned at the beginning of this chapter. Heavily employee-held Lowe's, Cos. rumored as a target in 1988, repurchased shares for its ESOP and adopted a shareholders' rights plan. The firm touts employee ownership as central to its culture.

The huge Long Island defense contractor Grumman Corp. (NYSE) was the subject of speculation as its stock shot up in March 1988, but Wertheim Schroder analyst Jerry Cantwell said that the ESOP, pension fund, and retired employees owned more than 50 percent of the company and "would probably insist on several conditions including the retention of current employees and maintenance of employment levels at Long Island facilities."

The Delchamps and Grumman examples were not, however, isolated occurrences. They portended a trend exhibiting a commitment toward employee

ownership that differs considerably from the systematic attempts by management
and board to jerry-rig employee ownership à la Podesta-HiShear-Frantz-Norlin-
Macmillan. In these cases, the overnight timing, manipulative voting structure,
total lack of communication with employees, and inattention to integrating employee ownership into the company's larger compensation system and culture—
all pointed less toward "employee ownership" than to the ownership of employees and their shareholder interest, which could be held on a tight leash and
completely dominated.

In 1988, the Kroger Company (NYSE) probably moved more energetically
than others in this direction. It combined a corporate culture based on employee
ownership and gain sharing with a plan to provide value to shareholders. On
September 26, the company rejected a $55 hostile bid from the Haft family,
and Kohlberg Kravis and Roberts said they would proceed with an offer of
$58.50, nearly $4 billion in cash and securities, including a special dividend
of $40. But the company decided to remain public and totally restructure itself
regarding *both* returning value to shareholders and improving the commitment
of all its employees. The company organized special dividends to shareholders
plus stock in the residual company. Through employee-share purchase plans and
open market trades, employee ownership was increased to about 35 percent, and
a company-wide profit-sharing plan for employees was developed.

In effect, the Kroger approach involves keeping a company public, paying
value to shareholders, but executing a partial leveraged buyout by the employees.
Kraft Inc. (formerly NYSE) considered this approach but was taken over. The
company was advised on its takeover defense by Goldman Sachs and Kraft's
press release on October 24, 1988, explains their thinking on this option:

> Because the restructured Kraft will have more than $12.4 billion in debt and
> require herculean efforts by our employees, the plan will replicate the structures
> currently in use in sponsored leveraged buyouts by providing significant equity
> incentives for employees in the form of stock options and an ESOP. This very
> important link between employee compensation and company performance will,
> we believe, endure the enormous efforts required to make the recapitalization a
> complete success.[50]

Polaroid: A Comprehensive Approach.   It was left to Polaroid Inc. (NYSE) to
combine these three strands: wage and benefit restructuring, a proposed associated share repurchase, and a corporate culture likely to enhance the productivity
effects of employee ownership. Polaroid claimed that its employee-ownership
plan was a coherent human resources approach designed to make employee
ownership shareholder neutral and to work synergistically with a company-wide
restructuring plan to provide more value to shareholders. As the Polaroid story
at the beginning of this chapter indicates, the Delaware Chancery Court basically accepted these arguments. Shamrock tried to make the coincidence of the
Polaroid board's meeting to adopt the larger ESOP with Shamrock's expression
of interest a key part of its case. But the Court was not critically concerned about

the takeover defense potential of the employee-ownership plan; rather, the court considered especially the structure and confidentiality of voting rights and the role of the trustee, the wage and benefit restructuring, the corporate cultural implications of the ESOP, the company's restructuring, and the company's longer-term interest in employee ownership and its fit with the company's corporate culture. The court did not deny that the employee ownership was emphasized as the takeover environment became evident.

The judicial outcome in Polaroid, like any case, needs to be viewed in light of the specific facts and circumstances of that situation. The reasoning of the court—consciously or unconsciously—pulled together several clear legal and social currents documented here.[51] But the Polaroid case has tremendous significance for the issues it raises and the social trends it captures.

A Scorecard for 1988–1990

In the two years after Polaroid more than 200 significant employee-ownership plans in public companies were established. What is the scorecard for 63 employee-ownership plans set up in takeover environments from 1988–1990 on which we were able to collect some information? Some startling findings emerge. First, not one corporation using significant employee ownership in either a specific or a general takeover environment was actually taken over in this period as a result of a tender offer or a proxy battle. Second, corporations implementing significant employee ownership used a variety of methods to reduce dilution to shareholders far more extensively than in the pre-1988 period, although, clearly, some corporations continued to ignore the dilution question completely. Third, lawsuits were filed against corporations using employee ownership in takeover environments; and although some of those suits are still pending, to date we have discovered not one lawsuit where the takeover investor or shareholders have prevailed and invalidated an employee-ownership plan.

In reviewing this period, we must caution the reader that the United States is not just one big court district, so that the latest court judgment on a matter will not necessarily predict how a court will rule next in a related matter. Court systems, state and federal, and individual courts sometimes have divergent views. Our focus is now on national trends.[52] Appendix H.1, Takeovers and Employee Ownerships, summarizes the specifics on the individual cases, such as whether wage and benefit restructuring or a share repurchase was used to address dilution and whether a lawsuit was filed according to available public information.

Let's look at the trends in some more detail. From 1988 to 1990, not one public company with a significant employee-ownership plan exposed to a takeover environment with either a specific takeover investor or a general threat, was actually taken over. This compares with takeovers of 28 percent of companies with specific takeover investors from 1981 to 1987. *The defensive aspect of employee ownership has become far more successful*. Why? We suggest that more companies are dealing directly with the issue of dilution caused by employee ownership. In the 1988–1990 period companies reported attempts to neutralize the cost of employee ownership for shareholders in over six out of ten cases in the presence of both a specific takeover investor and a general threat. This compares with *no* reported evidence on companies either restructuring wages/benefits or carrying out an associated share repurchase from 1981 to 1987. *Clearly, public companies implementing employee-ownership plans in takeover environments have radically changed their approach and seem to be paying more attention to shareholder value issues.* A clear pattern emerges. From 1988 to 1990, almost nine out of ten companies selling newly issued shares to employees took steps to neutralize the cost of employee ownership. In contrast, corporations whose employee-ownership plans bought shares on the open market to replace the ownership of public shareholders ("ownership replacement") attempted to neutralize the cost only about three out of ten times. By comparison from 1981 to 1988, companies selling newly issued shares to employees took no such actions, the financial innovation of using convertible preferred was not widely used, and very few companies restructured wage and benefit plans. In fact, when public companies sold newly issued shares to ESOPs in 1988–1990, in over half the cases they restructured both wages and benefits *and* announced a share repurchase. Please note that the value of an associated share repurchase can be significantly overrated because it is really wage and benefit restructuring, which addresses the main cause of dilution: Who pays for the new compensation expense represented by employee ownership? We include data on the associated share repurchase, since it may play a role in some cases.[53]

There is some evidence that suggests this complete switch in direction has had an impact on conflicts between boards/senior managements and shareholders/takeover investors over employee ownership. As we noted in Table 3.1, 73 percent of the companies taken over had a lawsuit filed against senior management/board and in *every* case some abuse of power vis-à-vis employee ownership or the shareholders was found by the courts. While some cases are undecided, the difference for the 1988 to 1990 period is startlingly dissimilar. There are lawsuits, but the changing structure of employee ownership seems to be associated with fewer victories by shareholders in invalidating employee ownership.

More information on the specific situations of each company is needed, but these trends suggest that after 1988 public corporations radically changed their approach to employee ownership. They focused more on the shareholder neutrality of employee ownership, more on the "employee" in employee ownership by avoiding structuring ESOPs to insure management entrenchment and control of the plans and instead instituting mirror voting plans, which gave confidential decisions directly to employees on how to vote in a tender offer or proxy contest. They clearly attracted lawsuits, but to date, the pre-1988 trend of employee-ownership lawsuits, where courts severely criticize management for manipulation, has all but disappeared from the public record.[54] The changing structure of employee ownership has altered the nature of management-board versus shareholders in conflicts over employee ownership. Ironically, management and boards have been more successful in integrating employee ownership into a potentially defensive environment for companies, but the price of this is that they are paying closer attention to shareholders and are generating a new kind of powerful shareholder, the employee shareholder, who is often faced with real choices and can now take his or her place alongside other shareholders.

Some New Developments

The total transformation in the shape and structure of employee ownership in takeover environments will be a stable part of the future of employee ownership in the country, because it satisfies the interests of three powerful groups who have objected to management manipulations of employee ownership in the pre-1988 period: shareholders, employees, and the courts. This transformation also begins to address some of the problems underscored by the Jensen position as we have applied it to employee ownership.[55] Is there room for more shareholder lawsuits and social criticism? Definitely. Look at the numbers again. There is a flip side to the coin. Since 1988, almost one third of the corporations with a specific takeover investor and the corporations in a general takeover environment have evidently not reported taking any steps to neutralize the cost of employee ownership to their shareholders.

The future attitudes of corporations will also depend on the outcome of five recent developments: evidence of the impact of employee ownership on share prices, the impact of increasing proxy battles for control of corporations with employee-ownership plans, the outcome of recent key court cases, and the impact of various state and federal policies, especially the State of Delaware's Antitakeover Statute.

The Impact of Employee-Ownership Plans on the Share Price of Sponsoring Companies.   One focal point about the meaning of the 1988–1990 employee-ownership surge in public corporations is how it affects the share prices of the companies, an issue which has been addressed by statistical studies. The bottom line is that employee-ownership plans in general do not have a negative impact on share prices in public corporations. Some of the evidence suggests that the impact is positive. There is thus little evidence that employee-ownership plans as a whole have diluted the market value of the shares of public shareholders. Let's look more closely at the evidence and examine some of the key questions and exceptions.

The first study was done by the Analysis Group, which looked at 94 ESOP establishments and expansions between January 1987 and July 1989. They looked at the movement of the company's share price within two days of the ESOP announcement net of the movement of the Standard & Poor's 500. There was no significant effect on shareholder wealth, although many of the companies showed a net-of-market increase in share price. Companies that adopted ESOPs under takeover pressure lost 3 to 5 percent of their market value within two days of the announcement. They then looked even more closely at the impact of ESOPs on corporate control. "Takeover ESOPs," which engendered a shift in outside control capable of giving the ESOP and inside shareholders veto power over an unwanted takeover bid, had a significant systematic negative effect on share prices, whereas ESOPs that did not have such control implications had a slight positive effect. Note, however, that only 20 percent of the 60 post-Polaroid ESOPs they tracked were able to engender a control transfer.

The Analysis Group observed that the establishment of any ESOP in a Delaware company tended to signal increased takeover activity and resulted in a significant share-price increase whereas noncontrol non-Delaware ESOPs had no impact on share prices. They concluded that "ESOPs can be used to align employee incentives and boost corporate productivity . . . [but] given the multiple purposes of ESOP plans, . . . examination of their average effects is likely to be meaningless."

A second study, which appeared in the journal *Financial Management*, examined 165 ESOP announcements and again found significant positive returns. The 32 firms using an ESOP as a takeover defense did have a dilution in share price, but it was not as large, or significant, as that discovered by the Analysis Group. But the study discovered that these firms were characterized by low profitability and low-managerial share ownership, which might be reasons for the ESOP defensive measure. In general, Chang found that when public companies use ESOPs to launch an internal LBO, to restructure wages, or to provide employee benefits, it is a wealth-increasing event. Subsequently, further analysis with two other scholars disclosed the same results.

A third study, recently completed by Michael Conte and Steven Isberg of the University of Baltimore, compared the total market returns for 23 public companies that established ESOPs between 1975 and 1987 to similar non-ESOP firms. Their total market returns were virtually the same before the adoption of the ESOP, but after, the ESOP firms returns soared to 35 percent. Thirty-one percent of this was from share-price increases and 4 percent from dividend increases. They claim that the share-price increase is directly explained by increased volume of trading by adding a major buyer to the market.

A fourth study, undertaken by Brigitte Jacob of Kent State University, also examined net-of-market share-price movements by ESOPs established in 1987–1988. Jacob's innovation was to begin measuring share-price movements 20 days before the ESOP announcement to allow for leakage of the information about the announcement and continue measuring it for 20 days after the announcement. ESOPs had no significant effect either way on share prices.

The most recent study is by the Investor Responsibility Research Center, which looked at ESOPs established in 1989. Their innovation was to compare the movement of the share price not only to the Standard & Poor's 500 but also to industry indexes. When they examined the share-price performance of public companies a day before and after an ESOP announcement, they found no significant differences from the industry index; however, several individual takeover-defense ESOPs did suffer significant share-price declines, such as Fairchild, Whitman, and the Tribune Company. They also found the small positive impacts on share-price movements for ESOPs in general when compared with the market, but, surprisingly, their sample of specific takeover ESOPs showed cumulative positive movements in share-price net of the market and insignificant negative movements one and two days after the announcement.[56]

These studies raise several crucial issues. First, shareholders simply do not think ESOPs in general are bad for public companies. That is good news for proponents of employee ownership. Second, the negative share-price impacts of ESOPs require a specific analysis of individual companies in takeover environments. But this raises a third problem. We suspect that the market may in fact be imperfect in some cases because shareholders are uninformed about what really causes dilution in a particular ESOP and how they analyze company information on the ESOP to figure out if dilution actually occurred.

Here is the fourth and knottiest issue. It is entirely possible that some dilutive ESOPs lead to share-price increases while some shareholder neutral ESOPs lead to share-price decreases net-of-market or even net-of-industry. Each individual company ESOP needs to be carefully examined to determine whether the combination of tax benefits, compensation increases to keep pace with the industry group, wage and benefit exchanges, productivity increases, and other actions by the company actually neutralize the cost of the ESOP from an accounting point of view. This determines whether an ESOP is shareholder neutral in its cost. But no research has yet told us whether a shareholder-neutral ESOP from an accounting standpoint will also be shareholder neutral from an economic perspective: that is, will its effect on share-price be predictable?

The upshot is that dilution—in the sense of who pays for employee ownership—is still a problem that public companies must confront out of fairness to shareholders no matter what happens to their share price. But the evidence of actual impacts on share prices does not indicate that an employee-ownership decision is necessarily bad for shareholders, especially if companies were to implement employee ownership when they are not in a takeover environment.

Proxy Battles.   The July/August 1990 issue of *Mergers and Acquisitions* reported the following in an article, "The Proxy Battle: Keeping Management on the Hot Seat":

> Early into 1990, it became apparent that forecasts of a demise in hostile takeover activity were grossly premature. . . . But a key question still to be answered is whether the proxy battle will be as potent as the tender—i.e., whether shareholders will be as receptive to giving their votes to an outsider as they usually are to giving their shares for cash.

Indeed, if the trend we have sketched of fewer successful takeovers of companies with employee ownership and fewer successful court challenges to companies using employee ownership in takeover environments endures, proxy battles may well become the new "courts" in which shareholders conduct public "trials" of management.[57] Proxy battles could be the new market for corporate control of management. In this new "court," shareholders become judge, jury, and lawyer all wrapped up in one. That may be a tactical advantage. But their tactical disadvantage surely is that this is not a trial by dollar bills: you can't just buy the votes of other shareholders in a proxy battle for a clear price, you have to persuade them of an idea. Another wild card in proxy battles is that, unlike most court suits the "employees"—especially in the new more democratic ESOPs of the post-1988 period—come to the table as shareholders in their own right, usually controlling the significant voting block in the company. *It's possible that in a fair context with real issues and wide divergence of opinion, employees may be persuaded to vote against the current management slate.* We may see the emergence of public shareholder–employee-shareholder coalitions. This is not a fantasy. It has already happened. The threat of a proxy fight with just such a coalition made up of Coniston Partners and United Air Lines' unions influenced the UAL board to accept the United Airlines Acquisition Corporation's (the union-salaried employee group) second bid late last spring. It is also possible that employee groups may themselves actually initiate proxy battles in some circumstances. Right now, observers can only list possibilities, as this area is in its infancy.

Three of these recent proxy battles involved employee-ownership plans: United, Armstrong, and Lockheed. The Belzbergs lost the proxy fight and their tender offer and dropped their court case against the Armstrong employee-ownership plan, but they did win one seat on the board of Armstrong. The new director: Harvard Professor Michael Jensen! Harold Simmons lost in the proxy fight with Lockheed Corp.'s management, but he has sued to nullify the election, raising many complaints about the employee-ownership plan. On May 10, 1990, Randall Smith of the *Wall Street Journal* accessed this new tool in an article, "Storming the Barricades with a Proxy: Takeover Defenses Prove to Be Flimsy."

> But as investors from Harold Simmons to Carl Icahn have learned, a proxy fight alone isn't enough to gain decisive shareholder support. Both men lost proxy challenges partly because they weren't making an offer for the target company. The battering ram that is working is the one-two combination of a takeover bid coupled with a proxy fight. . . . The reason proxy fights work against state laws and corporate defenses is that most such measures are crafted to stop hostile bids, meaning those opposed by the targets' directors. If the directors get replaced by a shareholder vote, the opposition ends. A proxy fight can even break through one anti-takeover measure specifically designed to block it, the staggered board, in which only one-third of the directors faces re-election annually. It turns out that even a 33% minority of directors, with backing from a shareholder majority, can

usually maneuver to gain control. John Wilcox, managing director of Georgeson & Co., a proxy solicitor, says that proxy fights are tapping a wellspring of support from big institutional investors that dominate the ownership of most large corporations. Those institutions have come to depend on a steady diet of takeover bids to boost stock market performance. "Institutions are going to be a major force for change down the line," says John Gavin, president of D.F. King & Co., another proxy solicitor.

This analysis suggests that employees could conceivably end up in one of four coalitions depending on their "business judgment": (1) with existing management; (2) alone opposed perhaps to existing management and/or a specific shareholder group; (3) aligned with a specific shareholder group, probably institutional investors holding employee pension funds; or (4) with a white knight, a new 5 percent or more shareholder of the company or another corporation. It is entirely possible that some employee groups will ask for independent legal and financial advisors to work with their employee-ownership plan trustee to help them evaluate how they should vote.

Indeed, advocates of shareholders' rights, especially the Washington-based United Shareholders Association founded by T. Boone Pickens and some institutional investors and takeover investors, have been fighting for proxy reform. The SEC makes rules about proxy solicitations and these groups view these rules as a deterrent to shareholder activism. Among other things, they are arguing for a "confidential proxy voting requirement, improved shareholder access to the proxy, shareholder approval of poison pills, golden parachutes, greenmail payments, and liberalization of the SECs proxy solicitation rules to facilitate communications among shareholders," according to Greg A. Jarrell, former chief economist for the SEC. The rise of institutional investor power through holdings in stock other than the employees' firm and employee ownership through holdings of stock in the employees' firm will combine with proxy activism to affect profoundly the role of shareholders in corporate decision making.[58]

Recent Conflicts. The outcome of three corporate conflicts will have an impact on how employee-ownership plans are perceived in public corporations. In December 1989, the press reported speculation concerning a possible takeover battle between Pennzoil Corporation (NYSE) and Chevron Corp. (NYSE). After Pennzoil disclosed that it had acquired an 8.8-percent stake in Chevron, the *New York Times* said that analysts expected an uneasy standoff lasting months, if not years. It paid almost $2.1 billion for about 31.5 million Chevron shares. Pennzoil indicated an interest in investing in Chevron all the $2.6 billion of proceeds it received from Texaco Inc. to settle their mammoth legal dispute. In November Chevron created a $1-billion ESOP, which would increase employee stock holdings from 11 percent to 16 percent. The company's ESOP bought newly issued shares, and the company announced plans to buy back an equal number of shares on the open market. Press reports said that the company will also offer employees an opportunity to invest 2 percent of their pay in Chevron Stock through a savings plan. Employee stock has confidential voting rights, and the new ESOP will be part of existing profit-sharing and savings plans.

Chevron was also reported to have launched a lawsuit against Pennzoil alleging violations of federal securities laws and asking the court to require Pennzoil to sell the stock Chevron alleges it acquired illegally. Chevron has also asked that various defensive measures taken by its board be approved. Although Pennzoil has raised questions about the Chevron employee-ownership plan, the plan is not a subject of the lawsuit. On July 16, 1990, Pennzoil announced that it intended to raise its stake to just under 10 percent by year end. In September, Pennzoil was granted summary judgment in the lawsuit, and it announced in early December that it would be free under federal antitrust law to purchase additional Chevron shares beginning December 14.[59]

On March 4, 1989, the *Wall Street Journal* reported that the employee-ownership plan of Lockheed Corp. (NYSE) would replace a portion of the company's 401(k) savings plan and its early retiree medical plan. The company announced a $500-million ESOP. Investor Harold Simmons was reported as owning a 5.3-percent stake. The company announced share repurchases to deal with the dilutive effect of the ESOP. By January 1990, Simmons stake had risen to 17.8 percent. By February, he was initiating a proxy fight for control of the board after management rejected his request for 6 of the 15 seats, saying he failed to outline a plan to improve the company's performance. Reports then discussed the company's difficult times. Simmons was rebuffed in his proxy fight after getting about 37 percent of the vote for his slate of directors. The *Journal* reported that he garnered only 12 percent of the votes outside his own stake and that he was experiencing a paper loss of $199 million on his original investment of $526 million, which had a current market value of $327 million in August 1990. He sued the company and its directors, challenging the fairness and legality of the election. As the *Wall Street Journal* reported, he argued that the directors had "manipulated the corporate machinery by placing millions of shares in friendly hands through an ESOP and then intimidated employees into voting in management's favor. . . . NL [Simmons's company] argues that if those votes were properly handled and the ESOP votes were thrown out, its director-nominees would have been elected. It asks the court to declare its slate the winner or to call a new election, in which the ESOP wouldn't be permitted to vote." Simmons specifically challenges the mirror-voting mechanism in the Lockheed ESOP in his suit in the United States District Court in the Central District of California. Finally, NCR Corp. set up an 8-percent ESOP in February 1991 as AT&T tried to gain control. A proxy fight and lawsuit are underway. AT&T won a suit in Federal court invalidating NCR's ESOP, which had the features that, we have noted, weaken an ESOP's case. And finally, Simmons sold most of his Lockheed stock.[60]

Impact of State and Federal Actions and Other Policies.   Delaware takeover laws and the U.S. Department of Labor will play a key role in the future of employee ownership.

A corporation may not enter into a business combination with a 15% share-holder for three years after the 15% acquisition unless (a) the acquirer had board approval ... or (b) ... the shareholder owned at least 85% of the outstanding voting stock not owned by employee-directors or employee stock plans which do not allow employees to decide confidentially whether to tender their shares; or (c) at the time of or after the 15 percent acquisition, the combination is approved by the board and two-thirds of the outstanding shares not owned by the potential acquirer at a special meeting and not by written consent.

—Delaware Code, Section 203, 1988.

The U.S. Department of Labor will be "particularly watchful for attempts by corporate management to utilize the assets of their own plans either as an offensive or a defensive tool in battles for corporate control."

—Joint Statement by the Departments of Labor and Treasury, 1989.

The rules that state governments and the federal government prescribe for corporate takeovers also have an enormous impact on the role of employee ownership in the market for corporate control. The Takeover Law of the State of Delaware has one set of rules governing how a corporate takeover that is not approved by the board can take place. It has dominated much of the "takeover-environment" discussion of employee ownership. Let's be clear. Delaware does not make takeovers impossible: it makes hostile takeovers answerable to certain thresholds and standards.[61] The core point for employee holdings in Delaware is that the state law explicitly mentions them and says that they are counted as disinterested holdings if employees really control these shares. *In effect, employees are viewed as any other shareholder if they have real shareholder rights.* In Delaware that means that employees can decide by themselves how to confidentially vote the entire employee holdings. Delaware *freezes out* an acquirer from taking over another corporation without board approval unless as a 15-percent shareholder it can gain ownership (in a tender offer) of at least 85 percent of the outstanding voting stock. Thus, as we have noted, a confidentially voted employee benefit plan owning more than 15 percent of a public corporation's stock can potentially block a hostile tender offer.

Six states—Georgia, Illinois, Kansas, Massachusetts, Pennsylvania, and South Dakota—have takeover provisions that approximate those of Delaware. Each state differently structures the number of years of the freeze-out, the percent of ownership necessary to trigger the statute, and the amount of stock the takeover investor must purchase in a tender offer to avoid the freeze-out. Table 3.3 indicates how closely these states follow Delaware.

But virtually every state with a takeover provision gives some power to employee-held shares by benefit plans, because a certain number of *all* share-holders need to approve specific procedures to allow a takeover. Since many of these states require a majority approval, more substantial employee holdings might be needed of these states if employees wish to block a takeover. On the other hand, where a takeover investor perceives a tender offer as impractical, he

TABLE 3.3 Comparisons of States with Takeover Statutes Similar to Those of Delaware

State	Waiting Period (years)	Trigger (%)	Amount to Avoid Freeze-out (%)	Employee-held Shares
Georgia	5	10	90	Same as Delaware
Illinois	3	15	85	Same as Delaware
Kansas	3	15	85	Same as Delaware
Massachusetts	3	5	90	Same as Delaware
Pennsylvania	5	20	80	Takeover must be approved by majority of outstanding shares not owned by acquirer. No mention of employee holdings.
South Dakota	4	10	80	Takeover must be approved by majority of outstanding shares not owned by acquirer. No mention of employee holdings.

Source: State Takeover Laws, compiled by Investor Responsibility Research Center. Analysis by Elana Hyman, 1990. [62]

or she may try a proxy contest and may find that a sizable employee-ownership stake with a sympathetic or unsympathetic employee group could turn the tide either way! Twenty-three states have fair price laws that regulate tender offers by "preventing a bidder from paying a high price for control and then buying the remaining shares for a lower price" without shareholder approval. Any employee-held shares would vote on this question. Twenty-six states have control-share acquisition laws, which compel an acquirer to have 10 percent, 33 percent, or 50 percent of a company's shares to win approval of a majority of outstanding shares and a majority of disinterested outstanding shares before it can exercise voting rights of the control stake. Twenty-five states have freeze-out laws, which "makes a control-share acquisition impossible for a bidder who needs the target's assets to service the debt incurred in the acquisition. Potential acquirers could circumvent the law's stringent requirements by launching a proxy contest." Eleven states plus the District of Columbia have no takeover laws.[63]

We expect the role of employee benefit plans to be a growing point of contention in takeover battles and in the drafting and changes of takeover laws once the full picture of employee holdings around the country becomes evident to companies, states, employees, and other shareholders. One central issue in these debates will be the structure of employee voting, an issue that has cropped up repeatedly in this chapter. Except for Delaware, Georgia, Illinois, Kansas, and Massachusetts, where employee stock plans clearly have the largest potential impact, no other states explicitly mention employee stock plans. In these five states, with one exception, the power of employee stock plans is clear: it derives from the voting being passed through from the plan trustee to individual employees on a confidential basis. But if proxy contests grow as a strategy of takeover investors, one can expect substantial debate and legal conflict over who votes the shares in employee stock plans in the other states, many of which have not defined the following considerations: Under what circumstances are the shares owned by employee stock plans treated as disinterested shares? Are management-dominated employee stock plans permitted to vote the shares? Should employees vote the shares individually? Are employees protected by confidentiality in their vote? Are unallocated shares in leveraged plans voted in proportion to allocated shares?

This final point—mirror voting—will probably be the main way the federal government influences the role of employee holdings in takeover environments. One can note that Delaware Section 203 and the state statutes following it closely only talk about *confidential voting* by individual employees, but there seems to be a reasonable modus operandi that insists upon mirror voting. The judge in the Polaroid case, Chancellor Carolyn Berger, said that "the ESOP provides for confidential and "mirrored" voting and tendering. . . . I find that the antitakeover aspect of the ESOP does not make it less than fair. Given its confidentiality provisions, it cannot be said that management controls employees tendering decisions."

The U.S. Department of Labor has recognized that mirror voting provisions can be valid, but they have also stressed that under certain circumstances a trustee may be able to override an employee vote if the trustee is aware it would violate its fiduciary responsibilities. Some legal authorities believe that mirror voting is valid. Washington attorney Steven Hester has some plain-spoken views on the subject: "The Department of Labor has said, in effect, that if your mirror voting comes up with the same decision a trustee would have come up with, it is legal, but in any case where it counts, it is illegal, so it is ok as long as it is irrelevant. They are saying that employees are too dumb, and the government must appoint a wise man to decide for them. This is really a shocking position and the DOL will lose if this view is tested. And if they win Congress may not stand for it. Their point of view is a victory of form over substance. It is right to let people decide about stock that they own."[64] Thus, there is conflict between the state and federal level here. Somehow, more clarity is needed on this point.

Another source of controversy, however, will be the impact of federal action on proxy voting on Employee Ownership, if indeed the Securities and Exchange Commission does reform proxy voting. Shareholders rights' groups may find themselves in the ironic—and some would say hypocritical—position of pressing the government to prevent mirror voting for employee stock plans with significant employee ownership to prevent employees from controlling the shares and having shareholder rights! The emerging state standards of fairness seem to be that an employee stock plan not controlled and manipulated by management deserves real shareholder rights. A federal standard based on principles of fairness and proper recognition of the shareholder rights of employees also needs to emerge. One possibility is that mirror voting would be declared legal if the employee-participants had independent legal and financial advisors who would use objective methods of analysis to support their position.[65] All these issues will have a powerful impact on what we call the takeover-defense silent majority.[66]

The Takeover-Defense Silent Majority.   There are many hundreds of publicly traded corporations in the Employee Ownership 1000 with a potential employee-ownership takeover defense that has never been discussed in the press or been the subject of a lawsuit. Takeover defense may not have been their motive for establishing employee ownership, and we expect that in many cases senior management, the employees, the shareholders, and the public are not even aware of the extent that their company is employee held. These companies dwarf those firms, which for one reason or another, have been publicly identified with employee ownership. Depending on the "rules of the takeover game" prescribed in the state where the company is incorporated *and* the percentage of shares held by nonofficer groups who might be expected to lean in this or another direction on a particular tender offer or proxy battle, each company has a unique situation into which its employee holdings fit. Specific companies with best estimates are contained in Appendix A.1. We do not know exactly how these companies structure the voting of employee holdings in company-sponsored benefit plans. This is a wild card because voting structure will likely be one crucial factor determining a potential role for employees in any contest. But there is more than a silent majority, there is an unknown minority.

The Unknown Minority and the Disclosure Crisis. In our opinion a startling discovery is that the actual percentage of employee ownership in many publicly held corporations cannot be easily discovered by a common investor using easily accessible means of research and information. We examined about 20 databases and found that each database simply had no information on many firms with substantial employee ownership. What started out as a technical challenge—how to get our hands on the highest quality public information on this issue—has become for us an indictment of the myth that an efficient public market for information on these companies exists. We believe that the expectations of public reporting and the advice lawyers and governmental bodies give companies on these issues has been oriented towards "insider-officer owners" or "outsider" five- or ten-percent owners, and that this issue has somehow fallen through the cracks. But the cracks seem to be huge. Remember, the employee-ownership phenomenon did not exist when the disclosure laws were written, so it is natural that the law may not effectively reflect new circumstances.

We suspected a problem when one of the coauthors was a consultant to a multibillion dollar company and had the opportunity to have dinner with the top financial brass. The company is generally sympathetic to employee holdings and has carried out several transactions over the years. He asked what percent of the company was employee held by benefit plans. The officers looked at each other in dismay. No one knew. One officer guessed it was 18 percent. The top man asked, "Didn't we usually have our defined-benefit plan hold a few percent?" Another officer said, "I'm not sure; I think Joe sold those shares." Even the people who prepared the Form 5500s (discussed below) for the company did not know. They provided the forms but could not reconstruct the figures. Shortly before this book came out, we requested a final number and was told the exact number, which was several percentage points less, but still over 10 percent! We later found it was not possible to reconstruct this information from any combination of all our databases. This example illustrates that the problem is not necessarily questionable behavior.

Every public company is supposed to file a Form 5500 with the Internal Revenue Service and the Department of Labor reporting annually on the holdings of each employee benefit plan. Yet, a modest percentage of the companies, which other sources reported had significant employee ownership before 1988, had no filing with the IRS and Labor Department. Every holder is required to file a Form 13D or 13G with the Securities and Exchange Commission, reporting all individuals, corporations or entities who are beneficial owners of more than 5 percent of the company's outstanding stock; yet many of the public corporations with individual plans holding more than 5 percent of their own stock had no record of such filings. If a person named Susan Smith owned 3 percent of a company in her Charles Schwab account and 3 percent in her Merrill Lynch account and 3 percent in her Chemical Bank IRA account and 3 percent in her Dean Witter account, she would own 12 percent of a company and would be considered *one holder* legally and would be breaking the law if she did not file as a 12-percent holder. Yet, if a company has four employee benefit plans, each owning 3 percent, clearly it is not required to file. There is ambiguity in the law or in interpretation of the law.[67]

Officers, directors and 10-percent principal stockholders of all public companies are required to file Form 3 or 4 with the SEC, yet most of individual employee benefit plans holding more than 10 percent have no records of filings. Institutional investment managers, such as those managing internal company-sponsored employee benefit plans who have combined equity assets of more than $100 million in securities are supposed to file Form 13F with the SEC. Specific equity holdings in individual companies below 10,000 shares and less than $200,000 are exempted. There is no record whatsoever of any filings by plans with significant employee holdings in this area.[68]

Other indications of the magnitude of this public-misinformation issue comes from examining the press. Remember there is no law saying media disclosure is required, but in light of the above discussion an argument can be made that it is material information. We estimate that most public companies whose employee benefit plans own more than 10 percent of the corporations have never disclosed this in a company press release, and it has never been mentioned in the *Wall Street Journal*.

What is more difficult to understand, however, is that formal company SEC filings are neglecting to make this information available. The Securities Exchange Act of 1934's principal trust was to insure public availability of adequate information about companies with publicly traded stocks. The government was so intent on this that it amended the act to include not only companies with securities listed on national securities exchanges but all companies with more than 500 shareholders and more than $1 million in assets. Companies must file an annual report on Form 10-K, a quarterly report on Form 10-Q and a current report for specified events on form 8-K. Companies must also file annual reports with shareholders and proxy solicitations before their annual meetings of shareholders.[69]

We have done a full text search of all SEC filings mentioned above of all public companies in the United States since 1986 and read each entry. A large percentage of the corporations with more than 4 percent employee ownership have evidently not mentioned this in their filings or in the President's Letter of their annual report. Also, the Investor Responsibility Research Center (IRRC) reviews annually all the proxy solicitation documents of the 1500 major public companies. A hefty percentage of these companies that seemingly have significant employee holdings in 1989 and in 1990 never revealed those holdings in their proxy solicitations. Finally, the auditing and accounting records of the top public companies are generally prepared by highly reputable accounting firms to insure accuracy. We printed out every reference to employee ownership from the National Automated Accounting Research System (NAARS) and discovered that it is impossible to reconstruct the actual percentage of employee holdings for most companies in the Employee Ownership 1000 from these accounting records. Clearly, there is some problem here.

Our final attempt was truly disturbing. We telephoned the top 300 companies of the Fortune 500 firms and explained that we were studying company stock owned by company-sponsored benefit plans and that this information was publicly available from the Department of Labor. Very few of the companies were cooperative. Most of the companies refused to disclose the figures, even when we requested IRS Form 5500 information that the public can order from the IRS. We then followed up these calls with letters to the CEOs of the Fortune 1000. Again, while some companies were extremely helpful, a sizable percentage did not respond or refused to cooperate.

These estimates, which, we are now confident, reflect actual circumstances, will be of enormous interest to many different groups. Governmental agencies may want to issue advisories to make disclosure requirements for employee benefit plans clear and specific and decide that companies are required to make public all sum-total employee benefit plan holdings in excess of 5 percent. Senior managers and boards may want to broadcast the news of their employee holdings as part of the company's culture, takeover-defense potential, or for other reasons. They may want to suppress the information or sell off all the holdings. Employees and unions will quickly perceive that they are the core shareholders in many of the companies in the Employee Ownership 1000 and may be interested in how voting and confidentiality is structured in these companies and whether management is going to take quick action to eliminate the stake because they are threatened. Employees in weak or risky companies will want to know how much of their pension plans are tied up in company stock. On this score in January 1991, it was rumored in the press that such was the case for the bankrupt Bank of New England. The record of employee ownership damage to employees in S&Ls makes adequate disclosure a priority in banking. Takeover investors and institutional investors will soon realize that they have no adequate up-to-date source of information on the takeover-defense potential of many companies. And states that protect corporations within their jurisdictions may rush to define the role of employee stock plans and confidential and mirrored voting in takeovers. We would like to stress that these numbers and estimates change monthly. It is the trends we have discovered in which we have confidence, given that information on specific companies may have already changed.[70]

Conclusion

The fact that a big block of stock in large public firms is locked up is a disadvantage to outside shareholders.

—Gregg Jarrell, University of Rochester economist

Here's my bottom line, simply stated: just as Quality was the watchword of the 80s in American business, so Ownership, I predict, will be the most significant issue of the 90s. As pressure for improved performance and increased shareholder value mounts, the question of who is going to participate in making the really important decisions in corporate America will move to the front burner. In a climate of perceived corporate inefficiency and wastefulness, of increased pressure on institutional investors for quick growth, and of increased demand from employees wanting a stronger voice in determining how their present and future security is going to be handled, the answer to the question of who is going to participate has the potential for dramatically reshaping the landscape of the American corporate enterprise in the closing decade of the 20th century.

—I.M. Booth, president and CEO, Polaroid Corp.

Employee ownership is not just about takeover defenses. Specific takeover environments explain only a fraction of the public company sponsorship of such plans. Where the plans have been used for takeover defenses, there is *life after the defense:* a changed company in which employees usually are the core shareholder whose confidential votes will play an important role in any future tender offer, proxy battle, consent solicitation, and perhaps, board election. The upshot of this is uncertain, because most of these public corporations have undergone this transformation in just the last five years.

Senior management and boards of directors initially tried terribly hard to emasculate employee ownership and use it like a stock trust of a senile old uncle whose votes and intentions they could control. Courts have continued the venerable Judge Beekman's tradition in *Steinway* v. *Steinway* by underlining that changing the relationship between employees and the company—in this case, the structure of ownership and involvement in corporations—does not *necessarily* disadvantage shareholders. But courts have drawn clear lines for "management entrenchment" employee-ownership plans, yet, as we have observed, there are still examples of seemingly outrageous attempts, that evidently never were challenged, at smothering employee shareholding and ignoring shareholders' interests.

Let's return to the questions raised by the Steinway case. Is employee ownership good for shareholders? That depends on how the plan was adopted, how it is structured, and the extent to which it is shareholder neutral and enhances the value of the corporation. It also depends on how much dilution there is. Nevertheless, we expect management entrenchment and shareholder disrespect to continue as a feature of a segment of employee-ownership plans. Let's not forget, however, that stock options for upper managers are also a significant source of dilution.

Actual takeover attempts and potential takeover environments have transformed the public corporation in a very short time. Whether takeover investors perceive this as a win or a loss for them, *de facto,* a group of employees, who now have inside knowledge of companies, and their management teams have now received a distribution of corporate power. We predict that institutional investors and takeover investors, whose initial knee-jerk reaction to employee ownership was to cry "entrenchment" in the eighties, may in some circumstances side with employees against managers in the nineties, as some nervous corporate boards refuse to make a long-term commitment to employee shareholding and move to buy out and terminate ESOPs in a future market when they are flush with cash.

Perhaps, employee ownership will be a part of a new structure of ownership for the next century, which returns patient yet knowledgeable investors to the corporation. Ironically, the soft underbelly of this "new vision" of the corporation is that there still is not enough managerial ownership in American companies to truly recreate the owner-manager incentive, which existed before the current period of entrenched professional managers. ESOPs and employee benefit plan purchases of stock alone cannot address this problem. We believe that the leveraged-equity purchase plan, popularized by corporate financial adviser G. Bennett Stewart, can be combined with these plans to build a seamless ownership imperative in public companies.

Writing in *The Quest For Value* (1990), Stewart has recommended that senior managers acquire a substantial amount of equity through stock purchases.[71] Most of the purchase price for the shares (say 90 percent) is financed through a loan from the company, secured by a pledge of the stock. The rest of the purchase price (say 10 percent) comes out of the managers' personal net worth and is put "at risk." As Stewart recognizes, "The managers' investments would be sizable enough to matter but not so large that they cannot afford to lose it—because they might. The loan from the company would accrue interest at a rate equal to the company's cost of capital less a discount to compensate managers for bearing market risk." Stewart says that this approach gets significant equity into the managers' hands without diluting shareholders, as occurs with the aggressive use of traditional stock options. He recommends structuring these ownership incentives in the individual business units of large corporations, creating a kind of internal LBO.

Stewart has supplied the missing link in the employee ownership and corporate control discussion. While public companies have been restructuring the wages and benefits of rank-and-file and salaried workforces to fund employee-ownership plans, how many have restructured stock options, which Stewart considers "just extra compensation, not effective incentives"? While nonentrenchment employee ownership has the potential of bringing the immediacy of "shareholder presence" back into the public corporation, the small amount of stock available in most ESOPs for senior managers and managers may not change what managers have at risk, also a critical part of the corporation. We believe that employees expect value-adding managers to be paid more than them and would welcome replacing the feudalism of perks and stock options with a more demanding "ownership culture."

What lessons might senior managers and boards take from this chapter? Employee ownership has a takeover-defense potential, but unlike takeover defenses it requires an approach and a price and a challenge for management. Above all, management and boards need to study the concept of dilution and understand fully its impact on their firms. They should make sure that employee ownership is paid for by a combination of tax savings, wage and benefit restructuring or planning, and reorganization of human resources or employee involvement programs to increase productivity. They should also be wary of the impact of associated share repurchases, because their effect on the core causes of dilution is not really evident, although they have attained an aura of grappling with the shareholder neutrality problem. We asked our legal research consultant, Elana Hyman, to crystallize the issues for management. She notes that a corporation should develop an interest in the concept as early as possible if there's any chance it will be adopted or fit corporate strategy. She adds that the more an employee-ownership plan is last-minute, fly-by-night, paternalistic, or manipulative, the greater the chances it will not be well received. It's best to create an ESOP when there is no struggle for ownership pending and to conduct serious, well documented discussions about the ESOP. In addition to clarifying these issues, she recommends the following:

> A client should be advised that the board of directors voting for the ESOP should consist of a majority of outside independent members. This eliminates claims about management entrenchment and conflict of interest. The client should insure that the stockholders are in no way harmed by the ESOP and are in some way benefitted by it. The client should make sure that the corporation itself benefits in some way from the creation of the ESOP. Treat the ESOP shareholders as you would any other shareholders. In future voting, do not think that it is safe to assume that workers will always vote with management.[72]

The evidence of this chapter indicates that the price of a potential employee-ownership takeover defense is, in fact, its unpredictability because courts have been deeply opposed to management-dominated voting of employees' shares. Employees must have a real choice. If management is running the corporation responsibly, employees and other patient investors may be satisfied with their performance. This returns again to the ideas of G. Bennett Stewart's *Remaking the Public Corporation from Within*. A democratically structured employee-ownership plan can serve either as an incentive or a penalty for management whereas a leveraged-equity purchase plan for management will add a compelling incentive. His message is that incentives should offer unlimited rewards for success and genuine penalties for poor performance. The challenge is to use employee ownership to expand the corporation through strategic acquisitions that maximize the benefits of decentralizing ownership and to change corporate governance and corporate culture, so that management becomes truly accountable and manages as Stewart says, "by motivation rather than mandate, by empowerment rather than punishment." These are the questions of the next chapter.[73]

The implications for employee groups are also wide-ranging. What can employees—union and nonunion—do in a takeover environment or a proxy battle? Again, there are different choices that will make sense in different situations. In almost any situation, it makes sense for the employee groups to form some kind of association, or coalition, so they can exchange views, analyze relevant information, and, if necessary, seek independent legal and investment banking advice. They should immediately realize that if wage and benefit planning and/or restructuring is taking place, they are really paying for the employee ownership; it is not a gift. They should adapt the attitudes of buyers and real shareholders in response to this situation. One option is prophylactic. Employees, concerned about an unfair and destructive takeover of their company, can initiate discussions about a suitable employee-ownership plan with senior management or even core shareholders and institutional investors. Another option for employee groups, who are convinced that management is the problem, is to join with a white knight or the takeover investor in conducting a joint campaign to change control of the company in return for a commitment to restructure the company using employee ownership. In some public companies, employees may desire to set up an acquisition corporation, retain lawyers and investment bankers, and make a bid of their own. They may be able to use the value of wage and benefit concessions, or excess assets in defined-benefit pension plans, or assets they control in 401(k) plans, or a partnership with an investor as a source of equity in the transaction. The employees' role in a takeover environment involving employee ownership does not necessarily have to be passive. For employees, the availability of these options may not be a pipedream. It was probably easier to work for a company in the 1950s and not worry about anything but picking up the paycheck on Friday. These are symptoms of the changing roles and functions of all the players in a corporation, which are driven by powerful market and social forces that are much bigger than employee ownership.

Notes

1. The court case is British Printing & Company v. Harcourt Brace Jovanovich 664 F. Supp 1519 (S.D.N.Y. July 24, 1987); *The Wall Street Journal,* May 27, 29, 1987, June 1, 1987, September 23, 1987, April 1, 1988; SEC filing December 1989 financial footnote.
2. *The Wall Street Journal,* September 12, 1985, October 6, 17, 1988.

3. From Shamrock Holdings v. Polaroid Corp., 559 A.2d, 257, 278 (Del. Ch., 1989); In re Polaroid Corporation Shareholders Litigation. Del. Supr., Hosey, J. (1989) (Order) [560 A.2d 491(table 1)]; "Polaroid ESOP Upheld," *Employee Ownership Report* (January-February 1989) 9(1): 1.

4. Letter sent from Frederick C. Dubinsky, J. Steve Smith, and Felix Isherwood to all United pilots on September 21, 1990.

5. Abridged from "Lockheed's Board Votes To Amend Poison Pill Plan," by Rick Wartzman with Jim Bartimo in Dallas contributing, *The Wall Street Journal,* September 25, 1990.

6. We are indebted to Steven Hester of Arnold & Porter for bringing this example to our attention and explaining its significance to us. Steinway v. Steinway & Sons et al., Supreme Court, Special Term, New York County, May 1896, 17 Misc. Rep. 43, 40 N.Y.S.: 718–725. In specific legal terminology, the stockholder claimed that the corporation's actions were *ultra vires* or beyond the scope of corporate powers. Following the book, *The Law of Corporations,* by Robert W. Hamilton (St. Paul, Minn.: West Publishing, 1987): 51–59, we note that the doctrine of *ultra vires* is now largely obsolete in modern corporation law. For the novice, we highly recommend this book as a roadmap to corporate law.

7. The law is referred to as Delaware Statute, Section 203, or "Delaware 203." The specific quote is "A corporation may not enter into a business combination with a 15% shareholder for three years after the 15% acquisition unless: (a) the acquiror had board approval for either the 15% acquisition or the proposed business combination before the acquiror gained a 15% interest; or (b) upon consummation of the 15% acquisition, the shareholder owned at least 85% of the outstanding voting stock not owned by employee-directors or employee stock plans which do not allow individual employees to decide confidentially whether to tender their shares; or (c) at the time of, or after the 15% acquisition, the combination is approved by the board and two-thirds of the outstanding shares not owned by the potential acquiror at a special meeting and not by written consent." See Del. Code Ann. tit. 8, Sec. 203 (1988). The law was adopted February 2, 1988, effective December 23, 1987. Please note that one motivation behind the three-year delay before a takeover can be consummated in this law is to prevent a takeover investor from proposing to buy part of a company's shares at a higher price in a partial tender offer and then later buy the rest of the shares at a lower price. There is some concern that all shareholders be treated equally and that such "two-tiered" offers, which are "front-loaded" in this fashion, be disallowed. One legal observer says that such transactions are "designed to panic shareholders into tendering their shares in the first step. . . . May such transactions be attacked on the ground that they lack any business purpose other than freezing or squeezing out a minority or are unfair to the minority?" Hamilton, 1988; 431. Note that these are "pure-vanilla" examples, all

things being equal. All things are always not equal and the specific facts of a case will determine how shareholders, courts, and the public views different situations.

8. This section paraphrases and summarizes Lazonick's historical introduction. *Controlling the Market for Corporate Control: The Historical Significance of Managerial Capitalism,* William Lazonick (New York: Barnard College, Department of Economics, April 1990).

9. Hamilton, 1987.

10. Hamilton, 1987: 269.

11. See Hamilton, 1987: 369–379 on the statutory rights to inspect corporate books and records of shareholders. In general this right is related to a "proper purpose," namely, a purpose that is reasonably relevant to the shareholder's interest as a shareholder. The Securities Exchange Act of 1934 requires that public and other SEC-filing companies must provide shareholders with annual reports, which contain audited financial information plus data on a quarterly basis.

12. Hamilton, 1987: 291. He notes that management's advantages in this "election" are as follows: it has the current list of shareholders while the insurgents must go to court to get it; it can generally finance its solicitation with corporate funds; and shareholders tend to have a promanagement bias because unhappy shareholders tend to disappear.

13. Michael C. Jensen, "Takeovers: Their Causes and Consequences," *Journal of Economic Perspectives* 2, no. 1 (Winter 1988): 22–23.

14. Jensen, 1988: 28–29.

15. Jensen, 1988: 28–29. Jensen footnotes Richard Roll, "Empirical Evidence on Takeover Activity and Corporate Wealth," in John Coffee and Louis Lowenstein and Susan Rose-Ackerman, eds., *Takeovers and Contests for Corporate Control* (New York: Oxford University Press, forthcoming) and Gordon Donaldson, *Managing Corporate Wealth* (New York: Praeger, 1984): 3, 22.

16. Hamilton, 1987: 380–404. A share dividend is not a true distribution of property or assets, since no property or cash leaves the corporation, the real worth of the corporation is not reduced, and the real worth of the shareholder is not increased. It simply increases the number of ownership units outstanding, but share dividends may adversely affect the rights of other classes of shareholders.

17. Hamilton, 1987: 310–323.

18. See Jensen, 1988: 42–43.

19. Lazonick, 1990: 42–79; Jensen, 1988: 29–31. Regarding critics of Jensen and some of his positions, see "Breach of Trust in Hostile Takeovers," by Andrei Shleifer and Lawrence H. Summers in Auerbach, 1988: 53. They conclude that, "transfers from stakeholders [employees and suppliers] to shareholders could make for a larger part of the takeover premium.

If takeovers are motivated by stock market undervaluations of assets, these transactions are rent distributions from the old shareholders to the buyer. Although evidence of the importance of such undervaluations is lacking, arguments that they are important is not. If, as appears to be the case, rent-transfers form a significant part of takeover gains, the combined share price change of the target and the buyer vastly overstates the efficiency gains from takeovers. . . . Previous academic work has tended to maintain that hostile takeovers are accompanied by increases in efficiency, but it has rarely been successful in isolating the sources of such gains."

20. Adapted from Jensen, 1988: 22. Jensen, as noted, believes that when a corporation has substantial free cash flow, managers may try to expand the firm in ways inefficient for returns to investors, thereby attracting challenges to their strategy from acquirers. Some observers suggest that one indicator of whether a company can be acquired would be a comparison of the company's purchase price with the replacement cost of the assets. The lower the ratio of market-value-to-replacement cost, the greater the bargain. This statistic is referred to as *Tobin's q*. The material in this note is taken from, "A Time-Series Analysis of Mergers and Acquisitions," by Devra L. Golbe and Lawrence J. White, in *Corporate Takeovers: Causes and Consequences,* ed. Alan J. Auerbach (Chicago: University of Chicago Press, 1988). We are developing only some broad themes necessary for the analysis of employee ownership. This article provides a historical analysis of the various factors behind mergers and acquisitions. For an excellent summary of recent economic research on takeovers, this volume is recommended.

21. The legitimacy of various takeover defenses changes rapidly with major new inventions of defensive tactics and court rulings on their propriety. For a current review of such defenses, see "Rule 14-a-8, Institutional Shareholder Proposals, and Shareholder Democracy," by Patrick J. Ryan, *Georgia Law Review* 23, no 1 (Fall 1988): 97–184 and "Corporate Directors and the Social Costs of Takeovers—Reflections in the Tin Parachute," by Patrick J. Ryan, *Tulane Law Review* 64 (1): 3–68.

22. Jensen, 1988: 43.

23. Buckhorn, Inc. v. Ropak Corp. 656 F. Supp. 209, 231 (S.D., Ohio) E.D., add'd February 24, 1987, in an unpublished decision, docket no. 87-3127 citing Norlin Corp. v. Rooney Pace, Inc., 744 F.2d 255, 266 (2d cir., 1984).

24. Recently, the ownership characteristics of the 1980 Fortune 500 firms that were acquired in the subsequent five years were closely examined. Compared to all Fortune 500 firms in 1980, the firms experiencing hostile takeover bids were smaller and older. They were less likely to be run by a founding family, and had lower officer-ownership than had the average firm, plus low market value, low growth, and investment, and a lower ratio of the firm's market value to the replacement cost of its tangible assets. Corporations that experienced friendly takeovers were smaller and younger

but were more likely to be run by a member of a founding family, and had high officer-ownership. This suggests that firms where managers' interests are more closely aligned with those of shareholders are less likely to be the target of hostile transactions. See Auerbach, 1988: 3, 127.

25. See American Institute of Certified Public Accountants (AICPA), Emerging Issues Task Force release 89-12.

26. Material relating to specific legal cases cited in this and following sections is based on the work of our legal research assistant, Elana Hyman, of the Rutgers University Camden Law School. Material relating to all other cases is from the Public Company Employee Ownership Database. Research materials that Ms. Hyman prepared include (1) Summaries of Major ESOP Cases (May 9, 1990a); (2) ESOPs As Corporate Takeover Defenses (May 25, 1990b; and (3) Employee Stock Ownership Plans: The Policy Issues at Stake (May 9, 1990c) and will be referred to as Hyman, 1990 a, b, or c. In this section we are not focusing on the legal implications of the cases and are merely excerpting "storyline" events from the cases. We caution readers that the use of employee benefit plans in corporate takeovers raise serious issues fiduciary questions upon which we only touch briefly. For a thorough review, see "Employee Stock Ownership Plans and Corporate Takeovers: Restraints on the Use of ESOPs by Corporate Officers and Directors to Avert Hostile Takeovers," by Margaret McLean, *Pepperdine Law Review* 10 (1983): 731–766. Our analysis combines social analysis of trends in employee-ownership transactions in takeover environments with summaries of directions in various related court cases. Our goal is two-fold: first, to suggest trends based on facts, and second, to observe possible connections between such trends and the general direction of court cases and legal opinion about this phenomenon. We understand that we cannot properly condense the facts of each court case or all cases together. When we tally up trends, we intend to show general directions and do not claim to indicate how potential judicial decisions will come out or how the many complex external situations will interact with these trends. There are other legal limitations on a narrative review of cases and news reports, which we shall comment on in greater detail in subsequent notes. See also Robert A. Profusek and Jeffrey S. Leavitt, "Dealing With Employee Benefit Plans, Part I: Roles in Hostile Takeovers and Part II. Points to Negotiate in Friendly Transaction," *Mergers & Acquisitions* (Winter 1984): 44–51.

27. The definitive review on this issue, which should be read by anyone interested in this subject is "Employee Benefit Plans in Control Contests: An Analysis of Participant "Pass Through" Arrangements," William P. Wade, *BNA Pension Reporter* 17 (1990): 1290–1306. The Department of Labor has not definitively supported "mirror voting," although it has become widespread in public corporations since 1988. It has said that mirror voting could be valid in a widely cited letter to the Polaroid Corporation, dated

February 23, 1989. The real issue is that in a tender offer in Delaware, or in a state that follows Delaware law, employees can have a say about only the shares in the employee benefit plan if those shares are voted completely by the employees, confidentially and with unallocated shares voted in proportion to allocated shares. The Department of Labor has traditionally opposed mirror voting because current employees get to vote the unallocated shares that may be allocated in the future to other employees. DOL argues why should "you" (current employees) make decisions about the value of the shares of "them" (future employees). The DOL's traditional position is now in conflict with the trend in state corporate law to give employee-shareholders fuller control over employee benefit-plan shares in their companies.

28. A relevant case dealing with an employee share-purchase plan is McPhail v. The L.S. Starrett Company, 257 F.2d 388, heard May 7, 1958, and decided July 1958, where the court ruled against a shareholder who claimed that an employee share-purchase plan disadvantaged him.

29. The Ninth Circuit Court said they would have upheld the injunction had not the shares already been transferred, but since they had, the court stated that "the egg has already been scrambled, and a delay in any possible disenfranchisement of the ESOT shares will not cause Klaus any irreparable harm." It decided to stabilize all parties' positions as far as possible, preventing each from gaining an advantage over one another until the court could resolve all the issues.

30. Podesta v. Calumet, Industries, et al., 94, 433. U.S. District Court, Northern District of Illinois, Eastern Division, No. 78. C 1005, May 9, 1978.

31. This paragraph draws directly from "Employee Stock Ownership Plans and other Defenses to Hostile Tender Offers," by Michael G. Galloway, *Washburn Law Journal* 21 (1982): 580–606. On Continental, Galloway refers to Defendant Continental Air Lines Memorandum of Law in Opposition to Motion for Preliminary Injunction, Texas International Airlines v. Continental Air Lines, Inc., Civ. No. 81–1131 LTL (Kx) (C.D. Cal. June 16, 1981) aff'd, No. 81–5514 (9th Cir. June 18, 1981) and Memorandum of Points and Authorities in Support of Plaintiff's Motion for Preliminary Injunction. As noted in another part of this book, the NYSE decided it would not list the company's stock without a shareholder vote and the Commissioner of Corporations for the State of California issued a stop order prohibiting issuance of any shares to the ESOP without shareholder approval. Continental tried to fight the Commissioner in court without success and efforts in the California legislature to overcome the stop order were unsuccessful according to Galloway, 1982: 603–604.

32. See Donovan v. Bierwirth, 680 F.2d 263 (2d Cir. 1982) aff'd. and modifying 538 F. Supp. 463 (E.D. N.Y. 1981). The court issued a preliminary injunction that prohibited the trustees of the pension plan from buying or

selling stock or exercising duties on behalf of the plan. It also appointed an investment manager to take charge of the fund while the case was undecided. The Court of Appeals reversed the appointment of this receiver and said the trustee's financial integrity was not at issue.

33. Ultimately, here is what happened to the shares in Bendix's savings plan. The battle was a four-way Bendix-Martin Marietta (MM)-Allied-United Technology corporate war. Originally, Bendix wanted to acquire 45 percent of MM's stock. Then, MM tried to acquire 50 percent of Bendix with a second step envisioned, where the balance of Bendix's shares would be exchanged for MM's stock. Then, United Technology launched a tender offer for 50.3 percent of Bendix acting as MM's ally, and the two companies agreed to divide up Bendix if either was successful. Bendix increased its offer for MM, which was rejected, and then rejected United's offer. United then tried to merge on a friendly basis, but this was declined. Bendix consummated its purchase of 70 percent of MM's stock and demanded that its board resign but MM refused. MM continued its offer for Bendix's stock and MM refused an offer of a peaceful solution. Then, Allied offered to merge with Bendix and Citibank withdrew the shares it had tendered to MM. MM bought 44 percent of Bendix's stock. Allied finally gained control of Bendix and struck an agreement with MM. This account was drawn from the article, "Employee Stock Ownership Plans and Corporate Takeovers: Restraints on the Use of ESOPs by Corporate Officers and Directors to Avert Hostile Takeovers," by Margaret McLean, *Pepperdine Law Review* 10 (1983): 731–766. See also, *The American Lawyer* (February 1983): 35–39. The court issued a temporary restraining order preventing the trustee from withdrawing the tendered shares unless ordered to do so by the employee-participants. Regarding a dismissal of Bendix's appeal, see Martin Marietta Corp. v. Bendix Corp., 697 F.2d 293 (2d Cir. 1982) and a denial of a subsequent request by Bendix for all the shares to be withdrawn, see Martin Marietta Corp. v. Bendix Corp. ['82-'83 Transfer Binder] Fed. Sec. L. Rep. (CCH) 99,058 (S.D.N.Y. 1982).

34. We have drawn this section directly from Wade, 1990: 1296. Wade's factual discussion of this unreported case is derived from the court records. See El Paso Co. v. Burlington Northern, Inc. (W.D. Tex., Dec. 30, 1982) for the order denying the temporary restraining order.

35. This term refers to the case of Unocal v. Mesa, 493 A.2d 946, 954 (Del. 1985).

36. References for companies mentioned are Cone: *The Wall Street Journal,* November 29, 1983, February 10, 1984; PR Newswire September 29, 1983, February 9, 1984; Lyon: *The Wall Street Journal,* April 18, 1984, February 27, 1985, March 21, 26, 1985; PR Newswire April 25, 30, 1985; Phillips: *The Wall Street Journal,* December 11, 24, 1984, March 5, 1985, June 28, 1985, July 1, 1985; TWA: *The Wall Street Journal,* June 19,

1985; New: *The Wall Street Journal,* September 27, 1985; Figgie: PR Newswire January 28, 1986; *The Wall Street Journal,* June 2, 1986, September 21, 1988, January 18, 1989; FMC: *The Wall Street Journal,* February 24, 1986; PR Newswire April 28, 1986; Rexnord: *The Wall Street Journal,* November 24, 1986, January 27, 1987; Holly: *The Wall Street Journal,* September 17, 1985, December 2, 1985, February 22, 1989; Greiner: *The Wall Street Journal,* June 10, 1986, December 16, 1986, September 21, 1987, October 14, 1987, SEC filing December 1989; Honeywell: *The Wall Street Journal,* February 19, 1986; Apogee: *The Wall Street Journal,* June 27, 1986; Texas: *The Wall Street Journal,* March 26, 1986, SEC filing 1986; Resorts: *The Wall Street Journal,* October 20, 1986, December 12, 15, 1986; GTE: *The Wall Street Journal,* November 7, 1986; Petro: PR Newswire January 15, 1985; *The Wall Street Journal,* January 16, 1985, July 25, 29, 1986, August 4, 1986; Bank: *The Wall Street Journal,* April 29, 1987, May 4, 1987; Crazy: *The Wall Street Journal,* October 20, 1987; Swank: *The Wall Street Journal,* September 30, 1987, JWT: *The Wall Street Journal,* June 15, 1987; Sooner: Public Company Employee Ownership Database, 1990; First Fulton: *The Wall Street Journal,* November 27, 1987; Trailways: WESJ June 22, 1987; Resdel: *The Wall Street Journal,* November 6, 1987; Frantz Manufacturing Company v. EAC Industries, 501 A.2d 401 (Del. Supr. Ct. Dec. 5, 1982); Anderson: *The Wall Street Journal,* February 10, 1986, June 6, 1986; In re: Anderson, Clayton Shareholders Litigation 519 A.2d 680 (Del. Ch. Ct. June 6, 1986); Chicago: *The Wall Street Journal,* April 15, 1985, March 20, 1986, April 10, 11, 17, 1986; PR Newswire April 1, 23, 1986, June 12, 1986; Danaher v. Chicago Pneumatic Tool, 633 F. Supp. 1066 (S.D.N.Y. April 10, 1986); Buckhorn: *The Wall Street Journal,* January 28, 1987, February 13, 21, 25, 1987; Buckhorn, Inc. v. Ropak Corp., 656 F. Supp. 209 (S.D. Ohio) Aff'd. E.D. February 24, 1987, in an unpublished decision, docket no. 87-3127.

37. See also Wade, 1990: 1297. See Danaher Corp. v. Chicago Pneumatic Tool Co., 635 F. Supp. 246 [7 EBC 1616] (S.D.N.Y. 1986) and 633 F. Supp. (S.D.N.Y. April 10, 1986). Wade reports that the company proposed that "there is no more representative group than the present employees of the interests of all employees, present and future [*sic*]" (p. 249) and suggested that employees decide on the tender offer, but the judge said that a trustee has a duty to exercise his or her own judgment and may not rely wholly on the advice of others. The court also noted that most of the ESOP shares were unallocated and that current employees had no vested right in voting for what would benefit future participants.

38. The basis of this chart is Appendix H.1 Chronology of Employee Ownership In Takeover Environments. The chart was constructed from our complete database files and is not a sample but represents the total population after an exhaustive search. We realize that somehow we may have overlooked

information in the public record; however, the results of this tally are so startling that we believe there is a very low probability that further data will materially change the results. Companies for which we have no information are Burlington Northern and Anderson Clayton. Lyons Metal Products is counted as a takeover despite the fact that the employees—not one of the takeover investors—actually took over the company from management, but a change in control did happen here. The specific raider that initiated takeover investing did not always take over a firm but, in our view, that is immaterial to the failure of an employee-ownership defense unless there was a friendly acquisition.

39. More details of the Carter Hawley Hale case are contained in Wade, 1990: 1296–1297, which discusses some facts of the unreported legal case. See also Vance v. Bank of America (Civ. no. 84-3359 (C.D. Cal., July 16, 1984).

40. To check this definitively would require a study of those companies in more detail. However, it seems fair to report that no significant transaction resulting in an immediate material premium to shareholders happened in these cases. What we cannot evaluate is whether such an occurrence would have been good for the company. This point returns us to the debate between the Jensen perspective and its critics over short-term versus long-term financial strategy, the value of debt, and the importance of patient investing, and financial commitment versus alternative investment expectations.

41. Acme: NCEO, Fall 1989, SEC filing December 1989; FirstCorp: *The Wall Street Journal*, July 15, 1988, SEC filing December 1989; Cabot: *The Wall Street Journal*, November 18, 1988; NCEO, Fall 1989; Medtronic: *The Wall Street Journal*, October 10, 1989; Horn: *The Wall Street Journal*, March 17, 1989; Fairchild: *The Wall Street Journal*, January 31, 1989, February 3, 9, 1989, April 13, 19, 1989. Carlyle charged that the transaction was arranged only to put a large block of stock in friendly hands, although it is not evident from previous cases that this alone would prejudice the ESOP.

42. Kansas: *The Wall Street Journal*, August 5, 1985, March 22, 1988; PR Newswire February 23, 1988; KMS: *The Wall Street Journal*, February 5, 1988; Farmers: *The Wall Street Journal*, March 11, 1988.

43. Charter: *The Wall Street Journal*, January 6, 1988, March 9, 1988, July 13, 1988; SEC filing December 1989; Macmillan: Mills Acquisition Co. v. Macmillan, 559 A.2d 1261 Del. Supr. Ct. oral decision, November 2, 1988, written decision, May 3, 1989. The Bass law suit is Bass v. Evans. In re: Macmillan, 552 A.2d 1227 in Delaware Chancery Court, June 29, 1988. See also, Securities and Exchange Commission v. Edward P. Evans, William F. Reilly, and Beverly C. Cheli, Civil Action no. 89-3285 (D.D.C. December 6, 1989). For the narrative, see *The Wall Street Journal*, June 25, 29, 1987, October 20, 1987, June 1, 10, 1988, July 22, 1988, November 4,

1988, December 7, 1989; PR Newswire May 31, 1988. The SEC said in its complaint that "the Commission wishes to emphasize that where disclosure is made or is required concerning the purchase of securities in an Employee Stock Ownership Plan, the person making the disclosure must carefully consider the need to disclose fully the purposes of the transaction and any plans or proposals served by the transaction, including, where applicable, any antitakeover or other defensive purposes, plans or proposals . . . under section 13(d) of the Exchange Act" (p. 2).

44. See Cottle v. Standard Brands Paint Co. (Del. Ch. Ct. November 17, 1988) (no. 9342 unpublished decision). See Polaroid addendum; *The Wall Street Journal,* January 4, 1988, January 2, 1990; Kysor: *The Wall Street Journal,* February 27, 1989, March 27, 1989, April 12, 1989, June 25, 1990; PR Newswire April 24, 1989.

45. Optical: *The Wall Street Journal,* January 6, 1988, February 1, 1988; PR Newswire, January 29, 1988; SEC filing December 1989; Interlake: PR Newswire August 11, 1989; *The Wall Street Journal,* August 14, 1989.

46. Champion: *The Wall Street Journal,* February 16, 22, 1988, April 14, 1988; SEC filing January 1987, SEC filing December 1989; Advest: *The Wall Street Journal,* December 8, 1988; Applied Power: *The Wall Street Journal,* August 30, 1988; Texaco: *The Wall Street Journal,* December 22, 1988; Citizens: *The Wall Street Journal,* July 10, 1989 with its savings and profit-sharing plan; Armstrong: *The Wall Street Journal,* June 29, 1989; Lockheed: *The Wall Street Journal,* April 5, 1989; PR Newswire April 4, 1989; Whitman: *The Wall Street Journal,* January 23, 1989; SPX: *The Wall Street Journal,* March 7, 1989; PR Newswire March 8, 1989, May 16, 1989; December 21, 1989; Bel: *The Wall Street Journal,* July 28, 1989, August 25, 31, 1989. Restructuring of benefits, which were not explained in detail, were done by Aristech Chemical Corp. (NYSE): PR Newswire January 17, 1989.

47. We are dividing takeover environments into two groups, *specific takeover investor* and *general takeover environment* because we categorized companies according to the available public information in our database. We want the reader to be able to judge whether lumping them together would have been misleading. We also wish to allow for the fact that specific takeover investors actually existed for companies we indicated were in general environments, although we had no way of knowing of the investor's identity. Our data suggests, however, that this distinction just does not make a material difference except when one examines the number of companies using both methods to address shareholder neutrality.

48. Greater: *The Wall Street Journal,* February 14, 1989; Emery: *The Wall Street Journal,* August 27, 1987, February 4, 11, 1988, June 17, 1988, February 13, 1989, SEC filing December 1989; Anchor: *The Wall Street Journal,* August 25, 1989. Although, please note, the range of material

dilution caused by a leveraged ESOP often depends on its size, a valid estimate cannot be inferred without financial analysis.

49. The Analysis Group of the Institutional Voting Research Service (Boston, 1990).

50. Grumman: *The Wall Street Journal,* March 28, 1989; Kraft: PR Newswire October 24, 1988. Goldman Sachs is mentioned in this release.

51. Robert F. Bruner and E. Richard Brownlee II study the shareholder-neutrality issue for Polaroid in detail in "Leveraged ESOPs, Wealth Transfers, and Shareholder Neutrality: The Case of Polaroid," *Financial Management* 19, no. 1 (Spring 1990): 59–64. They show that shareholders gained, although "the disparity in results between the simulated returns [(authors' note) in a model prepared by the Polaroid Corporation] and actual market-adjusted returns ($167 million) is provocative" and "some of the simulation assumptions are arguable" (p. 70). The researchers concluded that bondholders lost 11 percent during the ESOP restructuring. The U.S. Treasury lost tax revenues with an estimated net present value of $313 million. Finally, employees (the ESOP participants) "gained 28%—close enough to be called 'a wash'" (p. 71). Their wealth will depend mainly on their productivity improvements, since they paid for the ESOP with pay cuts.

52. Trends, however, do not mean you know what will happen when a specific court in a specific jurisdiction hears a case with a specific and unique set of facts. For example, in the federal system the trial courts are called district courts and the appeals courts are called circuit courts. Only within each circuit are the holdings of the circuit legally binding, while the holdings of other circuits are considered legally persuasive but do not constitute legal precedent. State and federal systems are wholly separate. Since corporate law is state law, state courts are not legally bound to follow each other's views, although certain state courts with extensive experience in this area receive special attention, for example, Delaware. I am indebted to Elana Hyman for her Memorandum on which this is based, Procedural Overview of State and Federal Courts, May 1, 1990.

53. The basis of these conclusions is Appendix H.1, Employee Ownership In Takeover Environments. The chart was constructed from our complete database files and is not a sample but represents the total population after an exhaustive search. We realize that somehow we may have overlooked information in the public record; however, the results of this tally are so startling that we believe there is a very low probability that further data will materially change the results.

54. Appendix H shows 14 lawsuits filed in the 1988–1990 period. We have no record of any court decisions against the company in any of these cases as this book goes to print. We caution the reader that the outcome for some of the companies listed as having lawsuits against their employee ownership plans and/or other takeover defenses is not yet settled.

55. It is impossible through these outside observations to see whether a protest or lawsuit has any merit whatsoever. It is possible that the companies took steps that have not been tracked by our database, and we caution any reader from jumping to legal or practical conclusions on specific companies without confirming information. It is also possible that companies discerned that such actions were unnecessary for various reasons.

56. See Analysis Group, 1990; Saeyoung Chang, "Employee Stock Ownership Plans and Shareholder Wealth: An Empirical Investigation," *Financial Management* 19, no. 1 (Spring 1990): 48–58. The follow-up study was done with Greg Niehaus of Northwestern University and Susan Chaplinsky of Michigan University and was quoted in The Employee Ownership Report, vol. 10, no. 6, pp. 3–4; Michael Conte and Steven Isberg, "Employee Stock Ownership Plans: A New View" (Baltimore, MD: University of Baltimore, 1990); Brigitte Jacob, "Abnormal Returns Associated with Employee Ownership of Public Corporations: An Empirical Investigation," Ph.D. diss., Kent State University, March 1991, Department of Finance. The Study by the Investor Responsibility Research Center will be released in spring-summer of 1991. We thank the Center for making a rough summary of their findings available to us.

57. To review issues of proxy battles, see Hamilton, 1987: 291–295.

58. An important collection on this topic is *Corporate Proxy Voting System, Hearings before the Subcommittee on Telecommunications and Finance, Committee on Energy and Commerce,* U.S. House of Representatives, August 2, 1989 (Washington, D.C.: Government Printing Office, Serial no. 101-72, 1989). This document contains many tough criticisms of the proxy voting system. Taken from "Shareholders Secret Victory," by Gregg A. Jarrell, *The Wall Street Journal,* June 22, 1990. These proposals and discussions and debates about the social trends fueling them were discussed in detail at a conference on "The Fiduciary Responsibilities of Institutional Investors" sponsored by the Salomon Brothers Center for the Study of Financial Institutions, New York University and the Center for Research in Financial Services and Regulated Industries, Rutgers–The State University of New Jersey, June 14–15, 1990. The proceedings are to be published as a book. See especially, Changes in Corporate Control and Governance Communicated through Proxy Power, by John J. Gavin, D.F. King & Co., Inc.; Proxy Contests: Strategic Tactics and Implications for Investors, by Natalie I. Koether, Keck Mahin Cate & Koether; Reforming Corporate Governance: Deregulation, Not More Regulation, by John Pound, Kennedy School of Government, Harvard University; A Proposed Substitute for Proxy Contests, by Robert A. G. Monks, Institutional Shareholder Services, Inc.; Are Institutional Investors a Likely Substitute for the Market for Corporate Control? by Leo Berzel, Mayer, Brown & Platt, Proxy Contests; and Institutional Investors, by Dennis J. Block, Weil, Gotshal, & Manges. See also, *Cor-*

porate Governance & Proxy Voting (New York: Institute for International Research, 1990).

59. Taken from "Pennzoil Mulled Acquiring Stake In BP or Mobil," *The Wall Street Journal,* December 18, 1989; "Pennzoil Feints; Chevron Weaves," *New York Times,* December 18, 1989, "Chevron Plans $1 billion Worker Stock Program," *Los Angeles Times,* 1989, "Chevron Moves Show Concern About Pennzoil," *The Wall Street Journal,* December 11, 1989, "Pennzoil To Increase Stake In Chevron to Nearly 10%," *The Wall Street Journal,* July 17, 1990. See also *The Wall Street Journal,* November 28, 1989, December 7, 1989, December 8, 1989, January 15, 1990, February 12, 1990, July 17, 1990.

60. Taken from *The Wall Street Journal,* April 4, 5, 1989, February 23, 1990, April 14, 1989, August 21, 1989, January 16, 1990, April 11, 14, 19, 1990, August 24, 1990; *Forbes,* February 5, 1990; PR Newswire July 13, 1989. See also, NL Industries, Inc. v. Lockheed Corporation, et al., no. 90 1950 RMT, (C.D. Cal.). NCR: *The Wall Street Journal* February 21, 22, 1991.

61. The research of our legal research consultant, Elana Hyman, was helpful to us in preparing this section, especially her Memorandum, Survey of State Takeover Laws, September 13, 1990. The text of the Delaware law has been challenged unsuccessfully so far by Black & Decker v. American Standard (DC Del. March 16, 1988), BNS Inc. v. Kopers, 683 F. Supp. 458 (D. Del. 1988), where Chief Judge Murray M. Schwartz found that Section 203 would probably be held constitutional under both the supremacy and commerce clauses of the U.S. Constitution, and PR Acquisition Corp. v. Staley Continental, 686 F. Supp. 476 (D. Del. 1988), and City Capital Associates Limited Partnership v. Interco, 696 F. Supp. 1551 (DC Del. 1988). See IRRC, 1990; Delaware pp. 8–9.

62. A useful source is State Takeover Laws (Washington, D.C.: Investor Responsibility Research Center, 1990). The IRRC provides regular updates and the material is easily accessible to the nonlawyer. We express our appreciation to the staff of the IRRC for providing us assistance.

63. Quotes are from IRRC, 1990: 5–13. This eight-page section is a good brief review of the types of state takeover laws. We have not dealt with some minor provisions that are not widespread.

64. Personal communication, September, 1990.

65. See Wade, 1990. See also Wiegley, "Section 13(d) and Employee Benefit Plans: A Maze of No-Action Letters," 90-53 SEC Today 1 (March 19, 1990). In Central Trust Co. v. American Avents Corp, 11EBC 1850 (S.D. Ohio, 1989) a court allowed a trustee to override the pass-through vote of employees. But as Wade says: "The critical feature of the American Avents pass-through was the requirement that American Avents as well as the affected participants had to approve any sale of the ESOP's stock. The

court concluded that implementing the pass-through would be a "vain act" because "even if all other participants voted in favor of the proposed sale, [the insiders] who are Board of Directors [of the company], and who admittedly seek to maintain control of [the company], would disapprove the sale." ... Consequently, although the case inevitably will be cited for the proposition that a trustee must override a pass-through when the economics of the situation suggest it is in the immediate financial best interests to do so, the writer believes the Central Trust Co. decision should be limited to its facts and should not be considered controlling precedent for a properly drawn pass-through, according to Wade, 1990: 1303–1304.

66. By the use of this term we do not mean to infer that any particular company was motivated by a takeover defense in adopting an employee-ownership plan. We are recognizing only that there is a takeover-defense potential, intentional or not.

67. The 13D is for persons who have rapidly acquired their shares, that is, at least 2 percent of the outstanding shares during a twelve-month period and the filings must be made within ten days of the event date and amendments must be filed for changes in ownership of at least 1 percent. Others file the 13G, that is, they meet the 5-percent rule but are otherwise exempted. They must file by December 31 and within 45 days after the end of each calendar year as long as the ownership percentage is at least 5 percent. A 14D-1 is made in conjunction with a formal tender offer of shares, but we have no way of estimating this filing regarding employee ownership.

68. As a result of the Securities Act amendments of 1975, a broad range of institutions applies here, including state and federal chartered banks, insurance companies, investment companies, independent investment advisors, internationally managed pension funds, endowments, and foundations.

69. For a full discussion of disclosure requirements, see *Securities Regulation,* by David L. Ratner (St. Paul, Minn.: West Publishing, 1988): 90–120, with sanctions discussed on 235–250.

70. The evidence we have given above also suggests that where our estimates and sources are incomplete, the major reason is that many companies do not provide information on this subject. This is why we have listed the source and year of our data for each company in Appendix A.1.

71. *The Quest for Value,* by G. Bennett Stewart (New York: Harper Business, HarperCollins, 1990). See also, Stewart, 1990: 127–128.

72. Memorandum, ESOPs as Corporate Takeover Defenses, May 25, 1990, Part 4, Advice to a Hypothetical Corporation Considering Establishing an ESOP, by Elana Hyman, Rutgers-State University of New Jersey, School of Law, Camden Campus.

73. Stewart, 1990: 128.

4

Corporate Culture/Governance

Xerox Corp., the subject of takeover rumors for months, announced it will buy back 11% of its stock, and set up an employee stock ownership plan. The office equipment and financial services company stated that the moves were designed to "enhance shareholder value," but a spokesman declined to elaborate. Clearly, these steps were undertaken, at least in part, to make a takeover tougher by buoying the stock price and getting more shares into friendly hands. Their stock had surged as high as $69 in April from a low of $56.75 in January on rumors that an investor such as Hanson PLC or Sir James Goldsmith was preparing to make a run on the company.... Xerox, based in Stamford, Conn., has been considered vulnerable, partly because its earnings and stock price have been lackluster. Xerox also invests heavily in research and development and someone buying the company could decide to cut that budget and pocket the funds. Xerox said the ESOP wouldn't dilute per-share earnings.... The ESOP will allocate shares to the 57,000 eligible U.S. employees out of a total U.S. workforce of 65,000.... The ESOP will borrow $785 million from banks.... The debt will be prepaid over 15 years, using largely the dividends that Xerox will pay the ESOP on the preferred. In addition, the ESOP will replace a savings plan available to many salaried employees and will partially replace the U.S. merit-pay increase budget for the next year, allowing those funds to be used to repay debt. The company has invested in efforts to increase employee involvement and product quality. When we called the company to ask if there was any connection between the ESOP and these programs, we were told there was none.[1]

In December 1988, Forbes *said that Charles Keating, Jr., then chairman of $7 billion (assets) American Continental Corp. (formerly OTC, in bankruptcy), has big problems. The Phoenix-based company, which owns California's Lincoln Savings & Loan Association, has cash-operating losses that even fancy bookkeeping can no longer cover up. The Securities & Exchange Commission is investigating whether the company's balance sheet and profit statement* *conform to reality.* Forbes *has said that the company's most recent quarterly report reads like a financial horror novel. American Continental, ostensibly a savings and loan holding company, is in reality a financial company dealing in speculative plays in leveraged buyouts, land development, junk bonds, currency trading, and heaven knows what else. Keating's solution to his woes: shoot the vultures. His ammunition: lending money to holders who are short-sellers, so that they can convert from margin accounts to cash accounts, drying up the shorts' pool of borrowable stock. He's also considering paying institutions so they will stop lending out their stock. It's amazing. A company running a cash deficit on its operations lends money against its own stock. Though American Continental is clearly vulnerable, shorting its stock isn't without risk. According to the company, insiders and their families own 8.34 million of the company's 16 million shares, and the employee stock ownership plan (ESOP) owns 4 million more, about 25%. That leaves just 3.66 million in the public float. On July 13, 1989, the company filed a draft reorganization plan in Federal Bankruptcy Court. On September 17, 1989, federal regulators launched a civil suit seeking more than $1.1 billion in damages from Keating. The suit alleges he and his family profited through insider dealing, illegal loans, sham real-estate transactions, and fraudulent sale of stock to employees of the parent company. A suit contends that he sold personal holdings to American Continental's ESOP and Lincoln S & L put up $15 million of its property as collateral for the loan that the ESOP needed to buy.*

Polaroid Corporation has prided itself on working toward being a participative company. Incorporated in 1939, it has 11,000 employees worldwide. From the beginning, company policy has emphasized openness and encouraged employee input. Over the years numerous employee participation groups have been active. In the fifties, the company developed an elected Employees' Committee. In the sixties, vertical and diagonal councils were formed to involve employees, and in the seventies, the company experimented with work teams and quality circles. In the eighties, the company moved away from involving employees in the traditional organization and in the direction of major efforts to totally change how the company was structured and how work was organized. Polaroid's program, called Total Quality Ownership, began with a series of 12 total-quality ownership conferences in which over 1200 employees participated. Nine companies explained their approach to total quality: Armstrong Corporation, Corning, Henry Ford Health Care Systems, McDonnell Douglas, Motorola, North American Philips, 3M, and Xerox Corporation. Three companies spoke about their way of integrating employee ownership into their company culture: closely held Avis Corporation, Science Application International Corporation, and publicly traded Weirton Steel Corporation. Polaroid's goal is reflected in its words, "combining the prescription of total quality with the empowerment of ownership." Owen Gaffney, Group Vice President for Human Resources, says that employee ownership means having "the right to relevant information and the responsibility to use that information to challenge the system within the scope of one's knowledge and expertise."[2]

Perini Corporation (AMEX) is 16% employee held. When Italian immigrant Bonfilio Perini established a construction company in the late 19th century, he could never imagine the company would constitute over $150 million in market value, thousands of employees, and almost $900 million in annual revenues. The ESOP has been created mainly to provide those employees on the corporate staff with an opportunity to invest in the company. Today, Perini says that employee ownership is a central part of the company's management plan to develop and motivate its employees. Perini's major projects include the development of industrial and commercial sites, oil pipelines, and utilities. Company officers say that the labor intensity of construction and the people factor of the business make employee ownership useful in retaining highly qualified personnel. The ESOP idea had been promoted by Louis Kelso when he once worked for the company. The Perini ESOP is open mainly to employees who comprise the corporate staff.[3]

The early stages of the United Air Lines failed employee buyout proved one major point: unions could make bids, raise financing, work with investment bankers and lawyers and be players in acquiring companies. Most observers have presumed that nonunion employees in a company without a union lacked sufficient organization and institutional power to be a player in a major employee-ownership transaction. But an important lesson of the early stages relates to nonunion employees. The nonunion employees created a group called the System Roundtable, which successfully appealed to United's management that they deserved input into all business transactions. They persuaded management to provide them with a budget for independent legal and financial advisors—First Chicago investment bankers and Fried, Frank, Harris, Shriver and Jacobson as legal advisors. The nonunion employees also negotiated an agreement with Keilin & Bloom, the key advisors representing the unions, to add one member to the new board of directors of the future employee-held company to represent their interests. These advisors worked at educating the nonunion employees about the transaction in a way that would be independent of management coercion and control. It was a minor event that established a major precedent. As unions continue to decline further and further below 13 percent of the private-sector United States workforce, this approach may also be repeated by nonunion employee groups as they observe partial acquisitions of their own companies by employee-ownership plans.

Introduction: Employee-Ownership Cultures

> *The findings in this book on the surprising extent of employee ownership in public companies are of major practical interest. It would be a mistake, however, to interpret these results to indicate that public companies or their employees have much interest in, or even awareness of, employee ownership as an organizing concept in their companies or their investment plans. Instead, employee ownership is simply a financial strategy for most of the companies. Rather than investing plan assets in IBM or treasury bonds, companies invest in their own stock, either because they think it is a good buy, because they want to bolster the market for their shares, because there are special tax advantages, or because they want to put more stock in friendly hands. Unless these companies start thinking of themselves as employee-ownership companies, and make an effort to involve employees as owners, the prevalence of company stock in employee benefit plans will have only negligible consequences for employees and companies.*
>
> *—Corey Rosen, National Center for Employee Ownership*

Are public companies with significant employee ownership different as organizations, workplaces, and corporations? One word of caution to the reader: When we use the term *employee* or *worker* we mean everyone in a company below senior management, that is, senior vice-president level. We do not have a working-class view of these terms, but rather a "shareholder view," which sees employees as the group other than the key personnel who run the company for the board. In our view vice presidents, as well as janitors, have the same reasons to be concerned about the question we raise here. What are the different ways public corporations approach employee ownership?

First, there is the *feudal culture,* espoused by companies that emphasize the differences between senior management and other employees. Employee ownership is strictly under the control of senior management and is viewed purely as a means. It has no importance in itself. The extent of this culture may even be hidden or unclear to most employees. The leaders in these companies are opposed to any attempts by employee ownership to change the company's fundamental organization. These corporations are inordinately threatened by any corporate governance role for employees.

Second, there is the *investor culture,* esteemed by companies that have traditional views of management but are open to, and proud of, employee ownership. They see ownership as a way to expand wages into a more long-term sharing in the company's economic future. Senior management in such companies often talk at length about employee ownership and their hopes that it will improve the company's success. Although their emphasis gives top billing to the motivation to work harder and the investment return of the stock, these companies do not go out of their way to empower employees with tools to improve their involvement and performance. They just hope it happens. A good number of these companies may have direct and confidential voting of shares by employeyss in tender offers and proxy fights with "mirror" voting for unallocated shares in leveraged ESOPs, but, in general, they view employees as they view most of their shareholders, as "passive investors" orchestrated by management.

Third, there is the *participatory culture,* valued by companies who take pride in employee ownership, as does the investor culture, but who go further. These companies are convinced that employee ownership is a good idea but recognize that it will make no difference in productivity or profitability unless they actively find ways to share information with employees at all levels and to manage energetically by promoting joint problem-solving teams composed of managers and rank-and-file employees from different departments. In addition to investing in consultants to help them figure out how to change their company, they educate and train executives and employees to bring about this process skillfully and successfully. These companies' approach to corporate governance is to see day-to-day employee involvement as the healthiest and most practical expression of shareholding. Shareholder rights is defined as employee responsibility.

Fourth, there is the *shareholder culture,* apparent in companies that have the qualities of pride in employee ownership of the investor culture and active involvement of the participatory culture. But the corporation treats the employees collectively as significant shareholders, according to the size of the employee holdings. The approach to shareholder rights explicitly recognizes that employees as a group are an active part of the "principals"—shareholders—who have some leverage over the "agents"—management. While the company's board and senior managers hope employees will be patient investors with a long-term focus, these companies treat employees as a group, as they would treat a 5-percent, 10-percent, 15-percent, 20-percent, or more shareholder entity. Employee-representatives have seats on the board of directors and thereby are involved in choosing senior management itself. These companies also allow employees to vote their ownership stake confidentially and have "mirror"-voting provisions, so that employees—not a trustee—vote the entire stake in a tender offer or proxy contest.

Fifth, there is an *entrepreneurial culture,* exhibited by a company that strives to make employee ownership part of an ongoing process to make the company the top competitor in its business and the best possible organization for which to work. Employee ownership is considered an important investment, a reason to encourage employee involvement, and a basis for shareholder rights. The real emphasis is not on providing things to employees as owners but on asking a great deal more responsibility and risk taking from them as owners. This corporation wants employees to be activist entrepreneurial workers and concerned, aggressive shareholders. They are companies committed to improving quality and customer focus, productivity, profitability, employee-management relations, and the overall organizational structure.

We will discuss the five ownership cultures and focus on a few key relevant issues: the implications of the risk of shareholding for workers, the significance of the decline of unions, the growth of a nonunion workforce, and the efforts required to enhance the value of employee holdings in their corporation. Before that, let's examine the big picture.

Trends

What are the facts or best estimates of key features of corporate culture and governance in the Employee Ownership 1000?

- Employees through their benefit plans are collectively the top shareholder in 41 percent of the Employee Ownership 1000![4]

- Employees through their benefit plans are one of the top three shareholders in 46 percent of the Employee Ownership 1000![5]

- About one-third of the companies have never made a public announcement about their employee holdings.[6]

- Employee holdings constitute what we will term an *investor stake*—that is, more than 10 percent of total common stock outstanding—in 57 percent of the Employee Ownership 1000, meaning that employees' retirement security is tied up in 10 percent of the total market value of these firms and they are one-tenth owners![7]

- About one-fifth of the companies make it extremely difficult to find out their level of employee holdings because of a lack of information in even customary places in which public companies talk about these holdings, such as in annual reports, routine SEC filings, proxy statements, and special SEC filings for more than 5-percent holders.[8]

- About 10 to 20 percent of corporate senior managers have publicly articulated the importance of employee ownership, based on our searches of their annual reports, president's letters, press releases, and national press articles.[9]

- Less than 5 percent of the companies, we estimate, are actively finding ways to encourage employee participation in the company and to train and empower employees to be involved in joint problem-solving teams.[10]

- Top ESOP and employee benefit plan lawyers estimate that a growing percentage of the companies have structured the company-sponsored benefit plans so that employees directly and confidentially can cast votes for all shares of stock in a tender offer or proxy contest with "mirror" voting.[11]

- Less than 1 percent of the companies have nonmanagerial workers serving on their boards of directors as representatives of employee shareholders. This represents less than 10 companies out of 1000 firms. Out of the companies where employee holdings represent the top holder, less than 10 of these companies, or about .5 percent, have employee representatives on the board of directors.[12]

These trends indicate that most public companies with significant employee ownership have feudal and investor cultures, and a small proportion of them espouse participatory cultures. Some emphasize shareholder rights for employee holders by the way they structure voting, but this scarcely means board representation. Let's understand the different employee-ownership cultures in more detail.

Feudal Culture

> *In many cases the objectives stated to employees for the employee-ownership plan are not the real objectives.*
>
> *—ESOP expert at a major U.S. accounting firm*

> *ESOPs, particularly KSOPs, are complicated and people need to examine them not only from a tax standpoint, but also in terms of their pay and compensation policies and larger corporate goals. Some were put in rather hastily . . . and people need to look at what they're doing, what they expect to get out of it, how it's going to be communicated, how it's going to be administered. They're powerful from a financial and tax perspective, but companies need to look at them more closely in terms of fitting into the overall company design. Once an employee-ownership plan holds significant amounts of stock, corporate governance becomes an important issue, particularly with different employee groups. This will become more important as employee-ownership plans mature and people realize what their power is.*
>
> *—Doug Tormey, national ESOP expert for Towers Perrin*

An estimated 20 to 30 percent of the Employee Ownership 1000 can be regarded as feudal employee-ownership culture, which sees employee ownership as a means, pure and simple. This estimate is based on the number of companies that have no public record disclosing information about significant levels of employee holdings or core employee ownership.[13] The plan is viewed more like the wage system in a highly traditional firm: strictly under the control of management with workers as recipients. The "means" tone comes across, for example, in the President's Letter to shareholders shortly after Harcourt Brace Jovanovich Inc. (NYSE) became 27.7 percent employee held in quick moves during a bitter takeover fight: "We did obtain $56 million in working capital from the sale of common stock to an ESOP for allocation to HBJ employees after having terminated our pension plan." Many companies follow the lead of a major NYSE company that is 20 percent employee held and has repeatedly said that it is simply "a cost-effective way of funding employee programs." Let's be clear: this company is taking an ideological stand on employee ownership by choosing the way it conceives of a 20-percent holder.

Treating workers as "serfs" is certainly not illegal, as long as one meets the right legal standards. Management in these companies may talk a good game about employee ownership and involvement in the company, and employees may brag about being stockholders, but there's little else to employee ownership in these companies but the stock and the talk. Sometimes employee ownership is plastered all over these companies, but it is basically a front. This is the way the employee-ownership plan at Charles Keating's Lincoln Savings and Loan came across: a financial convenience. Mostly, these companies want to deemphasize that employee holdings are a significant part of the company, or they take a very paternalistic approach whose main message is that employee ownership is a gift. That is just plain wrong: employee ownership under ERISA plans is deferred compensation, and it is no more a gift than a weekly paycheck is a gift. And if employees paid for an ESOP to keep the employee-ownership program "shareholder neutral," management has no right to act as if it *is* a gift.

Many employees have been trained to be passive and irresponsible; they blindly accept whatever they are told about their employee-ownership plan. These companies invest little energy in communicating about the employee ownership. When they do, the message is it's good for you but don't touch it; we'll hold on to it for you. Management goes out of its way to ensure employee ownership does not change the organization and is threatened by any notion of a more developed employee-owner identity by employees.

Employee ownership with a feudal culture can be a good investment for employees. It may involve rewards with little responsibility, depending on the rise or fall of the stock price. But it really comes down to a question of whether plans set up "for the exclusive benefit of employees" should take that chance. The major weakness of this view is that power corrupts and absolute power corrupts absolutely: there can be a temptation to use the employee-ownership plan as though it were merely another company bank account. Management chooses the trustee of the plan; it can choose itself or parties "friendly to it."

The case of CityFed Financial Group certainly raises some of these questions. CityFederal Financial Corporation, an OTC company, operating savings and loans in New Jersey, was one of the country's largest savings institutions, with assets of $10.5 billion, 108 full-service banking facilities in New Jersey and Florida and 120 mortgage loan production offices in 33 states.

In the mideighties the CEO, Gilbert Roessner, announced a major employee-ownership plan: "The ESOP will create a greater identity of interests between CityFed shareholders and our employees, all of whom will in the future be shareholders in their own right. As a result, our employees will have a higher stake in the future profitability and development of the company. Furthermore, compared to the cost of continuing the existing pension plan and due to the favorable tax-treatment afforded ESOPs, we have projected estimated after-tax savings of approximately $9.3 million between 1986 and 1995."[14] The company's ESOP owned 16.4 percent of outstanding common. In 1985, the Board of Directors approved employee benefit plan purchases up to 9.9 percent of its common stock on the open market. The pension plan was terminated and $5 million in excess assets was to be recovered, and a new floor plan was developed to guarantee existing benefits. In 1986, the corporation amended its loan agreement, which allows it to borrow funds to re-lend to ESOP, and increased the amount from $17 to 30 million. In 1987, the company said it will no longer make available stock for its thrift and profit-sharing plan, which will have to get their shares on the market. About 3000 people participated in the plan. The thrift plan, holding 5 percent of the company's stock was transformed into a 401(k) plan and held mainly employee contributions. According to a former company officer, when the company went belly up, employees lost all of this. The New Jersey bank was owned by CityFed Financial Corp., a North Palm Beach, Florida holding company, which planned to continue buying up other banks. A local real estate lawyer, who wishes to remain anonymous, alleges the bank was widely known for its lackadaisical attitude toward managing its assets and dealing with its accounts.

Before its demise, CityFed had constructed a wide array of takeover defenses, according to the Investor Responsibility Research Center, including 66.7 percent to approve a merger; 75 percent shareholder vote to amend bylaws and unequal voting rights; no shareholder rights to call special meetings, poison pills, golden parachutes; compensation plans with change in control provisions; director indemnification; and limited director liability. The New Jersey S & L went into receivership on December 8, 1989, and the shares are now traded at a negligible value. It is being managed by the Resolution Trust Corp. Some employees are livid. They feel cheated because they no longer have a defined-benefit pension plan. Sure they got annuities, but the company used excess assets to set up a leveraged ESOP, which bought 16.4 percent of the company's stock.

A former officer of the bank alleges that the ESOP trustee started making inquiries late in the game, but did nothing. He estimates that officers and directors owned about 25 percent, together with employees and the ESOP and thrift plan. He says that this experience has taught him that employees cannot be shareholders without having strong shareholder rights and board seats. They have too much at risk.[15] There may or may not have been illegal behavior in the CityFed case, but the point is that employee ownership in a feudal culture can be an enormous risk for employees. Regrettably, the now-weakened Bank of New England may have sizable holdings of its own stock in some employee benefit plans. We have discovered a number of situations where weak banks and S & Ls have significant employee ownership and insignificant employee monitoring. In general, employee ownership is now a necessary part of the retirement system of the country, but employees do not need to be both uninformed and powerless about their risk.

The feudal employee-ownership culture has several tell-tale signs: First, company officials turn employee ownership on and off like a faucet. They push the amount of employee holdings up high and then down low, depending on circumstances. Second, size of employee ownership means nothing; employees deserve little information, communication, and involvement, be it 4 percent or 40 percent. Third, there is no attempt to provide even meager special legal protection for employees. Respected employee-ownership lawyer, Marilyn Marchetti of the Chicago firm of Keck, Mahin, and Cate, has persuasively argued that for major transactions an ESOP trustee should appoint independent legal and financial counsel to help ensure that the employees' interests are being protected.[16] The Joint Economic Committee of Congress has recommended that all ESOPs have a representative committee of employees, which can meet with management to discuss the employee ownership. In such companies, these ideas are anathema.

To be realistic, we believe it is a sincere and reasonable position for a company to have a small ESOP or buy a small percentage of its own stock on behalf of a company-sponsored benefit plan without incurring negative consequences. It is, after all, a free country, free to be feudal, free to be anything else, as long as legal standards are followed.

There probably are numerous companies, however, where the feudal culture predominates and the employee-ownership plan is the major holder of the company's stock and/or controls a sizable amount of the company. Do workers really *want* to abandon shareholder responsibility in these companies? Let's not forget the corporate law of the last chapter, as these *are* public companies, not private fiefdoms. If, in addition to this, individuals with little ownership interests control the board of a company whose employees' retirement is tied up largely in company stock—and the company is grappling with a risky situation—does it then make sense for employees to be in the dark without shareholder rights? The senior management of CityFed Financial group insulated themselves from the appropriate power involvement of shareholders outside the company and shareholders inside the company. Arnold & Porter lawyer Steven Hester puts it bluntly: "This just shows how ludicrous the U.S. Department of Labor position is that a trustee must protect the employees. Is a trustee, off in some bank somewhere that has hundreds of trust accounts, in a better position to monitor the 'exclusive benefit of the employees' than the employees themselves who are right there at the company? No way. Let the employees protect themselves and have a board representative just as normal shareholders would."[17]

But the last chapter presented clearly documented cases of feudal employee-ownership culture gone haywire. In the management-entrenchment cases of Norlin, Macmillan, Buckhorn, and others, courts of law closely examined the facts and found that the attitudes that underlie a feudal employee-ownership culture can be carried too far.

Practically, the options for employees and managers who "want to let some air in" in feudal companies, determined to remain feudal, are modest: (1) try to persuade the company to share financial information with employees regularly; (2) create a volunteer Financial Performance Group, which monitors the company's performance through meetings with executives or—if the company is uncooperative—purchases the firm's SEC filings and employee benefit plan filings and compares it to similar companies in the same industry; (3) seek the choice of an independent employee-ownership plan trustee with whom the employees can have confidential meetings; (4) create an employees' association, which meets with senior management to discuss financial and workplace issues; (5) retain an attorney or investment banker—if these preceding actions are too risky—to act as an ombudsperson, who can represent employees' concerns without identifying them to management; (6) protect employees' interests while the company is involved in a risky transaction by bringing in an independent financial or legal advisor to the employee-ownership plan trustee; (7) file a class-action lawsuit, if the law has been broken; and (8) visit other Employee Ownership 1000 companies that have been successful with making the changes that are being considered. Many corporations with feudal employee-ownership cultures, who are otherwise sincere about employee ownership, will likely respond positively to nonconfrontative attempts to improve communications. It is those that do not communicate clearly and openly, whose employees have a real problem.

Investor Culture

There is a magic for people in owning stock in their employer. We've talked to people about how they feel about employee ownership. Some people will vote and don't think it makes a difference. Others say we vote as investors not employees. There are people who take a vacation to go to the shareholders meeting. Others say it is a set up. I think you have to have a very meaningful level of employee ownership for employees to participate. As a rule of thumb people have to be getting an amount of stock equal to 5% of pay. After 10 or 20 years you have stock at least equal to your annual income. Now that becomes a big financial asset for the employee.

—*Ken Lindberg, Hewitt Associates compensation consulting firm*

As our baby boom goes through the system, we'll find that things will be reversed and the concept of keeping employees for just a while and making no commitments to them won't work. Companies may have to create structures to create long-term commitment. The decline of defined-benefit pension plans and the rise of employee ownership is part of this concept and this trend.

—*Michael Lew, Coopers & Lybrand*

An estimated 60 to 75 percent of the Employee Ownership 1000 is part of the Investor Culture—an estimate based on public announcements by numerous companies whose employee holdings are more than a tenth of the entire market value of the company, constituting what we call an "investor stake."[18] The investor employee-ownership culture sees employee ownership as a mutual fund. The average employee holding of a public company is 12.14 percent, and almost 60 percent of public companies have an "investor stake," where employee benefit plans control at least a tenth of the company. The plan is viewed as a shared pool of capital at risk with other shareholders and management. Some companies define the holding simply as a "retirement vehicle." The common phrase is "aligning the interests of employees and shareholders." These companies often strive to make stock ownership a meaningful proportion of pay, and many have explicitly adopted a "pay-at-risk" philosophy that stresses the tie-in between company performance and employee reward. While these corporations have very traditional forms of management, they are sometimes proud of, and try to attract attention to, employee holdings. Employee ownership, frequently mentioned in the company's promotional literature, is described as an important part of personnel policies. In fact, in many of these companies it is viewed as the "rank-and-file" version of stock options to hold employees at the company. In companies where there is no defined-benefit plan, indeed, substantial employee holdings critically tie up the worker's retirement future in the stock of the company. One side effect of the large number of NYSE companies that have created such plans for their salaried workforce is that they have launched an essentially sophisticated form of employee retention as the nation enters a tight labor market. Al Salwen, a benefits consultant at William R. Mercer Co., recognized this: "Corporate America has experienced almost a traumatic downsizing in the past 5–10 years. As a result there's been a lot of employees shaken out of the tree . . . and, as a result, those who remain are much more important to the success of the organization. The extension of equity-type programs down in the organization is recognition that individual employees play a larger part and carry a larger burden."[19] The many "investor-culture" companies are the "Middle America" of employee ownership. Table 4.1 provides a sampling of the ways some senior managers talk about it.

The term *holders* best captures the attitude these companies have toward employees. Many of these companies, perhaps a very high percentage, probably provide employees with confidential "mirrored"-voting rights on the stock. But this provision does not imply that the companies wish employees to be active shareholders unless there is a crisis in control. This right-to-vote-the-stock usually takes place in a company culture where any form of investor activism—beyond that of an employee's personal enthusiasm about being a shareholder—would be viewed as inappropriate. The idea of employees' electing a board member would be considered strange, because these firms do not regard employees as shareholders on a par with public shareholders. Senior managers of these companies might not own up to this view, but it is proven by their behavior. From conversations with many executives, the reasoning here seems to be typically made up of one or both of the following components: (1) Management has an authority relationship with you as employees, one in which we direct the firm and you operate it; so too, we expect employee investors to cede the direction of their shareholder interests on a regular basis to management unless you are needed in a tender offer or a proxy battle; and (2) This company needs patient investors who aren't constantly breathing down management's back—investors who realize that sound strategic planning requires years of capital investment and careful husbandry. By being those patient investors,

TABLE 4.1 *Senior Managers Talk About Investor Culture*

Sara-Lee Corp. (NYSE) 10.40%

Employees as shareholders are very attractive. They have a slightly longer-term perspective.

CEO John Byran,
The Wall Street Journal, *March 12, 1990*

Xyvision Inc. (OTC) 7%

It is intended to ensure that Xyvision can attract and retain employees of the highest possible quality in a highly competitive market.

The Wall Street Journal, *June 16, 1989*

Borden Inc. (NYSE) 15%*

We seek not only deeper participation by Borden people in Borden progress, but deeper participation in its rewards through ownership. Over 13,000 Borden employees now own shares in the company, and we have established an ESOP that could help increase employee ownership to an ultimate target of 15% of the outstanding shares. There is no better and no surer way of sharing the gains of our common effort over the years to come.

President's Letter, *SEC filings, December 1989*

Sears Inc. (NYSE) 19.7%

We believe that increased ownership of Sears shares reinforces our employees' commitment to Sears success.

CEO Edward Brennan,
PR Newswire, *December 21, 1989*

Monarch Capital (NYSE) 6.9%

We are very excited that our employees will hold a substantial interest in the company, and feel this is an important step toward a goal of a more entrepreneurial work force. Employees will be able to share in the results of their efforts and will be able to see first-hand how new sales, improved productivity, and cost savings impact the corporation's earnings.

President's Letter, *SEC filings, December 1989*

Ruddick Inc. (AMEX) 40.50%

Management believes that the ESOP has worked successfully since its beginning in 1976 in encouraging all employee-shareholders to be more productive, thereby earning more profits for the company.

President's Letter, *SEC filings, July 1987*

Butler Manufacturing Inc. (OTC) 18.80%

The cornerstone of our programs to build better career-oriented employee commitment is our ESOP, which was established for all salaried and non-union hourly employees in 1983. Surplus pension funds have now all been transferred to the ESOP, and the value

(continued)

TABLE 4.1 *(Continued)*

of that Plan for the future will depend entirely on the level of corporate earnings that will support ESOP contributions and dividends, and on the market value of Butler stock.

President's Letter, *SEC filings, 1986*

Fireman's Fund Insurance Company** **(NYSE) 6.5%**

That is a matter of great, great pleasure to me. A step like this really helps a lot in getting our employees to think like owners.

James Byrne, Chairman
The Wall Street Journal, *March 8, 1988*

Michael Baker Corp. (AMEX) 33%

While the percentage level of ESOP holding will vary from time to time, the continuation of the ESOP concept is part of our long-term strategy.

SEC filings, December 1989

National Convenience Stores, Inc. (NYSE) 18.09%

National Convenience said the employee stock ownership plan should encourage employees to establish long-term employment with the company. In other actions, the board amended its bylaws relating to the calling of shareholders' meetings, the administration of consent solicitations and the procedures for nominating candidates for the board.

The Wall Street Journal, *May 15, 1985*

Kerr Glass Manufacturing Co. (NYSE) 25.50%

Roger W. Norian, chairman and president, said the holdings by the plans "would be reflective of shareholders with long-term investment objectives."

The Wall Street Journal, *October 27, 1987*

Frozen Food Express Industries Inc. (AMEX) 6.31%

We believe that the ESOP program will be a better benefit for our employees and the Company by allowing employees to participate in the future of the Company as investors.

President's Letter, *SEC filings, 1986*

---

*As an ultimate target.
**Management and the board sold the company in 1990.
Note: Percentages constitute the amount of employee ownership.
Source: Public Company Employee Ownership Database, 1990

employees contribute to the company's stability and the returns of nonemployee shareholders.

This surely is not an insincere position, because patient investor stock ownership has been generally profitable over the long term under conditions of relative investor passivity. Table 4.2 shows the conclusions of the data collected on securities prices since 1926.

TABLE 4.2 *Average Annual Rates of Return on Stocks, Bonds, and Government Securities from 1926–1985 (in percentages)*

Portfolio	Nominal Return	Real Return
Common stocks	12.0	8.8
Corporate bonds	5.1	2.1
Government bonds	4.4	1.4
Treasury bills	3.5	.4

Source: R. G. Ibbotson and R. A. Sinquefield, *Stocks, Bonds, Bills, and Inflation*, 1982, updated in *Stocks, Bonds, Bills, and Inflation: 1986 Yearbook*, Ibbotson Associates, Chicago, 1986, and based on a similar table in Richard A. Brealey and Stewart C. Myers, *Principles of Corporate Finance* (New York: McGraw Hill, 1988): 128.

The bottom line is that stocks have an average long-term return of 12 percent, far superior to all other securities and capital instruments. The Ibbotson numbers are figured for Standard & Poor's Composite Index, which represents a portfolio of common stocks for 500 large firms, and shows clearly that stocks are a superior long-term investment. Investment bankers setting up ESOPs in large companies have indicated that they are perfectly comfortable with the "risk issue," given the retirement horizon for most workers. Ibbotson Associates have also commented on the extraordinary advantages of being an employee-shareholder in your own company: you can avoid much of the transaction and management costs of the stock investment and defer taxes, since the capital appreciation and dividend income accumulate tax-free in any ERISA employee benefit plan. If the worker-shareholder were an individual investor, Ibbotson calculates that taxes would have eaten 70 percent of the return from 1970 to 1989 and 30 percent of the return in the period 1929 to 1989. But substantial risks *do* exist.

So there is another side of the coin. The arguments for companies with an investor culture providing greater shareholder rights to employees are as follows: (1) If employees are the core or one-tenth shareholders of the company, the passivity of the ma-and-pa investor seems excessive; (2) If employees have a large amount of their retirement tied up in the company stock and/or, if the firm is in a volatile, cyclical, or high-risk business, or if the company's stock is markedly unpredictable, employees may rightfully seek a higher-profile investor role, which allows them to more closely monitor the investment performance of assets on which they are so dependent; (3) If the employees as a group, or a relevant subgroup of employees mistrusts the senior management and/or the board of directors—for example, a raider, who takes over a company and preserves employee ownership but has no track record with employees—employees may require greater rights to actively protect their interest.

The options for an investor culture corporation that wishes to remain investor culture but wants to "let some air in" are indicative of a more trusting relationship between employees and management. Most likely, management as well as employees in investor companies will propose these ideas, since employee passivity is often as large a barrier to a more active investor role as management intransigence is in these firms: (1) revamping the company's bulletin board, video presentations, benefits, training, and in-house newspaper to allow for solid reporting to employees about the company's financial performance; (2) creating a special annual employee-shareholder meeting that includes comprehensive information and focuses on issues of special concern to them; (3) developing a training program to help all employees understand the financial fundamentals of the business; (4) organizing an Employee Investor Committee, which meets with senior management regularly and reports to employees; (5) establishing a nonvoting board-of-directors observer; (6) creating an ongoing independent financial advisor to the employee ownership plan trustee, who is accessible to employees on a confidential basis; (7) visiting other Employee Ownership 1000 companies that are successful with these innovations; and (8) starting an annual survey of employees' suggestions as investors.

The main drawback of even a vibrant employee-ownership culture can be summarized in one word: competition. As America's corporations enter a rapidly changing world, typified by freer markets and global competition for goods and services, why would a company not want to use employee ownership as leverage to improve employee-employer cooperation, quality, productivity, and profitability? We believe that many companies—with senior management who's open to, and sincere about, employee ownership—fear that the organizational changes required to diffuse information, authority, and responsibility throughout the company would substantially weaken it. In short, these companies still might have many feudal characteristics. The two that are particularly resistant to change, even in "good" companies, are ascribed status and ascribed reward. *Ascribed status* in these firms is the existence of an inflated management hierarchy with excessive perks and badges of prestige, which are unnecessary *for the business itself.* Status is ascribed because of your position, not your contribution. *Ascribed reward* in these companies is the belief that large differences in salaries are *necessary* for the success of the business, when in fact there is little evidence to support that case. In these companies, senior management has created essentially a private club devoted to maximizing its own siphoning of shareholder wealth. They are not rewarded for the performance of the company or its stock. Sometimes investor culture is a positive force in employee-held companies: employees and management really believe it is the way to run significant employee ownership. In other cases, investor culture is a way that management prevents employee-shareholders from challenging ascribed status and ascribed reward.

Participatory Culture

It was really beautiful. Hourlies and supervisors, pencil pushers and clock punchers, all gathered around the corporate foundry to forge a new relationship based on the idea that workers could play an active part in management. The new way entailed asking employees how their work might be improved and then letting them improve it, often in work teams. . . . The initial results were ROI-opening [Return on Investment]: A study of 101 industrial companies found that the participatively managed among them outscored the others on 13 of 14 financial measures. The consensus among academics, consultants, and managers is that most efforts to produce participation never make it. . . . The reason? Consensus here too: not the workers but management, upper, middle and lower. The concept was banished to the shop floor and, even if it flourished there, [was] never permitted to creep higher. Jump on the quality circle bandwagon? Sure, takers are everywhere. But change the behavior of managers or the organizational structure? Not this decade, thanks. The price of failure to establish a boiler-room-to-boardroom network of committed participative managers: battered circles, confusion among survivors, and the same old miscommunication between the ranks. . . . [A] human resources manager in [GE's] lighting group [says]: "Managers who think that their businesses are producing acceptable results aren't particularly interested in changing their ways." The failure or refusal by many organizations to make the necessary cultural conversion is hung up on the old issues of authority. . . . Information is power, and access to it remains a clear badge of rank to managers. . . . The skills required for the would-be participative manager—communicating, motivating, championing ideas—are sandy intrusions into the gearbox of many traditional executives.

—Bill Saporito
"The Revolt Against Working Smarter," Fortune

A lot of chairmen of public companies I have dealt with view the employee-ownership plan as a way to give employees a voice and some ownership, but a lot of transactions over the last two years are not in the spirit of employee ownership. They are just exchanging employee ownership for other benefits. It has been very short-sighted, just looking one or two months after the plan is installed. It's just tax and financial reasons. They should do things to change day-to-day management. It does not make me happy to see how little change there is among our corporate clients.

—ESOP investment banker at a major Wall Street bank
who wishes to remain anonymous

Anyone thinking about employee ownership and participative management needs to recognize that there are several "laws" that will determine their success. Blasi has reviewed the evidence for these in great detail in his book, *Employee*

Ownership: Revolution or Ripoff?, and these guidelines will be listed here to underscore their importance:[20]

- There is no evidence that employee ownership leads to participative management. Senior managers *and* employees must both decide to change from a hierarchical you-tell-me approach to team responsibility.

- There is no evidence whatsoever that employee ownership itself automatically causes improved productivity or profitability except when combined with employee involvement.

- Managers continually claim employee ownership improves productivity and exaggerate "the good feelings" employees have about employee ownership because they believe in a simplistic "money-causes-motivation-and-working-harder" approach to managing. These false beliefs lull them into thinking they do not have to institute participative management.

- Every major piece of research has shown that the only way to improve productivity and profitability with employee ownership is to combine it with a company-wide problem-solving team program, aimed at those strategic areas where value can be added in companies.[21]

- Despite the appeal of employee representatives on corporate boards and other mechanisms, such as confidential mirrored-voting rights, and the like, which are a response to employees' potential "shareholder rights," the evidence is that problem-solving teams, not high-level representation or "democratic window dressing" impact the bottom line.

- Employee involvement in strategic problem solving and work redesign, which completely revamps how jobs are structured, how tasks and departments are organized and managed, along with the scope of management and the level of the employees' responsibility, have a high probability of improving productivity and profitability independent of employee ownership, but ownership can help reward workers for the effort and keep workers and managers committed.

- Employees cannot be motivated to participate in such programs if their personal and group grievances are not dealt with. In short, management cannot expect employees to get enthusiastic about these programs if employees cannot resolve critical conflicts in the workplace with management.

An estimated 5 percent of the Employee Ownership 1000 can be said to have participatory culture because of the prevalence of wide-spread initiatives to involve more than 60 percent of the employees in solving problems that improve productivity, profitability, and quality.

Faced with this evidence and practical examples of employee involvement, organizational change, and work redesign, which is improving the results of companies, some corporations are embarking upon a participatory culture. But we found little evidence of Employee Ownership 1000 public companies' attempting to develop participative cultures and have decided to refrain from the normal practice of trendy business writers who cite inspiring stories of one quality circle's great contribution of saving one million dollars in one department of one facility of one company. There is no escaping it: participatory culture is in its infancy.

Some companies are *trying*. Some say they have concluded that both ideas make sense together as in Weirton Steel (NYSE), Standard Brands (NYSE), Hermann Miller (OTC), and EDO (NYSE). Some are adding employee ownership to an already participative company, as in Polaroid Corporation (NYSE) and Procter & Gamble (NYSE), and Federal-Mogul (NYSE), whose President, Dennis Gormley, has said, "This reorganization, combined with the establishment of an ESOP, will greatly enhance employee productivity and ultimately, company value. We believe people who have a stake in the company will perform better and that this expanded direct ownership opportunity, in conjunction with our long-established employee involvement programs will provide additional incentives."[22]

Thus, some highly developed investor culture companies are convinced that in fact employee ownership will not improve the bottom line without radically changing the way information is shared, management is organized, jobs are structured, problem-solving teams are trained and developed, and people from different departments cooperate. These companies are not committed to extensive shareholder rights—board representation, employee involvement in annual meetings or as employee-representatives in choosing senior management—rather, they see day-to-day employee involvement as the most practical, realistic, and healthy expression of shareholding. Much of the evidence presented here supports this position, which defines shareholder rights as increased employee responsibility. Nevertheless, many of the companies that call themselves participative companies are still working hard to "contain" participative management practices to the shop floor or the office floor.

It's no surprise that there has been little progress in harnessing employee ownership to improve the competitiveness of U.S. corporations. This remains a major source of untapped potential. A clear leader in manufacturing is unionized Weirton Steel Corporation (NYSE), whose intensive work at reorganization with its union and nonunion employees has been described elsewhere.[23] Although not publicly traded, Avis Inc. and Northwestern Steel & Wire (formerly NYSE), of which the first author is an employee-elected board member, have worked hard at combining employee ownership with labor-management cooperation. Nonunion Polaroid Corp. (NYSE) has been a company remarkably open to discussing the successes and tribulations of its effort. For example, in Polaroid's New Bedford manufacturing facility, the operation has been totally redesigned and organized with fewer levels of management, a small number of teams, including previously separate departments that organize their own work and monitor and cross-train one another. The plant has worked hard at decreasing the staff, eliminating management positions, and increasing productivity while depending on attrition and transfers to deal with the obvious drop in demand for people. Polaroid is slowly trying to implement these ideas in other facilities. A clear strength at Polaroid is that it has an elected Employees' Committee, which serves as a voice for workers and guarantees a grievance procedure that commits the company to resolving conflicts with employees in a fair and impartial manner. The mere thought of an Employees' Committee scares many nonunion companies, and few are willing to invest in fairness procedures. Procter & Gamble (NYSE) with 19.4 percent employee ownership is also a leader in participatory culture, but the company is closed mouth about its programs, since the participation programs are viewed as critical to its competitive edge. All these companies coordinate a corporation-wide effort for employee involvement and organizational change.

Companies that wish to strengthen and deepen a participatory culture can consider the following options: (1) visiting other Employee Ownership 1000 firms that have achieved their goals; (2) creating a corporation-wide participation team to develop a strategic change plan for the corporation with a budget, presentation to senior management and the board of directors; (3) evaluating why the current participation program may be stalled, if it is; (4) sending the union leaders on a tour of participative workplaces with unions, if the firm is unionized, and creating a joint labor-management committee to plan the program, hire consultants, and review progress; (5) establishing a fairness procedure to deal with grievances and conflict resolution, if the firm is nonunion; (6) training to develop problem-solving skills for all employees and managers.

The main drawback of this kind of energetic participatory culture is that it ignores the legal question of shareholder rights. That may in fact be a decision that both managers and employees wish to jointly choose, because a dynamic participative company may succeed in channeling information up and down the hierarchy in ways that attain the goals of formal legal participation. As some companies become largely employee held, management may choose participatory culture over shareholder culture as the ultimate vision that benefits the corporation in which they believe. Thus, it is *not* clear that every company that has shareholder culture will also be a participatory corporation.

Shareholder Culture

> In some cases employee ownership has been used to place stock in employee hands and to increase identification with the company. It's a useful way to create a commonality of interest between management and employees. I'm not sure how long that lasts before employees say this is all right, but we still don't have a vote on the board. The question is when do employees want to go from merely seeing stock in their account and having the right to vote their shares to wanting to take a more active role in management. I do not know if it will ever happen. If you've got a public company and you've got pass-through voting and if employees acted in concert, they'd control a large block of stock. What you end up with is employee ownership as the next step in workforce democracy, or a step in that direction. I'm not sure the unions are real thrilled with that.
>
> —Bernie Schaffer, lawyer at Hay Higgins/Hay Group consulting firm

Intervening in the process of selecting a chief executive? Going over the CEO's head to the board, his theoretical bosses? Agitating for more consultation and an "ongoing relationship" with directors? Is this any way for institutional investors to behave? Yes—at least sometimes. In fact, although the action now is confined to the squabble between public pension funds [and corporations], directors can expect to hear from unhappy investors much more frequently in the future. Such initiatives can be positive as long as shareholders don't overstep their bounds as owners and attempt to become managers. . . . Outside directors, after all, are supposed to be watching out for shareholder interests. What would be wrong with creating a link between owners and their representatives in the boardroom, particularly when corporate performance is wanting? . . . Yet too many . . . shareholder demands . . . would . . . prevent [American executives] from getting on with the task of managing.

—*Judith H. Dobrzynski*
"*A Shareholder's Place Is In the Boardroom—Sometimes*" Business Week

In response to the claim that workers will give themselves high wages instead of modernizing: "Job security is very important. If we modernize, it goes a long way" toward giving workers that protection.

—*Virgil Thompson, Independent Steelworkers Union President*
Weirton Steel Corporation

An estimated one half of 1 percent of the Employee Ownership 1000 have articulated a shareholder culture—a percentage based on the number of companies that report nonmanagerial employees on their board of directors and acknowledge they emphasize shareholder rights. Many of these companies, like Weirton Steel Corporation and Polaroid Corporation, have a developed investor culture, plus a growing emphasis on employee participation. But they have added a distinctly different element that does not happen by itself, unless senior management and/or a large number of employees actively will it: the idea that employees as a group deserve the shareholder rights corporate law gives to all shareholders. Our research consultant, Lawrence Greenberg, says, "Voting rights are a theoretical power. Shareholders hardly ever use them except in a crisis. They have no day-to-day effect. This is really a new version of taxation without representation. Only board representation can fix it." Table 4.3 shows the small number of public corporations that have employee board representatives as a result of employee ownership. But at Pan Am this idea has not been constructive.

Shareholder-culture companies clearly accept the *notion* that employees as a group are a real part of the "principals"—their shareholders, for whom management and the board serve as "agents." These companies would treat the employee group as they would treat any 5-percent, 10-percent, 15-percent, 20-percent or more shareholder. And that is the key, because some companies do not treat their core shareholders with much respect. Indeed, a major debate about the use of proxy battles is that securities law makes it very difficult for shareholders as a group to contact one another and band together to assert their "principal"

TABLE 4.3 *Nonmanagerial Employees on Corporate Boards in the Employee Ownership 1000*

Oregon Metallurgical Corporation
Pan AM
Polaroid Corporation
Weirton Steel Corporation

Source: Public Company Employee Ownership Database, 1990

rights. This is no different from the desire of many corporate managements to deal with employees "as if" they were merely isolated ma-and-pa investors. This in fact is the critical attitude that determines a shareholder culture: Does management see employees as a shareholder group? In most cases the answer is no. We have tried to show that persuasive reasons exist for both this attitude and this behavior. Therefore, most of the statements by chairmen and CEOs focusing on the employee-shareholder have common threads.

It might seem strange to think that senior management must "grant" to employees fundamental rights of shareholders that are, after all, the law or that employees must decide to articulate those rights. The reason is that most employee benefit plans were set up after World War II with an ideology of "managing assets for employees" as if they were banks managing savings deposits. No one really conceived that employee pensions would own so much of corporations where employees did not work or would own a substantial amount of corporations where they are employed, as in the Employee Ownership 1000. In the book, *Employee Ownership: Revolution or Ripoff?*, Blasi has analyzed exactly how an ideology unfriendly to employee-shareholder rights emerged from the way the laws affecting employee ownership were conceived, written, regulated, and interpreted. For the reader who wishes to understand these issues in depth, read "The Ideology of Bureaucracy in American Law" by Harvard Law Professor Gerald E. Frug, which appeared in the *Harvard Law Review* (1984). This cannot be seen wholly as an argument about employee-shareholder rights. Several analysts of corporate governance have made the same arguments about management's refusal to "grant" real rights to all shareholders and passive shareholders' refusals to accept responsibility for making critical inquiries and decisions about the corporation, which will influence their investments.[24]

But a number of developments that really have very little to do with employees or senior managers are radically changing all of this. This leavening about employee shareholding is neither a result mainly of management resistance to employee-shareholders nor of employees pushing for power in corporations. It is not a management conspiracy or a workers' revolt in most companies. If anything, there's evidence that many managers have willingly agreed that employee-ownership plans have confidential voting and tendering rights with mirrored provisions, largely because they probably trust the judgment of employees. And radical worker/shareholder activism has simply not caused any noteworthy examples of irresponsible shareholder behavior by employees. Everyone watched as publicly traded Weirton Steel Corporation asked its employee-shareholders to approve cuts in cash profit sharing in order to increase capital investment to make the company a world leader in steel. As usual, scores of neoclassical economists predicted the workers would be incapable of sacrificing short-term benefits for long-term economic gains. They were wrong. Weirton workers and managers and shareholders—all aligned their interests.[25] No, the shareholder activism in public companies is not a rebellion, but an evolution, affecting other parts of the entire financial ecosystem. It is a result of a change in the dynamic of the public corporation.

Shareholder rights themselves are evolving. The rise of takeover investors, hostile tenders, and proxy battles surely has its good and bad features, but one clear advantage is that core shareholders have realized that they can indeed assert themselves. The reform of the proxy solicitation process, now under debate, is one more symptom that this tide is rising. Let's not forget that many core shareholders' criticisms of corporate managements boil down to assertions of feudalism and lack of aggressive, competitive restructuring of the company. Proposals are being made to revitalize the independent role of boards of directors, bring back outside directors, emphasize board-audit committees, and allow more informal communication among shareholders without cumbersome SEC regulations. John Pound of the Kennedy School of Government at Harvard University has argued that SEC rules governing inside and controlling stockholders prevent shareholder rights:

> The correction is fairly straightforward. . . . Specifically, the rules governing both shareholder communication and the formation of groups must be rolled back significantly, so that investors can communicate, exchange ideas, and join together to bargain informally with management. Such deregulation would be consistent with the true spirit of corporate—and public—democracy. It would provide room for hundreds of new, informal ideas and initiatives to bloom, and for investors to develop true working partnerships between themselves and management. The development of such partnerships, and the initiatives that would be provoked by deregulation would, of course, not always be friendly and devoid of contention; some would doubtless make managements and even some investors uncomfortable. But once again, this is consistent with the essence of the democratic process.[26]

As these mechanisms develop, employee-shareholders will take advantage of them. They are following, not leading the shareholder rights movement. In the last six years the governmental and public attitude toward shareholder activism on behalf of employee benefit plans has changed significantly. A study in 1984 by the Employee Benefit Research Institute showed that some fund managers routinely voted with management, others capitulated to pressure from other clients and customers, and others simply did not vote the shares of the employee benefit plans. In 1984, the Department of Labor Assistant Secretary, responsible for national employee benefit plan policy, Robert A. G. Monks made it crystal clear to institutional shareholders that they had a legal responsibility to take and exercise their shareholder rights:

> In elections, persons who don't vote are making a purely personal decision. When institutional investors don't vote, or vote without paying close attention to the implications of their vote for the ultimate value of their holdings, they are hurting not only themselves but [also the] beneficiaries of the funds they hold in trust. [27]

The Department of Labor has continued this aggressive approach by stating explicitly in several letter rulings that fiduciaries must study the business when they make their decisions and evaluate the economic impact of various management proposals. DOL refined this to note that it does not require trustees to automatically accept a higher tender offer in a tender battle but that trustees are allowed to examine the underlying intrinsic value and the long-term business plan of a company. And if the investment manager does not vote the shares, they must exercise diligence and prudence in monitoring those that do. And who might *those* be? They may, in fact, be the employees of the company where the employee benefit plan is sponsored, if the plan explicitly reserves voting power for them. [28] This means that whether activist shareholder rights are exercised by employee benefit plans—for institutional shareholders and for employee-ownership plans—is no longer a choice for senior management. The federal government's policy on benefit plans in general may make shareholder rights for employee-shareholders a foregone conclusion. The upshot: senior managements are going to have to deal with either large institutional investors as their core shareholders or their employees as their core shareholders or both. Their only other alternative, if they wish to remain public companies, is to attract still passive European investors or Arab sheiks or the Japanese. Interestingly enough, the decline of unions will probably exacerbate employee interest in shareholder rights as they use corporate governance to enhance employee voice.

Entrepreneurial Culture

An estimated zero percent of the Employee Ownership 1000 espouses an entrepreneurial culture, because there is no persuasive evidence of a public company coherently striving toward this culture, although the National Center for Employee Ownership has identified a number of closely held firms that are moving in this direction.

Conclusion

Question: What will be the impact of employee ownership on employee rights?
Answer: I feel like I'm on a game show and ought to say pass.

> —Employee ownership investment banker at a major Wall Street bank

I think that employees' rights are probably equivalent to other shareholder rights and if the securities are properly structured, they will have these rights. The major move in the direction of shareholder rights is institutions. I think employees will be a good balancing force. I do not see employees in public companies organizing ESOP groups, but they all do have voting rights and they will get more communications and proxy statements and know what is going on and have a right to vote. [The compatibility of employee ownership and public shareholder ownership] will depend on how employee shareownership affects the company culture in the next 10 to 15 years. People used to think employee ownership was bad, but in a competitive world where we are competing not only amongst ourselves but with other countries, if people believe more in employee ownership, it will make them feel part of the organization and they will work harder.

—*Paul Mazzilli, Morgan Stanley & Company*

In examining this new trend, ESOP investment banker Adam Blumenthal of American Capital Strategies makes this argument:

The parallel with industrial development seems striking to me. Under early industrial law, workers had no serious employment rights but when management assembled them physically under conditions of mass production this created *de facto* power when they organized. This turned into the union movement. Similarly, under early employee-benefit plan law, workers also had few rights, but their ownership interests are now assembled by management in such a way that their *de facto* power will unavoidably organize.[29]

It is really impossible to predict how all these forces will interact over the coming decade, but shareholder rights will become a new focal point of the employer-employee relationship. Employees will not only play a role as "bankers" and "investors" to public corporations, but as shareholders they will have a "principal-agent" relationship with senior management and the board of directors. This innovation will have far-reaching implications in several areas of economic life. For one thing, the realization will be confusing and puzzling for the trade union movement, which has until now seen employee ownership as a tool mainly in worker buyouts and has comfortably avoided a society-wide policy on the question. That is no longer possible.

We predict all of these trends will generate modest moves by employee-shareholders to be formally recognized as "owners" in public companies. This will trigger the spread of many of the practical options we have mentioned in discussing each type of ownership culture. U.S. employees—rank-and-file and salaried—have no record of seriously challenging senior management or boards in companies except where they believe their economic interests and those of the company are severely threatened. The spread of employee ownership in both public and private corporations has workers subject mainly to adopting the "investor culture approach" or the "feudal approach." Figuring out responsible ways to express "participatory culture" and "shareholder culture" will be a formidable challenge for employees in their own right.

Indeed, the group that is bound to become truly rebellious, and worrisome for management, are core shareholders and institutional investors with whom many managers have no relationship, no ordered means of communication, no history, and no shared place or experience. This is why, after an initial resistance, some senior management and boards may become energetic proponents of employee-ownership "shareholder culture" as are employees themselves. The evidence of specific and general takeover environments involving employee ownership proves conclusively that senior managers and boards *have already decided* that employees are worthy of exercising confidential mirrored-voting rights on major corporate decisions, including tender offers and proxy campaigns.

However, this new situation will place a new responsibility on management's shoulders. They must persuade employee-shareholders that they are honest, competent, and successful for the corporation. They will not always succeed, but, under the circumstances, employees are less likely to want to harm the corporation and exploit the corporation as would break-up takeover raiders and greenmailers. Depending on the facts of each situation, employee shareholders can be expected in the coming years to vote against management in tender offers and proxy contests, to launch tender offers and proxy contests against their own boards and corporate policies, and to form coalitions and communication networks with institutional investors.

We do not expect employee-shareholders to "interfere in day-to-day management," but we do expect some slow-growing support for employee representatives on corporate boards of directors where employee holdings exceed 10 percent. In most companies, these directors will function less like cronies and golf club buddies of management and more like independent directors. At this point we expect corporations to divide into two camps. One camp will contain "feudal-style" managers, who will work mainly to contain employee-shareholders, other public shareholders, and independent directors as much as possible. They will try to dominate the corporation without truly listening to the feedback from these important groups. Another camp will attempt to move the company toward a sophisticated "investor culture," a competitive "participatory culture," or an aggressive, change-oriented "entrepreneurial culture" while recognizing and encouraging certain shareholder rights for employee-holders. All public corporation employee ownership will not be identical; a variety of models—some form of employee investor committee, employee association, employee-shareholder network, company union, or traditional union—will likely emerge.

In some companies these committees and/or board representatives present to senior management and/or the board suggestions on issues that unions have traditionally proposed to management. The decline of unions has not eliminated employee concern over how work is organized, how compensation is organized, how due process and fairness in the workplace is safeguarded, how health and safety are protected, and how employee involvement is developed and strengthened. Shareholder rights will lead to a new form of employee voice. For a decade, employee advocates have argued that national labor law has weakened.

Now, it will be partly replaced by none other than evolving corporate law, which endows employee-shareholders with a different form of influence. Regressive nonunion companies will fight this tooth and nail, terminate employee-ownership holdings left and right, and ignore the concerns and feedback being expressed. Progressive nonunion companies will develop a new format for employee voice and problem solving that will be different from both the company-dominated unions of the 1920s and the adversarial unions.

The two groups we expect to become most confused about this new cast of characters and roles are institutional investors/major outside stockholders/takeover investors, and unions. Institutional and takeover investors defend shareholder rights but sometimes are motivated by narrow, selfish, if not destructive, interests. They will now have to persuade employee-shareholders, who know and understand a great deal about the corporation's business and its short- and long-term prospects, in tender offers and proxy contests. They cannot depend on ventriloquist trustees, as in the past, who either do not vote the shares in employee benefit plans or always vote for management or invariably vote for the higher price and immediate premium. There is already some evidence that these activist shareholders want to dominate corporations themselves in place of managements and boards and do not welcome any role for employee-shareholders. Indeed, some of the noises from these quarters indicate they consider the whole idea of core employee-shareholders illegitimate and always a symptom of "management entrenchment." American employees will start to behave like bankers—that is, careful, judicious, conservative, and brutal in their economic analyses. They will not tolerate institutional investors arrogating to themselves the only right of independent and responsible shareholder activism.

This situation also presents a true watershed for the trade union movement. Please note, this movement will meanwhile be growing and expanding in the public sector, so it will not disappear. Public-sector unionization has increased significantly. How private-sector unions deal with employee ownership will determine their continued existence in the next half century. The total number of workers in public and closely held corporations with significant (more than 4 percent) employee ownership already outnumbers the entire private-sector trade union movement (Table 4 in the Introduction). By the year 2000, workers in companies with more than 10-percent employee ownership will dwarf private-sector union membership. And finally, the central tenet of unions—fixed wage increases—will have contributed much less to real income than would selective long-term investments in—you guessed it—corporate stock (Figure 2.1 and Table 4.2). Some unions will organize feudal culture firms with substantial employee ownership and poor attitudes toward employees. Other unions, like the United Steelworkers of America, which have the largest proportion of members in companies with significant employee ownership, may specialize in employee-ownership representation. They may help nonunion employee associations get started and organized, and use the unions' contacts with employee-ownership legal counsel and investment bankers to guide them toward a responsible shareholder role in their companies. Other unions may use employee ownership as an organizing tactic by cooperating with acquisition corporations and entities that will launch hostile tender offers and proxy battles of public companies and promise democratic employee ownership in the restructured corporation.

Employee ownership is not the only change affecting workplaces and corporations, but it is consistent with a general evolution in the corporate workplace. Employee ownership will probably be the province mainly of nonunion workers.

Notes

1. "Xerox Corp. Says It Plans To Buy Back 11% of Its Stock and Set Up An ESOP," *The Wall Street Journal*, July 11, 1989. Telephone interview with authors occurred in summer of 1990.

2. American Continental: *Forbes*, October 17, 1988, December 26, 1988; *The Wall Street Journal*, July 13, 1989, September 18, 1989. ESOP Association, 1990: 809–839. Summarized from the presentations of Owen Gaffney and Nick Pasquarosa.

3. Perini Corporation Profile, ESOP Association of America, 1987.

4. This estimate is based on counting through the Employee Ownership 1000 and recognizing as the top shareholder any employee benefit plan(s) that (1) the company said was the top shareholder in a recent 13D or 13G filing before the SEC; or (2) owned more than 15 percent of total shares outstanding. For 20 percent of the companies, we had a 13D or 13G statement.

5. This estimate is based on counting through the entire Employee Ownership 1000 and recognizing as a core shareolder—by which we mean one of the top three—any employee benefit plan(s) that (1) the company said was the first, second, or third largest shareholder in a recent 13D or 13G filing; or (2) owned more than 9 percent of the total shares outstanding. For 32 percent of the companies we had a 13D or 13G statement.

6. This estimate is based on a sampling of the Public Employee Ownership Database to see whether there was any record in a press article, a press release, or an SEC filing by a public company, on which we otherwise had information, as having significant employee holdings.

7. See the Introduction.

8. This estimate is based on computing the number of companies who file IRS form 5500 to report their employee benefit plan assets. Searching these forms is a useful way to estimate employee holdings and yields a relatively conservative number, because companies' stock is frequently also owned by employee share-purchase plans and employees directly. These forms of employee ownership are not ERISA plans and do not have to be reported to the IRS. In many firms it is hard for employees to find the real amount

of employee ownership. Employees are unlikely to look in proxies, SEC filings, and so forth, if a company does not discuss its employee holdings with them.

9. This estimate is based on electronically searching all SEC filings by a company as well as our Public Company Employee Ownership Database for such statements in the press or press releases.

10. This is a rough estimate. Many companies have a few quality circles or problem-solving teams in a work site or two. We are not impressed by such sprinkling and consider it insignificant. We agree with many other scholars who believe that the "trendiness" of such innovations makes companies exaggerate what they have and use smaller "attempts" as trophies. We realize that our estimate will be challenged as too low, so we are offering a standard against which it can be judged: a random survey of the Employee Ownership 1000 asking, "About how many of your corporation's employees are currently involved in quality circles or employee participation groups other than quality circles?" If more than 5 percent respond that they have most (61–80%) of their employees in such programs, then our estimates are disproved. (This question is based on the GAO survey mentioned below.) First, in searching our entire database and the files of the National Center for Employee Ownership, we could find evidence that only less than 1 percent of the companies fit this description. Our sources of information must be questioned because they focus mainly on employee ownership, not participation. We then searched for surveys of public companies on the participation issue. A U.S. General Accounting Office study surveyed the Fortune 1000 in 1988 and found that 3 percent of companies had 61 to 100 percent of their employees in quality circles and 6 percent of companies had the same number in employee participation groups other than quality circles. Since the Employee Ownership 1000 includes large and small companies, our estimate assumes that these firms have at least as much, and as little, participation programs as the nonemployee ownership companies. Finally, the U.S. General Accounting Office surveyed over 3000 ESOPs in 1985 on employee involvement. These firms were publicly traded and privately held firms, although the majority of the larger leveraged ESOPs (85%) in this study were privately held companies. Twenty-seven percent of the leveraged ESOPs—which are comparable to our study since they tend to be the higher employee ownership holdings—had some increased formal form of employee involvement although only 46 percent of these involved more responsibility than "making suggestions." One might then estimate that 12 percent of these firms had significant employee involvement. That, however, does not tell us whether most employees were involved. Indeed, the earlier GAO study clearly shows that only a very small number of firms reporting employee involvement indicate that most of their employees participate. In conclusion, none of these studies would suggest that our estimate is unreasonable. See, *Survey of*

Corporate Employee Involvement Efforts (Washington, D.C., U.S. General Accounting Office, 1988): 5 and *Employee Ownership Plans: Benefits and Costs of ESOP Tax Incentives for Broadening Stock Ownership* (Washington, D.C.: U.S. General Accounting Office, December 1986): 4i–43. The best recent research in the general prevalence of participation programs in union and nonunion firms is *Productivity-Enhancing Innovations in Work Organization: Compensation, and Employee Participation in the Union versus the Nonunion Sector,* by Adrienne E. Eaton and Paula B. Voos. (New Brunswick, N.J., Institute of Management and Labor Relations, September 1990) and "The New Human Resource Management in U.S. Workplaces: Is It Really New And Is It Only Nonunion?" by Casey Ichnioski, John Thomas Delaneuy, and David Lewin (New York: Columbia University Graduate School of Business, November 1988).

11. This is a guess, based on impressions from corporate lawyers with whom we have spoken.

12. Information on employee representatives come from the Public Company Employee Ownership Database's news reports and the files of the National Center for Employee Ownership.

13. Our estimates are just that, estimates. We are working with the extensive material we have collected, its strengths and its weaknesses. Nevertheless, discussions with practitioners in the field and a decade of reading local press reports on employee ownership from a national clipping service about companies that do emphasize their employee holdings, strongly support these views. We have been definitive when we can be. Here we are being suggestive, and we welcome more detailed data to support or disprove this estimate.

14. PR Newswire August 27, 1988.

15. *The Wall Street Journal,* December 22, 1985: PR Newswire August 27, 1986, October 21, 1987; interviews with former officers of the bank and local real estate lawyers; *Corporate Takeover Defenses,* compiled under the direction of Virginia K. Rosenbaum (Washington, D.C.: Investor Responsibility Research Center): 292. This annual report on takeover defenses is the most up-to-date treatment of the subject.

16. Personal communication, July 1990.

17. Personal communication, September 1990.

18. See the Introduction.

19. Personal communication, July–August 1990.

20. The research for these conclusions is based on mostly privately held companies with employee ownership and two key studies, one by the GAO, 1986; the other by Karen Young, *Beyond Taxes: Managing An Employee Ownership Company* (Oakland, Calif.: National Center for Employee Ownership, 1987). See also, the following National Center for Employee Ownership studies: *Employee Participation Programs in Employee Ownership Companies* and *Corporate Performance and Employee Ownership.*

21. We purposely chose the word *improve*. As we pointed out, one-time productivity increases can accrue from restructuring levels of management, staffing, and the organization of work.
22. *The Wall Street Journal,* January 10, 1989.
23. See Blasi, 1988: 212–216.
24. The three main chapters developing this point of view are Chapter 5, "The Law and Employee Rights," Chapter 6, "The Responsibilities of Capitalism," and Chapter 7, "Labor-Management Cooperation"; see Gerald E. Frug, *Harvard Law Review* 97, no. 6 (April 1984): 1277–1388. The best up-to-date review of these criticisms and analyses are the papers delivered at the "Conference on the Fiduciary Responsibilities of Institutional Investors" cosponsored by the Salomon Brothers Center at the New York University Stern School of Business and the Rutgers University Graduate School of Management.
25. Weirton: *The Wall Street Journal,* March 7, 1989, October 6, 1989, January 4, 1990.
26. *Rearming Corporate Governance: Deregulation, Not More Regulation,* by John Pound (Cambridge, Mass.: Harvard University Kennedy School of Government, 1990).
27. Martin, Brousseau, O'Connell, 1990.
28. The materials that follow contain documents of the shareholder rebellion. It is quite remarkable that such an important economic policy is contained in the nooks and crannies of DOL rulings and side letters here and there, but that is in fact the case. See page 3, How The Shareholder Proposal Is Influencing Corporate Structure, by David Martin, Partner, Hogan and Hartson (Washington, D.C.), John D. Brousseau, Special Counsel, Office of the Chief Counsel, Division of Corporate Finance, Securities and Exchange Commission, and Philip R. O'Connell, Senior Vice President, Champion International Corporation, for the Monks' quote. Mr. Monks is now head of Institutional Shareholder Services. See also, "Fulfilling Your Fiduciary Responsibilities," by Neil Minow, General Counsel, Institutional Shareholder Services, pp. 2–4. This paper is contained in the materials of the "Corporate Governance & Proxy Voting Conference," September 10 and 11, 1990. The entire collection of papers in the workshop book reviews these issues in full detail and is available from the Institute of International Research, 437 Madison Avenue, 23rd floor, New York, N.Y. 10022 (212-826-3340). In a February 23, 1988, letter to Avon Corp., DOL stated that "the decision as to how proxies are to be voted . . . are fiduciary acts of plan asset management." See also, Letter, Division of Corporate Finance, SEC, to Rio Grande Industries Inc., April 9, 1989; Letter, U.S. Department of Labor, Pension and Welfare Benefits Administration, to Robert A. G. Monks, January 23, 1990. Copies of these and other letters are available in the workshop book.
29. Personal communication, September 1990.

Conclusion

Where Is Employee Ownership Headed?

Employee ownership will play a decisive role in the future of the public corporation. Since 1974 the number of public corporations where the company's employees are the largest stockholder has grown by almost fifty times to almost 15 percent of all companies. The Employee Ownership 1000—the top 1000 by amount of employee ownership on all stock exchanges—now includes almost a third of the Fortune 500 Industrials and a fifth of the Fortune Service 500. It also encompasses many medium-sized corporations and a wide variety of smaller companies whose stock is traded Over The Counter. Firms with significant employee ownership account for almost a third of the market value and sales of all public companies and a fifth of the employment. The Employee Ownership Units of the top Wall Street investment banks have played a major role in this transformation led by Goldman, Sachs & Co., First Boston, and Morgan Stanley (in that order), which account for over 60 percent of the market share of publicly announced ESOP transactions since 1988 with roughly comparable proportions. To a lesser extent, J. P. Morgan, Salomon Brothers, Chemical Bank, Manufacturers Hanover, Merrill Lynch, Lehman Brothers, and Bankers Trust are involved. In 1990, Morgan Stanley eased ahead of Goldman Sachs and became the top ESOP advisor on leveraged ESOPs, convertible preferred ESOPs, and public financing of ESOP transactions.[1] The New Owners are typified by the size of their stake and its importance to the company. The average holding is about 12.2 percent and employees are the top shareholder in almost half of the Employee Ownership 1000.

Employee ownership will continue to grow. It has become a strategic imperative for public corporations. In a recent survey of Chief Financial Officers, *Business Week* found that companies are turning to employee-ownership plans as a prime source of patient capital and as a way to control benefit costs. Most CFO's said that employee ownership is likely to grow in the next five years.[2] By the year 2000, conservative projections would suggest that more than a quarter of all public corporations will be more than 15 percent owned by their employees, and a quarter of private-sector employees will be in such companies. As pension funds and other institutional investors expand their role, as both top shareholders in public corporations and a central force in the entire stock market, we expect employee-investors and institutional investors will increasingly see eye-to-eye about getting their justly deserved rights as shareholders.

Why Will Employee Ownership Continue to Grow?

The future of employee ownership on the corporate scene is generally assured because both the tools and the need are expected to expand. Companies can increase employee ownership through five distinct tools: (1) by using the assets of existing employee benefit plans to buy stock; (2) by setting up company-sponsored ESOPs, which borrow money to purchase the stock; (3) by encouraging employees to purchase stock with their own contributions to 401(k) and other thrift-based benefit plans; (4) by creating employee share-purchase programs, which encourage employees to buy stock directly on favorable terms underwritten by the corporation; and (5) by including greater numbers of employees in stock-option plans. Companies will thus be able to plan an "employee-ownership strategy" despite the general lending environment, the credit rating, and debt-to-equity ratio of any particular company. We have shown that about 50 percent of the Employee Ownership 1000's employee-held assets come from leveraged ESOPs while another half come from nonleveraged employee benefit plans or stock-purchase programs. Probably the pivotal engine propelling employee ownership in 401(k), profit sharing, and savings plans is that a corporation can easily amend *any* defined-contribution plan so that the plan can hold a substantial portion of its assets in company stock. Without such an amendment, ERISA usually limits employee ownership to 10 percent of a plan's assets. Investment bankers, compensation consultants, lawyers, accountants, managers, and workers themselves can be expected to come up with an array of new ideas and innovations for establishing and continuing employee ownership.

Corporations will continue to need the flexibility and patient capital that employee ownership offers. Stock buybacks, cashing out large holders, selling new shares, going private and going public, spinning-off units and restructurings, recapitalizations, and bankruptcies will continue to present many individual public companies with unique circumstances and challenges where employee ownership will often make good sense as a corporate finance option and as an employee benefit.

Partly as a response to the volatile takeover market of the eighties, many public corporations have been restructured as coalitions of employee-shareholders and public shareholders. Employee ownership is the hottest new approach to takeover threats, and it is being quietly introduced to many companies. Some corporations are seeking patient employee capital that will take long-term interests of the company into account in future takeover and proxy battles, while other corporate leaders may see this employee ownership as assured takeover protection. Other corporations view employee ownership as a way to create an "ownership" corporate culture or a more responsive form of corporate governance. No matter what the scenario, employee ownership has changed the rules of the takeover game forever. But corporations cannot always presume "their" employee-shareholders will side with them on all issues.

We expect employee ownership to become a potent force in mergers and acquisitions. More takeover investors will offer to establish significant employee-ownership plans after buying out the current employee holdings at a premium, as a way of winning employee support in a contest as T. Boone Pickens tried with the employees of Phillips Petroleum and as Shamrock Corporation hinted with Polaroid's employees. Robert M. Bass made the same offer to the employees of Macmillan Inc. Firms with significant employee ownership will merge, keeping the employee holdings intact, as recently happened with Avery International and Dennison Manufacturing. We expect to see a cottage industry in arranging such mergers, which may also function as takeover defenses. This was the case in the 1987 merger of Holly Sugar and Imperial Sugar. Finally, the unsuccessful acquisition of United Airlines by its unions will likely lead to further acquisition attempts by both union and nonunion employee groups, although such groups can be expected to team up with white knights with deep pockets next time around.

Competitive pressures will continue to intensify and companies will respond with multiple approaches to restructure wages and benefits. The new approach to benefits will be twofold: to tie company benefits to company performance and to structure benefits to minimize cost and increase the short-term cash flow of the corporation. We expect trading stock for wages, which started in unionized firms, will become commonplace in nonunion companies. Employee-ownership pension plans will be increasingly used to replace more expensive defined-benefit plans and deferred profit-sharing plans, and perhaps to fund retirement health benefits. The 401(k) plan with generous company matches in employee-held stock will probably become the dominant employee retirement plan. More and more companies will structure these and other defined-contribution plans, so that they invest mainly in the company's own stock. Now that a number of specific ways to restructure fixed wages and benefits have been quietly tried and understood, we expect more companies to follow the lead of the trailblazers mentioned in this book and use several approaches simultaneously to completely transform the whole idea and structure of "the wage" and "the benefit." The rigid fixed wage and benefit system will fall into permanent decline.

Notwithstanding all these trends, employee ownership will present corporate boards and senior managers, employees, and shareholders with some profound dilemmas.

The First Dilemma: Power and Corporate Governance

At the dawn of the corporate system, ownership was one reason why investors exercised board-level control in corporations. Their exclusion from ownership has been a key reason why employee board representation has made little sense to American observers of the corporate scene. As America's corporations became widely held by many individual shareholders, corporate managers began to handpick their own boards who served as "trustees" for shareholders. Accusations of abuse of corporate power and the fox guarding the chicken coop have increased under this system. Now, employee-investors and institutional investors in many corporations have fewer reasons to be convinced that handpicked corporate boards any longer serve their interests and they will question this Trusteeship model.

While employees are the top shareholder in almost half of the Employee Ownership 1000, they have nonmanagerial board representation in only four public corporations! If capitalism has any meaning, this ownership deserves representation rights, and the corporate elite is going to have to stop the double standard. We expect some core investors will challenge corporate leaders to practice the capitalism they preach. The main issue will be for employees to first figure out that they are core investors and then decide that it matters to them. In many companies the "employee ownership" is really a passive investment option and both management and employees are truly committed to a Trusteeship point of view. But once employees understand the concept of dilution, they will see that they actually pay for their employee ownership in many companies. It is not a gift, and management can no longer continue to use the myth that it is "free" in order to justify stripping them of shareholder rights.

What can we look forward to in the Employee Ownership 1000? Once employees in most of these companies realize that they hold often decisive judgment about whether management will win or lose a takeover or a proxy fight, we expect some will become more involved in knowing what is really happening in their company. We also expect that senior managements that wish to encourage an "ownership" culture will follow the lead of Polaroid Corporation and others and initiate employee board representation. In companies where the "employee ownership" is just a front for management entrenchment, the raising of this issue will lead to severe conflict and perhaps a move by management to quickly undo employee-ownership plans. One can also expect some unique court battles and standoffs between managements and employees.

The Second Dilemma: Risk and Wealth

> *With their benefits tied up in company stock, employees are victims of the swings of the market. Since the market can go either way, enormous risk may be involved, but the payoff can also be better than simple wages.*
>
> —*Shane Williams*

In more and more companies, employee ownership will become far more than another little program. In these firms a large percentage of wages and/or a major portion of the retirement benefit will be tied up in company stock. We believe that this restructuring of wages and benefits will lead more employees and managers to seek board representation for employee-shareholders. Where the employee ownership involves a critical risk, employees will simply develop a rational self-interest in having informed representatives other than their supervising managers be present to protect their investment. This concern will be enhanced because employees will be fully aware that, unlike defined-benefit pension plans, which are insured by the U.S. Pension Benefit Guarantee Corporation, most employee-ownership plans do not have a safety net. But there will also be a positive motivation. Because stock has the potential of real appreciation far beyond the real value of fixed wage increases, employees will rightfully see their "employee-ownership estate" as their chance to get rich. Once educated, many employees will not be keen to turn away and check back in twenty years!

Excessive and unreasonable risk is the main abuse of bad employee owner-ship. The problem for employees of public corporations is that the worst risk often takes place at the moment of the least knowledge: when a transaction begins. As the decision-makers of the corporation, management can initiate any number of employee-ownership transactions without the knowledge of most nonunion workforces. Employees need to find ways to be informed at the begin-ning *and* during the unfolding story of employee ownership. We believe that the practice of providing the trustee of the employee benefit plan or ESOP employ-ees with independent legal and financial advice before a major transaction is the first step. Later, we recommend that each company have an employee-ownership information effort run by an advisory committee representing a cross-section of employees along with formal board representation.

The employee-ownership world will be an uncomfortable world for many managers and workers because their fortunes will be tied together more obvi-ously. U.S. companies will no longer be purely dominant in their markets and able to pass regular fixed wage and benefit increases onto consumers in high prices. It is a world where only value that gets created gets shared. Employees who do not wish to will have to worry about the condition and operations of the company in more detail, and managers who prefer not to do it, will have to spend more time speaking with and sharing responsibility with employees. Long-held attitudes and ways of behaving for both managers and workers will come under stress.

Nevertheless, we believe that the fixed wage and benefit system has really not served either the American worker or the American corporation as well as we might think. Real wages have stood still or gone up very little since 1970 while the average real rate of return on stocks has been 8.8 percent from 1926 to 1985. Most fixed wage and benefit increases won by workers were eaten away by inflation, but in the same period employee stock ownership investments in many companies would have appreciated significantly! Yes, competitive pres-sures are forcing companies to restructure their compensation systems for the benefit of the company. But we are arguing, in addition, that a way needs to be found to allow workers to share in the significant advantages of capital and stock appreciation, so that they can both contribute more to corporations and increase their personal wealth. Thus, we expect workers to demand employee ownership as they watch automatic annual wage increases moderate and lose their inflation-adjusted value.

Employee ownership might also change the wage system in the direction of Martin Weitzman's ideas in *The Share Economy*.[3] To the extent that employee ownership represents a sharing of profits with employees and substitutes for other wages and benefits, which is often the case, when a firm is hit with bad times, the cost per worker of employing labor will go down (since dividends and stock value are part of pay), and the firm should then lay off fewer workers than a comparable firm. Employment may be more stable in employee-held firms if the cost per worker varies with firm performance.

The transformation of the fixed wage and benefit system will not be easy or clear-cut, because there are really three distinct worlds of public company employee ownership. Replacing the fixed wage and benefit system with a large proportion of employee ownership makes sense only where a reasonable chance of a bigger returns exists. The problem: How do workers tell the difference? We see the risk of employee ownership interacting differently with the push for ownership rights in each of the three worlds. This is traditional in capitalist securities markets, where greater risk and higher potential return has generally meant greater rights.

The First World of Employee Ownership includes most of America's leading corporations where credit ratings are excellent, dividends are strong, stock appreciation has been regular, and the company has both the strength and the ability to weather some bad times. Many of the large ESOPs we read about in the *Wall Street Journal* are in such companies and they will give employee ownership a good name. Employees are often overjoyed at the employee-ownership announcement in these firms. Successful business as usual may encourage management and employees into viewing the employee holdings mainly as a passive investment. The stock price and dividend performance itself serves as the energizer for employee ownership. Interest in employee involvement programs may be very low. Where present, it may have more to do with improving quality and winning the Malcolm Baldridge Award than with the employee-ownership idea. Risk may be low, especially if the company guarantees a minimum floor value of the stock, and reward may be high. The better firms will combine employee ownership with an employee involvement culture.

The Second World of Employee Ownership is the struggling companies in transition. Sometimes the adoption of significant employee ownership happens when a company moves from the First to the Second World and both fears a takeover and tries to control costs. These firms, which have had excellent periods, are not usually failing, but they are under enormous competitive pressure and often face a series of special crises that must be rapidly overcome. More often than not, employee ownership is a mixed bag, frequently accompanied by layoffs, cost cutting, and an extensive restructuring of a once easy and generous wage and benefit program. Employees pay dearly for employee ownership because management is defensive about accusations that the plan caused dilution and was not shareholder neutral. In these firms, management can either lead toward an "ownership culture" or sit back and allow a cynicism toward ownership that makes workers feel like victims. If employees can be involved in turning the company around, the employee ownership can be used as a glue to hold everyone together and energize an employee involvement program, which will help solve business problems and increase productivity. We expect that board representation will interest both workers and managers in this type of company. Unfortunately, these companies usually give lip service to employee ownership, and the concept is merged in people's minds with everything they dislike about the company and its situation.

The Third World of Employee Ownership are firms in a high-risk situation, facing an opportunity of impending success or a real chance of economic disaster. They may be very new or very small or may be emerging from or going into bankruptcy. These companies have poor credit, high debt, irregular earnings, and no history of regular stock appreciation. Payrolls and benefits are tight. Some of these firms are NYSE, AMEX, or NASDAQ companies, but we suspect that many of them are small Over-The-Counter corporations whose stock is irregularly traded on "pink slips." Some of these firms have been, or are on the brink of being, delisted by the Exchanges for a variety of reasons. They may miss their SEC filings. A very large proportion of employees' entire retirement estate may be invested in company stock. These companies are almost always nonunion. If this firm becomes a great success, employees may truly strike it rich, but they could represent disaster for employees as the employee-owners of the S&Ls City Federal Financial and Lincoln Savings & Loan—along with those from the recent debacle at the Bank of New England—discovered with their paternalistic and risky employee-ownership adventures (p. 211 and p. 218). These firms usually need the financial flexibility of employee ownership the most, but this ownership creates the greatest risk often under conditions of the least knowledge and responsible involvement by employees. We expect that efforts at employee involvement programs, board representation, and employee-ownership communications will cause the most tension, yet yield the greatest payoffs in such firms. When a corporation is on the skids, however, employees and trustees of benefit plans should rush to see whether they have significant employee ownership. We have recently compared the Employee Ownership 1000 List with the Thompson Bankwatch and Standard & Poors List of risky banks and S&Ls, and we were distressed to find some potential problems. The question of risk raises broader issues.

In response to some of these difficulties, Adam Chinn of the New York law firm Wachtell, Lipton, Rosen & Katz has written a useful guide to the special problems and liabilities that may face companies owned by, or with substantial, ESOPs. It reviews the role of ESOPs in workout situations. Several other firms have become involved in class-action suits by employees where arguments arose over the doers of leveraged-buyout deals of the eighties and employee-holders of company stock, including Hill, Parker, Franklin, Cardwell, and Jones, and

J. C. Nickens and Associates of Houston, Texas. Members of the Amalgamated Clothing and Textile Workers union are now involved in a class-action suit with the Cone Mills Corp. The Office of Fiduciary Litigation of the U.S. Department of Labor Pension Welfare Benefits Administration is also involved in several cases.[4]

The Third Dilemma: Sharing the Bed with Public Shareholders

Will employee-shareholders and public shareholders love or hate each other? The real problem is that the belief that public shareholders can quickly and accurately determine the amount of employee ownership—which may have a significant bearing on takeover battles, proxy fights, dilution, and corporate policies—in an "efficient public market" seems to be pure fiction in many companies. We do not understand why a company with three separate employee-ownership plans, each owning 4 percent of its stock, does not have to reveal this top 12 percent holder to the public in a way that is conveniently accessible. The tremendous disagreement between public sources on the amount of employee ownership prevalent in companies is a critical issue. It is also magnified by the fact that many companies encourage direct stock ownership through stock-purchase programs, stock grants, or options, whose total employee ownership stake does not *have* to be reported (pp. 302–306 reviews this problem).

The main barrier to responsible employee ownership is that many public shareholders, institutional investors, *and employees* are usually in the dark about just how much employee ownership a company really has. Many CEOs of public corporations quickly and helpfully responded to letters we sent to 750 of the Fortune 1000 companies in January 1991 on which we had no information. We were astounded, however, that a large proportion of the companies ignored the letters and some were very uncooperative when we tried to make telephone contact. Of the over twenty databases we used to track employee ownership, we were also shocked that information on significant employee ownership was simply unavailable on many corporations in most databases. This was most serious when corporate proxies, SEC filings, and employee benefit plan reports to the IRS ignored the information. Finally, many companies encourage employee ownership through employee share-purchase plans. While shareholders usually approve such plans which are reported in SEC filings, companies do not have to report to anyone how much employee ownership they create because they are not ERISA benefit plans. Thus, there is a whole hidden layer of employee ownership. Some companies believe it is an invasion of privacy to track how much stock their employees purchase. But the impact on shareholder openness can be seen. One of the largest companies in the United States reported to us that their benefit plans owned about 2 percent of their stock while a senior executive told us that actual employee ownership through stock purchase plans and direct purchases by employees amounted to over 20 percent!

The explosion of enormous amounts of employee ownership in many forms will mean that management and public shareholders and financial analysts will scrutinize these transactions for signs of dilution. (See p. 37.) Transactions that fell through the cracks a few years ago will now create visible conflict. Investment bankers who can carefully analyze and manage the dilution problem will be more frequently used. We expect that employee-ownership transactions will be regularly combined with accurate statements of the tax benefits, wage and benefit restructuring, restructuring and productivity improvement programs, and evaluations of the compensation packages of comparable corporations, so that senior management can demonstrate that employees are paying for employee ownership. Finally, the Investor Responsibility Research Center reports that

> current SEC and stock exchange regulations do not require shareholder approval for the creation or addition of stock to an Employee Stock Ownership Plan. The 1990 voting survey asked institutions whether they think the creation of an ESOP should be subject to shareholder approval. Overall, 86 percent of the survey respondents said that ESOPs should be put to a shareholder vote. Of the pension funds responding, 95 percent of the public pension funds and 67 percent of the private pension funds said that ESOPs should be subject to shareholder approval. Eighty-three percent of universities and foundations indicated support for an ESOP vote, and 86 percent of investment managers said they would back the requirement. [5]

In corporations where the disclosure and the dilution problems are managed, we predict a novel turn of events. Institutional shareholders will support and recommend proposals for board representation for employee-holders as a group to make corporate governance more responsible and less entrenched. Advisory committees of employee-holders will begin meeting with institutional shareholders and even takeover investors. We expect to see novel coalitions of institutional shareholders and employee-shareholders, such as mutual funds that invest only in firms with significant employee ownership and receive capital only from employee-ownership plans. Through such funds, employees can both diversify their investments and expand their capital involvement in their company. We expect that soon someone will propose to a mutual fund company, like Fidelity or Vanguard, that they establish Employee-Ownership Funds for investors who wish to be involved in such firms.

Employee groups will demand more voice and input as employee-owners as they realize the tremendous, often decisive power they hold to effect the outcome of takeover battles and proxy contests. It is not inconceivable that irresponsible and dictatorial management teams will be driven from power by institutional shareholder-employee shareholder coalitions. Remember, this is how former UAL Chairman Richard Ferris lost his job when United's unions and potential employee-owners teamed up with institutional shareholders. In short, the Employee Ownership 1000 will serve as yet another force in the mounting activism in corporate governance, which is being escalated by both institutional investors and core shareholders.

The Fourth Dilemma: Increased Productivity and Employee Empowerment

Will significant employee ownership improve profits and productivity in public corporations? The answer is yes, if it is done right. All the studies point toward one simple formula: shower employees with information as owners; teach them how to make sense of this new knowledge; create an "ownership culture," using practices, rituals, and symbols unique to your company; and establish a wide-ranging employee involvement program that brings employees, managers, and members of different departments together in problem-solving teams that work on the firm's knottiest problems in productivity, quality, and profit. In short, make your company do what Malcolm Baldridge Award winners do. It is important to distinguish between this kind of practical involvement and empowerment and board-level representation for employees. Board representation may be important as a shareholder right, and employee board representatives may offer perspectives and information that help the company work as a more effective team, but board representation is unlikely to have the same effect on economic performance as employee involvement and quality improvement programs have.

Few public corporations have engaged the full potential of employee ownership. Significant employee ownership creates a partnership and an identification between employees and the company. It is a long-term way to share the wealth that comes from successful corporate performance. When it is used without opportunities for practical employee involvement, employee ownership is simply a way to make employees investors. It is important that companies not exaggerate the impact of this stake as many do: investors have a share and are passively waiting for a return. We expect that employees with significant ownership stakes and other investors will begin pressing management to let employee ownership make a difference through employee empowerment.

The way this issue unfolds may determine what labor-management relations looks like in the next century. Already, workers in companies with significant employee ownership are mostly nonunion and outnumber workers in the total private-sector trade union movement! By the year 2000, workers in companies more than 10 percent employee-held will dwarf the entire membership of the trade union movement. Thus, no matter how it develops the new labor-management system will have a substantial employee-ownership sector. Workers in companies that remain nonunion may decide that their dominant ownership gives them a mechanism to get involved in corporate governance to represent their interests as both employees and shareholders.

We expect a new form of employee-shareholder representation to emerge in many nonunion companies that will include board representation, employee advisory committees, employee involvement programs, independent legal and financial advisors to employee ownership trustees, and perhaps employee associations with officers who meet regularly with management. The same pattern is emerging in some unionized companies. Nonunion Polaroid Corporation and union Weirton Steel Corporation and Northwestern Steel and Wire Co. are important harbingers of where this is going.

One possibility is that unions will stay committed to the fixed wage system, which garners wage increases, but not real income increases, as another form of worker representation evolves; unions may become an anachronism as the best economic returns for workers become available in the employee-ownership sector. Unions may decide to make employee ownership part of their program for both economic gains and expanded worker rights in companies by aggressively bargaining a variety of employee-ownership features into contracts and then by systematically establishing many aspects of employee-shareholder representation.

At the extremes, we expect some nasty conflicts. In the end, a variety of mechanisms for a worker voice will emerge in America. There will be a fight in the trade union movement over how to respond to the influence of the employee-ownership sector. Some nonunion employee groups will encounter severe conflicts in attempting to implement employee-shareholder representation and will be forced to set up unions. Unions will court employee groups in firms with feudal managers. But where senior managers and supervisors are open to employee empowerment, they will actually strengthen the nonunion employee-ownership sector.

The Fifth Dilemma: What Will the Government Do?

The sheer extent and depth of employee ownership we have discovered and its potentially crucial role in leading corporations, stock markets, takeovers, retirement security, corporate governance, labor-management relations, and the economy as a whole, merit a more comprehensive examination by federal and state governments. Following is our laundry list of the most sensible actions the government can take and the evidence supporting these moves.

First, there should be no further cuts in ESOP tax incentives. ESOP tax incentives create a loss of revenues for the federal government of approximately $800 million annually,[6] and the incentives were cut back to the bone in 1989. They have been a decisive factor in creating an employee-ownership sector in the U.S. economy. Our study indicates that any cut in the ability of corporations to deduct principal payments that serve as contributions to leveraged ESOPs and/or dividend payments to employees in leveraged ESOPs would gut the employee-ownership trend in the United States. Make no mistake about it, such a move in Congress would be a vote for the concentration of wealth and an act against salaried and rank-and-file workers and lower-level managers. The main reason against cuts is that they would represent a policy decision by the U.S. Government to eliminate employee ownership from the corporate economy at the time when citizens are most concerned about shrinking real wages, tighter benefit programs, and inequalities in the distribution of wealth. Also, given the decline in defined-benefit pension plans and the cost of other forms of employee benefits, employee ownership with proper tax incentives has now become an important and necessary form of retirement security. It now must be seen as integral to the retirement security policy of the nation. Stop it and you take away benefits.

Second, tax incentives for non-ESOP forms of employee ownership should be expanded. We now know these plans represent about half of national employee ownership. Because they are not dependent on leverage, they should be a meaningful part of any national policy. We recommend that companies that establish employee share-purchase programs, which include all employees and provide a greater than 10 percent discount on the stock purchase price, be allowed to exclude three times the discount from taxable income. Also, there should be more extensive tax incentives for stock ownership plans, such as the Pepsi and Dupont stock-option plans. This expansion would allow the government to radically increase the amount of employee ownership in the economy and bring more and more citizens into capital ownership through relatively inexpensive tax incentives.

Third, ESOP tax incentives should be expanded significantly to improve both the quantity and quality of employee ownership. The two most serious problems about making employee ownership an ongoing part of the U.S. labor-management system are the exclusion of many workers from employee-ownership plans and the temporariness of employee ownership. Unionized employees are regularly excluded from such plans, and we estimate that only 4.3 million of the 8.6 million employees in public corporations are actually members of the employee-ownership plans. And employee-ownership leader, Robert Beyster, Chairman of Science Application International Corporation of LaJolla, California, fears that once most leveraged ESOPs, established in the late eighties, allocate their stock to employees, old employees will simply sell their stock and new employees will have no way to get involved. We believe that corporations should get special added ESOP tax incentives for implementing high-quality employee-ownership plans that would have the following characteristics: (1) all full-time employees would be included; (2) successor employee-ownership plans would maintain at least 20 percent employee ownership at all times; (3) employees would receive board representation proportional to the stake; (4) the company would establish a broad-based advisory task force of employees to develop a written plan and budget for employee involvement, and the budget of this plan would be equal to at least 10 percent of the ESOP tax benefit.[7]

The Sixth Dilemma: Changing the Concentration of Wealth

Despite the fact that employee ownership has grown enormously and brought opportunity for greater real wealth appreciation to millions of employees who have been stuck in the fixed wage system, employee ownership has still not significantly changed the concentration of wealth in the United States. Total employee-held assets in public and closely held corporations now constitute only 3 percent of the value of all corporate stock.[8] At first glance, the common response is that 60 percent of all corporate stock is owned by households, so mom and pop still own America (see Stock Ownership Patterns, Table 1.1). But that is wrong. Ninety percent of the stock owned by households is owned by the richest 10 percent of households and 60 percent is owned by the richest 1 percent of households, according to the Joint Economic Committee of Congress.[9] This widespread exclusion of the population from the capitalist system is nothing short of feudalism, and it threatens to turn American capitalism into a cruel hoax. Wage serfdom would not be so bad for most Americans, if real wages were not standing still as the real returns to capital bound forward. Republican political strategist Kevin Phillips says that this concentration of wealth will provoke a watershed change in American politics.[10] Phillips's evidence suggests that the inequality is growing—not declining—and is more pronounced in the United States than in other countries, especially in the gap between what executives and other employees are paid in this country.

Many of the elite that control the U.S. Congress and the Executive Branch have shown themselves to be completely derelict in confronting the concentration of wealth, even though the figures have been put before them year after year for most of this century. The time has come for an organized public confrontation with entrenched politicians who just do not care about this issue. It is time for the creation of a national Campaign for Economic Democracy with broad-based support from many groups and parties based around one simple question: Are you in favor of modest changes in federal law to make widespread employee ownership a reality for most Americans in the near future?

We can now say definitively that employee ownership can serve as an efficient and practical mechanism to expand the involvement of a large percentage of the working population in the capitalist system. We have presented extensive evidence that Corporate America can fit employee ownership into its agenda; in fact, corporations can potentially improve their competitiveness and their compensation systems with the addition of employee ownership. We think that modest ESOP and non-ESOP tax incentives for employee ownership could be immediately expanded, with a goal of achieving 25 percent employee ownership of the entire corporate system by the year 2000. The ownership would be paid for by exchanges with other forms of compensation, tax incentives, and potential productivity increases. The approach is twofold: first, the central insight of Louis Kelso—figuring out ways for companies to use credit to purchase stock for workers; and, second, encouraging workers to invest very modest amounts of fixed wages in stock in worthy companies while continuing to encourage the responsible investment of employee benefit plan assets in company stock. The goal cannot be complete employee ownership of corporations, because a vibrant competitive capitalism requires flexible access of these companies to equity and bond markets and the pressure of investors on corporate managers. Most public corporations will probably find that 15 to 40 percent employee ownership is optimal, although such tax incentives would likely lead to majority employee ownership in many closely held companies.

The emergence of the Employee Ownership 1000 in the United States has huge implications for the debate about the economic structure of the Soviet Union, Eastern Europe, and other nations that will seek ways to combine capitalism with economic justice and democracy. The U.S. experience has proven that a flagship corporate sector with significant employee ownership is a realistic possibility. Each country is different, but in general the American experience suggests that extensive and secure employee ownership requires orderly stock markets with public disclosure, innovative investment bankers and consultants, and strong government support through tax incentives that (1) reward corporations for using credit to buy company stock for workers in large blocks; (2) allow employee benefit plans to invest in company stock over the long term; (3) encourage stock-purchase plans for small personal investments of modest amounts of worker wages; and (4) mandate that corporations must include all employees in the employee ownership and give them real shareholder rights in order to get the tax incentives.

If the United States succeeds in expanding employee ownership of the American capitalist system deeply and quickly—and it can succeed with minor adjustments made at little cost—then it will have a major impact on how capitalism is regarded around the world, yielding powerful implications for foreign policy.[11] If American corporations and workers succeed in combining employee ownership with more activism in corporate governance and greater employee involvement in improving company performance, they will surely create the seeds of a new model of labor-management relations and capitalist production. It would be a departure from imperial capitalism, which has been marked by relations between workers and managers and corporations and shareholders that can only be called feudal. It would be entrepreneurial capitalism, capitalism with a human face.

Notes

1. We asked each of the major investment banks to rank themselves and their competitors according to their market share of ESOP Advisory assignments since 1988. Our ranking is a summary of the data provided to us.
2. *Business Week,* October 22, 1990: 100. The survey was done by New York-based consulting firm A.T. Kearney Inc. Fifty percent of the 60 companies covered by this portion of the survey had an ESOP with an average 7.9 percent of equity. This suggests that we have uncovered far more employee ownership than commonly believed to exist.
3. Cambridge, Mass.: Harvard University Press, 1984.
4. See Adam D. Chinn, *ESOPs in Trouble* (NY: Wachtell, Lipton, Rosen & Katz, 1991). Hill, Parker, and Nickens represented the employees of Rexene Inc. in a class-action suit against the company, which was settled out of court. Regarding Cone Mills, see "Lawsuit Sparks Tension at Cone,"

Greensboro News & Record, December 11, 1989, and "Workers File Suit over ESOP," *Pension and Investments,* November 12, 1990, p. 13.

5. "Voting by Institutional Investors," on *Corporate Governance Issues on The 1990 Proxy Season,* by Jeffrey W. Biersach (Washington, D.C.: Investor Responsibility Research Center, Corporate Governance Service, October, 1990.)

6. This is an estimate for 1990, based on computations from the ESOP Association in Washington, D.C. It does not include tax incentives available in ESOPs that would be available through other employee benefit plans under ERISA. If a firm did not implement an ESOP, it could get comparable tax deductions for creating other types of employee benefits.

7. Examples of added incentives would be: (1) the ability to deduct contributions for all employee benefit plans (including ESOPs) above existing limits; (2) the ability to allocate above the existing limits in stock value to employees' accounts annually; (3) the ability of the firm's lender to deduct interest on a loan to an employee-ownership plan and pass on the savings in lower than prime interest rates if the firm is more than 15 percent employee held, rather than the 50 percent now required; (4) the ability to deduct 120 percent of dividends paid on employee-ownership stock; and (5) the ability to exempt from the excise tax for recovering excess pension assets on those assets transferred to an ESOP.

8. This estimate was arrived at by adding the total market value of the Employee Ownership 1000 (about $100 billion for these public corporations) to the National Center for Employee Ownership's estimate of the total market value of all closely held employee ownership, more than 4 percent ($30 billion). This $120 billion is the total employee-ownership market value for the economy and is 3 percent of the total value of all public and closely held corporate stock estimated by the Federal Reserve to be $4.339 trillion for the second quarter of 1990. Please note, these estimates do not include employee-ownership market value for employee holdings of less than 4 percent in public and closely held companies. For public corporations, this amount may be significant, but we are unable to estimate it at this time.

9. *Concentration of Wealth in the United States.* (Washington, D.C.: Joint Economic Committee of Congress, July 1986). We use revised estimates that corrected an earlier error. Reproduced in Blasi, 1988: 109, Table 4.4.

10. Kevin Phillips, *The Politics of Rich and Poor* (New York: Random House, 1990).

11. A Presidential Task Force established by Ronald Reagan explored this issue in *High Road to Economic Justice: U.S. Encouragement of Employee Stock Ownership in Central America and the Caribbean* (Washington, D.C.: CESJ- Center for Economic and Social Justice, October 1986). Contact Norman Kurland at the Center for more information. CESJ, the National Center for Employee Ownership in Oakland, California, and the ESOP Association in Washington, D.C. monitor efforts of countries to institute employee ownership. Contact Margaret Lund at 415-272-9461 for more information.

Appendix A

The Employee Ownership 1000

The *Employee Ownership 1000* is an alphabetical list of 1000 companies in which employees own more than 4 percent of the stock of a corporation traded by the New York Stock Exchange, the American Stock Exchange, or Over The Counter (OTC). The OTC companies include those listed by the National Association of Securities Dealers (NASDAQ) and the "Pink-Sheet" firms listed by the National Quotation Bureau. Corporations recently delisted by the Exchanges are also included, so that recent changes can be identified. Read across the Employee Ownership 1000 list and observe the ticker symbol, the company name, the percentage of employee ownership, the exchange, the state, the best available recent source for employee-ownership information, and the Employee Ownership 1000 rank. Companies were ranked in order of the size of their employee-ownership holdings, starting at one for the largest. Companies with the same stakes have the same ranking and delisted companies are not ranked.

A legend at the end of the Employee Ownership 1000 describes the sources of information and their abbreviations in the list. Because the amount of employee ownership can change for any number of reasons and publicly available sources are not always reliable, the authors disclaim any use of this information for other than descriptive or research purposes.

An Employee Ownership 1000 Database on Disk is available. It includes company address, recent market value, number of employees, and the dollar size of the employee stake. Quarterly hard copy updates of the Employee Ownership 1000 are also available. Write, telephone, or fax the authors at: Institute of Management and Labor Relations, Rutgers University, Levin Building, Livingston Campus, New Brunswick, N.J. 08903-5062. Telephone: 908-932-5444. Fax: 609-924-2629.

Company Name	Percent	Exchange	State	Ticker	Source of Data	Rank
A.P. Green Industries Inc.	10.91	OTC	MO	APGI	SEC, 12/90	344
AAR Corp.	4.14	NYSE	IL	AIR	SEC, 12/90 estimate	865
Abbott Laboratories	6.50	NYSE	IL	ABT	Spectrum 5, 7/90	617
Acme Steel Co.	8.00	OTC	IL	ACME	IRS, '88	529
Action Savings Bank SLA	5.29	OTC	NJ	ANSL	SEC, '90	750
Adams-Russell Electronics Co.	15.70	OTC/NQB	MA	AEI	SEC, 3/89	189
Advanced Computer Techniques Corp.	12.90	OTC	NY	ACTP	Spectrum 5, '90	271
Advest Group Inc.	7.40	NYSE	CT	ADV	SEC, 12/90	561
Aequitron Medical Inc.	11.90	OTC	MN	AQTN	SEC, 5/90	311
Aetna Life & Casualty Co.	4.30	NYSE	CT	AET	IRS, '88	857
Affiliated Bancshares of Colorado Inc.	7.40	OTC	CO	AFBK	Spectrum 5, '90	561
Alaska Air Group Inc.	6.20	NYSE	WA	ALK	IRRC, '90	637
Albany International Corp. CL A	18.99	NYSE	NY	AIN	SEC, '89	137
ALCO Standard Corp.	12.57	NYSE	PA	ASN	Verbal	286
Alex Brown	42.10	OTC	MD	ABSB	Spectrum 5, '90	15
Alexander & Alexander Services Inc.	4.91	NYSE	NY	AAL	IRS, '88-'89	810
Allegheny Power System Inc. [a]	3.51	NYSE	NY	AYP	IRS, '87	894
Allen Group Inc.	8.59	NYSE	NY	ALN	IRS, '88-'89	492
Allied Group Inc.	37.00	OTC	IA	ALGR	SEC, '90	28
Allied Products Corp.	10.70	NYSE	IL	ADP	IRRC, '90	352
Allied-Signal Inc.	15.80	NYSE	NJ	ALGR	IRRC, '90	188
Aloette Cosmetics Inc.	6.28	OTC	PA	ALET	IRS, '87	634
Alpha Industries Inc.	4.40	AMEX	MA	AHA	IRS, '87	850
Aluminum Company of America	5.00	NYSE	PA	AA	Company estimate	786

Company	Price	Exchange	State	Ticker	Source	No.
Alza Corp.	6.10	AMEX	CA	AZA	Spectrum 5, '90	650
AM International Inc.	9.10	NYSE	IL	AM	IRRC, '91	456
Ambase Corp.	10.40	NYSE	DE	ABC	SEC, 12/90	363
AMC Entertainment Inc.	4.68	AMEX	MO	AEN	SEC, 12/90 estimate	834
Amcast Industrial Corp.	5.20	NYSE	OH	AIZ	Spectrum 5, '90	754
Amerco	5.20	OTC/NOB	AZ	3AMRN	Spectrum 5, '90	754
Ameribanc Investors Group	36.20	OTC	VA	AINVS	Spectrum 5	31
America West Airlines Inc.	36.44	OTC	AZ	AWAL	SEC, 12/90	30
American Bankers Insurance Group Inc.	11.20	OTC	FL	ABIG	SEC, 12/90	334
American Building Maintenance Industries	25.39	NYSE	CA	ABM	SEC, 12/90	64
American Business Products Inc.	38.09	NYSE	GA	ABP	IRS, '88-'89	23
American Capital & Research Corp.	21.89	OTC	VA	ACRCA	SEC, '89	103
American Continental Corp.^k	25.00	OTC/NQB	AZ	AMCC	SEC, 5/90	69
American Electric Power Co. Inc.	4.03	NYSE	OH	AEP	IRS, '88-'89	873
American Express Co.	4.50	NYSE	NY	AXP	WSJ, 10/29/85	846
American Family Corp.	6.10	NYS	GA	AFL	SEC, 8/89	650
American Greetings Corp.^g	4.00	PSE	OH	AGREA	Company	875
American Information Technologies	4.60	NYSE	IL	AMII	SEC, 12/90	837
American Nursery Products Inc.	6.10	OTC	OK	ANSY	Spectrum 5, '90	650
American Pacesetter	22.10	OTC	CA	AEC	IRS, 87	100
American Petrofina Inc. CL A	4.54	AMEX	TX	APIA	IRS, '88-'89	844
American Recreation Centers, Inc.	14.22	OTC	CA	AMRC	SEC, 12/90	226
American Savings Bank FSB	4.70	NYSE	NY	ASB	SEC, 12/90	830
American Stores Co.	5.03	NYSE	UT	ASC	IRS, '88-'89	781
American Telephone & Telegraph Co.	11.00	NYSE	NY	T	Verbal	342
American Video Imaging Inc.	5.60	OTC/NQB	IL	AVII	SEC, '89	705
American Water Works Inc.^b	3.57	NYSE	NJ	AWK	IRS, 87	893

A.1 (Continued)

Company Name	Percent	Exchange	State	Ticker	Source of Data	Rank
American Western Corp.	14.80	OTC/NQB	SD	AWST	SEC, 6/89	212
Ameritrust Corp.	13.50	OTC	OH	AMTR	SEC, '90	250
Amoco Corp.	6.23	NYSE	IL	AN	IRS, '88-'89	636
Amrep Corp.	19.80	NYSE	NY	AXR	IRRC, '91	120
Amvestors Financial Corp.	9.10	OTC	KS	AVFC	SEC, 4/90	456
Analysis & Technology, Inc.	25.30	OTC	CT	AATI	Spectrum 5, '90	65
Andrew Corp.	5.70	OTC	IL	ANDW	SEC, 8/89	695
Anheuser-Busch Companies Inc.	15.70	NYSE	MO	BUD	SEC, '90	189
Anthony Industries Inc.	22.10	NYSE	CA	ANT	SEC, 8/90	100
AON Corp.	8.80	NYSE	IL	AOC	NAARS	476
Apple Computer Inc.	24.00	OTC	CA	AAPL	Franklin Research, '90	83
Applied Power Inc.	34.78	OTC	WI	APWRA	SEC, 12/90	34
Arden Group Inc.	24.90	OTC	CA	ARDNA	Spectrum 5, '90	77
Armco Inc.	7.80	NYSE	NJ	AS	IRRC, '90	541
Armstrong World Industries Inc. CONV PFD	12.00	NYSE	PA	ACK	IRRC, '91	299
Arrow Electronics Inc.	12.10	NYSE	NY	ARW	Spectrum 5 & 6	296
Arvin Industries Inc.	9.94	NYSE	IN	ARV	IRS, '88-'89	415
Ashland Oil Inc.	23.00	NYSE	KY	ASH	IRRC, '90	92
Atkinson (Guy F.) Co. of California	18.50	OTC	CA	ATKN	IRRC, '90	144
Atlanta Gas Light Co.	10.56	NYSE	GA	ATG	SEC, 12/90 estimate	358
Atlantic Richfield	9.00	NYSE	CA	ARC	Verbal	461
Audiotronics Corp.	27.50	AMEX	CA	ADO	Spectrum 5, '90	57
Automatic Data Processing Inc.	7.19	NYSE	NJ	AUD	SEC, 12/90 estimate	577
Avery International Corp. [h]	5.90	NYS	CA	AVY	SEC, 11/90	678
Avondale Industries Inc.	45.10	OTC	LA	AVDL	Spectrum 5, '90	12
B.I. Inc.	5.10	OTC	CO	BIAC	SEC, 5/90	771

260

Company	Price	Exchange	State	Ticker	Source	No.
Badger Meter Inc.	13.40	AMEX	WI	BMI	Business Wire 10/15/90	254
Baker (Michael) Corp.	33.00	AMEX	PA	BKR	PR, 6/19/90	39
Baldor Electric Co.	5.80	NYSE	AR	BEZ	IRRC, '90	689
Balfour Maclaine Corp.	4.34	AMEX	VA	BML	IRS, '88	855
Ball Corp.	10.00	NYSE	IN	BLL	Morgan Stanley, 1990	384
Baltimore Gas & Electric Co.	5.69	NYSE	MD	BGE	IRS, '87	703
Bancflorida Financial Corp.	16.22	NYSE	FL	BFL	SEC, 12/90	180
Banco Popular De Puerto Rico	15.00	OTC	PR	BPOP	Verbal	204
Bancorp New Jersey Inc.	7.00	OTC	NJ	BCNJ	Spectrum 5, '90	587
Bank of Gonzales Holding Co.	11.90	OTC/NQB	LA	N/A	Spectrum 5, '90	311
Bank of New York Co.	12.89	NYSE	NY	BK	SEC, 12/90	277
Bank of San Francisco Holding Co.	9.70	AMEX	CA	BOF	SEC, 12/90	431
Bank South Corp.	8.17	OTC	GA	BKSO	IRRC, '90	522
Bankamerica Corp.	6.00	NYSE	CA	BAC	Verbal	665
Bankers Corp.	4.00	OTC	NJ	BKCO	BWR 1/22/91 estimate	875
Bankers First Corporation	9.88	OTC	GA	BNKF	NAARS	425
Banks of Mid-America Inc.	5.56	OTC	OK	BOMA	SEC, '90	718
Banner Industries Inc.	5.60	NYSE	OH	BNR	SEC, 8/90	705
Bariod Corp.	4.44	NYSE	TX	BRC	IRS, '88-'89	848
Barnes Group Inc.	17.61	NYSE	CT	B	NAARS	152
Barnett Banks Inc.	13.63	NYSE	FL	BBI	Goldman & IRS '87	246
Bassett Furniture Industries Inc.	5.50	OTC	VA	BBSET	IRRC, '90	724
BayBanks Inc.	7.80	OTC	MA	BBNK	IRRC, '90	541
Becton, Dickinson & Co.	20.00	NYSE	NJ	BDX	NCEO	112
Bel Fuse Inc.	15.00	OTC	NJ	BELF	WSJ, 7/28/89	204
Bell Atlantic Corp.	5.90	NYSE	PA	BEL	Morgan Stanley	678
BELL National Corp.	24.12	OTC/NQB	CA	BELL	SEC, 5/89	82

A.1 (Continued)

Company Name	Percent	Exchange	State	Ticker	Source of Data	Rank
BellSouth Corp.	7.11	NYSE	GA	BLS	PR 1/25/90 & SEC 12/90	579
Bemis Co. Inc.	11.20	NYSE	MN	BMS	SEC, '89	334
Betz Laboratories Inc. [b]	3.50	OTC	PA	BETZ	IRRC, '91	895
Big O Tires Inc.	4.80	OTC	CO	BIGO	Spectrum 5	821
Binks Manufacturing Co.	13.00	AMEX	IL	BIN	Verbal	263
Bird Inc.	4.98	OTC	MA	BIRD	IRS, '88-'89	803
Bishop Inc.	4.29	OTC	CA	BISH	IRS, '87	858
BMA Corp.	8.80	OTC	MO	BMAC	IRRC, '90	476
Boise Cascade Corp.	15.00	NYSE	ID	BCC	IRRC, '90	204
Boston Bancorp	10.21	OTC	MA	SBOS	NAARS	371
Boston Five Bancorp Inc.	8.00	OTC	MA	BFCS	SEC, 12/90	529
Bowater Inc. [a]	3.50	NYSE	CT	BOW	Company	895
Brooklyn Union Gas Co.	16.50	NYSE	NY	BU	IRRC, '90	173
Brown & Sharpe Manufacturing Co.	20.00	NYSE	RI	BNS	IRRC, '90	112
Brunswick Corp.	7.43	NYSE	IL	BC	SEC, 12/90	560
BSB Bancorp Inc.	5.56	OTC/NQB	NY	BSBN	SEC, 6/89	718
Buckeye Financial Corp.	5.07	OTC	OH	BCKY	SEC, 6/90	777
Buffton Corporation	5.42	AMEX	TX	BUFF	SEC, '90	737
Builders Transport Inc.	13.90	OTC	SC	TRUK	Spectrum 5	237
Burr-Brown Corp.	5.50	OTC	AZ	BBRC	Spectrum 5	724
Businessland Inc.	5.08	NYSE	CA	BLI	SEC, 4/90	776
Butler Manufacturing Co.	19.30	OTC	MO	BTLR	Spectrum 5	127
Cabot Corp.	4.85	NYSE	MA	CBT	SEC, 12/90	817
Cambrex Corp.	5.70	OTC	NJ	CBAM	SEC, 5/90	695
Capital Bancshares Inc.	29.30	OTC/NQB	LA	CBRR	Spectrum 5	47

262

Company	Price	Exchange	State	Ticker	Source	No.
Capital Cities/ABC Inc. [c]	2.33	NYSE	NY	CCB	IRS, '88-'89	908
Cardinal Financial Group Inc.	8.62	OTC	KY	CAFS	SEC, 12/90	486
Careercom Corp.	5.10	NYSE	PA	CCM	SEC, 12/90 estimate	771
Carolina Power & Light Co.	7.83	NYSE	NC	CPL	SEC, 12/90	539
Carpenter Technology Corp.	3.50	NYSE	PA	CRS	Company	895
Carter Hawley Hale Stores Inc.	40.00	NYSE	CA	CHH	NCEO	19
Casey's General Stores Inc.	14.90	OTC	IA	CASY	SEC, 6/89	211
Cato Corp. CL A	16.63	OTC	NC	CACOA	Spectrum 6, 1/90	171
CB Bancshares Inc.	18.66	OTC/NQB	HI	CBB	SEC, 12/90	143
CBI Industries Inc.	22.40	NYSE	IL	CBH	IRRC, '90	97
CCX Inc.	29.95	NYSE	NJ	CCX	IRS, '87	45
Celina Financial Corp.	4.90	OTC	OH	CELNA	IRS, '87	811
Central & South West Corp.	17.31	NYSE	TX	CSR	IRS, '88 & Morgan Stanley	156
Central Bancshares of the South, Inc.	7.00	OTC	AL	CBSS	Spectrum 5	587
Central Banking System Inc.	15.30	OTC	CA	CSYS	SEC, 10/90	199
Central Fidelity Banks Inc.	14.50	OTC	VA	CFBS	IRS, '88-'89	219
Central Freight Lines Inc.	46.10	OTC	TX	CTLF	Spectrum 5	11
Central Lousiana Electric Co.	5.90	NYSE	LA	CNL	IRS, '87	678
Central Steel & Wire Co.	17.10	OTC/NQB	IL	CERW	Spectrum 5	158
Centrust Bank	15.60	OTC/NQB	FL	DLP	SEC, '90	192
Century Telephone Enterprises Inc.	39.30	NYSE	LA	CTL	IRRC, '91	21
CF&I Steel Corp. [1]	38.92	OTC	CO	CFIP	SEC, 5/90	22
Champion Parts Inc.	13.40	OTC	IL	CREB	SEC, 12/90	254
Check Technology Corp.	8.50	OTC	MN	CTCQ	SEC, 6/90	495
Chemed Corp.	19.40	NYSE	OH	CHE	IRRC, '90	125
Chemical Leaman Corp.	8.04	OTC	PA	CLEA	SEC, 12/90 estimate	526
Chester Valley Bancorp	9.90	OTC	PA	CVAL	SEC, 12/90	418

A.1 (Continued)

Company Name	Percent	Exchange	State	Ticker	Source of Data	Rank
Chevron Corp.	16.00	NYSE	CA	CHV	IRRC, '90	182
Chicago Rivet & Machine Co.	11.30	AMEX	IL	CVR	SEC, 5/89	329
Chieftain International Inc.	10.09	OTH	Canada	CID	SEC, 4/89	381
Chock Full O'Nuts	5.20	NYSE	NY	CHF	IRRC, '91	754
Chris-Craft Industries Inc.	3.40	NYSE	NY	CCN	Spectrum 5	898
Chris-Craft Industries Inc. CL B	4.90	NYSE	NY	3CCNDB	Spectrum 5	811
Chris-Craft Industries Inc. CONV PFD ᵐ	1.00	NYSE	NY	CCNB	Spectrum 5	912
Chubb Corp.	4.56	NYSE	NJ	CB	SEC, 12/90	842
CIGNA Corp.	8.89	NYSE	PA	CI	IRS, '87	475
Cilcorp Inc.	10.00	NYSE	IL	CER	NCEO	384
Cimco Inc.	5.60	OTC	Canada	CIMC	Spectrum 5, '90	705
Cincinnati Bell Inc.	10.53	NYSE	OH	CSN	NCEO & Morgan Stanley	359
Cincinnati Gas & Electric Co.	12.79	NYSE	OH	CIN	IRS, '88-'89	281
Cincinnati Milacron, Inc.	9.90	NYSE	OH	CMZ	IRRC, '89	418
Cincinnati Milacron, Inc. PFD	18.50	NYSE	OH	N/A	IRRC, '91	144
Circuit City Stores Inc.	5.03	NYSE	VA	CC	SEC, 12/90 estimate	781
Circus Circus Enterprises Inc.	13.00	NYSE	NV	CIR	SEC, '89	263
Citizens and Southern Corp.	5.00	NYSE	GA	CTZ	Morgan Stanley	786
Citizens Savings Financial Corp.	9.90	OTC	FL	CSFCB	Spectrum 5, '90	418
City National Corp.	5.00	OTC	CA	CTYN	Spectrum 5, '90	786
Citytrust Bancorp Inc.	4.80	NYSE	CT	CYT	IRRC, '90	821
Clark Equipment Co.	18.26	NYSE	MI	CKL	Spectrum 5, '90	146
Clayton Homes Inc.	4.84	NYSE	TN	CMH	SEC, 12/90 estimate	819
CMS Energy Corp.	6.20	NYSE	MI	CMS	Company	637
CNL Financial Corp.	20.20	OTC	GA	CNLF	SEC, 6/90	109
Coast Distribution System	4.98	AMEX	CA	CRV	SEC, 12/90 estimate	803

264

Company						
Coastal Corp.	29.40	NYSE	TX	CGP	SEC, 6/90	46
Coca-Cola Co. [c]	1.60	NYSE	GA	KO	IRS, '87	911
Colgate-Palmolive Co.	8.80	NYSE	NY	CL	IRRC, '91	476
Columbia Gas System Inc.	14.25	NYSE	DE	CG	IRS, '88-'89	225
Comarco Inc.	9.40	OTC	CA	CMRO	SEC, '90	448
Comdisco Inc.	7.71	NYSE	IL	CDO	SEC, 12/90 estimate	548
Comfed Bancorp Inc.	12.76	AMEX	MA	CFK	SEC, 12/90	282
Commerce Bancorp Inc.	19.68	OTC	DC	COBA	PR, 8/17/89	122
Commerce Bancshares Inc.	10.20	OTC	MO	CBSH	IRS, '88	372
Commerce Group Corp.	19.10	BSE	WI	CGCO	Spectrum 5, '90	131
Commercial Federal Corp.	6.90	OTC	NE	CFCN	Spectrum 5, '90	595
Commercial Intertech Corp.	6.71	OTC	OH	CTEK	PR, 2/15/90	608
Commercial Metals Co.	11.70	NYSE	TX	CMC	PR, 11/23/87	320
Commonwealth Energy Systems	20.10	NYSE	MA	CES	IRRC, '91	110
Communications Systems Inc.	5.20	OTC	MN	CSII	Spectrum 5, '90	754
Community Bancorp Inc.	6.40	OTC	PA	CBPA	Spectrum 5, '90	621
Community Bancshares Inc.	8.50	OTC	TN	CBOG	Spectrum 5	495
Computer Task Group Inc.	15.42	NYSE	NY	TSK	SEC, 12/90 estimate	195
Computrac Inc.	5.16	AMEX	TX	LLB	SEC, 12/90 estimate	766
Comstock Group Inc.	6.00	OTC/NQB	CT	CSTK	SEC, 4/89	665
Conagra Inc.	10.00	NYSE	NE	CAG	Company	384
Connecticut Natural Gas Corp.	4.26	NYSE	CT	CTG	IRS, '88-'89	860
Connelly Containers Inc.	13.63	PSE	PA	CON	SEC, 8/89	246
Consolidated Edison Co. of NY Inc. [c]	2.90	NYSE	NY	ED	IRS, '87	904
Consolidated Equities Corp.	11.20	OTC/NQB	GA	CNEG	SEC, 4/90	334
Consolidated Freightways Inc. [i]	19.54	NYSE	CA	CNF	WSJ, 2/13/89	123
Consolidated Natural Gas Co.	13.00	NYSE	PA	CNG	IRRC, '91	263

265

A.1 (Continued)

Company Name	Percent	Exchange	State	Ticker	Source of Data	Rank
Consolidated Papers Inc.	13.00	OTC	WI	CPER	IRRC, '90	263
Consolidated Rail Corp.	10.00	NYSE	PA	CRR	IRRC, '90	384
Consumers Financial Corp.	11.90	OTC	PA	CFIN	Spectrum 5, '90	311
Contel Corp.	5.03	NYSE	GA	CTC	SEC, 12/90 estimate	781
Convex Computer Corp.	6.06	NYSE	TX	CNVXG	SEC, 12/90 estimate	661
Cooker Restaurant Corp.	9.90	OTC	OH	COKR	Spectrum 5, '90	418
Cooper Industries Inc.	5.00	NYSE	TX	CBE	IRRC, '90	786
Cooper Tire & Rubber Co.	15.36	NYSE	OH	CTB	IRRC, '91	198
Coral Companies Inc.	10.00	OTH	CO	COCI	SEC, 8/89	384
Corcap Inc.	14.20	AMEX	CT	CCP	SEC, '90	228
Corning Inc.	12.02	NYSE	NY	GLW	IRRC, '91	298
Corroon & Black Corp.	6.90	NYSE	NY	CBL	IRS, '88-'89	595
Courier Corp.	5.90	OTC	MA	CRRC	Spectrum 5, '90	678
CPB Inc.	8.40	OTC	HI	CPBI	SEC, 5/90	503
CPC International Inc.	8.40	NYSE	NJ	CPC	SEC, 8/90	503
CPT Corp.	12.70	OTC	MN	CPTC	IRRC, '91	284
Craftmatic/Contour Industries Inc.	28.35	OTC	PA	CRCC	SEC, 12/90	52
Crestar Financial Corp.	7.80	PSE	VA	UVBK	SEC, 6/90	541
Crompton & Knowles Corp.	4.76	NYSE	CT	CNK	IRS, '88-'89	828
Crossland Savings FSB	10.63	NYSE	NY	CRLD	SEC, 12/90 estimate	357
Crown Central Petroleum Corp.	5.85	AMEX	MD	CNPA	IRS, '87	686
Crown Crafts Inc.	19.10	AMEX	GA	CRW	SEC, 12/90	131
Crystal Brands Inc.	21.79	NYSE	CT	CBR	IRS, '87	104
CTS Corp.	5.50	NYSE	IN	CTS	IRRC, '90	724
Cullen/Frost Bankers Inc.	9.60	OTC	TX	CFBI	IRRC, '90	436
Cummins Engine Co.	11.60	NYSE	IN	CUM	IRRC, '90	322

Company						
CyCare Systems Inc.	24.52	NYSE	AZ	CYS	SEC, 12/90	80
Cyprus Minerals Co.	13.90	NYSE	CO	CYM	IRRC, '90	237
Dahlberg Inc.	8.90	OTC	MN	DAHL	SEC, '90	473
Dana Corp.	10.00	NYSE	OH	DCN	Company	384
Data General Corp.	10.90	NYSE	MA	DGN	IRRC, '90	345
Datapoint Corp.	4.86	NYSE	TX	DPT	IRS, '87	816
Dayton-Hudson Corp.	6.20	NYSE	MN	DH	Spectrum 5	637
DBA Systems Inc.	19.00	OTC	FL	DBAS	NCEO	133
Deerfield Federal Savings & Loan Association	8.30	OTC	IL	DEER	PR, 4/90	516
Del Laboratories Inc.	6.20	AMEX	NY	DLI	SEC, '90	637
Delaware Savings Bank FSB	5.32	OTC/NQB	DE	DESB	SEC, 12/90	744
Delchamps Inc.	25.00	OTC	AL	DLCH	WSJ, 10/6/88	69
Delmarva Power & Light Co.	5.04	NYSE	DE	DEW	IRS, '88-89	780
Delmed Inc.	6.36	AMEX	NJ	DMD	SEC, 12/90 estimate	629
Delta Air Lines, Inc.	16.50	NYSE	GA	DAL	IRRC, '91	173
Deluxe Corp.	8.49	NYSE	MN	DLX	SEC, 12/90 est.	499
Dennison Manufacturing Co. [h]	18.67	NYSE	MA	DSN	IRRC, '90	142
DeSoto Inc.	10.70	NYSE	IL	DSO	Spectrum 5, '90	352
DFSoutheastern Inc.	8.80	OTC	GA	DFSE	SEC, 12/90	476
Diamond Shamrock Inc.	13.30	NYSE	TX	DRM	IRRC, '91	256
Digital Sound Corp.	8.40	OTC	CA	DGSD	SEC, 5/90	503
Diversified Energies Inc.	11.80	NYSE	MN	DEI	IRS, '88-89	316
Donaldson Co. Inc.	12.00	NYSE	MN	DCI	IRRC, '91	299
Drew Industries Inc.	11.00	BSE	NY	DREW	SEC, 5/88	341
DynCorp	35.00	OTC/NQB	VA	DYNP	NCEO, '90	32
E-Systems Inc.	22.30	NYSE	TX	ESY	SEC, '90, IRRC 90	98
Eagle Bancorp Inc.	4.65	OTC	WV	EBCI	SEC, 12/89	835

267

A.1 (Continued)

Company Name	Percent	Exchange	State	Ticker	Source of Data	Rank
Eagle Financial Corp.	5.06	AMS	CT	EAG	NAARS	778
Eastern Co.	5.32	AMEX	CT	EML	IRS, '88-'89	744
Eastern Enterprises	5.90	NYS	MA	EFU	SEC, 4/89	678
Eastland Financial Corp.	5.50	OTC	RI	EAFC	Spectrum 5	724
Eaton Corp.	7.00	NYSE	OH	ETN	IRRC, '91	587
ECC International Corp.	4.06	NYSE	PA	ECC	SEC, 12/90 estimate	870
Eckerd (Jack) Corp.	6.10	BSE	FL	ECK	SEC, 6/90	650
Economy Savings Bank	5.60	OTC	PA	ESBB	SEC, 11/90	705
Edac Technologies Corp.	28.40	OTC	CT	EDAC	Spectrum 5	51
Edo Corp.	25.80	NYSE	NY	EDO	IRRC, '91	61
Ekco Group Inc.	10.80	NYSE	NH	EKO	IRRC, '91	347
El Paso Electric Co.	4.92	OTC	TX	ELPA	IRS, '87	809
Elco Industries Inc.	5.00	OTC	IL	ELCN	Spectrum 5	786
Elcor Corp.	11.26	NYSE	TX	ELK	SEC, 12/90	332
Eldorado Bancorp	6.10	AMEX	CA	ELB	SEC, '90	650
Empire Banc Corp.	15.00	OTC/NQS	MI	3EMBM	NCEO	204
Empire National Bank of Traverse City	15.00	OTC/NQB	MI	DYNPP	NCEO, '90	204
Energy Ventures Inc.	10.00	OTC	TX	ENGY	DJNW 7/30/90	384
Engineered Support Systems Inc.	8.36	OTC	MO	EASI	NAARS	511
Engraph Inc.	5.55	OTC	GA	ENGH	NCEO	720
Ennis Business Forms Inc.	9.60	NYSE	TX	EBF	IRRC, '90	436
Enron Corp.	22.30	NYSE	TX	ENE	IRRC, '91	98
Enserch Corp.	5.60	NYSE	TX	ENS	IRRC, '90	705
Entertainment Publishing Corp.	5.11	AMEX	MI	ENT	SEC, 12/90 estimate	769
Entronics Corp.	4.95	OTC	TX	ENTC	SEC, 12/90 estimate	806
Enviropact Inc.	15.00	AMEX	FL	ENV	NCEO	204

268

Company						
Equifax Inc.	8.00	NYSE	GA	EFX	IRRC, '90	529
ERC Industries Inc.	5.90	OTC/NQB	TX	ERCI	SEC, 5/89	678
ESELCO Inc.	6.60	OTC	MI	EDSE	IRS, '88-'89	614
Espey Manufacturing & Electronics Corp.	23.50	AMEX	NY	ESP	Spectrum 5, '90	90
Essex Corp.	5.81	OTC	VA	ESEX	SEC, 7/90	688
Essex County Gas Co.	10.52	OTC	MA	ECGC	SEC, '89, NAARS	360
Ethyl Corp.	7.12	NYSE	VA	EY	NCEO	578
Evans Inc.	4.05	OTC	IL	EVAN	IRS, '88-'89	872
Excel Industries Inc.	8.60	AMEX	IN	EXC	SEC, 5/90	489
Exolon-Esk Co.	8.60	BSE	NY	EXL	SEC, 8/89	489
Exxon Corp.	9.35	NYSE	NY	XON	WSJ, 6/4/90	452
F F O Financial Group Inc.	5.41	OTC	FL	FFFG	SEC, 6/90	738
Fair, Isaac and Company Inc.	12.71	OTC	CA	FICI	NAARS	283
Fairchild Industries Inc.	18.90	BSE	VA	FEN	SEC, 8/89	138
Fairfield Communities Inc.	4.36	NYSE	AR	FCI	NCEO	853
Far West Financial Corp.	9.00	NYSE	CA	FWF	NCEO	461
Farr Co.	7.20	OTC	CA	FARC	SEC, 12/90 estimate	572
Federal Express Corp.	10.00	NYSE	TN	FDX	Morgan Stanley	384
Federal Mogul Corp.	8.20	NYSE	MI	FMO	IRRC, '91	518
Federal Paper Board Co. Inc.	4.00	NYSE	NJ	FBO	NCEO	875
Ferro Corp.	7.80	NYSE	OH	FOE	IRRC, '90	541
FHP International Corp.	4.70	OTC	CA	FHPC	IRRC, '91	830
Fidelity National Financial Inc.	12.10	AMEX	CA	FNF	SEC, 12/90 estimate	296
Fidelity Savings Association	10.00	OTC	PA	FSVA	SEC, '90	384
Figgie International Inc. CL B	34.50	OTC	OH	FIGI	IRRC, '91	36
Filtertek Inc.	9.80	NYSE	IL	FTK	SEC, 8/89	426
Financial Benefit Group Inc.	14.30	OTC	FL	FBGIB	SEC, 8/90	224

A.1 (Continued)

Company Name	Percent	Exchange	State	Ticker	Source of Data	Rank
First Albany Companies Inc.	11.76	OTC	NY	FACT	SEC, 5/90	318
First American Financial Corp.	24.34	OTC	CA	FAMR	IRS, '88-'89	81
First Bank System Inc.	7.20	NYSE	MN	FBS	SEC, 6/90	572
First Capital Financial Corp.	8.50	OTC/NQB	CO	FCFI	SEC, 12/90	495
First Capital Holdings Corp.	6.40	NYSE	CA	FCH	SEC, '89	621
First City Bancorp Inc.	10.00	OTC	GA	CITY	DJNW 7/10/90	384
First Colonial Group Inc.	11.90	OTC/NQB	PA	FCGR	Spectrum 5	311
First Commerce Corp.	5.80	OTC	LA	FCOM	IRS, '88-'89	689
First Connecticut Small Business Invest. Co.	10.13	AMEX	CT	FCO	IRS, '87	377
First Federal Capital Corp.	6.10	OTC	WI	FTFC	SEC, 12/90	650
First Federal Financial Corp.	9.90	OTC	KY	FFKY	SEC, 12/90	418
First Federal S & L Assoc. of Lenawee County	7.02	OTC	MI	LFSA	SEC, '89	586
First Federal Savings Bank of Tennessee	11.23	OTC	TN	FTSB	SEC, 12/90	333
First Federal Savings Bank Utah	19.20	OTC	UT	FFUT	SEC, '89	129
First Fidelity Bancorporation	10.20	NYSE	NJ	FFB	SEC, 12/90	372
First Franklin Corp.	4.70	OTC	OH	FFHS	Spectrum 5	830
First Hawaiian Inc.	14.22	OTC	HI	FHWN	IRS, '88-'89	226
First Mutual Savings Bank	10.70	OTC	WA	FMSB	DJNW 7/10/90	352
First Northern Savings	5.20	OTC	WI	FNGB	SEC, 3/90	754
First of Michigan Capital Corp.	4.90	OTC	MI	FMG	Spectrum 5	811
First Republic Bancorp Inc.	13.30	AMEX	CA	FRC	Spectrum 5	256
First Savings Bancorp	11.44	OTC	OH	FFNS	SEC, 12/90	326
First Security Corp.	4.57	OTC	UT	FSCO	IRS, '87	841
First State Financial Services Inc.	9.00	OTC	NJ	FSFI	Spectrum 5	461
First Tennessee National Corp.	6.43	OTC	TN	FTEN	IRS, '88-'89	620
Firstar Corp.	13.30	NYSE	WI	FSR	IRRC, '91	256

Company	Price	Exchange	State	Ticker	Source	No.
Firstcorp Inc.	25.00	AMEX	NC	FCR	WSJ, 7/15/88	69
Firstfed Financial Corp.	9.72	NYSE	CA	FED	SEC, 12/90	430
FMC Corp.	25.30	NYSE	IL	FMC	IRRC, '91	65
FMS Financial Corp.	6.62	OTC	NJ	FMCO	SEC, 12/90	613
Foote, Cone & Belding Communications Inc.	14.10	NYSE	IL	FCB	Spectrum 6, 6/30/90	229
Ford Motor Co.	11.73	NYSE	MI	F	IRS, '88-'89	319
Forest Oil Corp.	5.87	OTC	PA	FOIL	IRS, '88-'89	685
Foxboro Co.	8.03	NYSE	NY	FOX	IRS, '87	527
FPL Group Inc.	9.30	NYSE	FL	FPL	Goldman Sachs 7/17/90	454
Franklin Electric Co. Inc.	7.00	OTC	IN	FELE	NCEO	587
Frequency Electronics Inc.	13.61	AMEX	NY	FEI	SEC, 12/90	248
Frozen Food Express Industries Inc.	6.31	AMEX	TX	JIT	SEC, 12/90	630
Fuller (H.B.) Co.	9.58	OTC	MN	FULL	IRS, '87	439
Fund American Companies, Inc.	12.00	NYSE	CT	FFC	IRRC, '91	299
G.R.I. Corp.	8.59	AMEX	IL	GRR	SEC, 6/89	492
GEICO Corp.	8.00	NYSE	DC	GEC	IRRC, '90	529
Gelman Sciences Inc.	6.19	AMEX	MI	GSC	NAARS	647
Gencorp Inc.	9.48	NYSE	OH	GY	SEC, 12/90	444
General Aircraft Corp.	20.00	OTC/NQB	MA	GAIR	SEC, 6/90	112
General Dynamics Corp.	8.10	NYSE	MO	GD	IRRC, '90	524
General Electric Co. [a]	3.50	NYSE	CT	GE	Company	895
General Mills Inc. [c]	2.10	NYSE	MN	GIS	Morgan Stanley	909
General Motors	9.47	NYSE	MI	GMH	IRS, '88-'89	445
Genesco Inc.	5.48	NYSE	TN	GCO	IRS, '87	732
Genrad Inc.	17.50	NYSE	MA	GEN	NCEO	153
George Washington Corp.	11.90	OTC	FL	GWSH	Spectrum 5, '90	311

A.1 (Continued)

Company Name	Percent	Exchange	State	Ticker	Source of Data	Rank
Geothermal Resources International Inc.	5.50	CSE	CA	GSX	SEC, 7/89	724
Gerber Products Co.	5.60	NYSE	MI	GEB	Spectrum 5, '90	705
Giant Industries Inc.	15.92	NYSE	AZ	GI	SEC, 12/90	187
Gibson (C.R.) Co.	13.70	AMEX	CT	GIB	Spectrum 6	244
Gilbert Associates Inc. CL A	11.10	OTC	PA	GILBA	NCEO	338
Gillette Co.	6.20	NYSE	MA	GS	IRRC, '90	637
Gleason Corp.	6.80	NYSE	NY	GLE	SEC, 5/90	603
Glenfed Inc.	5.20	AMEX	CA	GLN	SEC, 10/89	754
GNW Financial Corp.	6.40	OTC	WA	GNFW	Spectrum 5, '90	621
Golden Enterprises	7.90	OTC	AL	GLDC	Spectrum 5	537
Good Guys Inc.	6.00	OTC	CA	GGUY	SEC, 12/90	665
Goodrich (B.F.) Co.	5.70	NYSE	OH	GR	IRRC, '90	695
Graco Inc.	11.03	NYSE	MN	GGG	SEC, 12/90	340
Graham Corp.	7.39	AMEX	NY	GHM	WSJ, 8/09/90	566
Granite Construction Inc.	50.60	OTC	CA	GCCO	SEC, 12/90	7
Granite State Bankshares Inc.	5.10	OTC	NH	GSBI	Spectrum 5, '90	771
Great Lakes Bancorp, FSB	17.40	OTC	MI	GLBC	IRRC, '91	154
Great Southern Bancorp Inc.	10.00	OTC	MO	GSEC	Spectrum 5	384
Greater New York Savings Bank	12.20	OTC	NY	GRTR	IRRC, '90	294
Greenwich Financial Corp.	8.70	OTC	CT	GFCT	SEC, 12/90	481
Greiner Engineering Inc.	16.90	AMEX	TX	GII	SEC, 12/90	162
Grey Advertising Inc.	6.03	OTC	NY	GREY	SEC, '89	662
Greyhound Dial Corp. [a]	3.00	NYSE	AZ	G	Morgan Stanley estimate	902
Grow Group Inc.	6.00	NYSE	NY	GRO	IRRC, '91	665
Grumman Corp.	42.85	NYSE	NY	GQ	IRRC, '91	14
GTE Corp.	8.64	NYSE	CT	GTE	SEC, 12/90 estimated	485

Company						
Gyrodyne Co. of America Inc.	6.74	OTC	NY	GYRO	IRS, '87	607
Hadson Corp.	8.20	NYSE	OK	HAD	SEC, 12/90	518
Hamptons Bancshares Inc.	7.50	OTC	NY	HBSI	SEC, 12/90	553
Handschy Industries Inc.	10.00	OTC/NQB	IL	3HNDS	Spectrum 5	384
Harcourt Brace Jovanovich Inc. j	19.30	NYSE	FL	HBJ	Spectrum 5	127
Harmon Industries Inc.	5.60	OTC	MO	HRMN	Spectrum 5	705
Harmonia Bankcorp Inc.	5.90	OTC/NQB	NJ	HBIC	Spectrum 5	678
Harnischfeger Industries Inc.	7.10	NYSE	WI	HPH	SEC, 5/89	580
Hartford Steam Boiler Inspection & Insurance Co.	5.40	NYSE	CT	HBOL	IRRC, '91	739
Hartmarx Corp.	11.50	NYSE	IL	HMX	IRRC, '90	325
Hawaiian Electric Industries Inc.	17.00	NYSE	HI	HE	NAARS	160
Hawkeye Bancorporation	10.20	OTC	IA	HWKB	Spectrum 5	372
Hawkins Chemical Inc.	25.00	OTC	MN	HWKN	Spectrum 5	69
Hawthorne Financial Corp.	8.91	OTC	CA	HTHR	SEC, 12/90	472
Haywood Savings & Loan Association Inc.	9.98	OTC	NC	HWNC	SEC, 12/90	414
Heart Federal Savings & Loan Association	8.20	OTC/NQB	CA	HFED	SEC, 8/89	518
Heico Corp.	4.59	AMEX	FL	HEI	IRS, '88	839
Hi-Shear Industries Inc.	43.87	NYSE	NY	HSI	SEC, 12/90 estimate	13
High Point Financial Corp.	13.70	OTC/NQB	NJ	HPFC	Spectrum 5	244
Hinderliter Industries Inc.	12.30	OTC/NQB	OK	HND	SEC, '89	293
Hipotronics Inc.	4.90	AMEX	NY	HIP	SEC, 12/90	811
Holly Corp.	16.80	AMEX	TX	HOC	IRRC, '91	164
Home & City Savings Bank	6.50	OTC	NY	HCSB	PR, 7/29/89	617
Home Federal Savings Bank	6.37	OTC	SC	HFSA	SEC, 4/90	628
Home Federal Savings Bank of Georgia	8.26	OTC	GA	HFGA	SEC, '89	517
HomeFed Corp.	10.00	NYSE	CA	HFD	IRRC, '89	384
Honeywell Inc.	5.00	NYSE	MN	HON	IRS, '87	786

A.1 (Continued)

Company Name	Percent	Exchange	State	Ticker	Source of Data	Rank
Hormel (Geo. A.) & Co.	6.20	NYSE	MN	HRL	Spectrum 5	637
Horn & Hardart Co.	7.06	NYSE	NV	HOR	SEC, 12/90	584
Houghton Mifflin Co.	4.59	NYSE	MA	HTN	IRS, '87	839
Household International Inc.	4.00	NYSE	IL	HI	IRS, '88-'89	875
Houston Industries Inc.	7.81	NYSE	TX	HOU	PR Newswire 10/10/90	540
Howell Industries Inc.	16.00	AMEX	MI	HOW	SEC, 12/90	182
Hughes Supply Inc.	14.00	NYSE	FL	HUG	IRS, '88-'89	233
Humana Inc. [a]	3.44	NYSE	KY	HUM	IRS, '87	897
Hunter Environmental Services, Inc.	13.30	OTC	OH	HESI	WSJ, 12/23/88	256
Huntington Bancshares Inc.	5.16	OTC	OH	HBAN	IRS, '88-'89	766
Idaho Power Co.	9.44	NYSE	ID	IDA	SEC, 12/90 estimate	446
Illinois Power Co. [a]	3.50	NYSE	IL	IPC	IRS, '87	895
Imperial Holly Corp.	32.40	AMEX	TX	IHK	Spectrum 5	43
INB Financial Corp.	9.00	OTC	IN	INBF	IRRC, '91	461
Independent Bank Corp.	5.30	OTC	MI	IBCP	Spectrum 5	746
Indiana Federal Corp.	5.34	OTC	IN	IFSL	WSJ, 4/26/89	743
Industrial Training Systems Corp.	8.70	OTC	NJ	ITSC	SEC, '87	481
Informix Corp.	8.62	OTC	CA	IFMX	SEC, 12/90 estimate	486
Ingersoll-Rand Co.	4.95	NYSE	NJ	IR	IRS, '87	806
Ingles Markets, Inc.	15.60	OTC	NC	IMKTA	SEC, 5/89	192
Initio Inc.	6.02	OTC	NV	INTO	IRS, '87	664
Inland Steel Industries Inc.	11.30	NYSE	IL	IAD	IRRC, '90	329
Instrument Systems Corp.	9.80	AMEX	NY	ISY	Spectrum 5	426
Integra Financial Corp.	4.00	OTC	PA	ITGR	WSJ, 1/27/89	875
Inter-Regional Financial Group Inc.	37.58	NYSE	MN	IFG	IRS, '88-'89	24
Interand Corp.	14.60	OTC/NQB	IL	IRND	SEC, 4/90	218

Company	Price	Exchange	State	Ticker	Source	No.
Interchange Financial Services Corp.	11.05	OTC	NJ	ISB	SEC, 12/90	339
Intergraph Corp.	14.10	OTC	AL	INGR	SEC, 12/90	229
Interlake (The), Corp.	10.50	NYSE	IL	IK	IRRC, '90	361
Intermet Corp.	8.40	OTC	GA	INMT	SEC, 10/90	503
Intermetrics Inc.	4.00	OTC	MA	IMET	IRS, '87	875
International Business Machines Corp. ᶠ	0.27	NYSE	NY	IBM	IRS, '87	913
International Holding Capital Corp.	10.04	OTC/NQB	HI	ISLH	SEC, 12/90	383
International Mercantile Corp.	29.10	OTC/NQB	MO	INME	SEC, 6/90	48
International Multifoods Corp.	5.30	NYSE	MN	IMC	IRRC, '90	746
International Paper Co.	7.30	NYSE	NY	IP	Verbal	567
International Research & Development Corp.	20.10	OTC	MI	IRDV	Spectrum 5	110
Investors Financial Corp.	4.56	OTC	VA	INVF	NAARS	842
Iomega Corp.	6.70	OTC	UT	IOMG	DJNW 8/3/90	609
Iowa Illinois Gas & Electric Inc.	5.63	NYSE	IA	IWG	IRS, '88-'89	704
Iowa Southern Inc.	6.57	OTC	IA	IUTL	NAARS	616
Ipalco Enterprises Inc.	7.60	NYSE	IN	IPL	IRRC, '90	551
Iroquois Bancorp Inc.	9.94	OTC	NY	IROQ	SEC, 3/90	415
IRT Corp.	6.30	AMEX	CA	IX	Spectrum 5, '90	·631
ITT Corp.	10.30	NYSE	NY	ITT	IRRC, '90	368
Jaclyn Inc.	5.20	AMEX	NJ	JLN	SEC, '89	754
Jacobson Stores Inc.	4.22	OTC	MI	JCBS	IRS, '87	862
James River Corp. of Virginia	11.40	NYSE	VA	JR	Spectrum 5, '90	327
JB's Restaurants Inc.	5.10	OTC	UT	JBBB	SEC, '88	771
Jefferies Group, Inc.	13.80	OTC	CA	JEFG	SEC, '89	241
Jetronic Industries Inc.	9.70	AMEX	PA	JET	SEC, 5/89	431
Johnson Controls Inc.	12.00	NYSE	WI	JCI	Morgan Stanley, 1990	299
Joslyn Corp.	6.90	OTC	IL	JOSL	SEC, 7/90	595

A.1 (Continued)

Company Name	Percent	Exchange	State	Ticker	Source of Data	Rank
Justin Industries Inc.	16.09	OTC	TX	JSTN	SEC, '90	181
K mart Corp.	4.00	NYSE	MI	KM	Verbal	875
K N Energy Inc.	9.49	NYSE	CO	KNE	SEC, 6/90	443
Kaman Corp. CL A	5.00	OTC	CT	KAMNA	Company	786
Kansas City Southern Industries, Inc.	7.90	NYSE	MO	KSU	IRRC, '89	537
Kansas Power & Light Co.	4.64	NYSE	KS	KAN	IRS, '87	836
Kaplan Industries Inc.	7.10	OTC/NQB	FL	KAPL	SEC, 8/89	580
Kay Jewelers Inc.	8.50	NYSE	VA	KJI	SEC, '90	495
Kentucky Utilities Co.	5.30	NYSE	KY	KU	IRRC, '89	746
Kerr Glass Manufacturing Corp.	25.70	NYSE	CA	KGM	SEC, '90	62
Kerr-McGee Corp.	14.40	NYSE	OK	KMG	SEC, 3/89	223
Kevlin Microwave Corp.	14.10	OTC	MA	KVLM	SEC, 8/90	229
Key Tronic Corp.	6.20	OTC	WA	KTCC	Spectrum 6, 7/90	637
KeyData Corp.	18.00	OTC/NQB	MA	KEYD	SEC, 5/89	148
Killearn Properties Inc.	7.50	AMEX	FL	KPI	Spectrum 5, 7/90	553
Kimball International - CL B	12.90	OTC	IN	KBALB	IRS, '87	271
Kimberly-Clark Corp.	5.30	NYSE	TX	KMB	Spectrum 5, 7/90	746
Kimmins Environmental Service Corp.	4.60	NYSE	FL	KVN	NAARS	837
Kinnard Investments Inc.	14.50	OTC	MN	KINN	Spectrum 5	219
KMS Industries Inc.	28.20	OTC	MI	KMSI	SEC, '90	54
Knape & Vogt Manufacturing Co.	6.08	OTC	MI	KNAP	IRS, '87	660
Knight-Ridder Inc.	14.00	NYSE	FL	KRI	WSJ, 11/29/88	233
Koger Properties Inc.	4.00	NYSE	FL	KOG	IRS, '88-'89	875
Koss Corp.	10.90	OTC	WI	KOSS	Spectrum 5	345
Kroger Co.	34.60	NYSE	OH	KR	IRRC, '90	35
KRUG International Corp.	5.57	OTC	OH	KRUG	IRS, '88-'89	717

Company	Price	Exchange	State	Ticker	Source	No.
Kysor Industrial Corp.	23.00	NYSE	MI	KZ	Spectrum 5, 11/90	92
LaBarge Inc.	8.70	AMEX	MO	LB	Spectrum 5, 7/90	481
Lama (Tony) Co. Inc.	20.00	OTC	TX	TLAM	NCEO	112
Landmark Savings Association	10.00	AMEX	PA	LSA	NCEO	384
Lee Pharmaceuticals	5.06	AMEX	CA	LPH	IRS, '88-'89	778
Legg Mason Inc.	9.50	NYSE	MD	LM	SEC, '89	441
Leggett & Platt Inc.	6.75	NYSE	MO	LEG	SEC, 6/89	605
Lesco Inc.	12.50	OTC	OH	LSCO	Verbal	287
Liberty National Bancorp Inc.	8.51	OTC	KY	LNBC	SEC, 3/90	494
Lillian Vernon Corp.	28.00	AMEX	NY	LVC	Franklin Research, '90	55
Liqui-Box Corp.	7.22	OTC	OH	LIQB	IRS, '88-'89	571
Loan America Financial Corp. CL B	7.20	OTC	FL	LAFCB	Spectrum 5	572
Lockheed Corp.	18.90	NYSE	CA	LK	IRRC, '91	138
Logitek Inc.	19.00	OTC	NY	LGTK	SEC, '89	133
Longs Drug Stores Corp.	15.60	NYSE	CA	LDG	IRRC, '90	192
Louisiana General Services Inc.	29.10	NYSE	LA	LGS	Spectrum 6	48
Louisiana-Pacific Corp.	11.60	NYSE	OR	LPX	IRRC, '91	322
Lowe's Companies Inc.	24.00	NYSE	NC	LOW	IRRC, '91	83
Lubrizol Corp.	4.00	NYSE	OH	LZ	IRS, '87	875
Lukens Inc.	12.00	NYSE	PA	LUC	IRRC	299
Lydall Inc.	19.00	AMEX	CT	LDL	SEC, 1989	133
M/A-Com Inc.	7.46	NYSE	MA	MAI	NAARS	559
M/A/R/C Inc.	7.40	OTC	TX	MARC	SEC, '90	561
MacDermid Inc.	22.91	OTC	CT	MACD	SEC, 6/90	94
Madison Financial Corp.	8.80	OTC/NQB	IL	MFLC	SEC, 6/90	476
Madison Gas & Electric Co.	12.80	OTC	WI	MDSN	IRS, '87	278
Magna International Inc CL A	16.00	OTC	Canada	MAGAF	SEC, 6/90	182

A.1 (Continued)

Company Name	Percent	Exchange	State	Ticker	Source of Data	Rank
Manitowoc Co. Inc.	16.87	OTC	WI	MANT	SEC, 6/90	163
Manufacturers Hanover Corp.	8.00	NYSE	NY	MHC	IRRC, '90	529
Mapco Inc.	7.40	NYSE	OK	MDA	IRRC, '90	561
Marathon Office Supply Inc.	4.00	AMEX	CA	MAO	IRS, '87	875
Mark Controls Corp.	7.10	OTC	IL	MRCC	Spectrum 5	580
Marsh & McLennan Companies Inc.	10.10	NYSE	NY	MMC	IRRC, '91	378
Marsh Supermarkets, Inc.	20.00	OTC	IN	MARS	SEC, 1986	112
Martin Marietta Corp.	6.00	NYSE	MD	ML	Company	665
Maui Land & Pineapple Co Inc.	10.75	OTC/NQB	HI	MAUI	SEC, 3/89	351
Maxxam Inc.	8.20	AMEX	CA	MXM	SEC, 10/90	518
May Department Stores Co.	25.00	NYSE	MO	MA	IRRC, '91	69
Maytag Corp. [a]	3.00	NYSE	IA	MYG	Morgan Stanley estimate	902
McCormick & Co. Inc.	26.30	OTC	MD	MCCRK	IRRC, '89	60
McDonald & Co. Investments Inc.	8.48	NYSE	OH	MDD	SEC, 12/89	500
McDonald's Corp.	9.80	NYSE	IL	MCD	Analysis Group, 3/90	426
McDonnell Douglas Corp.	32.60	NYSE	MO	MD	IRRC, '90	41
MCI Communications Corp. [c]	2.42	OTC	DC	MCIC	IRS, '88-'89	906
McKesson Corp.	20.40	NYSE	CA	MCK	IRRC, '90	108
MCORP	17.07	NYSE	TX	M	IRS, '87	159
MDU Resources Group Inc.	8.62	NYSE	ND	MDU	IRS, '88-'89	486
Mead Corp.	4.77	NYSE	OH	MEA	IRS, '87	827
Media General Inc. CL A	10.70	AMEX	VA	MEGA	Spectrum 5	352
Melville Corp.	6.10	NYSE	NY	MES	IRRC, '91	650
Mercantile Stores Co. Inc.	5.70	NYSE	DE	MST	IRRC, '90	695
Merchants Bancorp Inc.	5.25	OTC	CT	NMBC	SEC, 6/90	751
Merchants Bancshares Inc.	9.39	OTC	VT	MBVT	SEC, '90	451

Company	Price	Exchange	State	Symbol	Source	No.
Merchants National Corp.	15.37	OTC	IN	MCHN	IRS, '88 & WSJ 5/15/90	197
Meret Inc.	31.40	OTC	OH	MRET	Spectrum 5	44
Meridian Bancorp Inc.	8.00	OTC	PA	MRDN	PR, 6/28/89	529
Merrill Lynch & Co. Inc.	25.00	NYSE	NY	MER	WSJ, 1/24/89	69
Merrimack Bancorp Inc.	7.50	OTC	MA	MRMK	SEC, '89	553
Met-Coil Systems Corp.	14.70	OTC	IA	METS	Spectrum 5	215
Met-Pro Corp.	7.50	OTC/NQB	PA	MPR	SEC, 5/89	553
Methode Electronics Inc.	13.04	OTC	IL	METHA	IRS, '88-'89	262
MetroBank Financial Group Inc.	15.67	OTC/NQB	NJ	MFGR	SEC, '90	191
Michigan National Corp.	9.00	OTC	MI	MNCO	IRRC, '90	461
MicroAge Inc.	7.50	OTC	AZ	MICA	Spectrum 5	553
Mid-American Lines Inc.	9.50	OTC	KS	MAML	Spectrum 5	442
Midwest Grain Products Inc.	13.80	OTC	KS	MWGP	Spectrum 5	241
Miller (Herman) Inc.	35.00	OTC	MI	MLHR	IRRC, '89	32
Milton Roy Co.	6.00	NYSE	FL	MRC	WSJ, 7/20/89	665
3M [b]	3.40	NYSE	MN	MMM	Morgan Stanley	898
Minnesota Power & Light Co.	6.70	NYSE	MN	MPL	WSJ, 11/28/89	609
Minnetonka Corp.	14.69	OTC/NQB	MN	MINL	SEC, 8/89	217
MNX Inc.	12.40	OTC	MO	MNXI	Spectrum 5	291
Mobile Corp. [c]	2.50	NYSE	NY	MOB	Morgan Stanley	905
Modine Mfg Co.	17.38	OTC	WI	MODI	SEC, 8/90	155
Monarch Capital Corp.	6.90	NYSE	MA	MON	IRRC, '91	595
Monsanto Co.	5.53	NYSE	MO	MTC	IRS, '88-'89	721
Montana Power Co.	8.00	NYSE	MT	MTP	PR, 1/11/90	529
Moog Inc. CL A	7.80	AMEX	NY	MOGA	Spectrum 5	541
Mor-Flo Industries Inc. CL B	13.80	OTC	OH	MORF	Spectrum 5	241
Morgan Stanley Group Inc.	57.20	NYSE	NY	MS	Morgan Stanley Group	5

A.1 (Continued)

Company Name	Percent	Exchange	State	Ticker	Source of Data	Rank
Morrison-Knudsen Corp.	9.70	NYSE	ID	MRN	IRRC, '90	431
Motorola Inc.	9.00	NYSE	IL	MOT	Verbal	461
Nalco Chemical Co.	16.70	NYSE	IL	NLC	IRRC, '91	168
National Banc of Commerce Co.	6.30	OTC	WV	NBCC	Spectrum 5	631
National Commerce Bancorporation	6.10	OTC	TN	NCBC	SEC, '90	650
National Computer Systems Inc.	10.00	OTC	MN	NLCS	IRRC, '91	384
National Convenience Stores Inc.	18.09	NYSE	TX	NCS	IRRC, '91	147
National Fuel Gas Co.	20.00	NYSE	NY	NFG	NCEO	112
National Healthcorp L.P.	17.90	AMEX	TN	NHC	Spectrum 5	149
National Security Group Inc.	7.40	OTC/NQB	N/A	NSEC	Spectrum 5	561
National Security Insurance Co.	9.90	OTC	AL	NSIC	Spectrum 5	418
National-Standard Co.	22.00	NYSE	MI	NSD	SEC, '90	102
Nature's Bounty Inc.	5.60	OTC	NY	NBTY	WSJ, 12/4/84	705
Nature's Sunshine Products Inc.	7.20	OTC	UT	NATR	SEC, 3/89	572
Nelson (L.B.) Corp.	33.10	OTC/NQB	CA	LBN	SEC, '90	38
Nelson (Thomas) Inc.	8.36	OTC	TN	TNEL	IRS, '88-'89	511
Network Systems Corp.	5.11	PSE	MN	NSCO	PR Newswire 11/1/90	769
New Jersey Resources Corp.	4.80	NYSE	NJ	NJR	NCEO	821
New London Inc.	4.00	OTC	TX	NLON	IRS, '87	875
New York Bancorp Inc.	6.09	OTC	NY	NYBC	SEC, '89	659
Newport Electronics Inc.	4.83	OTC	CA	NEWE	IRS, '88-'89	820
Niagara Mohawk Power Corp.	9.92	NYSE	NY	NMK	IRRC, '91	417
Nortek Inc.	11.80	NYSE	RI	NTK	SEC, '90	316
Northeast Bancorp Inc.	9.20	OTC	CT	NBIC	IRRC, '91	455
Northeast Savings F.A.	19.00	NYSE	CT	NSB	IRRC, '89	133
Northern States Power Co.	7.50	NYSE	MA	NSP	IRRC, '90	553

Northern Trust Co.	16.70	OTC	IL	NTRS	IRRC, '90	168
Northrop Corp.	16.40	NYSE	CA	NOC	IRRC, '90	176
Norwest Corp.	10.80	NYSE	MN	NOB	IRRC, '91	347
Nucor Corp.	4.23	NYSE	NC	NUE	IRS, '88-'89	861
NUI Corp.	6.85	NYSE	NJ	NUI	IRS, '88-'89	602
Nynex Corp.	9.57	NYSE	NY	NYN	Morgan Stanley 6/18/90	440
Oakwood Homes Corp.	13.50	NYSE	NC	OH	SEC, 6/90	250
Occidental Petroleum Corp.	4.73	NYSE	CA	OXY	IRS, '88-'89	829
Odetics Inc. CL A	15.40	AMEX	CA	O.A	Spectrum 5	196
Oglebay Norton Co.	9.40	OTC	OH	OGLE	WSJ, 5/31/89	448
Ohio Edison Co.	5.96	NYSE	OH	OEC	Morgan Stanley Group	675
Oilgear Co.	39.40	OTC	WI	OLGR	Spectrum 5	20
Oklahoma Gas & Electric Co.	5.70	NYSE	OK	OGE	IRS, '88-'89	695
Old Republic International Corp.	10.10	OTC	IL	OLDR	Spectrum 5	378
Old Stone Corp.	37.20	OTC	RI	OSTN	IRRC, '91	26
Olin Corp.	23.60	NYSE	CT	OLN	IRRC, '90	89
Olympic Savings Bank	8.12	OTC	WA	OSBW	SEC, 4/90	523
OMI Corp.	12.00	AMEX	NY	OMM	SEC, '89	299
Omni Capital Group Inc.	6.70	OTC	NC	OCGI	Spectrum 5	609
Omnicare Inc.	5.00	NYSE	OH	OCR	SEC, '89	786
On-Line Software International Inc.	4.50	NYSE	NJ	OSI	IRS, '88-'89	846
Oneida Ltd.	14.50	NYSE	NY	OCQ	IRRC, '90	219
Oneok Inc.	10.00	NYSE	OK	OKE	NCEO	384
Optical Coating Laboratory Inc.	22.50	OTC	CA	OCLI	SEC, 11/90	96
Oregon Metallurgical Corp.	67.40	OTC	OR	OREM	SEC, '89	3
Oregon Steel Mills Inc.	47.30	AMEX	OR	OS	SEC, '90	9
ORYX Energy Corp. [a]	3.30	NYSE	TX	ORX	Morgan Stanley	900

A.1 (Continued)

Company Name	Percent	Exchange	State	Ticker	Source of Data	Rank
Otter Tail Power Co.	7.30	OTC	MN	OTTR	Spectrum 5	567
Overland Express Co.	10.16	OTC	IN	OVER	IRS, '87	376
Owens-Corning Fiberglas Corp.	14.50	NYSE	OH	OCF	Company	219
Oxboro Medical International Inc.	11.40	OTC/NQB	MN	LIFL	SEC, 11/90	327
Pacific Enterprises	24.00	NYSE	CA.	PET	IRRC, '90	83
Pacific Gas & Electric Co.	12.80	NYSE	CA	PCG	IRRC, '90	278
Pacific Telesis Group ᵃ	3.72	NYSE	CA	PAC	IRRC, '91	892
PacifiCorp.	4.29	NYSE	OR	PPW	WSJ, 1/4/88	858
Paine Webber Group Inc.	12.13	NYSE	NY	PWJ	IRS, '88–'89	295
Pamrapo Bancorp, Inc.	6.30	OTC	NJ	PBCI	Spectrum 5	631
Pan Am Corp.	13.00	NYSE	NY	PN	NCEO	263
Panhandle Eastern Corp.	6.40	NYSE	TX	PEL	IRRC, '90	621
Parker-Hannifin Corp.	5.21	NYSE	OH	PH	WSJ, 2/23/89	752
Parkvale Financial Corp.	8.47	OTC	PA	PVSA	SEC, 11/90	501
Penn Virginia Corp.	5.44	OTC	PA	PVIR	IRS, '88–'89	736
Penney J.C. Co. Inc.	32.50	NYSE	TX	JCP	IRRC, '91	42
Pennwalt Corp.	8.40	BSE	PA	PSM	SEC, 4/89	503
Pentair Inc.	14.70	OTC	MN	PNTA	WSJ, 3/7/90	215
Penwest Ltd.	5.00	OTC	WA	PENW	WSJ, 12/13/89	786
Peoples Energy Corp.	5.74	NYSE	IL	PGL	IRS, '88–'89	693
Perini Corp.	16.00	AMEX	MA	PCR	IRRC, '91	182
Perpetual Financial Corp.	6.76	OTC	VA	PFCP	SEC, 12/90 estimate	604
Petroleum Equipment Tools Co.	9.00	OTC	TX	PTCO	SEC, '88	461
Petrolite Corp.	10.80	OTC	MO	PLIT	NCEO	347
Pfizer Inc.	4.00	NYSE	NY	PFE	Company	875
Phillips Petroleum Co.	23.90	NYSE	OK	P	Business Wire 9/17/90	87

Company	Price	Exchange	State	Ticker	Source	No.
Phillips-Van Heusen Corp.	5.60	NYSE	NY	PVH	Spectrum 5	705
Pioneer Federal Bancorp Inc.	9.00	OTC	HI	PFBC	Spectrum 5	461
Piper Jaffray Inc.	46.75	OTC	MN	PIPR	SEC, 5/89	10
Plenum Publishing Corp.	11.30	OTC	NY	PLEN	IRS, '87	329
PLM International Inc.	60.60	AMEX	CA	PLM	Goldman Sachs	4
Ply-Gem Industries Inc.	6.90	AMEX	CA	PGI	SEC, '90	595
PNC Financial Corp.	4.00	NYSE	PA	PNC	WSJ, 1/5/90	875
Polaroid Corp.	19.20	NYSE	MA	PRD	IRRC, '91	129
Polifly Financial Corp.	4.80	OTC	NJ	PFLY	Spectrum 5	821
Portec Inc.	12.50	NYSE	IL	POR	SEC, 5/89	287
Portland General Corp.	4.85	NYSE	OR	PGN	WSJ, 9/26/90	817
Potlatch Corp.	4.00	NYSE	CA	PCH	IRS, '88-'89	875
Potomac Electric Power Co.	4.20	NYSE	DC	POM	NCEO	863
Poughkeepsie Savings Bank, FSB	10.00	OTC	NY	PKPS	NCEO	384
PPG Industries Inc.	14.00	NYSE	PA	PPG	IRRC	233
Premier Financial Services Inc.	9.70	OTC	IL	PREM	Spectrum 5	431
Preston Corp.	4.95	OTC	MD	PTRK	NCEO	806
Prima Energy Corp.	10.50	OTC	CO	PENG	Spectrum 5	361
Primark Corp.	6.00	NYSE	VA	PMK	PR, 1/1/89	665
Procter & Gamble Co.	13.20	NYSE	OH	PG	IRRC, '91	260
Production Operators Corp.	5.20	OTC	TX	PROP	Spectrum 5, '90	754
Products Research & Chemicals	20.00	NYSE	GA	PRC	Franklin Research, '90	112
Profit Systems Inc.	7.80	OTC	NY	PFTS	SEC, 5/88	541
Protective Life Corp.	4.00	OTC	AL	PROT	NCEO	875
PS Group Inc.	8.00	NYSE	CA	PSG	Spectrum 5	529
Public Service of New Mexico	4.03	NYSE	NM	PNM	IRS, '87	873
Publix Super Markets Inc.	16.55	OTC/NQB	FL	3PUSH	SEC, 12/90	172

A.1 (Continued)

Company Name	Percent	Exchange	State	Ticker	Source of Data	Rank
Puerto Rican Cement Co., Inc.	5.14	NYSE	PR	PRN	NCEO	768
Puget Sound & Light Co.	4.06	NYSE	WA	PSD	IRS, '88-'89	870
Puget Sound Bancorp	4.10	OTC	WA	PSNB	IRS, '88	868
QSR Inc.	5.40	OTC	FL	TVIV	SEC, '88	739
Quadrex Corp.	5.40	OTC	CA	QUAD	SEC, 6/89	739
Quaker Oats Co.	4.00	NYSE	IL	OAT	WSJ, 1/18/89	875
Quality Mills Inc.	16.40	OTC/NQB	NC	QLTYP	SEC, 5/88	176
Quantum Chemical Corp.	12.50	NYSE	NY	CUE	SEC, '90	287
Questar Corp.	12.40	NYSE	UT	STR	IRRC, '90	291
Radiation Systems Inc.	11.70	OTC	VA	RADS	PR Newswire 10/10/90	320
Ralston Purina Co.	9.40	NYSE	MO	RAL	Spectrum 5	448
Raritan Bancorp Inc.	4.35	OTC	NJ	RARB	NAARS	854
Ravens-Metal Products Inc.	6.10	OTC/NQB	WV	RAVE	SEC, '90	650
Raychem Corp.	5.40	NYSE	CA	RYC	Company	739
Raymond James Financial Inc.	10.00	NYSE	FL	RJF	NCEO	384
RB&W Corp.	7.51	AMEX	OH	RBW	SEC, 12/90 estimate	552
Reading & Bates Corp.	6.12	NYSE	TX	RB	NCEO	649
Recognition Equipment Inc.	8.98	NYSE	TX	REC	SEC, '89	461
Repap Enterprises Corp.	10.97	OTC	Canada	RPAPF	SEC, 11/90	343
Repco Inc.	6.60	OTC	FL	RPCO	SEC, 4/89	614
Republic Gypsum Co.	9.00	NYSE	TX	RGC	NCEO	461
Resorts International Inc.	10.00	BSE	NJ	RT.A	WSJ, 11/13/89	384
Resource America Inc.	9.06	OTC	OH	REXI	SEC, '90	460
Rexworks Inc.	12.90	OTC	WI	REXW	Spectrum 5	271
Reynolds & Reynolds Co. CL A	13.61	NYSE	OH	REYNA	NCEO	248
Reynolds Metals Co.	5.84	NYSE	VA	RLM	IRS, '87	687

284

Company	Price	Exchange	State	Ticker	Source	No.
RF&P Corp.	16.40	OTC/NQB	VA	RFPC	SEC, 6/90	176
Rhodes (M.H.) Inc.	48.90	OTC/NQB	CT	N/A	Spectrum 5	8
Riverside Group Inc.	5.20	OTC	FL	RSGI	Spectrum 5	754
RLI Corp.	27.19	NYSE	IL	RLI	SEC, '90	59
Roadway Services Inc.	17.22	OTC	OH	ROAD	IRRC, '91	157
Robinson Nugent Inc.	4.31	PSE	IN	RNIC	IRS, '87	856
Roblin Industries Inc.	10.06	OTC/NQB	NY	RBL	SEC, 5/88	382
Rochester Community Savings Bank	7.70	OTC	NY	RCSB	IRRC, '90	549
Rockwell International Corp.	41.10	NYSE	CA	ROK	IRRC, '90	17
Rodman & Renshaw Capital Group Inc.	10.40	NYSE	IL	RR	SEC, 6/90	363
Rohm & Haas Co.	17.64	NYSE	PA	ROH	IRRC, '91	151
Ronson Corp.	6.20	BSE	NJ	RONC	SEC, 6/90	637
Rorer Group Inc.	4.80	NYSE	PA	ROR	First Boston 1990	821
Roseville Telephone Co.	9.10	OTC/NQB	CA	RSTE	Spectrum 5	456
Rospatch Corp.	12.90	OTC	MI	RPCH	Spectrum 5	271
Ross Industries Inc.	5.10	OTC	VA	ROSX	SEC, '89	771
Ross Stores Inc.	10.40	OTC	CA	ROST	SEC, 5/90	363
Rowe Furniture Corp.	9.70	AMEX	VA	ROW	SEC, '87	431
Ruddick Corp.	40.50	AMEX	NC	RDK	IRRC, '90	18
Ryland Group Inc.	10.00	NYSE	MD	RYL	IRRC, '91	384
S T V Engineers Inc.	41.70	OTC	PA	STVI	SEC, 5/90	16
S.N.L. Financial Corp. CL A	5.60	OTC	UT	SNLF	Spectrum 5	705
S.N.L. Financial Corp. CL C	20.70	OTC	UT	N/A	Spectrum 5	106
Safeco Corp.	4.08	PSE	WA	SAFC	IRS, '88-'89	869
Sage Broadcasting Corp.	28.60	OTC	CT	SAGB	SEC, 4/90	50
Sage Drilling Co., Inc.	15.10	OTC	KS	SAGE	Spectrum 5	202
San Diego Gas & Electric Co.	7.80	NYSE	CA	SDO	Verbal	541

A.1 (Continued)

Company Name	Percent	Exchange	State	Ticker	Source of Data	Rank
Sanderson Farms Inc.	6.20	OTC	MS	SAFM	SEC, '89	637
Sanmark-Stardust Inc.	16.71	AMEX	NY	SMK	SEC, '90	167
Sara Lee Corp.	5.00	NYSE	IL	SLE	IRRC, '91	786
Savannah Foods & Industries, Inc.	10.80	OTC	GA	SVAN	Spectrum 5, '90	347
Scan-Optics, Inc.	4.13	OTC	CT	SOCR	IRS, '88-'89	866
Scana Corp.	6.13	NYSE	SC	SCG	IRS, '88-'89	648
Sceptre Resources, Ltd.	5.50	AMEX	Canada	SRL	SEC, 4/89	724
Schultz Sav-O Stores Inc.	20.80	OTC	WI	SAVO	Spectrum 5, '90	105
Schwab (Charles) Corp.	10.40	NYSE	CA	SCH	Spectrum 5, 5/8/90	363
Science Management Corp.	8.10	AMEX	NJ	SMQ	Spectrum 5	524
Scientific Software-Intercomp Inc.	10.00	OTC	CO	SSFT	SEC, '90	384
Scott's Liquid Gold Inc.	10.70	OTC	CO	SLIQ	Spectrum 5, '90	352
Scottish Heritable Inc.	14.77	OTC	VA	SHER	SEC, '88	214
Seagull Energy Corp.	5.70	NYSE	TX	SGO	IRRC, '91	695
Sealright Co., Inc.	16.44	OTC	MO	SRCO	IRS, '87	175
Sears, Roebuck Co.	15.10	NYSE	IL	S	IRRC, '91	202
Security American Financial Enterprises Inc.	12.50	OTC/NQB	MN	SAFE	SEC, 6/90	287
Security Financial Group Inc.	10.30	OTC	MI	SFGI	Spectrum 5, '90	368
Seneca Foods Corp.	6.75	OTC	NY	SENE	IRS, '87	605
Servotronics Inc.	37.50	AMEX	NY	SVT	Spectrum 5	25
SFE Technologies	4.00	OTC	CA	SFEM	IRS, '87	875
Shearson Lehman Hutton Holdings Inc. °	9.43	NYSE	NY	SLH	SEC, 12/90 estimate	447
Sherwin-Williams Co.	16.30	NYSE	OH	SHW	IRRC, '90	179
Sherwood Group, Inc.	5.70	AMEX	NY	SHD	SEC, '90	695
Simmons First National Corp.	9.00	OTC	AR	SFNCA	Spectrum 5	461
Smucker (J.M.) Co.	4.20	NYSE	OH	SJM	IRRC, '91	863

286

Company	Price	Exchange	State	Ticker	Source	No.
Society Corp.	9.31	PSE	OH	SOCI	IRS, '88-'89	453
Somerset Bankshares Inc.	10.10	OTC	MA	SOSA	Spectrum 5	378
South Carolina National Corp.	13.90	OTC	SC	SCNC	IRRC, '90	237
South Jersey Industries, Inc.	11.52	NYSE	NJ	SJI	IRS, '88-'89	324
Southeastern Michigan Gas Enterprises, Inc.	12.60	OTC	MI	SMGS	SEC, '89	285
Southern New England Telecommunications, Corp.	7.70	NYSE	CT	SNG	IRRC, '91	549
Southside Bancshares Corp.	19.90	OTC/NQB	MO	SOBN	Spectrum 5	119
Southwest Airlines Co.	8.34	NYSE	TX	LUV	IRS, '88-'89	514
Southwest Gas Corp.	5.94	NYSE	NV	SWX	IRS, '88-'89	676
Southwestern Bell Corp.	5.00	NYSE	MO	SBC	NCEO	786
Southwestern Public Service Co.	4.37	NYSE	TX	SPS	IRS, '88-'89	852
SPS Technologies Inc.	10.00	NYSE	PA	ST	WSJ, 9/9/89	384
SPX Corp.	12.00	NYSE	MI	SPW	IRRC, '90	299
Square D Co.	6.80	NYSE	IL	SQD	IRRC, '91	603
St. Paul Bancorp Inc.	5.01	OTC	IL	SPBC	SEC, 2/90	784
St. Paul Companies, Inc.	7.04	PSE	MN	STPL	NAARS	585
Standard Brands Paint Co.	18.90	NYSE	CA	SBP	IRRC, '91	138
Standard Motor Products, Inc.	6.90	NYSE	NY	SMP	IRRC, '91	595
Standex International Corp.	12.00	NYSE	NH	SXI	IRRC, '91	299
Stanley Works	28.30	NYSE	CT	SWK	Company	53
Starrett (L.S.), Co. CL A	22.91	NYSE	MA	SCX	SEC, '89	94
Statesman Group, Inc.	10.00	OTC	IA	STTG	SEC, '90	384
Sterling Chemicals, Inc.	25.00	NYSE	TX	STX	Verbal	69
Stone & Webster, Inc.	51.60	NYSE	NY	SW	IRRC, '91	6
Sun City Industries, Inc.	23.92	AMEX	FL	SNI	WSJ, 4/5/90	86
Sungroup, Inc.	7.20	OTC/NQB	TN	SUNNC	SEC, 5/90	572
Sunstar Foods Inc.	8.02	OTC	MN	SUNF	IRS, '87	528

A.1 (Continued)

Company Name	Percent	Exchange	State	Ticker	Source of Data	Rank
SunTrust Banks Inc.	5.00	NYSE	GA	STI	IRRC, '89	786
Superior Holding Corp.	7.10	OTC/NQB	GA	SPRCC	SEC, 6/90	580
Superior Teletec, Inc.	16.00	AMEX	GA	STT	NCEO	182
Swank Inc.	71.60	OTC	MA	SNKI	Spectrum 5	2
Syncor International Corp.	13.00	OTC	CA	SCOR	WSJ, 11/22/89	263
Systems & Computer Technology Corp.	8.31	OTC	PA	SCTC	Verbal	515
Tab Products Co.	5.72	AMEX	CA	TBP	SEC, 6/89	694
Tal-Cap Inc.	24.70	OTC/NQB	MN	TALC	SEC, 6/89	79
Talley Industries, Inc. CL B	17.90	NYSE	AZ	TAL	Spectrum 5	149
Tandy Brands, Inc.	12.00	AMEX	TX	TAB	SEC, 6/90	299
Tandycrafts, Inc.	37.20	NYSE	TX	TAC	SEC, 10/90	26
TCF Financial Corp.	7.60	NYSE	MN	TCB	Spectrum 5	551
TCI International Inc.	25.30	OTC	CA	TCII	Spectrum 5, 6/30/90	65
Team Inc.	5.21	AMEX	TX	TMI	SEC, 12/89	752
Technical Coatings Inc.	9.60	OTC/NQB	TX	TCIC	SEC, 9/89	436
Technical Communications Corp.	15.00	OTC	MA	TCCO	NCEO, '90	204
Technology Development Corp.	12.00	OTC	TX	TDCX	SEC, '88	299
TECO Energy, Inc.	6.00	NYSE	FL	TE	IRRC, '91	665
Tennant Co.	13.50	OTC	MN	TANT	Spectrum 5	250
Tenneco Inc. [a]	3.25	NYSE	TX	TGT	IRS, '88-'89	901
Termiflex Corp.	25.48	OTC	NH	TFLX	SEC, '90	63
Texaco Inc.	7.00	NYSE	NY	TX	IRRC, '91	587
Texas Instruments Inc.	13.18	NYSE	TX	TXN	IRRC, '91	261
Texas Utilities Co.	6.00	NYSE	TX	TXU	NCEO	665
Textron Inc.	19.80	NYSE	RI	TXT	IRRC, '91	120
Time Warner Inc. [c]	2.00	NYSE	NY	TL	IRS, '88-'89	910

288

Company	Price	Exchange	State	Ticker	Source	No.
Times-Mirror Co.	7.30	NYSE	CA	TMC	IRRC, '91	567
Timken Co.	5.20	NYSE	OH	TKR	IRS, '88-'89	754
Titan Corp.	5.70	NYSE	CA	TTN	IRS, '88	695
TJ International Inc.	15.20	OTC	ID	TJCO	Business Wire 9/18/90	200
Tokheim Corp.	14.80	NYSE	IN	TOK	IRRC, '91	212
Topps Company Inc.	36.70	OTC	NY	TOPPC	Barron's 12/14/87	29
Toro Co.	20.50	NYSE	MN	TTC	IRRC, '91	107
Trans-Industries Inc.	5.60	OTC	MI	TRNI	SEC, 8/90	705
Transamerica Corp.	5.45	NYSE	CA	TA	IRS, '88-'89	735
Transco Energy Co.	12.90	NYSE	TX	E	IRRC, '90	271
Travelers Corp.	4.80	NYSE	CT	TIC	Morgan Stanley	821
Tribune Co.	10.00	NYSE	IL	TRB	IRRC, '91	384
TRW Inc.	16.70	NYSE	OH	TRW	IRRC, '91	168
Tucson Electric Power Co.	4.13	NYSE	AZ	TEP	IRS, '87	866
Turner Corp.	15.20	AMEX	NY	TUR	IRRC, '91	200
Tyler Corp.	34.00	NYSE	TX	TYL	IRRC, '90	37
Tyson Foods	25.00	OTC	AR	TYSNA	NCEO, '90	69
U S West Inc.	13.50	NYSE	CO	USW	Analysis Group, 3/90	250
U.S. Bancorp	14.10	OTC	OR	USBC	IRRC, '91	229
U.S. Healthcare Inc.	10.00	PSE	PA	USHC	SEC, 5/89	384
U.S. Trust Corp.	12.80	OTC	NY	USTC	SEC, '90	278
Ultimap International Corp.	8.35	OTC	MN	UMAP	SEC, 6/90	513
UMC Electronics Co	16.80	OTC/NQB	CT	UMCE	SEC, 7/87	164
Union Camp Corp.	6.40	NYSE	NJ	UCC	%EO EST	621
Union Carbide Corp.	10.00	NYSE	CT	UK	Morgan Stanley, '90	384
Union Electric Co.	4.38	NYSE	MO	UEP	IRS, '87	851
Union Planters Corp.	4.70	NYSE	TN	UPC	IRRC, '90	830

A.1 (Continued)

Company Name	Percent	Exchange	State	Ticker	Source of Data	Rank
Unisys Corp.	5.80	NYSE	PA	UIS	Morgan Stanley	689
United Bancorp	17.00	OTC/NQB	OR	UORE	SEC, 6/90	160
United Banks of Colorado	10.20	OTC	CO	UBKS	IRS, '88-'89	372
United Carolina Bancshares Corp.	6.03	OTC	NC	UCAR	NAARS	662
United Companies Financial Corp.	19.40	OTC	LA	UNCF	IRRC, '91	125
United Missouri Bancshares Inc.	7.00	OTC	MO	UMSB	IRRC, '91	587
United Oklahoma Bankshares, Inc.	23.30	OTC/NQB	OK	UOBI	Spectrum 5	91
United Technologies Corp.	12.00	NYSE	CT	UTX	Company estimate	299
United Telecommunications	4.53	NYSE	KS	UT	IRS, '88-'89	845
Unitel Video Inc.	5.51	AMEX	NY	UNV	NAARS	723
Unitog Co.	6.50	OTC	MO	UTOG	SEC, 6/90	617
Universal Corp.	5.00	NYSE	VA	UVV	IRRC, '91	786
Unocal Corp.	8.40	NYSE	CA	UCL	IRRC, '91	503
Upjohn Co.	5.20	NYSE	MI	UPJ	Morgan Stanley, 6/19/90	754
USAir Group Inc.	5.00	NYSE	DC	U	Goldman Sachs, '90	786
USG Corp.	18.80	NYSE	IL	USG	IRRC, '90	141
USLICO Corp.	5.60	NYSE	VA	USC	SEC, '86	705
USX Corp.	13.00	NYSE	PA	X	Company	263
UTL Corp.	10.40	OTC	TX	UTLC	SEC, '90	363
Valero Energy Corp.	6.40	NYSE	TX	VLO	IRRC, '90	621
Valley Bancorporation	12.90	OTC	WI	VYBN	IRRC, '90	271
Valley Federal Savings & Loan Association	8.40	OTC	CA	VFEDC	SEC, 11/90	503
Valspar Corp.	10.00	AMEX	MN	VAL	IRRC, '90	384
VanFed Bancorp	8.70	OTC	WA	VANF	SEC, '89	481
Varian Associates	5.00	NYSE	CA	VAR	Company	786
Velobind Inc.	27.30	OTC	CA	VBND	SEC, 12/90	58

Venturian Corp.	5.80	OTC	MN	VENT	EO DCP 87	689
VF Corp.	6.70	NYSE	PA	VFC	Company	609
Vista Chemical Co.	6.27	NYSE	TX	VC	NAARS	635
VSB Bancorp Inc.	5.47	OTC	NJ	VSBC	SEC, '90	734
VSE Corp.	16.80	OTC	VA	VSEC	SEC, '90	164
Walbro Corp.	6.40	OTC	MI	WALB	SEC, '90	621
Wall Street Financial Corp.	5.50	OTC	CA	WSFC	SEC, 6/90	724
Walmart Stores Inc. c	2.40	NYSE	AK	WMT	IRS, '87	907
Warren Bancorp Inc.	5.50	OTC	MA	WRNB	SEC, 6/90	724
Washington Bancorp Inc.	5.98	OTC	NJ	WNBC	SEC, '90	674
Waterhouse Investors Services Inc.	8.90	OTC	NY	WHOO	Spectrum 5, '90	473
Webster Financial Corp.	6.20	OTC	CT	WBST	SEC, '89	637
Weirton Steel Corp.	73.40	NYSE	VA	WS	IRRC, '91	1
Westamerica Bancorporation	9.90	AMEX	CA	WAB	Spectrum 5, '90	418
Western Digital Corp.	8.40	AMEX	CA	WDC	IRRC, '91	503
Western Federal Savings Bank	5.01	OTC	CA	WFPR	SEC, 8/89	784
Western Union	10.00	NYSE	NJ	WU	NCEO	384
Westmoreland Coal Co.	9.07	OTC	PA	WMOR	IRS, '88-'89	459
Weston (Roy F.) Inc.	25.10	OTC/NQB	PA	WSTNA	SEC, '89	68
Westvaco Corp.	14.00	NYSE	NY	W	IRRC, '90	233
Wetterau Inc.	11.10	OTC	MO	WETT	IRRC, '91	337
Weyerhaeuser Co.	4.41	NYSE	WA	WY	Company	849
Wheeling-Pittsburgh Steel Corp.	33.00	NYSE	WV	QWHX	NCEO	39
Whitman Corp.	10.00	NYSE	IL	WH	IRRC, '91	384
Whittaker Corp.	7.00	NYSE	CA	WKR	Company	587
Wichita River Oil Corp. Colorado	27.90	AMEX	CO	WRO	SEC, 12/90 estimate	56
Wilfred American Educational Corp.	8.60	NYSE	NY	WAE	Spectrum 5	489

A.1 (Continued)

Company Name	Percent	Exchange	State	Ticker	Source of Data	Rank
Willamette Industries, Inc.	12.00	OTC	OR	WMTT	SEC, '90	299
Williams Companies Inc.	10.30	NYSE	OK	WMB	IRRC, '90	368
Wisconsin Energy Corp.	5.48	NYSE	WI	WEC	IRS, '88-'89	732
Wisconsin Public Service Corp.	5.00	NYSE	WI	WSP	IRRC, '91	786
Wolohan Lumber Co.	4.96	OTC	MI	WLHN	IRS, '87	805
Woodward Governor Co	19.50	OTC/NQB	IL	WGOV	SEC, 8/90	124
Workingmens Corp.	5.91	OTC	MA	WCBK	SEC, 5/89	677
WorldCorp Inc.	6.90	NYSE	VA	WOA	SEC, '90	595
Worldwide Computer Services Inc.	13.90	OTC	NJ	WCSI	SEC, 5/90	237
Worthington Industries, Inc.	5.20	PSE	OH	WTHG	IRRC, '90	754
WPL Holdings Inc.	5.00	NYSE	WI	WPH	IRRC	786
Wrigley (Wm.) Jr. Co.	4.90	NYSE	IL	WWY	IRS, '88-'89	811
Xerox Corp.	10.00	NYSE	CT	XRX	IRRC, '91	384
Xyvision Inc.	7.00	OTC	MA	XYVI	NCEO, 6/16/89	587
Yellow Freight System	23.90	OTC	KS	YELL	IRRC, '91	87
York Research Corp.	5.52	OTC	CT	YORK	NAARS	722
Zions Bancorporation	13.00	OTC	UT	ZION	IRRC, '89	263

292

Additional Companies

Company						N/A
Angeles Corp.	50.00	AMEX	CA	ANG	Company	N/A
ARX Inc.	4.00	NYSE	NY	ARX	SEC, 1/91 estimate	N/A
Bancorp of Mississippi Inc.	10.51	OTC	MS	BOMS	Verbal	N/A
Basic Earth Sciences System Inc.	13.00	OTC	CO	BSIC	Verbal	N/A
Bay View Capital Corp.	5.95	NYSE	CA	BVFS	BWR 1/28/91	N/A
Benguet Corp.	17.08	NYSE	PH	BE	SEC, 1/91 estimate	N/A
Bethlehem Steel Corp.	5.60	NYSE	PA	BS	Company	N/A
BFS Bankorp Inc.	5.00	OTC	NY	BFSI	Verbal	N/A
Boeing Co. [d]	1.05	NYSE	WA	BA	IRS, '88 estimate	N/A
Bristol-Myers Squibb Co. [c]	1.70	NYSE	NY	BMY	Company	N/A
BSD Bancorp Inc.	4.10	AMEX	CA	BSD	Company	N/A
Builders Transport, Inc.	13.90	OTC	SC	TRUK	Spectrum, 1/91	N/A
Cablevision Inc. [b]	3.65	AMEX	NY	CVC	Company	N/A
Capital Bancorp Inc. Florida	5.60	OTC/NQB	FL	CAPL	Spectrum 5	N/A
Carriage Industries Inc.	4.00	NYSE	GA	CGE	SEC Proxy, 3/90	N/A
Caspen Oil Inc.	20.30	AMEX	TX	CNO	Spectrum, 1/91	N/A
Centerior Energy Corp. [a]	3.70	NYSE	OH	CX	Company	N/A
Central Cooperative Bank	6.88	OTC	MA	CEBK	BWR, 2/25/91	N/A
Chesapeake Utilities Corp.	4.00	OTC	DE	CHPK	IRS, '88 estimate	N/A
Chrysler Corp. [c]	1.79	NYSE	MI	C	IRS, '88 estimate	N/A
Cochrane Furniture Inc.	11.30	OTC/NQB	NC	3CFUR	Spectrum, 1/91	N/A
CPB Inc.	8.80	OTC	HI	CPBI	Spectrum, 1/91	N/A
Crown Cork & Seal Co., Inc. [a]	3.14	NYSE	PA	CCK	IRS, '88 estimate	N/A
DCB Corp.	8.30	OTC/NQB	IN	3DCBC	Spectrum, 1/91	N/A
Distribuco Inc.	10.60	OTC/NQB	CA	N/A	Spectrum, 1/91	N/A
Dominion Resources Inc.	4.00	NYSE	VA	D	Company	N/A

A.1 (Continued)

Company Name	Percent	Exchange	State	Ticker	Source of Data	Rank
Du Pont (E.I.) De Nemours & Co., Inc. [c]	1.52	NYSE	DE	DD	IRS, '88 estimate	N/A
Duke Power Co.	8.30	NYSE	NC	DUK	Company	N/A
Eastman Kodak Co. [c]	2.77	NYSE	NY	EK	IRS, '88 estimate	N/A
Entergy Services [b]	3.86	NYSE	LA	ETR	Company	N/A
Excel Bancorp Inc.	36.00	OTC	MA	XCEL	BWR, 2/19/91 estimate	N/A
First Citizens Bankshare Inc.	18.40	OTC	NC	FCNCB	Spectrum, 1/91	N/A
Flemington National Bank & Trust Co.	5.27	OTC/NQB	NJ	3FLNB	IRS, '88 estimate	N/A
Fluor Corp	4.01	NYSE	CA	FLR	Company	N/A
Franklin Savings Association	4.00	OTC/NQB	KS	3FSAK	WSJ, 9/6/90	N/A
Fremont General Corp.	12.10	OTC	CA	FRMT	Spectrum 5	N/A
General Datacomm Industries Inc.	9.57	NYSE	CT	GDC	SEC Proxy, 3/90	N/A
General Motors CL E	13.00	NYSE	TX	GME	Company	N/A
General Re Corp. [a,n]	3.05	NYSE	CT	GRN	Company	N/A
Grant Industries Inc.	16.90	OTC/NQB	NY	N/A	Spectrum, 1/91	N/A
Gray Communications Systems Inc.	6.20	OTC/NQB	GA	3GCOM	Spectrum, 1/91	N/A
Harsco Corp.	4.00	NYSE	PA	HSC	IRS, '88 estimate	N/A
Haverfield Corp.	6.26	OTC	OH	HVFD	WSJ, 2/28/91	N/A
Hazelton National Bank	4.66	OTC/NQB	PA	N/A	IRS, '88 estimate	N/A
Heico Corp.	5.14	AMEX	FL	HEI	Company, estimate	N/A
Hewlett-Packard Co.	5.41	NYSE	CA	HWP	Company, estimate	N/A
Jesup Group Inc.	8.50	OTC	CT	JGRPC	Spectrum, 1/91	N/A
Lancaster Colony Corp.	4.00	OTC	OH	LANC	ESOP, 11/12/90	N/A
McRae Industries Inc. CL A	17.70	AMEX	NC	MRI.A	SEC Proxy, 3/90	N/A
McRae Industries Inc. CL B	16.40	AMEX	NC	MRI.B	SEC Proxy, 3/90	N/A
Metro Bancshares Inc.	6.90	OTC	NY	MTBS	Spectrum, 1/91	N/A
Mitchell Energy & Development Corp.	4.00	AMEX	TX	MND	IRS, '88 estimate	N/A

Company						
MNC Financial Inc. [d]	1.20	NYSE	MD	MNC	IRS, '88 estimate	N/A
Momentum Distribution Inc.	7.65	NYSE	WA	MMDI	PR, 4/25/90 estimate	N/A
Mutual Savings Life Insurance Co.	55.50	OTC/NQB	AL	3MUTS	Spectrum, 1/91	N/A
National Savings Bank of Albany	6.04	OTC	NY	NSBA	WSJ, 12/28/90	N/A
NCR Corp.	8.00	NYSE	OH	NCR	Company, 2/21/91	N/A
Northbay Financial Corp.	5.10	AMEX	CA	NBF	Company	N/A
NWNL Cos.	8.40	OTC	MN	NWNL	WSJ, 1/3/91 estimate	N/A
Nycom Information Services, Inc.	15.00	AMEX	CT	NYCM	Company	N/A
Ohio Casualty Corp.	9.00	NYSE	OH	OCAS	Company	N/A
Pepsico Inc. [c]	2.94	NYSE	NY	PEP	Company	N/A
Philip Morris Cos. Inc. [c]	2.00	NYSE	NY	MO	Company	N/A
Pinnacle West Capital Corp. [a]	3.59	NYSE	AZ	PNW	Company	N/A
Premier Bank	8.46	OTC	LA	PRBC	Company	N/A
Robeson Savings Bank, Inc.	7.27	OTC/NQB	NC	N/A	IRS, '88 estimate	N/A
SCE Corp. (Southern California Edison Co.)	11.00	NYSE	CA	SCE	Company	N/A
Simetco Inc.	16.70	OTC	OH	SMET	Spectrum, 1/91	N/A
Sonat Inc. [ac]	3.00	NYSE	AL	SNT	IRS, '88 estimate	N/A
The Waltham Corp.	4.41	OTC	MA	WLBK	PR, 1/25/91 estimate	N/A
Tribune/Swab-Fox Cos., Inc.	6.10	OTC	OK	TSFC	IRS, '88 estimate	N/A
U.S. West Inc. [d]	1.45	NYSE	CO	USW	IRS, '88 estimate	N/A
Union Pacific Corp. [c]	1.62	NYSE	PA	UNP	IRS, '88 estimate	N/A
United Federal Bancorp Inc.	5.00	OTC	PA	UFBK	DJNW, 3/12/91	N/A
Univar Corp.	4.00	NYSE	WA	UVX	IRS, '88 estimate	N/A
Ventura County National	12.56	OTC	CA	VCNB	WSJ, 12/28/90 estimate	N/A
Waste Management Inc. [d]	1.06	NYSE	IL	WMX	Company, estimate	N/A
Wisconsin Savings Association	11.15	OTC/NQB	WI	3WISA	IRS, '88 estimate	N/A
Zenith Electronics Corp.	4.00	NYSE	IL	ZE	NCEO	N/A

Companies Delisted

Company Name	Percent	Exchange	State	Ticker	Source of Data
Adams Russell Electronics Co. Inc.	15.70	AMEX	MA	D.AIF	SEC, 8/90
Alamo Savings Association of Texas	11.24	OTC	TX	D.AIX	SEC, 7/90
AME Inc.	35.73	OTC	CA	D.AOU	SEC, 5/88
Amerco	5.18	OTC	NV	D.ADK	SEC, 5/90
American Capital & Research Corp.	21.80	OTC	VA	D.APR	SEC, 5/90
American Carriers Inc.	6.74	OTC	KS	D.ADQ	IRS, '88-'89
American Western Corp.	14.80	OTC	SD	D.ABK	SEC, 12/90
Anchor Financial Corp.	5.20	OTC	SC	D.APH	Spectrum 5, 8/90
Arthur D. Little Inc.	5.33	OTC	MA	D.ANL	SEC, 6/90
AST General Corp.	11.10	OTC	TX	D.AFE	SEC, 8/90
Atlantic Financial Federal	20.80	OTC	PA	D.ALF	SEC, 12/90
Avant Garde Computing Inc.	5.37	OTC	NJ	AVGAQ	IRS, '88-'89
Baddour Inc.	7.05	OTC	TN	D.BPX	SEC, 90
Bank Building & Equipment Corp. of America	32.80	AMEX	MO	D.BBL	SEC, 12/90
Barry Wright Corp.	15.60	NYSE	MA	D.BYN	IRRC, '90
Baruch Foster Corp.	8.56	AMEX	TX	BFO	IRS, '88-'89
Begley Co.	31.02	OTC	KY	D.BWA	SEC, 8/90
Bozzuto's Inc.	15.55	OTC	CT	D.BFT	IRS, '88-'89
Care Enterprises Inc.	6.70	AMEX	CA	D.CST	Spectrum 5
CDK Holding Corp.	5.29	OTC	N/A	D.CPF	SEC, '90
Centrust Bank	13.80	AMEX	FL	DLP	SEC, 7/90
Charter Crellin Inc.	18.50	OTC	NY	D.CWH	SEC, 8/90
Charter Medical Corp.	68.40	AMEX	GA	D.CJO	SEC, 10/90

Citizens Western Corp.	11.91	OTC	CA	D.CGT	SEC, 12/90
Clark Consolidated Industries	21.42	AMEX	OH	D.CEN	SEC, 5/88
Coltec Industries Inc.	29.00	BSE	NY	D.COT	SEC, 5/88
Columbus Energy Corp.	10.80	OTC	CO	D.CVY	SEC, '90
Commerce Group Inc.	16.50	OTC	MA	D.C46	SEC, 12/90
Commercial Bancshares Inc.	9.71	OTC	WV	D.CBO	SEC, 10/90
Community Bancorp Inc.	5.64	OTC	NY	D.CEA	SEC, 12/90
Community Bankshares Inc.	8.56	OTC/DQS	AL	D.CBH	SEC, 12/90
Community Bankshares Inc. Virginia	6.57	OTC/DQS	VA	D.CBT	SEC, 8/90
Compiler Technology Inc.	13.40	OTC	MS	D.CKV	SEC, 4/90
Computer Aided Timeshare Inc.	6.28	OTC	MN	D.CPI	SEC, '90
Cone Mills	21.40	OTC	NC	COE	SEC, 12/90
Consolidated Capital Equities Corp.	51.00	AMEX	TX	N/A	SEC, '90
Cullinet Software Inc.	8.28	NYSE	MA	D.CTA	SEC, 12/90
Daubert Industries Inc.	46.30	OTC	IL	D.DPF	SEC, 10/90
DCB Corp.	8.40	OTC	IN	D.DBI	SEC, 8/90
Deer Park Financial	22.67	OTC	OH	D.DRE	SEC, 12/90
Delaware Savings Bank FSB	5.32	OTC/DQS	DE	D.DTK	SEC, 10/90
Develcon Electronics Ltd	17.42	OTC	Canada	D.DDR	NAARS
DST Systems Inc.	9.49	OTC	MO	DSTS	IRS, '88-'89
East Texas Capital Corp.	6.20	OTC	TX	D.ECT	SEC, 12/90
Economy Savings Bank	5.60	OTC	PA	D.EQF	SEC, 8/90
Emery Air Freight Corp.[i]	17.98	NYSE	CT	D.EFH	SEC, '89
Empire Banc Corp.	12.90	OTC	MI	D.EAI	SEC, 7/90
Empire of America FSB	5.60	AMEX	NY	D.ERI	WSJ 1/8/88

A.1 Delisted (Continued)

Company Name	Percent	Exchange	State	Ticker	Source of Data
Epic Healthcare Group Inc.	59.77	OTC	N/A	D.EAR	SEC, '90
ERC International Inc.	4.00	NYSE	VA	ERC	IRS, '88-'89
Financial Guardian Group Inc.	24.70	OTC	N/A	D.FBS	Spectrum 5
Fireman's Fund	6.10	NYSE	CA	D.FDU	SEC, 12/90
First & Ocean Bancorp	5.38	OTC/DQS	MA	D.FKU	SEC, 12/90
First Bank Corp.	10.94	OTC/DQS	MI	D.FUW	SEC, 12/90
First Community Bancshares Inc.	5.35	OTC	WV	D.FDZ	SEC, 12/90 estimate
First Financial Corp.	9.80	OTC	IN	D.FQM	Spectrum 5
First Financial of Russellville Inc.	8.90	OTC	KY	D.FGW	SEC, 12/90
First Financial Shares Inc.	10.00	OTC	KY	D.FBG	SEC, 12/90
First Independence Corp.	13.70	OTC	N/A	D.FBX	Spectrum 5
First-Citizens National Bank of Dyersburg	18.10	OTC/DQS	TN	D.FPX	SEC, 12/90
Flying J Inc.	11.14	OTC	UT	D.FCP	SEC, 10/90
Forum RE Group Bermuda Ltd	36.50	OTC	Bermuda	D.FLD	SEC, 12/90
Genway Corp.	12.60	OTC	IL	D.GCB	SEC, '90
GMX Communications	75.14	OTC/DQS	FL	D.GMXE	SEC, 5/89
Hardinge Brothers Inc.	11.40	OTC	NY	D.HOE	Spectrum 5
Harvest Financial Corp.	10.00	OTC	IA	D.HTS	SEC, 12/90
Hauserman Inc.	4.53	OTC	OH	HASRQ	IRS, '88-'89
Heritage Bancorp Inc.	6.50	OTC	MI	D.HQI	SEC, 12/90
Hofmann Industries Inc.	5.00	AMEX	PA	HOF	Company
Home Owners Federal Savings & Loan Association	7.00	NYSE	MA	D.HDR	SEC, 12/90
Horizon Bancorp	7.77	OTC/DQS	IN	D.HPP	SEC, 4/90
Indspec Chemical Corp.	11.70	OTC	PA	D.IDO	SEC, 8/90

298

Company	Price	Exchange	State	Ticker	Source
Infergene Co.	7.70	OTC/DQS	CA	D.IUR	Spectrum 5, 90
Jorgensen (Earle M.) Co.	12.25	NYSE	CA	JOR	IRS, '88-'89
Kaiser Steel Resources Inc.	48.80	OTC	CA	D.KFJ	SEC, 8/90
Kettle Restaurants Inc.	23.60	OTC	TX	D.KAX	SEC, 10/90
Latshaw Enterprises Inc.	11.00	AMEX	KS	LAT	IRS, '88-'89
LCB Bancorp Inc.	10.62	OTC/DQS	OH	D.LGH	SEC, 10/90
Macmillan Inc.	9.60	NYS	NY	D.MIY	SEC, 5/90
Marquette Electronics Inc.	20.50	OTC	WI	D.MNO	SEC, 10/90
Maxxam Inc.	35.50	OTC	CA	D.MLM	SEC, 4/90
Minnetonka Corp.	14.69	OTC	MN	D.MHK	SEC, 10/90
Mohasco Corp.	7.03	NYSE	VA	D.MLQ	IRS, '87
Monat Capital Corp.	43.50	OTC	MO	D.MFR	SEC, '90
Monitor Technologies Inc.	11.11	OTC	CA	D.MHO	IRS, '88-'89
Monolith Portland Cement Co.	45.00	OTC/DQS	CA	D.MIJ	SEC, '90
Moore (Benjamin) & Co.	5.30	OTC/DQS	NJ	D.BBX	SEC, 10/90
Moran (J.T.) Financial Corp.	7.70	NYSE	NY	D.JPD	SEC, 10/90
Morsemere Financial Group Inc.	15.67	OTC	NJ	D.MBW	SEC, 10/90
Mosler Inc.	9.40	OTC	OH	X.MOS	SEC, 11/90
NBT Bancorp Inc.	7.54	OTC/DQS	NY	D.NNN	SEC, 2/90
North Valley Bancorp	5.40	OTC/DQS	CA	D.NEM	SEC, 5/89
Norton Co.	6.14	NYSE	MA	NRT	IRS, '88-'89
Palmetto Bancshares Inc.	6.48	OTC	SE	D.PEQ	SEC, 10/90
Parkvale Savings Association	7.50	OTC/DQS	PA	D.PCE	SEC, 3/89
Paxton (Frank) Co. CL A	9.08	OTC	MO	PAXTA	IRS, '88-'89
Peoples Savings Bank of Brockton	7.04	OTC	MA	D.PWY	SEC, 10/90 estimate

A.1 Delisted (Continued)

Company Name	Percent	Exchange	State	Ticker	Source of Data
Peoria Journal Star Inc.	32.54	OTC	IL	D.PMG	SEC, 5/90
Scicom Data Services	67.00	OTC	MN	D.SIK	SEC, '90
Scotty's Inc.	6.92	NYSE	FL	D.SII	SEC, 10/90
Search Natural Resources Inc.	26.23	OTC/DQS	CO	D.SJA	SEC, 2/90
Security American Financial Enterprises Inc.	12.50	OTC	MN	D.SJI	SEC, 10/90
Security Savings & Loan Association	12.99	OTC/DQS	CT	D.SPW	SEC, 10/90
Seeburg Corp.	6.00	NYSE	IL	D.SUF	SEC, 12/90
Shawsville Bancorp Inc.	23.00	OTC	VA	D.SDD	SEC, 10/90
SICO Inc.	88.00	OTC	IN	D.SBQ	SEC, 7/90
Sigma Form Corp.	5.77	OTC	CA	D.SGMA	SEC, '89
Smithkline Beckman Corp.	5.00	NYSE	PA	D.SCG	Company estimate
Sorg Inc.	5.00	AMEX	NY	SRG	IRS, '88-'89
Southeastern Michigan Gas Co.	12.60	OTC	MI	D.S21	SEC, 7/90
Sovran Financial Corp.	5.00	NYSE	VA	SOV	IRS, '88-'89
Sterling Financial Corp.	6.67	OTC	PA	D.SIP	SEC, 7/90
Sunstar Foods Inc.	8.70	OTC	MN	D.SNP	SEC, '87
System Integrators Inc.	5.60	MID	CA	D.SCF	SEC, '90
Trans World Airlines Inc.	6.00	CSE	NY	D.TCQ	SEC, 10/90
Tri City Bankshares Corp.	17.90	OTC/DQS	WI	D.TDV	SEC, 7/87
Trico Brancshares	10.00	OTC/DQS	CA	D.TEH	SEC, 5/90
US Bancorp Inc.	5.50	OTC	OR	D.ULJ	IRS, '87
Utah Power & Light Co.	5.08	NYSE	UT	D.UAJ	IRS, '88-'89
UTL Corp.	10.40	OTC	CA	D.UOB	SEC, 11/90

Western Federal Savings & Loan Association	9.95	OTC/DQS	CA	D.WDY	SEC, 11/90
Western Financial Savings Bank	13.20	OTC	N/A	D.WNL	SEC, '90
Western Savings & Loan Association	7.20	NYSE	AZ	D.WNO	IRS, 88-'89
WestFed Holdings Inc.	9.65	OTC	CA	D.WOA	SEC, 12/90

Notes

Special circumstances which have come to the authors' attention are discussed in the footnotes. Also, Employee ownership by employee benefit plans which constitutes less than four percent of the market value of a select number of companies is reported. These are companies whose employee holdings are enormous in dollar value relative to their total market value.

a. Over $1 Billion and over 3%
b. Over $500 Million and over 3.5%
c. Over $5 Billion and over 1.5%
d. Over $10 Billion and over 1%
e. Over $25 Billion and over .5%
f. Over $50 Billion and over .25%
g. Employees hold 1% of stock and 4% of voting power. This may also be true with other companies, but the information was not available.
h. Avery International Corp. and Dennison Manufacturing Co. have merged, but no further information was available.
i. Emery Air Freight Corp. and Consolidated Freightways Inc. have merged, but no further information was available.
j. In January 1991 the company announced that it would be acquired by General Cinema Corp. No further information was available.
k. Company has recently filed for bankruptcy.
l. Company has recently filed for bankruptcy.
m. Total employee ownership of this company exceeds four percent when all classes of stock are taken into account.
n. This represents preferred shares. Company savings plan owns .15% of common shares.
o. Company was recently taken private by American Express.

Table by Shane Williams

Legend

Following is a description of headings, stock exchanges, and Table A.1, sources of information used for the **Employee Ownership 1000,** and the **Public Company Employee Ownership Database.**

I.   Headings (Columns) in the Employee Ownership 1000

Ticker.   This symbol identifies a corporation's stock and is typically listed in the *Wall Street Journal*. It can be used to find out information on the stock price and the company on electronic databases, such as the Dow Jones News Service (Telephone 609-452-1511) and Prodigy (1-800-822-6922). Ticker symbols and stocks for which prices are not quoted in the "Money and Investing" (Section C) portion of the *Wall Street Journal* are not traded enough to be reported. Information on these stocks may be available from broker/dealers who subscribe to the National Daily Quotation Service "Pink Sheets" (described below) or from the OTC Bulletin Board of the National Association of Securities Dealers (202-728-8000). A "3" preceding a ticker symbol refers to the symbol for a stock listed on the "Pink Sheets" of the National Daily Quotation Service (201-435-9000).

Company Name.   This is the name of the company as it typically appears for the purposes of stock trading. *CL A* or *CL B* refers to Class A or B common stock. *PFD* or *CONV PFD* refers to preferred or convertible preferred stock. A state abbreviation after a company name refers to the state of incorporation. *FSB* means Federal Savings Bank.

EO%.   The *employee-ownership percentage* is the presumed amount of the company's stock owned by the company's employees *as reported or estimated from the public source(s) cited*. Information for each public company was searched in each source, or database, as described below from January 1990 to February 1991. References to employee ownership from all sources were then examined for each company record, and the most recent source, which in our judgment was most reliable, was chosen. These numbers are for research and descriptive purposes only and should be confirmed before being used as a basis for any material decision.

Exchange.   This is the exchange on which the corporation's stock is traded. OTC/NQB means that the stock is traded through a network of traders whose firms are listed on the "Pink Sheets" of the National Quotation Bureau. Information on these companies may also be available from the OTC Bulletin Board.

State.   Two-letter state abbreviation.

Source.   Source of the employee-ownership percentage.

II.   The Stock Exchanges

NYSE.   This is the New York Stock Exchange, listing almost 1800 corporations. Trading is done "on the floor" in New York City. Information on companies trading in this marketplace, including total market value and number of shares outstanding, is available in printed form by calling the Research Department at 212-656-3000.

AMEX.   This is the American Stock Exchange, listing almost 850 corporations. Trading is done in New York City. Information on companies trading in this marketplace, including total market value and number of shares outstanding, is available by calling the Research Department at 212-306-1000 for the *AMEX Fact Book.*

OTC. This is the Over-The-Counter market, which has no physical trading floor. Traders are linked by telephone lines and computers. The most actively traded 4000 or so stocks are listed by the National Association of Securities Dealers (NASD) on its Automated Quotation system (referred to as NASDAQ), which allows a trader to look on a screen to monitor the market price for a stock. A "NASDAQ Symbol Explanation," appearing daily in the lower right-hand corner of *Wall Street Journal's* NASDAQ listings, explains how to interpret important information contained in the company ticker symbol. Information on companies trading in this marketplace, including total market value and total numbers of shares outstanding, is available in printed form by calling Information Services at 301-590-6500. NASDAQ also publishes the *NASDAQ Company Directory.*

OTC/NQB. This is also the Over-The-Counter market, but several tens of thousands of smaller company stocks traded in this marketplace are not traded enough to be listed on a major exchange. The ticker symbol is sometimes preceded by the number *3.* They are compiled by the National Quotation Bureau in Jersey City, New Jersey. Each night a daily "telephone book of stocks" printed on thin pink paper is sent out to investment and trading houses around the country, which list the stock, its ticker symbol, the bid and the asked price, and the name and telephone number of a firm trading that security. Thus, these are called "Pink-Sheet" companies. In January and July of each year, NQB publishes *The National Stock Summary,* which summarizes all the companies that have appeared in the National Daily Quotation Service. This book is the indispensable source on the OTC market and also an excellent source for company name and address changes and bankruptcy information. NASD is automating some of these listings in its OTC Bulletin Board.

BSE. This is a regional stock exchange located in Boston. Regional exchanges, which list stocks of other exchanges plus stocks in their own region, are also located in Chicago (Midwest Stock Exchange) and in Los Angeles (Pacific Stock Exchange).

CSE. This is the Cincinnati Stock Exchange.

PSE. This is the Philadelphia Stock Exchange.

N/A. *Not Available* is used mainly for delisted companies, for which information on the exchange is not readily available.

D., or Delisted. A *D.* preceding a ticker symbol means that the company is delisted from a stock exchange. Companies are delisted for these reasons: they have been sold; they have filed for bankruptcy, or have been liquidated; they have violated exchange rules; they have been taken private; or they are delinquent in filing reports to the U.S. Securities and Exchange Commission.

III. SOURCES

This column lists the public sources for the employee-ownership percentage with the abbreviations used in the Employee Ownership 1000 list. *The sources are listed in the order we generally considered the most useful.* These sources are also used to construct the *Public Company Employee Ownership Database,* on which the chapters of the book are based. That database contains a text storyline of each company's employee-ownership history. Potential limitations of each source are discussed. Generally, employee ownership through employee benefit plans that did not involve a leveraged-ESOP transaction are not announced in databases except in the U.S. Department of Labor, Form 5500, Report of Employee Benefit Plan and Spectrum 5. The extent of the limitations suggests to the authors that there is considerably more significant employee ownership in public companies, which has not yet been identified. This also explains how the Employee Ownership 1000 database was constructed. The reader is provided with information, so that he or she can independently access all these sources. Using these sources with a computer modem and a good reference library, an employee or investor can compile substantial information on a company.

Company. In December 1990 to January 1991, personal letters were sent to the chief executive officers of about 750 of the Fortune 1000 firms and all AMEX firms, for which we were unable to find employee-ownership information, and requested data for use in this book. This information was kindly and generously provided by the corporate officers or their staff members. A limitation is that many companies with employee share-purchase programs do not compile, or will not release, the number of shares directly bought by employees. Also, over 75 percent of the CEOs did not respond to the letter.

Verbal. From October 1990 to December 1990, research assistants telephoned the investor relations or benefits departments of Fortune 1000 corporations. and corporations, for which our only source was an old and unreliable *Report on Employee Benefit Plan* (IRS Form 5500). A limitation is that most public corporations would not provide information over the telephone, while many companies refused to cooperate or neglected to get back to us with the information as they promised they would.

SEC. Reports that all public corporations in the United States from 1986 to January 1991 are required to make to the U.S. Securities and Exchange Commission were searched. These include Annual Reports, President's Letter, Management Discussion, Financial Footnotes, Proxy Materials, and disclosure of more than 5 percent owners of the company's stock. All references to any form of employee ownership were identified and read for every public company for every year. Compact Disclosure and Disclosure Database, both trademarks of Disclosure Incorporated of Bethesda, Maryland, computerize these SEC filings and make them available through many business libraries and electronic databases. It is also available on the Dow Jones News Service. Their phone number is 301-951-1300. Paper and microfiche copies of all corporate documents can be obtained overnight or by fax by calling 1-800-874-4337 or 202-789-2233. The date cited is the date of the month that the data was retrieved, not the date of the corporate report. A limitation is that more than 50 percent of the corporations did not report to the SEC significant employee ownership *referred to in other public sources* or provide actual percentages or detailed information from which such percentages could be estimated and information on employee share-purchase plan holdings is generally completely unavailable.

IRRC. Corporate proxy statements are materials sent to shareholders before the annual meeting. The Investor Responsibility Research Center of Washington, D.C. (202-939-6500) monitors this and other shareholder information for 1500 corporations and publishes the results annually in *Corporate Takeover Defenses,* compiled by Virginia Rosenbaum. The limitation is that about 50 percent of these corporations are not disclosing significant employee ownership in their corporate proxies.

Spectrum 5. *All public corporations* are required to file Schedules 13D, 13G, and 14D-1, describing all individuals or entities who are beneficial owners of 5 percent or more of their stock with the U.S. Securities and Exchange Commission. All filings for all corporations were examined from July 1989 to January 1990. The most recent filing, even if it occurred in 1988 or 1989, is included. These filings are computerized by CDA Investment Technologies of Rockville, Maryland, and are available through a monthly subscription service by calling 301-975-9600. Their limitation is that 80 percent of public companies with significant employee ownership do not disclose it to the Securities and Exchange Commission through these reports. One explanation is that some companies have multiple employee-ownership plans, which individually are under 5-percent holders, although many companies may be confused about whether employee holdings should be filed.

Spectrum 6. Officers, directors, and 10 percent principal stockholders ("insiders") are required to file Forms 3 and 4 as periodic reports with the SEC. A semiannual report is published by CDA Investment Technologies. A limitation is that less than 5 percent of public corporations report employee benefit plan holdings in these filings.

PR. PR Newswire of New York City (212-832-9400) collects and makes available press releases of over 15,000 corporations and organizations. All press releases were read. Current press releases from 1989 are available on the Dow Jones News Service, and an archive of press releases since 1980 is available on LEXIS of Mead Data Central (800-543-6862 or 513-859-1608). More than 50 percent of the companies do not issue press releases about major employee-ownership transactions or developments.

BWR. Business Wire, another corporate press release newswire representing 11,000 companies, is also available on the Dow Jones News Service. All press releases were read. Same limitations as above.

Wall Street Journal. All articles since June 1969 were printed out on the Dow Jones News Service and read. The limitation is that AMEX and OTC companies and non-leveraged employee ownership is generally underreported. Even for Fortune 1000 firms, it is estimated that at least 40 percent of significant employee-ownership stakes and transactions are never reported.

Dow Jones News Service. This service makes available articles and news not always printed in the *Wall Street Journal*. All releases since 1979 were read. Same limitations as above.

We searched and read every article on employee ownership in *Business Week* (since 1985), the *Washington Post* (since January 1984), *Fortune, Forbes,* and the *American Banker.* A limitation is that none of these publications ever served as the sole independent source of employee-ownership information, although they contain many useful analytical articles.

NAARS. The National Automated Accounting Research System contains annual reports with recent accounting information from more than 4200 publicly traded companies made available by the American Institute of Certified Public Accountants. It is available on LEXIS. All employee-ownership transactions were examined for 1989. A limitation is that NAARS deals mainly with large companies and reports on transactions.

Investment Banks. Investment banks, which advise public corporations on leveraged ESOPs, maintain lists of announced transactions. Morgan Stanley, First Boston, and Goldman Sachs provided the most useful lists.

IRS 1988–1989. Every company must report an Annual Return Form 5500/Report of Employee Benefit Plan for all employee benefit plans covered by ERISA. Form 5500C is filed for small plans with under 100 employee participants. Ownership of company securities is provided and we have computed estimates based on this information. The main limitation is that computer access to this information involves a 1–2-year lag, so that recent employee ownership cannot be identified. Also, we estimate that over 25 percent of significant employee ownership is not reported. But the most recent individual reports are available for inspection or purchase at the Department of Labor (202-523-8771).

NCEO.   The National Center for Employee Ownership (415-272-9461), a nonprofit research and information center, tracks employee ownership and publishes company lists based largely on a national clipping service of newspapers and magazines, which it markets for a modest fee. The Center's *Employee Ownership Report* examines company developments bimonthly and its *Journal of Employee Ownership Law and Finance* has many articles dealing with public companies. The clipping service is the best bimonthly source of company news on employee ownership, but over 50 percent of the Employee Ownership 1000 are not mentioned there. All the above were examined.

ESOP Association.   This is the national lobbying organization for ESOP companies located in Washington, D.C. (202-293-2971). *The ESOP Report* contains a section, "ESOP News from the States," which reports on public companies. Only major recent employee-ownership transactions are reported.

Barron's.   *Barron's* articles and references to employee ownership in corporations were examined from July 1987 through the Dow Jones News Service. A limitation is that most transactions are not mentioned in *Barron's,* although its analytical reporting led to several important discoveries.

Analysis Group.   This institutional investor research group (617-489-4200) published a study of employee ownership and takeover defenses, which included employee ownership percentages. The report is limited to large companies and transactions from 1988 to 1990.

Franklin Research.   This investor research group (617-423-6655) published a study of employee ownership in major companies. The report is limited to examples.

Datatimes.   Contains the full text of over 100 U.S. and Canadian newspapers and magazines. Its strength is regional coverage and smaller newspapers. All publications were searched and read from September 1990 to January 1991 in order to monitor small-company transactions not available through the clipping service, which has a two-month delay in delivery. A limitation is that over 50 percent of company transactions are not covered by the regional press.

IRS '87.   Same as IRS '88–'89, except this is an older database. In this year it was not possible to distinguish between employee benefit plan investments that held company real estate and those that held company stock, although we estimated that over 80 percent of employee holdings were in stock. IRS '88–'89 has improved recording, which largely eliminates this problem. This should be confirmed when it is the only source.

Estimate.   An estimate is the least reliable source. It is based on taking a publicly reported dollar value of employee holdings (usually reported as the size of a leveraged-ESOP loan in an SEC filing) or a publicly reported figure on the number of shares held by an employee plan and computing that as a percentage of most recent figures for total market value or total shares outstanding. Estimates should be confirmed. The reason for our letters to the CEOs of Fortune 1000 firms was to confirm such estimates.

Appendix B

Employee Ownership and Stock Buybacks

TABLE B.1 *Employee Ownership and Stock Buybacks with Year, Exchange, Share Type, and Takeover Environment Noted*

Year	Company	Exchange	Type of Shares	Takeover
'80	E-Systems Inc.	NYSE	Common	No
'80	Florida Steel Corp.	NYSE	Common	No
'80	Leggett & Platt	NYSE	Common	No
'81	Elcor Corp.	NYSE	Common	No
'82	Perini Corp.	AMEX	Common	No
'82	Koss Corp.	OTC	Common	No
'82	Tosco Corp.	NYSE	Common	No
'82	Anthony Industries Inc.	NYSE	Common	No
'83	Bank South Corp.	OTC	Common	No
'83	Odetics Inc. CL B	AMEX	Common	Yes
'84	CPT Corp.	OTC	Common	Yes
'84	American First Corp.	OTC	Common	No
'84	Nature's Bounty Inc.	OTC	Common	No
'84	AT&T	NYSE	Common	No
'84	M.D.C. Holdings Inc.	NYSE	Common	No
'84	Rangaire Corp.	OTC	Common	No
'84	Avon Products	NYSE	Common	No
'84	Butler Manufacturing	OTC	Common	No
'84	Syscon Corp.	N/A	Common	No
'85	Kansas City Southern Inc.	NYSE	Common	No
'85	American Express	NYSE	Common	No
'85	Landmark Savings Association	AMEX	Common	No
'85	Midcon Corp.	N/A	Common	No
'85	New Jersey Resources Corp.	NYSE	Common	Yes

(*continued*)

TABLE B.1 *(Continued)*

Year	Company	Exchange	Type of Shares	Takeover
'85	NAFCO Financial Group	N/A	Common	No
'86	Bank of New York	NYSE	Common	No
'86	Figgie International	OTC	Common	No
'86	GTE	NYSE	Common	Yes
'86	AEL Industries	OTC	Common	No
'86	America West Airlines	OTC	Common	No
'86	Resorts International Inc.	AMEX	Common	Yes
'86	Valspar Corp.	AMEX	Common	No
'86	Vermont American Corp.	AMEX	Common	No
'86	Honeywell Inc.	NYSE	Common	Yes
'87	Tokheim Corp.	NYSE	Conv. Pfd.	No
'87	CBI Industries	NYSE	Common	No
'87	Carlisle Cos.	N/A	Common	No
'87	Clinical Data Inc.	OTC	Common	No
'87	Comfed Bancorp	AMEX	Common	No
'87	Bank Building & Equipment Corp.	AMEX	Common	Yes
'87	Boston Five Bancorp	OTC	Common	Yes
'87	Rochester Community Savings Bank	OTC	Common	No
'87	Foote Cone & Belding Communications	NYSE	Common	No
'87	Atlantic Financial Federal Inc.	N/A	Common	No
'88	EDO Corp.	NYSE	Conv. Pfd.	No
'88	Jefferies Group Inc.	OTC	Common	Yes
'88	Northern Trust Co.	OTC	Common	No
'88	Tandycrafts Inc.	NYSE	Common	Yes
'88	Chemed Corp.	NYSE	Common	No
'88	Capital Federal Savings & Loan	OTC	Common	No
'88	Lowe's Cos.	NYSE	Common	Yes
'88	Baldor Electric Co.	NYSE	Common	No
'88	Bell Industries Inc.	NYSE	Common	No
'88	Cape Cod Bank & Trust Co.	OTC	Common	No
'88	Cayuga Savings Bank	OTC	Common	No
'88	DBA Systems Inc.	OTC	Common	Yes
'88	First Republic Bancorp	AMEX	Common	No
'88	James Madison Ltd.	AMEX	Common	No
'88	Knight-Ridder	NYSE	Common	No
'88	Home Depot Inc.	NYSE	Common	No
'88	Advest Group Inc.	NYSE	Common	Yes
'88	Charter One Financial Inc.	OTC	Common	No

(continued)

TABLE B.1 *(Continued)*

Year	Company	Exchange	Type of Shares	Takeover
'88	AmVestors Financial Corp.	N/A	Common	No
'89	Barnett Banks	NYSE	Common	No
'89	Elko Industries	OTC	Common	No
'89	Big O Tires	OTC	Common	No
'89	Frequency Electronics	AMEX	Common	No
'89	Craftmatic-Contour Industries	OTC	Conv. Pfd.	No
'89	MicroAge	OTC	Common	No
'89	Chambers Development Co.	AMEX	Common	No
'89	Chesapeake Corp.	NYSE	Common	No
'89	Contel Cellular Inc.	NYSE	Common	No
'89	McDonald & Co. Investments	NYSE	Common	No
'89	Financial Benefits Group	OTC	Common	No
'89	Gerber Products	NYSE	Common	No
'89	Kerr-McGee Corp.	NYSE	Common	Yes
'89	Grow Group Inc.	NYSE	Common	No
'89	Hammond Co.	OTC	Common	No
'89	Indiana Federal Corp.	OTC	Common	No
'89	Integra Financial Corp.	OTC	Common	No
'89	Inter-Regional Financial Grp	NYSE	Common	No
'89	Lincoln Telecommunications	OTC	Common	Yes
'89	Minnesota Power & Light Co.	NYSE	Common	No
'89	Moog Inc.	AMEX	Common	No
'89	National Computer Systems Inc.	OTC	Common	No
'89	Nu Horizons Electronics Corp.	AMEX	Common	No
'89	Continental Bank Corp.	NYSE	Common	No
'89	Oryx Energy Co.	NYSE	Common	No
'89	Pacific Bancorp	OTC	Common	No
'89	Parker-Hannifin	NYSE	Common	No
'89	Peoples Federal Savings Bank	OTC	Common	No
'89	Sears, Roebuck & Co.	NYSE	Common	Yes
'89	Polifly Financial Corp.	OTC	Common	No
'89	Quaker Oats Co.	NYSE	Conv. Pfd.	No
'89	TCBY Enterprises Inc.	NYSE	Common	No
'89	Waterhouse Investors Services	OTC	Common	No
'89	Valero Energy Corp.	NYSE	Common	No
'89	Standard Motor Products	NYSE	Common	No
'89	Fluorocarbon Co.	N/A	Common	No
'89	Instrument Systems Corp.	AMEX	Common	No
'89	Boston Bancorp	OTC	Common	No
'89	Glaco Inc.	NYSE	Common	No
'89	Idaho Power Co.	NYSE	Common	No

(continued)

TABLE B.1 *(Continued)*

Year	Company	Exchange	Type of Shares	Takeover
'89	U.S. Trust Corp.	OTC	Common	Yes
'89	LecTec Corp.	N/A	Common	No
'89	BayBanks Inc.	OTC	Common	No
'89	BellSouth Corp.	NYSE	Common	No
'89	Bowater Inc.	NYSE	Common	Yes
'89	Brunswick Corp.	NYSE	Common	No
'89	Buffton Corp.	AMEX	Common	No
'89	Ameritech Corp.*	NYSE	Common	No
'89	Commerce Bancorp, Inc.	OTC	Common	No
'90	Cincinnati Bell Inc.	NYSE	Common	No
'90	Graham Corp.	AMEX	Common	No
'90	Pentair Inc.	OTC	Conv. Pfd.	No
'90	St. Paul Cos.	OTC	Conv. Pfd.	No
'90	Aon Corp.	NYSE	Common	No
'90	Radiation Systems	OTC	Common	No
'90	PNC Financial Corp.	NYSE	Common	No
'90	Nynex	NYSE	Common	No
'90	Montana Power Co.	NYSE	Common	No
'90	Farr Co.	OTC	Common	No
'90	Central Bancshares of the South	OTC	Common	Yes
'90	Buckeye Financial Corp.	OTC	Common	No

*American Information Technologies Corp.

Appendix C

Employee Ownership and Cashing out Large Shareholders

TABLE C.1 *Employee Ownership and Cashing out Large Holders by Year, Exchange, and Takeover Environment*

Company	Exchange	Takeover Environment	Year
Adams-Russell Electronics	AMEX	Yes	1988
ALCO Standard Corp.	NYSE	No	1982
Allied Group	OTC	No	1990
American Western Corp.	OTC	No	1989
Anderson Clayton & Co.	NYSE	No	1986
Artra Group Inc.	NYSE	No	1989
Badger Meter Inc.	AMEX	No	1984
Bell National Corp.	OTC	No	1984
Bonneville Pacific Corp.	OTC	No	1989
C.R. Gibson Co.	AMEX	No	1988
Circus Circus Enterprises	NYSE	No	1989
Continental Bank Corp.	NYSE	No	1983
Cooker Restaurant Corp.	OTC	No	1989
Craftmatic-Contour Industries	OTC	No	1989
Diamond Shamrock Inc.	NYSE	No	1989
Fairchild Industries	NYSE	No	1989
Flight International Group (The)	OTC	No	1989
Flow International Corp.	OTC	No	1989
Gannett	NYSE	Yes	1990
Glaco Inc.	NYSE	No	1989
Graham Corp.	AMEX	No	1990
Hach Co.	OTC	No	1989
Horn & Hardart	NYSE	Yes	1989
Integrity Entertainment Corp.	AMEX	No	1983

(continued)

TABLE C.1 *(Continued)*

Company	Exchange	Takeover Environment	Year
Jaclyn Inc.	AMEX	No	1989
Methode Electronics	OTC	No	1981
Mobile Telecommunications Technologies	OTC	No	1984
Outboard Marine	NYSE	No	1984
Pitt-Des Moines Inc.	AMEX	No	1990
Production Operators Corp.	OTC	No	1989
Rangaire Corp.	OTC	No	1986
Republic Gypsum	NYSE	No	1986
Resorts International	AMEX	Yes	1986
Rohm & Haas	NYSE	No	1990
Sage Drilling Co.	OTC	No	1985
Sanmark-Stardust Inc.	AMEX	No	1985
Seagull Energy Corp.	NYSE	No	1989
Synalloy Corp.	AMEX	No	1989
Syncor International	OTC	No	1989
Synergen	OTC	No	1988
Termiflex Corp.	OTC	No	1987
WorldCorp	NYSE	No	1989

Appendix D

Employee Ownership and Newly Issued Shares

TABLE D.1 *Employee Ownership and Newly Issued Shares by Year, Takeover Environment, Use of an Antidilution Buyback, Type of Shares Used, and Dollar Value*

Mo	Yr	Company	Exchange	Dollar Value	Type of Shares	T[a]	A[b]
1	'81	AT&T	NYSE	$100,000,000	Common	No	No
10	'81	Exxon	NYSE	$173,800,000	Common	No	No
7	'81	Lowe's Cos.	NYSE	$14,000,000	Common	Yes	No
10	'82	Cox Communications	NYSE	$2,800,000	Common	Yes	Yes
5	'82	Perini Corp.	AMEX	$6,081,800	Common	No	No
9	'82	Phillips Petroleum	NYSE	N/A	Common	No	No
11	'82	Swank Inc.	NYSE	$7,475,104	Conv. Pfd.	Yes	No
3	'83	Butler Manufacturing	OTC	$9,200,000	Common	No	Yes
4	'83	Columbia Gas System	NYSE	$100,000,000	Common	No	No
4	'83	General Mills	NYSE	$95,000,000	Common	No	Yes
9	'83	Primark Corp.	NYSE	$8,000,000	Common	No	No
10	'83	Scotty's Inc.	NYSE	N/A	Common	Yes	No
11	'84	Starrett (L.S.) CL A	NYSE	N/A	Common	No	Yes
1	'85	Brown & Sharpe	NYSE	$6,000,000	Common	No	No
9	'85	Clark Equipment	NYSE	$85,000,000	Common	No	No
6	'85	Connecticut Energy Corp.	NYSE	N/A	Common	No	No
7	'85	Federal Express	NYSE	$50,000,000	Common	No	No
6	'85	Freedom Savings & Loan	OTC	N/A	Conv. Pfd.	No	No

(continued)

TABLE D.1 *(Continued)*

Mo	Yr	Company	Exchange	Dollar Value	Type of Shares	T[a]	A[b]
9	'85	Holly Corp.	AMEX	$1,287,300	Common	Yes	No
8	'85	Kansas City Southern Industries	NYSE	$70,000,000	Common	No	No
7	'85	Michigan National Corp.	OTC	$43,300,000	Common	No	No
5	'85	National Convenience Stores	NYSE	$30,000,000	Common	No	Yes
7	'85	Ogden Corp.	NYSE	$90,000,000	Conv. Pfd.	No	No
6	'85	Ply-Gem Industries	AMEX	N/A	Common	No	No
10	'85	Profit Systems Inc.	OTC	N/A	Common	No	No
4	'85	Times Mirror -DEL.	NYSE	$150,000,000	Common	No	No
6	'86	Apogee Enterprises	OTC	N/A	Common	Yes	No
1	'86	Bank of New York	NYSE	$25,500,000	Common	No	No
6	'86	Cincinnati Bell	NYSE	$75,000,000	Common	No	No
1	'86	Figgie International	OTC	$12,000,000	Common	No	No
11	'86	GTE	NYSE	$474,800,000	Common	Yes	No
3	'86	Texas American Energy Corp.	OTC	$6,000,000	Conv. Pfd.	Yes	No
7	'86	VF Corp.	NYSE	$65,000,000	Conv. Pfd.	No	No
8	'87	Affiliated Bank Corp.	OTC	$13,000,000	Conv. Pfd.	Yes	No
5	'87	Diamond Shamrock R&M Corp.	NYSE	$60,000,000	Common	Yes	No
7	'87	Donaldson Co.	NYSE	$21,000,000	Common	No	Yes
8	'87	Emery Air Freight	NYSE	$20,800,000	Common	Yes	No
12	'87	First Republic Bancorp	AMEX	12 percent	Common	No	No
11	'87	FMC Corp. Valisys Corp.	N/A	20 percent	Common	No	No
5	'87	Harcourt Brace Jovanovich	NYSE	$151,352,000	Conv. Pfd.	Yes	No
10	'87	Imperial Holly Corp.	AMEX	$150,000,000	Common	Yes	No
10	'87	Macmillan	NYSE	$60,000,000	Common	Yes	No
11	'87	Moog Inc. -CL A	AMEX	N/A	Common	No	No
12	'87	Moseley Holding Corp.	OTC	N/A	Common	No	No
7	'87	National Standard	NYSE	$12,000,000	Common	No	No
10	'87	NBS Bancorp Inc.		$671,600,000	Common	No	No
1	'87	NBSC Corp.	OTC	N/A	Common	No	No

(continued)

TABLE D.1 *(Continued)*

Mo	Yr	Company	Exchange	Dollar Value	Type of Shares	T[a]	A[b]
6	'87	Oneida Ltd.	NYSE	$12,500,000	Common	No	No
1	'87	Public Service Co. of Colorado	NYSE	$1,100,000	Common	No	No
10	'87	Statesman Group Inc.	OTC	$9,000,000	Conv. Pfd.	No	Yes
4	'87	Texaco Inc.	NYSE	$500,000,000	Conv. Pfd.	Yes	No
10	'87	Tokheim Corp.	NYSE	$26,000,000	Conv. Pfd.	No	No
12	'87	Wesbanco Inc.	OTC	N/A	Common	No	No
12	'88	American Bankers Insurance Group	OTC	$20,000,000	Conv. Pfd.	No	No
4	'88	Aristech Chemical Corp.	NYSE	$60,000,000	Common	No	No
1	'88	Barry Wright Corp.	NYSE	$50,000,000	Common	No	No
11	'88	Cabot Corp.	NYSE	$75,000,000	Conv. Pfd.	No	Yes
2	'88	Champion Parts Rebuilders	OTC	$36,000,000	Common	Yes	No
1	'88	Charter-Crellin Inc.	OTC	$3,500,000	Common	Yes	No
4	'88	Dahlberg Inc.	OTC	$2,875,000	Common	No	No
10	'88	EDO Corp.	NYSE	$19,200,000	Conv. Pfd.	No	Yes
10	'88	Forum Re Group Bermuda Limited	OTC	$5,000,000	Common	No	No
12	'88	Idaho Power Co.	NYSE	$22,428,048	Common	No	No
8	'88	J. C. Penney	NYSE	$700,000,000	Conv. Pfd.	No	Yes
4	'88	Jefferies Group	OTC	$9,000,000	Common	Yes	No
10	'88	Merrill Lynch	NYSE	$220,000,000	Common	No	No
1	'88	Minnetonka Corp.	OTC	$30,000,000	Common	Yes	No
11	'88	Northern Trust Co.	OTC	$75,000,000	Common	No	Yes
4	'88	Old Stone Corp.	OTC	$25,000,000	Conv. Pfd.	No	No
1	'88	Optical Coating Laboratory	OTC	$1,100,000	Conv. Pfd.	Yes	No
3	'88	Polaroid	NYSE	N/A	Common	Yes	Yes
1	'88	Quantum Chemical	NYSE	$13,600,000	Common	No	Yes
11	'88	Ralston Purina	NYSE	$500,000,000	Conv. Pfd.	No	Yes
1	'88	Southwest Gas Corp.	NYSE	N/A	Common	No	No
1	'88	Tandycrafts	NYSE	$21,900,000	Common	Yes	No
11	'88	Tribune Co.	NYSE	N/A	Common	No	Yes
10	'88	Tyler Corp.	NYSE	N/A	Common	No	No
7	'89	A. P. Green Industries	OTC	9.2 percent	Common	Yes	Yes
10	'89	Allied Group	OTC	$36,000,000	Conv. Pfd.	No	No

(continued)

TABLE D.1 *(Continued)*

Mo	Yr	Company	Exchange	Dollar Value	Type of Shares	T[a]	A[b]
5	'89	Ameritrust	OTC	$71,700,000	Common	No	Yes
4	'89	Anheuser-Busch	NYSE	$500,000,000	Common	No	Yes
6	'89	Armstrong World Industries	NYSE	$270,000,000	Conv. Pfd.	No	Yes
5	'89	Ball Corp.	NYSE	$70,000,000	Conv. Pfd.	No	Yes
11	'89	Barnett Banks	NYSE	$175,000,000	Common	No	Yes
7	'89	Beeba's Creations Inc.	OTC	$5,000,000	Conv. Pfd.	No	Yes
10	'89	Bell Atlantic	NYSE	$1,000,000,000	Common	No	No
6	'89	Betz Laboratories	OTC	$100,000,000	Conv. Pfd.	No	No
12	'89	Big O Tires	OTC	$2,500,000	Common	No	No
5	'89	Boise Cascade	NYSE	$300,000,000	Conv. Pfd.	No	Yes
4	'89	Brunswick Corp.	NYSE	$100,000,000	Common	No	Yes
10	'89	Carolina Power & Light	NYSE	$300,000,000	Common	No	No
11	'89	Chevron	NYSE	$1,000,000,000	Common	No	Yes
9	'89	Chubb	NYSE	$150,000,000	Common	No	No
12	'89	Cincinnati Gas & Electric	NYSE	$5,088,000	Common	No	No
6	'89	Colgate Palmolive	NYSE	$410,000,000	Conv. Pfd.	Yes	Yes
8	'89	Commerce Bancorp	OTC	$7,500,000	Common	No	No
2	'89	Consolidated Freightways	NYSE	$150,000,000	Conv. Pfd.	Yes	Yes
8	'89	Corning Inc.	NYSE	$50,000,000	Conv. Pfd.	No	No
5	'89	CPC International	NYSE	$200,000,000	Conv. Pfd.	No	Yes
12	'89	Craftmatic-Contour Industries	OTC	$6,237,000	Conv. Pfd.	No	No
7	'89	Cummins Engine	NYSE	$75,000,000	Common	Yes	Yes
7	'89	Delta Air Lines	NYSE	$500,000,000	Conv. Pfd.	Yes	Yes
4	'89	Dunkin' Donuts	OTC	$300,000,000	Common	Yes	Yes
7	'89	Eaton Corp.	NYSE	$150,000,000	Conv. Pfd.	No	Yes
2	'89	Ecko Group Inc.	NYSE	$18,300,000	Conv. Pfd.	Yes	Yes
10	'89	Elko Industries Inc.	OTC	$3,600,000	Common	No	No
1	'89	Federal-Mogul Corp.	NYSE	$62,000,000	Conv. Pfd.	Yes	Yes
4	'89	Ferro Corp.	NYSE	$70,500,000	Conv. Pfd.	Yes	Yes
12	'89	Frequency Electronics	AMEX	$5,000,000	Common	No	No
7	'89	General Re Corp.	NYSE	$150,000,000	Conv. Pfd.	No	Yes
7	'89	Gerber Products	NYSE	$21,000,000	Common	No	No

(continued)

TABLE D.1 *(Continued)*

Mo	Yr	Company	Exchange	Dollar Value	Type of Shares	Tª	Aᵇ
2	'89	Greater New York Savings Bank	OTC	$22,900,000	Common	Yes	No
6	'89	Greyhound	NYSE	$40,000,000	Common	Yes	No
6	'89	Hathaway Corp.	OTC	$1,500,000	Common	Yes	No
7	'89	Inland Steel	NYSE	$150,000,000	Conv. Pfd.	No	Yes
2	'89	Inter-regional Financial Group	NYSE	$5,600,000	Common	No	No
8	'89	Interlake Corp.	NYSE	N/A	Common	No	No
5	'89	ITT	NYSE	$700,000,000	Conv. Pfd.	Yes	Yes
5	'89	Johnson Controls	NYSE	$175,000,000	Conv. Pfd.	Yes	No
2	'89	Kysor Industrial	NYSE	$20,000,000	Conv. Pfd.	No	Yes
12	'89	Landmark Bancshares Corp.	NYSE	N/A	Common	No	No
12	'89	Latshaw Enterprises Inc.	AMEX	$1,400,000	Common	No	No
4	'89	Lockheed	NYSE	$500,000,000	Common	Yes	Yes
3	'89	Longs Drug Stores Corp.	NYSE	$25,200,000	Common	No	No
6	'89	Lukens	NYSE	$33,100,000	Conv. Pfd.	No	No
4	'89	Mapco Inc.	NYSE	N/A	Common	No	Yes
3	'89	May Department Stores	NYSE	$500,000,000	Conv. Pfd.	No	Yes
6	'89	Maytag	NYSE	$65,000,000	Common	No	Yes
5	'89	McDonald's	NYSE	$100,000,000	Conv. Pfd.	No	No
10	'89	Medtronic	NYSE	$40,000,000	Common	Yes	Yes
6	'89	Melville Corp.	NYSE	$357,500,000	Conv. Pfd.	No	Yes
6	'89	Meridian Bancorp	OTC	$65,000,000	Conv. Pfd.	No	Yes
4	'89	MicroAge	OTC	$1,100,000	Common	No	No
7	'89	Milton Roy Co.	NYSE	$6,000,000	Common	No	Yes
12	'89	Mobil Corp.	NYSE	$800,000,000	Conv. Pfd.	No	Yes
11	'89	Morrison Knudsen Corp.	NYSE	N/A	Common	No	No
5	'89	Nalco Chemical Co.	NYSE	$200,000,000	Conv. Pfd.	No	Yes
3	'89	Norwest	NYSE	$44,000,000	Common	No	No
5	'89	Oglebay Norton	OTC	$2,900,000	Common	No	No
5	'89	Olin Corp.	NYSE	$100,000,000	Conv. Pfd.	No	Yes
12	'89	Pacific Telesis Group	NYSE	N/A	Common	No	No
8	'89	PLM International	AMEX	$64,000,000	Conv. Pfd.	No	No
1	'89	PPG Industries	NYSE	$252,000,000	Common	No	Yes
1	'89	Procter & Gamble	NYSE	$1,000,000,000	Conv. Pfd.	No	Yes

(continued)

TABLE D.1   *(Continued)*

Mo	Yr	Company	Exchange	Dollar Value	Type of Shares	T[a]	A[b]
6	'89	Questar Inc.	NYSE	$35,000,000	Common	No	Yes
7	'89	Rorer Group	NYSE	$72,000,000	Conv. Pfd.	No	No
8	'89	Ryland Group	NYSE	$40,000,000	Conv. Pfd.	No	Yes
4	'89	Sara Lee	NYSE	$350,000,000	Conv. Pfd.	No	No
12	'89	Secor Bank Federal Savings Bank	OTC	N/A	Conv. Pfd.	No	No
3	'89	SPX Corp.	NYSE	$50,000,000	Common	Yes	Yes
7	'89	Square D Co.	NYSE	$125,000,000	Conv. Pfd.	No	Yes
6	'89	Stanley Works	NYSE	$95,000,000	Common	No	Yes
7	'89	Tandem Computers	NYSE	$50,000,000	Common	No	Yes
6	'89	Textron	NYSE	$100,000,000	Common	No	Yes
6	'89	Travelers	NYSE	$200,000,000	Conv. Pfd.	No	No
7	'89	Turner Corp.	AMEX	$16,000,000	Conv. Pfd.	No	No
7	'89	United Technologies	NYSE	$660,000,000	Conv. Pfd.	No	No
6	'89	Upjohn	NYSE	$300,000,000	Conv. Pfd.	No	Yes
8	'89	USAir Group	NYSE	$113,600,000	Common	Yes	No
1	'89	Whitman Corp.	NYSE	$500,000,000	Conv. Pfd.	Yes	No
7	'89	Xerox Corp.	NYSE	$785,000,000	Conv. Pfd.	Yes	Yes
6	'90	American Information	NYSE	$700,000,000	Common	No	No
1	'90	Becton Dickinson	NYSE	$60,000,000	Conv. Pfd.	No	No
2	'90	Commercial Intertech Corp.	OTC	$25,000,000	Conv. Pfd.	Yes	Yes
3	'90	County Bank, FSB	OTC	$10,000,000	Conv. Pfd.	No	No
2	'90	Cyprus Minerals	NYSE	$94,000,000	Common	Yes	No
7	'90	FPL Group Inc.	NYSE	$400,000,000	Common	No	No
1	'90	Gillette	NYSE	$100,000,000	Conv. Pfd.	No	Yes
5	'90	Graham Corp.	AMEX	N/A	Common	No	No
5	'90	Kelley Oil Corp.	OTC	$1,500,000	Conv. Pfd.	No	No
3	'90	Pentair Inc.	OTC	$57,000,000	Conv. Pfd.	No	No
6	'90	Union Camp Corp.	NYSE	$160,000,000	Conv. Pfd.	No	Yes
1	'90	Worldwide Computer Services	OTC	N/A	Common	No	No

[a] T = Takeover Environment
[b] A = Antidilution Buyback of Shares Announced

Appendix E

Public Companies Going Private with Employee Ownership

TABLE E.1 *Public Companies Going Private with Year, Exchange, and Takeover Environment Noted*

Year	Company	Exchange	Takeover
1989	A.M.E. Inc.	OTC	Yes
1988	American Standard	NYSE	Yes
1984	American Sterilizer Co.	NYSE	No
1989	American Sterilizer Co.	NYSE	No
1988	Arthur D. Little	OTC	Yes
1985	Amsted Industries	N/A	Yes
1984	Blue Bell Inc.	NYSE	No
1987	Charter Medical Corp.	AMEX	No
1988	Commonwealth Savings Association	N/A	No
1987	Dyncorp	OTC	Yes
1987	Imperial Holly Corp.	AMEX	Yes
1990	Kroy Inc.	N/A	No
1985	Lyon Metal Products	N/A	Yes
1982	McLouth Steel Corp.	N/A	Yes
1989	Medical Properties Inc.	AMEX	Yes
1981	National Spinning Co.	N/A	Yes
1988	Northwestern Steel & Wire	NYSE	Yes
1984	Parsons Corp.	N/A	No
1981	Pamida Inc.	N/A	No
1983	Raymond International	N/A	Yes
1989	Scicom Data Services	OTC	Yes
1989	Security American Financial Enterprises	N/A	No
1987	TWA	NYSE	Yes
1983	U.S. Sugar Corp.	N/A	No

Appendix F

Employee Buyouts
(and Some Spinoffs)

TABLE F.1 *Employee Buyouts and Some Spinoffs of Units to Various Management and Employee Groupings*

Public Corporation	Unit	Location	Business	Exchange	Completed
1981					
Macmillan	Alco-Gravure	Glen Burnie, MD	printing	NYSE	Yes
General Motors	Hyatt-Clark Industries	Clark, NJ	roller bearings	NYSE	Yes
Ford Motor	Aluminum Casting Plant	Sheffield, AL		NYSE	No
1982					
Phillips Petroleum	Duraco	Streamwood, IL	plastics	NYSE	Yes
1983					
Control Data	Kerotest Manufacturing Corp.	Pittsburgh, PA.	valve mfr.	NYSE	Yes
National Intergroup	Weirton Steel Corp.	Weirton, WV	steel	NYSE	Yes
Louisiana Pacific	Ketchikan Pulp Mill	Ketchikan, AL	wood products	NYSE	No
1984					
Eaton	Yale Material Handling Group	New Haven	small trucks	NYSE	No

(*continued*)

TABLE F.1   *(Continued)*

Public Corporation	Unit	Location	Business	Exchange	Completed
Allegheny International	Timet	Toronto, OH	titanium	NYSE	Yes (but ESOP not major)
1985					
Allegheny Beverage	N/A	N/A	beverage	NYSE	No
Ogden	Avondale Shipyards	Boston, MA	shipbuilding	NYSE	Yes
American Express	Fireman's Fund	Novato, CA	insurance	NYSE	Yes (not a buyout, 8% ESOP)
LTV*	Steel Plant	Gladsden, AL	steel	NYSE	No
Colt Industries	Crucible Materials Corp.	Syracuse, NY	steel	NYSE	Yes
IU International	Ryder/ P-I-E	Jacksonville, FL	trucking	(not public, part ESOP)	
Overmyer	Overmyer Mould	Winchester, IN	molds	NASD	(part ESOP)
LTV	Gulf State Steel Corp.	N/A	steel	NYSE	No (nonunion)
LTV	Republic Containeer	Nitro, WV	steel	NYSE	Yes
National Distillers	Seymour Specialty Wire	Seymour, CT	wire	NYSE	Yes
1986					
American Standard	Mosler Safe	Hamilton, OH	safes	NYSE	Yes (partial ESOP)
General Dynamics	Quincy Shipyard	Quincy, MA	shipbuilding	NYSE	No
LTV	Republic Storage	Canton, OH	locker mfr.	NYSE	Yes
British Petroleum	Chase Brass	Cleveland, OH	brass	NYSE	Yes
1987					
Owens-Corning Fiberglas Corp.	Oregon Metallurgical Corp.	Albany, OR	titanium	NYSE	Yes

(continued)

TABLE F.1 *(Continued)*

Public Corporation	Unit	Location	Business	Exchange	Completed
Diamond Shamrock	Diamond Shamrock R&M Corp.**	Dallas, TX	oil refining	NYSE	No
Hospital Corporation of America	HealthTrust Inc.	Nashville, TN	hospitals	NYSE	Yes
DeKalb Energy	Heinhold Hog Marketing	DeKalb, IL	hog buying	NYSE	Yes
National Health	National Health Corp. ESOP Eight Health Care Centers	Murfreesboro, TN	healthcare	NYSE	Yes
McDermott International Inc.*	Babcock & Wilcox Steel	PA	steel	NYSE	No
National Standard	Forged Products Unit	Havana, IL Buchanan, MI		NYSE	No (no record)
Athlone*	Rhode Island Forging			NYSE	
Martin Marietta	Columbia Aluminum (Martin Marietta first sold it to an Australian fruit company)	Goldendale, CA	aluminum		(partial—33%)
1988					
American Medical International	EPIC Health Group Inc.	Irving, TX	hospitals	NYSE	Yes
Ampco-Pittsburgh Corp.	Pittsburgh Forgings Co. Parnell Precision Products	Corropolis, PA	steel	NYSE	Yes
Zenith Electronics*	Consumer Electronics Unit	Springfield, MO	electronics	NYSE	No

(continued)

TABLE F.1 *(Continued)*

Public Corporation	Unit	Location	Business	Exchange	Completed
Crown Zellerbach***	Omak Wood Products	Omak, WA	wood products	NYSE	Yes
Quaker Fabric Co.	Claremont, NH & Leominster, MA Plants	Claremont, NH	upholstery	NYSE	Yes
Levi Strauss	Colt Enterprises	Tyler, TX ACTU	jeans mfg.	NYSE	Yes
CSX	Pittsburgh & Lake Erie RR	Pittsburgh, PA	railroad	NYSE	No
Lorimar	Bozell	N/A	N/A	N/A	N/A
1989					
Sears Roebuck	Coldwell Banker Commercial Unit**	Los Angeles, CA	real estate	NYSE	Yes
Weyerhauser Co.	Wright Nurseries	Cairo, GA	nursey	NYSE	No
LTV Corp.	Republic Engineered Steel Inc.	Masillon, OH	steel	NYSE	Yes
American Medical International	Professional Health Care Unit	Los Angeles, CA	healthcare	NYSE	(sold to Epic)
Farley Inc.*	Cluett Peabody & Co.	Chicago, IL	textile	not public	No
National Heritage Inc.*	Nursing Homes Mgt. Business	(no record, but no deal)		NYSE	No
Cyclops Corp.	Cyclops Steel	Pittsburgh, PA	steel	NYSE	No
Hospital Corp. of America*	Psychiatric Unit	Nashville, TN	healthcare	NYSE	No
Republic Health Corp.	Houston Northwest Medical Center	Houston, TX	healthcare	private	Yes
CRS Sirrine Inc.	Sirrine Environmental Consultants	N/A	N/A	private	N/A

(continued)

TABLE F.1 *(Continued)*

Public Corporation	Unit	Location	Business	Exchange	Completed
Mutual of New York	Financial Services Corp.	N/A	N/A	NYSE	N/A
Control Data Corp.	Burke Marketing	N/A	N/A	NYSE	N/A
Cigna	Individual Financial Services Division	N/A	N/A	N/A	N/A
Lloyds Lumber	Lumberyard	Altoona, PA	lumber	N/A	N/A
Cyclops Industries	Cytemp division	N/A	N/A	N/A	No
Morrison Knudsen Corp.	National Steel & Shipbuilding	San Diego, CA	shipbuilding	NYSE	Yes
American Maize Products	Your Building Centers	Altoona, PA	retailer	AMEX	Yes
1990					
GenCorp	Textileather Unit	Toledo, OH	vinyl	NYSE	Yes
Ashland Oil Corp.	Ashland Technology Unit New Name: Aecom Technology Corp.	Los Angeles, CA	engineering management	NYSE	Yes
PPG	Maryland Brush	Baltimore, MD	paint brushes	NYSE	Yes

Note: The main purpose of this table is to list employee buyouts. Some transactions that are not employee buyouts are included to illustrate the use of employee ownership by public corporations.

Appendix G
Wage and Benefit Restructuring

TABLE G.1 *Wage and Benefit Restructuring ESOPs by Year, Type, Presence of Takeover Environment, and Other Factors*

Year	Company	Exchange	Type	T[a]	AD[b]	NIS[c]
1979	Chrysler	NYSE	1	No	Yes	No
1981	Pan Am Corp.	NYSE	1	No	No	No
1982	Continental Steel	N/A	1	No	No	No
1983	Branch Industries	N/A	1	No	No	No
1983	Dunes Hotels & Casinos, Inc.	NYSE	1	No	No	No
1983	Eastern Airlines	NYSE	1	Yes	No	No
1983	Interstate Motor Freight Systems	OTC	1	No	No	No
1983	Republic Airlines	N/A	1	No	No	No
1983	Western Airlines	N/A	1	No	No	No
1983	Wilson Foods Corp.	N/A	1	No	No	No
1984	Frontier Holdings		1	Yes	No	No
1985	IU International Corp.	NYSE	1	No	No	No
1985	Kaiser Aluminum and Chemical	NYSE	1	No	No	No
1985	Smith's Transfer Corp.	NYSE	1	No	No	No
1986	Bethlehem Steel	NYSE	1	No	No	No
1986	CF&I Steel Corp.	OTC	1	No	No	No
1986	LTV	NYSE	1	No	No	No
1987	Moseley Holding Corp.	OTC	1	No	No	Yes
1987	Trailways	NYSE	1	Yes	No	No
1988	Arkansas Best Corp.	OTC	1	No	No	No
1988	Polaroid Corp.	NYSE	1	Yes	Yes	Yes
1989	PLM International Inc.	AMEX	1	No	No	Yes
1989	Rexene Corporation	NYSE	1	No	No	No
1989	Salomon Inc.	NYSE	1	No	No	No
1989	Transcon Inc.	NYSE	1	No	No	No
1990	Bear Stearns	NYSE	1	No	No	No
1989	Armstrong World Industries	NYSE	2	No	Yes	Yes
1989	Boise Cascade	NYSE	2	No	Yes	Yes

(continued)

TABLE G.1   *(Continued)*

Year	Company	Exchange	Type	T[a]	AD[b]	NIS[c]
1989	Builders Transport Inc.	OTC	2	Yes	No	No
1989	Lincoln Telecommunications Co.	OTC	2	Yes	No	No
1989	Lockheed	NYSE	2	Yes	Yes	Yes
1989	Sara Lee	NYSE	2	No	No	Yes
1989	SPS Technologies	NYSE	2	No	No	No
1989	Whitman Corp.	NYSE	2	Yes	Yes	Yes
1990	Gillette	NYSE	2	No	Yes	Yes
1986	Advest Group	NYSE	3	No	No	No
1987	Donaldson Co.	NYSE	3	No	Yes	Yes
1987	Greiner Engineering	AMEX	3	No	No	No
1987	Radiation Systems	OTC	3	No	Yes	No
1988	Champion Parts Rebuilders	OTC	3	Yes	No	Yes
1988	Charter-Crellin	OTC	3	Yes	No	Yes
1988	Jefferies Group	OTC	3	Yes	No	Yes
1988	Team Inc.	AMEX	3	No	No	No
1989	BayBanks, Inc.	OTC	3	No	No	No
1989	Chubb	NYSE	3	No	No	Yes
1989	Fairchild Industries	NYSE	3	No	No	Yes
1989	Hach Co.	OTC	3	No	No	No
1989	McRae Industries—CL A	AMEX	3	No	No	No
1989	Peoples FSB of Dekalb City	OTC	3	No	No	No
1989	Procter & Gamble	NYSE	3	No	Yes	Yes
1989	Quaker Oats Co.	NYSE	3	No	No	Yes
1989	Sara Lee	NYSE	3	No	No	Yes
1989	Sears Roebuck & Co.	NYSE	3	No	No	No
1983	Columbia Gas System	NYSE	4	No	No	Yes
1983	General Mills	NYSE	4	No	Yes	Yes
1983	Michael Baker Corp.	AMEX	4	No	No	No
1987	McKesson Corp.	NYSE	4	No	Yes	Yes
1987	Moog Inc.-CL A	AMEX	4	No	No	Yes
1987	Rochester Community Savings Bank	OTC	4	No	No	No
1987	Texaco	NYSE	4	Yes	No	Yes
1988	Cabot Corp.	NYSE	4	No	Yes	Yes
1988	Circle Express	OTC	4	No	No	No
1988	Dahlberg Inc.	OTC	4	No	No	Yes
1988	Guardian Bancorp	AMEX	4	No	No	No
1988	J. C. Penney	NYSE	4	No	Yes	Yes
1988	Nerco Inc.	NYSE	4	No	No	No
1988	Northern Trust Co.	OTC	4	No	Yes	Yes
1988	Ralston Purina	NYSE	4	No	Yes	Yes
1988	Tandycrafts Inc.	NYSE	4	Yes	No	Yes
1988	Tribune Co.	NYSE	4	No	Yes	Yes

(continued)

TABLE G.1 *(Continued)*

Year	Company	Exchange	Type	T[a]	AD[b]	NIS[c]
1989	Barnett Banks Inc.	NYSE	4	No	Yes	Yes
1989	Bell Atlantic	NYSE	4	No	No	Yes
1989	BellSouth	NYSE	4	No	No	No
1989	Brunswick Corp.	NYSE	4	No	Yes	Yes
1989	Consolidated Freightways	NYSE	4	Yes	Yes	Yes
1989	Cummins Engine Co.	NYSE	4	Yes	Yes	Yes
1989	Delta Air Lines	NYSE	4	Yes	Yes	Yes
1989	Eaton Corp.	NYSE	4	No	Yes	Yes
1989	Federal-Mogul Corp.	NYSE	4	Yes	Yes	Yes
1989	Financial Benefits Group	OTC	4	No	No	No
1989	Gerber Products Co.	NYSE	4	No	No	Yes
1989	Greyhound	NYSE	4	Yes	No	Yes
1989	Hartmarx Corp.	NYSE	4	No	No	Yes
1989	Inland Steel	NYSE	4	No	Yes	Yes
1989	ITT	NYSE	4	Yes	Yes	Yes
1989	Kerr-McGee	NYSE	4	Yes	Yes	No
1989	Landmark Bancshares Corp.	NYSE	4	No	No	Yes
1989	Lockheed	NYSE	4	Yes	Yes	Yes
1989	Lukens	NYSE	4	No	No	Yes
1989	Maytag Corp.	NYSE	4	No	Yes	Yes
1989	Meridian Bancorp	OTC	4	No	Yes	Yes
1989	Minnesota Mining & Manufacturing Co.	NYSE	4	No	Yes	Yes
1989	Norwest Corp.	NYSE	4	No	No	Yes
1989	Olin Corp.	NYSE	4	No	Yes	Yes
1989	Questar Inc.	NYSE	4	No	Yes	Yes
1989	Sara Lee	NYSE	4	No	No	Yes
1989	Southwestern Bell Corp.	NYSE	4	No	No	No
1989	Square D Co.	NYSE	4	No	Yes	Yes
1989	Syncor International Corp.	OTC	4	No	No	No
1989	U.S. West	NYSE	4	No	No	No
1989	United Technologies Corp.	NYSE	4	No	No	Yes
1989	Xerox Corp.	NYSE	4	Yes	Yes	Yes
1990	Alaska Air Group	NYSE	4	No	No	No
1990	Commercial Intertech Corp.	OTC	4	Yes	Yes	Yes
1990	FPL Group	NYSE	4	No	No	Yes
1990	Gannett	NYSE	4	No	No	Yes
1990	Merchants National Corp.	OTC	4	No	No	No
1990	PNC Financial Corp.	NYSE	4	No	No	No
1990	Rohm & Haas Co.	NYSE	4	No	No	No
1990	Southern New England Telecommunications	NYSE	4	No	No	No
1990	Union Camp Corp.	NYSE	4	No	Yes	Yes

(continued)

TABLE G.1   *(Continued)*

Year	Company	Exchange	Type	T[a]	AD[b]	NIS[c]
N/A	INB Financial CP	OTC	4	No	No	Yes
1983	Dan River Mills	NYSE	5	Yes	No	No
1983	Graniteville	NYSE	5	Yes	No	No
1983	Michael Baker Corp.	AMEX	5	Yes	No	No
1983	Primark Corp.	NYSE	5	No	No	Yes
1984	Equimark Corp.	NYSE	5	No	No	No
1984	Lyon Metal Products	NYSE	5	Yes	No	No
1984	Northwestern Financial Corp.	N/A	5	No	No	No
1985	Avondale Industries	OTC	5	No	No	No
1985	Clark Equipment Co.	NYSE	5	No	No	Yes
1986	Bank of New York Co.	NYSE	5	No	No	No
1986	Enron Corp.	NYSE	5	No	No	No
1986	Figgie International Inc.	OTC	5	No	No	Yes
1986	Frozen Food Express Industries	NYSE	5	No	No	No
1986	Merchants Bancorp	OTC	5	No	No	No
1986	Rexnord Inc.	NYSE	5	Yes	No	No
1987	Ashland Oil Inc.	NYSE	5	Yes	No	No
1987	Bank Building & Equip. Corp. of America	AMEX	5	Yes	No	No
1987	Brown & Sharpe	NYSE	5	No	No	Yes
1987	CBI Industries	NYSE	5	No	No	No
1987	Cullen-Frost Bankers	OTC	5	No	No	No
1987	Emery Air Freight	NYSE	5	Yes	No	Yes
1987	National Standard Co.	NYSE	5	No	No	Yes
1987	Poughkeepsie Savings Bank, FSB (The)	OTC	5	No	No	No
1987	Roper Corp.	NYSE	5	No	No	No
1987	Union Special Corp.	N/A	5	No	No	No
1988	Applied Power	OTC	5	No	No	No
1988	Barry Wright Corp.	NYSE	5	No	No	Yes
1988	Courier Corp.	OTC	5	No	No	No
1988	Merrill Lynch	NYSE	5	No	No	Yes
1988	Monarch Capital Corp.	NYSE	5	No	No	No
1988	R B & W Corp.	AMEX	5	No	No	No
1988	Roadmaster Industries	OTC	5	No	No	No
1988	Universal Foods Corp.	NYSE	5	Yes	No	No
1989	Allied Group	OTC	5	No	No	Yes
1989	Indiana Federal Corp.	OTC	5	No	No	No
1989	Lowe's Cos.	NYSE	5	No	No	Yes
1989	Nalco Chemical Co.	NYSE	5	No	Yes	Yes
1989	Nu Horizons Electronics Corp.	AMEX	5	No	No	No

(continued)

TABLE G.1   *(Continued)*

Year	Company	Exchange	Type	T[a]	AD[b]	NIS[c]
1989	Pacific Western Bancshares	N/A	5	No	No	No
1989	Robertson (H.H.) Co.	NYSE	5	No	No	No
1990	Mid-State, FSB	OTC	5	No	No	No

T[a]   = Takeover environment
AD[b] = Announced use of antidilution buyback to cancel out possible dilution to earnings per shares of newly issued shares purchased by ESOP (only applies if newly issued shares were used)
NIS[c] = Use of newly issued shares in ESOP

Types
1 Trading Stock for Wages
2 Restructuring Retiree Health Benefits
3 Restructuring Profit-Sharing Plans
4 Prefunding 401(k) Savings Plans with Leveraged ESOPs
5 Terminating Defined-Benefit Pension Plans

Appendix H

Takeovers and Employee Ownership

TABLE H.1 *Takeovers and Employee Ownership*

Year	Company	Exchange	Raider	ESOP Size (%)
'81	United Cos. Financial	OTC	Louisiana General Associates	
'83	Michael Baker Corp.	AMEX	Century Engineering	39.00
'83	Odetics Inc. CL B.	AMEX	General	
'83	Graniteville	N/A	Southeastern Public Service Co.	
'84	Carter Hawley Hale Stores	NYSE	Limited	20.00
'84	CPT Corp.	OTC	General	
'84	Phillips Petroleum	NYSE	Mesa Partners	
'84	Norlin Corp.	N/A	Piezo Electric Products & Rooney Pace Inc.	
'84	Lyon Metal Products	N/A		68.00
'84	Cone Mills	NYSE	Western Pacific Industries	
'85	Marsh & McLennan	NYSE	General	
'85	New Jersey Resources	NYSE	NUI Corp.	07.00
'85	Scotty's Inc.	NYSE	General	
'85	TWA Inc.	NYSE	Carl Icahn/Texas Air	
'86	Figgie International	OTC	General	10.50
'86	FMC Corp.	NYSE	General	29.00
'86	Greiner Engineering	AMEX	STV Engineers	13.00
'86	GTE	NYSE	Belzberg's	
'86	Honeywell	NYSE	General	
'86	Resorts International	AMEX	Pratt Hotel Corp.	
'86	Texas American Energy	OTC	Shamrock / Hecco Ventures	15.20

Total ESOP (%)	NIS[a]	Share Repurchase	WB[b] Rest. Type	Takeover[c] Type	Lawsuit[d]	Prop.[e] Only
	No	No	5	Private EO[f]	Yes	No
33.00	No	No	5		No	No
5.00	No		No		No	No
	No		No	Public Outsider	Yes	No
40.00	No		No		No	No
12.66	No		No		Yes	No
10.80	No		No		Yes	No
	Yes	No	No	Delisted	No	No
	No		No	Private EO	Yes	No
	No		No	Private EO	No	No
10.30	No		No		No	Yes
6.90	No		No		No	No
6.92	Yes	No	No		No	No
	No		No		No	No
12.50	No		No		No	No
25.60	No		No		Yes	No
17.05	No		No		Yes	No
4.12	Yes	No	No		No	No
5.00	No		No		No	No
10.00	No		No		No	Yes
15.20	Yes	No	No		Yes	No

(continued)

TABLE H.1 *(Continued)*

Year	Company	Exchange	Raider	ESOP Size (%)
'86	Eastern Airlines	NYSE	Texas Air	
'86	Apogee International	OTC	General	
'86	Petro-Lewis Corp.	NYSE	Kidder Peabody & Freeport	
'87	Bank Building & Equipment Corp. of America	AMEX	Amcat	40.00
'87	Crazy Eddie Inc.	OTC	General	
'87	Diamond Shamrock R&M Corp.	NYSE	General	
'87	Enron Corp.	NYSE	General	27.00
'87	Foote Cone & Belding Communications Inc.	NYSE	General	
'87	Harcourt Brace Jovanovich	NYSE	British Printing	
'87	Imperial Holly	AMEX	Imperial Sugar / Shamrock	
'87	Integrity Entertainment	AMEX	Shamrock	
'87	JWT Group	NYSE	WPP Group PLC	
'87	Macmillan	NYSE	Maxwell Communication / Robert Bass	
'87	Swank Inc.	NYSE	Henry Salzhaver	
'87	Western Savings & Loan Association	NYSE	General	10.00
'87	Sooner Federal Savings & Loan Association	OTC	Robin Buerge	
'87	First Fulton Bancshares		Barnett Banks	
'87	Rexnord	NYSE	Banner Industries Inc.	30.00
'87	Trailways		Greyhound	
'87	Resdel Industries	OTC	Reliance Financial Corp.	
'88	Acme Steel	OTC	General	
'88	Cabot Corp.	NYSE	General	07.50
'88	Charter-Crellin Inc.	OTC	Atlantis Group	
'88	Delchamps Inc.	OTC	A&P	25.00
'88	Farmers Group	OTC	Bat Group PLC	
'88	Firstcorp	AMEX	General	23.20
'88	Grumman	NYSE	General	
'88	Jefferies Group	OTC	General	11.00
'88	Kansas City Southern Industries	NYSE	Howard Kaskal	07.90
'88	KMS Industries	OTC	Burmah / Oil Public Limited Co.	09.70

Total ESOP (%)	NIS[a]	Share Repurchase	WB[b] Rest. Type	Takeover[c] Type	Lawsuit[d]	Prop.[e] Only
	No	No	1		Yes	No
	Yes	No	No		No	No
	No		No	Private Outsider & EO	No	No
32.80	No	No	5		Yes	No
	No		No	Delisted	No	No
13.29	Yes	No	No		No	No
17.35	No		No		No	No
14.10	No		No		No	No
27.70	Yes	No	No		No	No
22.50	No		No		No	No
8.50	No		No		No	No
	No		No	Delisted	No	Yes
9.60	Yes	No	No		No	No
71.60	Yes	No	No		No	No
7.38	No		No		No	No
	No	No	No	Private	No	No
	No	No	No		No	Yes
33.00	No	No	5	Private	No	No
	No		No	Public Outsider	No	No
	No		No	Delisted	No	No
8.00	No	No	7		No	No
11.00	No		No		No	No
18.50	Yes	No	3		Yes	No
25.00	No		No		Yes	No
			No		No	Yes
25.00	No		No		No	No
43.25	No		No		No	No
10.04	Yes	No	3		No	No
7.90	No		No		No	No
29.30	No		No		No	No

(*continued*)

TABLE H.1   *(Continued)*

Year	Company	Exchange	Raider	ESOP Size (%)
'88	Kroger Co.	NYSE	Haft / Kohlberg Roberts	06.30
'88	Lowe's Cos.	NYSE	General	
'88	Optical Coating Laboratory	OTC	Alpine Group	
'88	Polaroid	NYSE	Roy Disney	06.80
'88	Texaco	NYSE	Carl Icahn	03.00
'88	Kraft	NYSE	Philip Morris	
'88	Champion Parts Rebuilders	OTC	General Refactories	19.00
'88	Universal Foods	NYSE	Prudential-Bache	
'88	Northwestern Steel & Wire	NYSE	Bennett LeBow	
'89	A. P. Green Industries	OTC	East Rock Partners	09.20
'89	Advest Group	NYSE	General	
'89	Applied Power	OTC	General	34.00
'89	Aristech Chemical	NYSE	General	15.00
'89	Armstrong World Industries	NYSE	Belzberg's	12.00
'89	Bel Fuse	OTC	Santa Monica Partners & Initio Inc.	
'89	Brunswick Corp.	NYSE	General	05.20
'89	Builders Transport	OTC	Walentas & Dinstein	13.90
'89	Chevron Corp.	NYSE	General	04.20
'89	Citizens & Southern	NYSE	NCNB	05.00
'89	Colgate Palmolive	NYSE	General	06.00
'89	Delta Air Lines	NYSE	NWA	
'89	Ecko Group	NYSE	Sonar Partners	40.00
'89	Fairchild Industries	NYSE	Carlyle Group	23.00
'89	Ferro Corp.	NYSE	General	10.00
'89	Greater New York Savings Bank	OTC	Emigrant Savings Bank	12.20
'89	Greyhound	NYSE	General	02.90
'89	Horn & Hardart	NYSE	Riese Organization	06.90
'89	Interlake Corp.	NYSE	Mark IV Industries	09.90
'89	ITT	NYSE	General	05.00
'89	Johnson Controls	NYSE	General	08.00
'89	Kerr-McGee	NYSE	General	05.00
'89	Kysor Industrial	NYSE	Kaufman Alsberg & Co.	15.00
'89	Lockheed	NYSE	Harold Simmons	17.00
'89	Minnetonka	OTC	Calvin Klein & Barry Schwartz	13.00
'89	Procter & Gamble	NYSE	General	08.00

Total ESOP (%)	NIS[a]	Share Repurchase	WB[b] Rest. Type	Takeover[c] Type	Lawsuit[d]	Prop.[e] Only
35.00	No		No		No	No
22.70	Yes	No	No		No	No
22.50	Yes	No	No		No	No
19.37	Yes	Yes	6,1		Yes	No
7.00	Yes	No	4		Yes	No
	No	No	No		No	No
13.80	Yes	No	3		No	No
	No	No	5		No	No
	No		No	Private EO	No	No
9.20	Yes	Yes	No		Yes	No
7.35	No		No		No	No
34.00	No		No		No	No
16.00	Yes	No	7		No	No
12.00	No		No		Yes	No
15.00	No		No		No	No
7.00	No		No		No	No
13.90	No	No	2		Yes	No
15.20	No		No		Yes	No
5.00	No		No		No	No
11.00	Yes	Yes	No		No	No
14.00	Yes	Yes	4		No	No
9.00	Yes	Yes	No		No	No
18.90	No		No		No	No
10.00	Yes	Yes	No		No	No
12.20	Yes	No	No		No	No
2.90	Yes	No	4		No	No
6.90	No		No		No	No
9.90	No		No		No	No
11.00	Yes	Yes	4		No	No
12.00	Yes	No	No		No	No
5.00	No	Yes	4		No	No
16.00	No		No		Yes	No
17.00	Yes	Yes	4,2		Yes	No
14.69			No		No	No
19.40	No		No		No	No

(*continued*)

TABLE H.1 *(Continued)*

Year	Company	Exchange	Raider	ESOP Size (%)
'89	SPX Corp.	NYSE	General	09.20
'89	St. Paul Bancorp	OTC	General	05.01
'89	Tech-Sym Corp.	NYSE	Mason Best Co.	07.27
'89	USAir Group	NYSE	Steinhardt Partners	05.00
'89	Whitman	NYSE	Zeus Partners	10.00
'89	Xerox	NYSE	Hanson PLC/ Sir James Goldsmith	11.00
'89	Holly	AMEX	General	18.00
'89	Hathaway	OTC	TBG Investment Co.	02.97
'89	Medtonic Inc.	NYSE	General	02.20
'89	Emery Air Freight	NYSE	Consolidated Freightways	
'89	Anchor Glass Container	NYSE	Vitro Sociedad Anonima	
'90	Commercial Intertech	OTC	General	20.00
'90	Cummins Engine	NYSE	Miller Family	11.40
'90	Cyprus Minerals	NYSE	Robert Holms	10.00
'90	Federal-Mogul	NYSE	Nortek	10.00
'90	J.C. Penny	NYSE	General	09.00
'90	Justin Industries	OTC	Perry Southerland	17.20
'90	Tandycrafts	NYSE	General	38.00

a. Newly Issued Shares
b. Wage and Benefit Restructuring Types:
   1. Trading stock for wages
   2. Postretirement health benefits
   3. Use of profit-sharing contributions to fund ESOP
   4. Leveraged ESOP to prefund match to 401(k) or savings plan
   5. Terminate defined-benefit pension plan and use excess assets in ESOP
   6. Offset plan
   7. Miscellaneous
   No: No wages or benefit restructuring
c. Results of Attempted Takeover
d. Lawsuit Filed?
e. ESOP Only Proposed?
f. Going Private with Employee Ownership

Total ESOP (%)	NIS[a]	Share Repurchase	WB[b] Rest. Type	Takeover[c] Type	Lawsuit[d]	Prop.[e] Only
11.30	Yes	Yes	7		Yes	No
5.01	No		No		No	No
	No		No		No	Yes
5.00	Yes	No	No		No	No
10.20	Yes	Yes	2		No	No
11.00	Yes	Yes	4		No	No
18.10	Yes	No	No		No	Yes
20.97	Yes	No	No		No	No
2.20	Yes	Yes	No		No	No
	Yes	No	No	Public Outsider	No	No
	No		No		Yes	Yes
6.71	Yes	Yes	4		No	No
11.40	Yes	Yes	4		Yes	No
10.00	Yes	No	No		Yes	No
9.00	Yes	Yes	4		No	No
24.70	No		No		No	No
17.20	No		No		No	No
38.00	Yes	No	4		No	No

Index

A&P, 139–140
Abuse of power, 168–169, 172, 180, 245
Accounting issues, 69–71
Acme Steel, 170
Adams-Russell Electronics, 48
Advest Group Inc., 174
AECOM, 62
AFL-CIO, 140
Agee, William, 161
Agency costs, 149
Airline industry, 101, 102–104, 141
Airline Pilots Association, 101, 103, 142
Air Transit Employees, 103
Allegheny Ludlum Corp., 63
Allied Corp., 161
Allied Group Inc., 110
Allied Signal Inc., 75
Alpine Group, 67, 173
Amalgamated Clothing and Textile Workers, 249
Amcat Corp., 166
American Capital Strategies, 64, 66, 235
American Carriers Corp., 101
American Continental Corp., 211–212
American Express Inc., 67
American Financial Corp., 60
American Institute of Certified Public Accountants (AICPA) Statement of Position 76–83, 86
American Standard Inc., 58
American Steel & Wire, 61
American Stock Exchange (AMEX), 3, 7, 302
America West Airlines, 61
Ameritech, 46
AMPCO Pittsburgh Corporation, 63
Amsted Industries Inc., 58, 63
Analysis Group, The, 177, 181, 182, 306

Anchor Glass Container Corp., 177
Anderson Clayton Corp., 167–168, 205
Annual reports, 6, 8, 192, 199, 216
Antitakeover laws, 186–190
Antitrust laws, 186
A. P. Green Industries, 54, 176
Apogee Enterprises Inc., 165
Applied Power Inc., 174
Armstrong World Industries, 116, 118, 174, 184, 212
Arnold & Porter, 5, 61, 220
Arthur D. Little Inc., 58
Ascribed reward, 226
Ascribed status, 226
Ashland Oil Company, 110
Association of Flight Attendants, 103, 141
Association for Private Pension and Welfare Plans, 107
AT&T, 120, 123, 186
Atlantis Group, 171
Avery International, 244
Avis Inc., 212, 229
Avondale Shipbuilding, 63

Badger Meter Co., 48
Baker, Deborah, 119
Bank Building & Equipment Corp. of America, 166
Bankers Trust, 74
Banking, 73. See also specific banks
Bank loans, 73
Bank of America, 44, 163
Bank of New England, 193, 219, 248
Bank of New York, 110
Bankruptcy, 56, 63, 64, 68, 98, 100, 101, 105, 109, 248
Banks of Mid-America, 110

Barber, Randy, 102
Barry Wright Corporation, 55, 67, 110
Bass Brothers, 58
Beekman, Judge J., 143, 194
Bel Fuse Inc., 174
Bell, Alexander Graham, 146
Bell National Corporation, 48
BellSouth, 123
Belzberg family, 89, 174
Bendix Corporation, 161, 203
Berger, Carolyn, 140, 189
Berle, Adolph, 2
Bethlehem Steel, 105
Beyster, Robert, 71, 125, 253
Black & Decker, 58
Blank-check preferred shares, 172
Bloated management, 98
Bloom, Ronald, 106. See also Keilin and
    Bloom
Blue Bell Inc., 57
Blumenthal, Adam, 235. See also American
    Capital Strategies
Board of directors:
  and business judgment, 152–153
  diversity on, 3
  duty of, 148–149
  election of, 150
  employee representation on, 34, 105, 134,
      164, 215, 216, 219, 222, 231, 246,
      251
  implications of employee ownership for, 80
  nonmanagerial employees on, 232, 245
  power of, 148
  shareholder representation on, 151
Boesky, Ivan, 58
Boise Cascade, 49, 51, 116, 117, 120
Booth, I. M., 194
Borden Inc., 223
Borman, Frank, 102
Boston Bancorp, 47
Boston Stock Exchange (BSE), 303
Branch Industries, 101
Brealey, Richard A., 78, 79, 80
Bridge loan, 76
British Printing Company, 139
Brunswick Corp., 76
Bryan, Charlie, 102
Buckhorn Corp., 155, 167, 220
Burke Marketing Services, 63
Burlington Industries, 11
Burlington Northern Inc., 161, 205
Burmah Oil Public Limited Co., 171
Business judgment rule, 152–153, 169, 185

Business Wire, 305
Butler, David, 48
Butler Manufacturing Co., 47, 223
Buyouts. See Employee buyouts

Cabot Corp., 170, 176
California Public Employees' Retirement
    System, 142
Calloway, D. Wayne, 90
Calumet Industries, 159–160
Campaign for Economic Democracy, 254
Candrilli, Al, 123
Cantwell, Jerry, 177
Cape Cod Bank and Trust, 47
Capitalism, 5, 7, 245, 254, 255–256
Capitol Federal Savings and Loan Association
    of Colorado, 47
Caribe, 159
Carlucci, Frank, 66
Carlyle Group, 171
Carnegie, Andrew, 146
Carter Hawley Hale, 162–163, 169
Cash flow, 38, 85, 91, 128, 153
Cashing out large shareholders, 28, 38,
    48–49, 50
  by year, exchange, and takeover
      environment, 311–312
Cash profit sharing, 25, 28, 114
Cayuga Savings Bank, 47
Central Bancshares of the South Inc., 46
Century Engineering, 161
CF&I Steel Corp., 105
Champion Parts Rebuilders Inc., 55, 174
Chapter 11 reorganization, 64, 104. See also
    Bankruptcy
Charter-Crellin Inc., 171
Charter Medical Corp., 58
Chase Manhattan Bank, 74–75
Chemical Bank of New York, 73, 119, 242
Chevron Corp., 174, 185–186
Chicago Pneumatic Tool, 167, 168
Chicago School, 149
Chicago West Pullman Corp., 61
Chief executive officer (CEO), 150
Chinn, Adam, 248
Chrysler Corporation, 99–100
Chrysler Loan Guarantee Act of 1979, 99
Chubb Corp., 114
Cigna Corporation, 66
Cincinnati Stock Exchange (CSE), 303
Circus Circus Enterprises Inc., 48
Citibank, 161
Citicorp, 73

Citizens and Southern Corp., 174
City Federal Financial Corporation, 218–219, 248
CityFed Financial Group, 218–219
Class-action lawsuits, 163, 177, 221, 248, 249
Closely held companies. *See* Private companies
Coalition of Unions of Republic Employees (CURE), 103
COLAs (cost-of-living adjustments), 94, 95, 98, 103, 132
Coldwell Banker Commercial Real Estate, 64, 66
Colgate Palmolive Co., 54, 174
Collective bargaining, 12, 14, 63, 98, 109, 132
Columbia Aluminum, 64
Columbia Institutional Investor Project, 2
Commerce Bancorp, 47
Commfed Bancorp Inc., 47
Commission, 28
Common stock, 34, 51, 56, 147
  average annual rates of return on, 225
Commonwealth Mortgage Corp., 58
Commonwealth Savings Association, 58
Compagnie Oris Industry, 122
Compensation:
  absorb-the-fat approach, 93
  average annual wages adjusted for inflation, 92
  history of fixed-wage system, 90–94
Comte, Michael, 182
Concessionary ESOPs in the airline industry, 102–104
Concession bargaining, 3, 65, 97–107
  in nonunion companies, 106–107
Cone Mills Corp., 162, 249
Confidential voting, 189, 194, 232
Conflict of interest, 49, 149, 153, 168, 196
Coniston Partners, 184
Conrail, 89, 120, 122
Conrail Privatization Act, 89
Consolidated Capital Equities Corp., 67
Consolidated Freightways, 67, 122, 177
Continental Airlines, 97, 100–101, 160
Continental Airlines v. *Texas Air*, 168
Continental Bank Corp., 49
Continental Steel, 105
Contra-equity account, 86
Contribution risk, 4
Control, 5–6
Control Data Corp., 63

Control-share acquisition laws, 189
Conversion ratio, 56
Convertible Compensation Fund (Quaker Oats), 112
Convertible preferred stock, 53, 56, 88, 180
  four key aspects of, 56
  to offset dilution, 39, 41, 51
Coopers and Lybrand, 95, 221
Copper Range Inc., 61
Core shareholders, 236
Corning, 105, 212
Corporate bonds, average annual rates of return on, 225
Corporate control, market for, 147, 153–154, 155
  arguments over, 151–152
Corporate culture, 42, 145, 176, 177–178
  entrepreneurial, 215, 234
  feudal, 214, 217–222
  investor, 214–215, 221–227
  participatory, 215, 227–230
  shareholder, 215, 230–234
  as a takeover defense, 177–178
  trends, 216–217
Corporate finance uses for employee ownership:
  cashing out large holders, 48–49, 50
  employee buyouts, 62–66
  employee-ownership buybacks, 44–47
  going private, 57–59
  going public, 60–62
  issuing new shares to employees, 49–62
  restructuring companies, 66–68
Corporate governance, 2, 12, 134. *See also* Corporate culture; Voting rights
  power and, 244–245
  trends in, 216–217, 244
Corporate law, 148–153, 220, 231, 237
Corporate Partners L.P., 141
Corporate power, 148, 195
Corporate pyramid, 91
Corporate raiders, 57, 153, 154, 168, 176, 205, 226, 236
Corporate restructuring, 66–68
Corporation and Private Property, The (Berle and Means), 2
CPC International, 76
CPT Corporation, 163
Crazy Eddie Inc., 166
Credit rating agencies, 70, 86–87
Credit ratings, 70–71, 128, 243
Cummins Engine Co., 122
Currency trading, 212

Dahlberg Inc., 55, 122
Danaher v. *Chicago Pneumatic Tool*, 168
Dan River Textiles, 58, 109
Davis, Donald, 44
Dayton Hudson, 122
Debt, 3, 69, 75, 78, 153, 205
Deferred profit sharing, 25, 69, 114
Deficit Reduction Act of 1984, 73, 86
Defined-benefit plans, 4, 21, 26, 69, 95, 134
    compared with employee-stock ownership
        plans, 109
    costs of, 107
    as employee retention devices, 222
    replacing, 107–111
    trends, 107, 109
Defined-contribution plans, 4, 22–23
    increasing use of, 93–94
    401(k), 24, 119–123, 244
    profit-sharing plans, 25, 111–116
    risk of, 3–4, 131–134
    types of, 23
Delaware Chancery Court, rulings by, 33, 106,
        140–141, 172, 178
Delchamps, Jr., Alfred, 140
Delchamps Inc., 139, 177
Delisted companies and employee ownership,
        296–301
Delta Air Lines, 103, 122, 174
Dennison Manufacturing, 244
Deregulation, 101, 102, 151
D. F. King & Co., 185
DIAL (Direct Immediate Allocation Loan),
        74–75
Dilution, 80, 106, 128, 170, 179, 183, 245
    and cashing out large shareholders, 49
    cash purchase and, 41
    caused by ESOP stock buybacks, 47
    caused by selling newly issued shares, 51,
        53, 175, 313–318
    and company matching contributions, 120
    convertible preferred shares to offset, 51
    in earnings per share, 37–38
    examples of, 38–41
    in the market value of the stock, 38
    during 1973–1987 period, 170
    during 1988–1990 period, 179
    offsetting, 41–43
    probability of, 41
    shareholder concern about, 111
    share repurchases to offset, 54, 177
    and share price, 31–34, 181–183
    takeovers and, 178–181, 330–337
    types of, 37–38

    in voting power, 38
    wage and benefit restructuring to offset, 54,
        107–123, 130, 174–177, 330–337
Disclosure, 8, 69, 73, 75–76, 159, 172,
        191–193, 199, 250
    insufficient public announcements about
        employee ownership, 56
Disney, Roy, 140
Dividends:
    on common stock, 56
    decision to pay, 152
    on employee-held stock, 24
    on individual stock purchases, 27
    on preferred stock, 56
    share, 199
    used to repay ESOP debt, 31, 85–86, 138
Dobrzynski, Judith H., 231
Donaldson, Gordon, 147
Dow Jones News Service, 302, 305
Drexel Burnham Lambert, 74, 102
Dubinsky, Frederick C., 142
Duty of care, 148
Duty of loyalty, 149
Dune's Hotels and Casinos, 66, 106
Dwyer III, Joe, 44

Earnings per share, 37–38, 128, 156
Eastern Air Lines, 101, 102–103
Eastern Air Lines Acquisition Corp., 165
East Rock Partners, 176
Edwards, Doug, 115
Efficiency, 5, 153, 154
Efficient public market, 249
El Paso Company, 161
Emery Air Freight, 66–67, 110, 122, 177
Emery Worldwide, 67
Employee activism, 3, 111, 233
Employee associations, 3, 221, 236, 237
Employee benefit plans, 21, 35
    as sources of capital for employee
        ownership, 71, 80, 244
    employee-held assets in, 23
Employee Benefit Research Institute, 94, 233
Employee buyouts, 62–68, 320–324
    to avoid bankruptcy, 64
    defined, 62
    encouraged by public companies, 63–64
    examples of, 63–64
    growth of, 64
        annual, 65
    of healthy companies, 64
    industry concentration of, 65
    management's role in, 84

prospects for, 65–66
reasons for, 63–64
total worth of, 62
Employee communication, 34, 178, 218, 219, 226
Employee groups, 250
Employee Investor Committee, 226
Employee involvement, 4, 57, 80, 102, 118, 216, 227–234
  nonmanagerial employees on corporate boards, 232
  to offset dilution, 43
  in problem solving, 228
  and productivity, 53, 93, 228
  in specific companies, 140, 212, 229
  statistics concerning, 239–240
Employee-owned corporation, defined, 7
Employee ownership. *See also* Wage and benefit restructuring
  as an acceptable practice, 20
  accounting for, 69–71
  amount of, 11–12
  assets held in, 31
  in bankruptcy reorganization, 68
  banks and, 73
  barriers to effective, 249
  and the bottom line, 144
  buybacks, 39, 44–47. *See also* Share repurchases
    dilution caused by, 47
    reasons for, 46
    and takeover environments, 45
    tax laws affecting, 46
    with year, exchange, share type, and takeover environment noted, 307–310
  CEO backing for, 126
  competitive pressures and, 244
  concentration of by business sector, 10
  conversion of thrifts from mutual to stock corporations, 62
  cost of, 44, 80
  defensive aspect of, 179–180
  defined, 7
  dilemmas facing:
    concentration of wealth, 253–255
    government reaction, 252–253
    increased productivity and employee empowerment, 251–252
    power and corporate governance, 244–245
    risk and wealth, 245–249
    sharing the bed with public shareholders, 249–250
  distribution of in U.S. workforce, 13

distribution in employee benefits, 23
  employees excluded from, 7, 12, 13, 30
  employees' role in, 81, 127, 158–164
  factors to consider in establishing, 128–130
  in Fortune 500 companies, 14–20
  over 4 percent in public corporations, 257–304
  under 4 percent in public corporations, 20, 301
  future of, 20–28
  geographical distribution of, 11
  growth of, 1–2, 11, 21, 95, 97, 242, 243–244
    role of takeovers in, 243–244
    using newly issued shares, 51–54
  human resources staff and, 126
  impact on share price of sponsoring companies, 181–183
  implications of, 80
  investment bankers in, 125–127
  "laws" that determine success, 227–228
  making the decision about, 125–130
  management attitude toward, 129, 236, 246
  management manipulation of, 171–172
  media coverage of, 98, 169
  among over-the-counter corporations, 95
  percentage of, in a public company, 302
  power of, 144
  predictions concerning, 3–4, 12–13, 242, 243
  to rescue failing firms, 11
  to restructure companies, 66–68
  and shareholders, 81, 144, 156
  strategy for, 71
  in takeover environments, 144, 157–158, 330–336
    growth of, 161–163
  varieties of, 21–22
  wrong motives for, 159–160
Employee ownership and cashing out large shareholders, 311–312
Employee-ownership capital market, 71, 80
Employee-ownership objective, 71
Employee Ownership 1000, 6, 8, 9–20, 193, 257–304
  as a basis for analysis, 29
  compared to employee-ownership sector of the economy, 11–14
  distribution among the three stock exchanges, 10
  headings, 302
  as a percent of all public companies, 6, 242
  as a percent of U.S. economy, 6, 242

Employee Ownership 1000 (*continued*)
  plans, 23
  significance of, 8
  sources, 81–82, 304–306. *See also*
    Disclosure; Insufficient public
    announcements about employee
    ownership
  Analysis Group, The, 306
  annual reports, 6
  Barron's, 306
  Business News Wire, 305
  company, 304
  Datatimes, 306
  Dow Jones News Service, 305
  ESOP Association, 306
  estimate, 306
  Franklin Research, 306
  Internal Revenue Service, 6, 305–306
  investment banks, 305
  IRRC, 304
  NAARS, 305
  NCEO, 305
  Press Release Wire, 305
  Securities and Exchange Commission,
    6, 304
  Spectrum 5 (13D), 304–305
  Spectrum 6, 305
  verbal, 304
  Wall Street Journal, The, 6, 305
  stock exchanges, 302–304
Employee Ownership: Revolution or Ripoff?
  (Blasi), 6, 7, 43, 227–228, 232
Employee ownership and stock buybacks,
  307–310
Employee participation. *See* Employee
  involvement
Employee passivity, 226
Employee Retirement Income Security Act
  of 1974 (ERISA), 22, 23, 71, 82,
  95, 127, 163, 225, 238, 243
Employee shareholding, size of, 11, 12
Employee share-purchase plans, 3, 72
  amount of employee ownership not
    accurately reported, 249
  as a tool to increase employee ownership in
    the economy, 72
Employee stock-purchase plans, 25–26
Employee stock-ownership plans (ESOPs):
  abusive, 173
  buybacks, 45–46
  as defined by the Internal Revenue Code, 23
  dividends, 24
  legislation concerning, 21

  leveraged, 23–24, 50, 69
  misconceptions about, 1
  neutralizing cost of, 183
  for new capital formation, 52
  nonleveraged, 26. *See also* Stock-bonus
    plans
  orchestrating financial, strategic, and
    benefits objectives in one plan (J. C.
    Penney example), 54
  to rescue a failing firm, 97
  risk, 4
  tax incentives, 23–24, 28, 40, 42, 79–80,
    85–86, 252–253
  total market return for firms adopting,
    182–183
  as a way to reduce taxes, 28
Employee Stock Ownership Trust (ESOT), 127
Employees, defined, 84, 91, 214
Empowerment, 197
Encyclopedia Britannica, 58
Enron Corp., 74, 110
Entertainment Publications Inc., 67
Entrepreneurial culture, 215, 234
Equimark Corp., 110
ESOP Notes, 74, 75
ESOPs. *See* Employee stock-ownership plans
"Excessive" ownership, 172
External financing, 78
Exxon, 55

Fairchild Industries, 171, 183
Fair price laws, 189
Farmers Group, 171
Farr Co., 46
Federal Express, 123
Federal Home Loan Bank Board, 166
Federal-Mogul, 229
Federal Savings & Loan Association, 166
Feldman, Alvin, 100
Ferris, Richard, 250
Feudal culture, 214, 217–221, 235
Fidelity mutual funds, 250
Fiduciary duties, 149
Figgie International, 110
Financial Accounting Standards Board (FASB):
  accounting rules for retirement benefits,
    115–116
  Emerging Issues Task Force (EITF),
    39, 86
  standard for income taxes (SFAS No. 96),
    86
Financial Corporation of America, 67
Financial Performance Group, 220

Financing, 3
  accounting effects, 69
  bank loans, 73
  external, 78, 79
  private placements, 73–76
  public capital market, 76–77
  to purchase employee shares, 51
  self-liquidating, 79
  straight employee investments, 72
  structuring *vs.* finding, 127
Fireman's Fund Insurance Company,
      67, 224
First Boston, 54, 120, 167, 242
First Chicago, 213
FirstCorp Inc., 170
First Federal Bank of Durham, 170
First Fulton Bancshares Inc., 167
Fixed-benefit plans, 2, 22, 91, 98, 244, 246.
      See also Defined-benefit plans
Fixed costs, 91
Fixed retirement system, 131, 132
Flight International Group, The, 49
FMC Corp., 165
FMS Corp., 62
Ford Motor Company, 11
Foreign tax credit, 24, 32
Fortune 100 companies:
  employee holdings in, 14–17
  profit-sharing plans in, 112
Fortune 500 companies, 11, 124
  employee holdings in, 14–20
  incorporation in Delaware, 144
  as information sources, 193
  ownership characteristics of acquired,
      200–201
Fortune Service 500 companies, employee
      holdings in, 17–20
Forum Re Group Bermuda Limited, 62
Forum Reinsurance, 62
Foster Higgins, 115
401(k) plans, 3, 69, 72, 94, 106, 117
  company matching contributions to, 24, 89,
      119–123
  overview of, 24–25
  tax incentives, 25
Franklin Research, 306
Frantz Manufacturing, 167
Fraser, Douglas, 100
Free cash flow, 151–152, 200
Freedom Savings and Loan Association, 55
Freeman, Brian, 2, 89, 102, 104
Freeport-McMoRan Inc., 166
Freeze-out laws, 187, 189

FRESOP (Floating Rate Employee Stock
      Ownership Plan) Notes, 74
Fried, Frank, Harris, Shriver and Jacobson,
      213
Frontier Airlines, 101, 103–104
Frozen Food Express Industries Inc., 48, 224
Frug, Gerald E., 232

Gabelli & Co., 48
GAF Corp., 170
Gaffney, Owen, 213
GAMCO Investors, 48
Gannett Co., 48
Gannett Foundation, 48
Gates, Jeffrey, 78
Gavin, John, 185
General Refractories, 55
Georgeson & Co., 185
Getty, Jr., Gordon, 68
Getty Oil Company, 68
Globalization, 152
Global competition, 65, 72, 93, 131, 226
Going private, 57–59, 170
  examples of, 58
  trends toward, 59
  with year, exchange, and takeover
      environment noted, 319
Going public, 60–62
Golden parachutes, 155, 172, 185, 219
Goldman, Sachs & Co., 178, 242
Goldsmith, Sir James, 102, 211
Gordon, Lilli, 177
Gorman, Robert, 35
Gormley, Dennis, 229
Government bonds, average annual rates
      of return on, 225
Government deficits, 93
Graniteville Corporation, 162
Great Merger Movement, 147
Greenberg, Lawrence, 231
Greenmail, 164, 165, 166, 185, 236
Greiner Engineering, 114, 165
Greyhound Bus Lines, 107
Greyhound Corp., 174
Grievance procedures, 230
Growth Finance Corp., 101
Grumman Aerospace Corp., 160, 177
GTE Corp., 120, 165, 166
Guardian Bancorp, 122
Gutfreund, John, 88

Hach Co., 114
Halls Motor Transit, 101

Hamilton, Robert W., 148, 149, 151, 152
Hanson PLC, 211
Harcourt Brace Jovanovich Inc., 55, 67, 110, 139, 168, 171, 217
Hawley, Philip, 162, 163
Hay Higgins/Hay Group, 124, 230
Health insurance costs, 93, 118. *See also* Postretirement medical benefits
HealthTrust, 64
Henry Ford Health Care Systems, 212
Hermann Miller, 229
Hester, Steven, 5, 61, 109, 190, 220. *See also* Arnold & Porter
Hewitt Associates, 20, 221
Hill, Parker, Franklin, Cardwell, and Jones, 248
Hi-Shear Corporation, 159
H. H. Robertson Company, 110
Holders, 222
Holly Corp., 165
Holly Sugar Corp., 110, 166, 244
Honeywell Inc., 46, 165
Horn & Hardart Co., 171
Hospital Corporation of America, 64
Hostile takeovers, 8, 39, 40, 58, 100, 233
Hostile tender offers, 150, 153, 154, 161
Houlihan, Lokey, Howard and Zukin, 127
Hurwitz, Charles, 58
Hyman, Elana, 196

Iacocca, Lee, 100
Ibbotson Associates, 225
Icahn, Carl, 58, 59, 104, 164, 165, 184
Imperial Sugar Corp., 110, 166, 244
INB Financial, 122
Incentives, 195, 196–197
  added, 256
Incentive stock options (ISOs), 27
Independent Steelworkers Union, 231
Indiana Federal Corp., 47, 110
Individual Retirement Accounts (IRAs), 31
Industrial Equity Limited, 122
Industrial Training Systems, 61
Inflation, 132
Inflation risk, 4
Information leaks, 182
Information Systems Group, 186
Insider dealing, 212
Insider officer-owners, 191
Institutional investors, 2, 185, 192, 230–234, 236, 249–250
Integra Financial Corp., 47
Integrity Entertainment Corp., 166

Interlake Corp., 173–174
Internally generated cash, 78
Internal corporate struggles, 68
Internal Revenue Service (IRS):
  databases, 305, 306
  elimination of interest income deduction, 75
  Form 5500, 6, 191, 193, 238
  Revenue Ruling 89-76, 75
International Association of Machinists (IAM), 102, 103, 141
International Brotherhood of Teamsters (IBT), 103, 104
International Minerals & Chemical Corporation, 125
Interstate Motor Freight Systems, 101
Invasion of privacy, 249
Investment bankers, 107, 125–127
  criteria used to advise public companies about employee ownership, 128–130
Investment banks, 305
  "bakeoff" to choose employee-ownership advisor, 126–127
  market share in employee ownership transactions, 242
Investment managers, 26
Investment risk, 3–4
Investor activism, 222
Investor culture, 214–215, 221–227, 235
Investor Responsibility Research Center (IRRC), 182, 192, 219, 250, 304
Investor stake, 216, 221
Iron-clad agreement (Carnegie), 146
Isberg, Steven, 182
ITT Corp., 174
IU International Corporation, 101

Jacob, Brigitte, 182
Jacobs, Irwin, 111, 164
Jakonson Kass Partners, 166
Jarrell, Greg A., 185, 194
J. C. Nickens, 249
J. C. Penney Inc., 54, 120, 170, 176
Jeffries Group Inc., 170–171
Jensen, Michael C., 151–152, 153, 154, 155, 166, 169, 181, 184
John G. Kinnard & Co., 67
Joint Economic Committee of Congress, 220, 254
Junk bonds, 3, 73–74, 212
JWT Corp., 167

Kaiser Aluminum and Chemical, 105
Kaiser Steel Corp., 100

Kansas City Southern Industries, 171
Kaskel, Howard, 171
Kaufmann Alsberg & Co., 173
Keating, Charles, 211–212, 218
Keck, Mahin, and Cate, 220
Keilin, Eugene, 106
Keilin and Bloom, 61, 66, 106, 213
Kelso, Louis, xi, 21, 52, 61, 78, 80, 213, 254
Kelso & Company, 57, 58
Kerr Glass Manufacturing Co., 224
Kinnard Investments Inc., 67
K mart Corp., 8
KMS Industries Inc., 171
Kodak, 140
Kohlberg, Kravis and Roberts, 60, 172, 178
Kraft Inc., 178
Kroger Company, 67, 178
Kroy Inc., 58
Kruse, Douglas, 13, 29
KSOPs, 25, 119, 217. *See also* 401(k) plans
Kurland, Norman, 78, 256
Kysor Industrial Corp., 173

Labor, U.S. Department of, 220
    actions against pension plans, 160, 162, 163
    employee statistics, 11
    filing requirements of, 191
    information available from, 193
    and management use of employee
        ownership, 168, 172
    opposition to mirror voting, 190, 202
    Pension Welfare Benefits Administration,
        249
Labor costs, 93. *See also* Compensation;
        Wage and benefit restructuring; Wages
        and benefits
Labor laws, 3, 14, 236
Labor-management participation teams, 106
Labor-management relations, 98, 102, 105,
        131, 133
Law of Corporations, The (Hamilton), 148
Lawrence, Paul, 133
Lawsuits:
    class-action, 163, 177, 221, 248, 249
    by employees, 163
    limiting management's power to use
        employee ownership, 167–168
    outcome for 1988–1990, 179, 180
    by shareholders, 150–151, 154, 181
    trends, 207
Lazonick, William, 146, 147, 153, 154
LeBow, Bennett, 58
Lee, Lawrence H., 103

Letter of credit, 172
Leverage, 3, 21, 28, 74, 80
Leveraged buyout (LBO), 21, 60, 84, 111,
        164, 178, 212, 248. *See also* Employee
        buyouts
Leveraged Employee Stock Ownership Plan
        (LESOP), 23–24, 50
Lew, Michael I., 90, 95, 221
Lincoln Savings and Loan Association, 211,
        218, 248
Lincoln Telecommunications, 120
Lindberg, Ken, 20, 221
Lockheed Corp., 120, 142, 174, 184, 186
Loeb, Walter F., 170
Long, Sen. Russell, xi, 21
Lorenzo, Frank, 97, 100, 102–103, 104, 135,
        165
Lowe's Companies, 55–56
LTV Corp., 63, 64, 105, 106, 109, 160
Lydall Corp., 114
Lyons, Judy, 60
Lyons Metal Products, 58, 110, 159, 163–164,
        205

Macmillan Inc., 67, 171–172, 177, 220, 244
Macmillan Information, 172
Macmillan Publishing, 172
Malcolm Baldridge Award, 247, 251
Management, as agents of shareholders,
        149–150
Management buyout, 84
Management entrenchment, 149–150, 155,
        164, 165, 173, 194–195, 196, 237
Manufacturers Hanover Trust Company
        of New York, 73, 242
Marchetti, Marilyn, 220
Mark, Reuben, 54
Market equity, 40
Martin, J. Landis, 142
Martin Marietta Corp., 161, 203
Master wage agreement, 105
Matching contributions:
    advantages to employer/employee, 123
    ESOP stock as, 138
    to 401(k) plans, 24, 89, 128
    takeovers and, 122
    trends in, 120, 121
Maxwell, Robert, 55, 110, 139, 172
Maxwell Communications, 172
May, 122
Mazzilli, Paul, 1, 56, 235
McClouth Steel, 105
McRae Industries, 114

McDonald's, 122
McDonnell-Douglas, 11, 212
Means, Gardner, 2
Media disclosure, 192
Medtronic Inc., 171
Mercer, William M., 111
Merchants Bancorp, 110
Mergers, 102, 147, 154, 166
Merrill Lynch & Co., 33, 55, 72, 106
Merrill Lynch Capital Markets, 76
Mesa Partners, 164
Metall Mining Corporation, 61
Met-Coil Systems Corp., 61
Michael Baker Corp., 110, 161, 224
Mills Acquisitions, 172
Minnesota Mining & Manufacturing (3M), 212
Minstar Corp., 164
Mirror voting, 158, 173, 180, 189–190,
    201–202, 215, 216, 222, 228, 235
Mismanagement, 98
Mobile Telecommunications Technologies Inc.,
    48
Mobil Oil Corp., 39, 122
Monarch Capital Corp., 110, 223
Money-center banks, 73, 74
Monks, Robert A. G., 234
Moody's Investor Services, 70, 128, 147
Morgan, Frank, 111
Morgan, J. P., 147, 242
Morgan Stanley & Company, 1, 56, 70, 76,
    77, 85, 89, 123, 170, 235, 242
Morris, III, Robert, 165
Moseley Holding Corp., 106
Motorola, 212
Mulligan, John, 1
Multi-investor buyout, 57–58
Mutual funds, 250
Myers, Stewart C., 78, 79, 80

NASDAQ Exchange, 7, 303. See also
    Over-The-Counter Market (OTC)
National Association of Securities Dealers
    (NASDAQ), 257
National Automated Accounting Research
    System (NAARS), 193, 305
National Center for Employee Ownership
    (NCEO):
    as an information source, 256, 306. See also
    Corey Rosen and Karen Young
    statistics from 13, 27, 61, 62, 64, 84, 125,
    214, 234, 239
National Convenience Stores Inc., 224
National Daily Quotation Service, 302, 303

National Health Corp., 63
National Intergroup of Pittsburgh, 34
National Master Freight Agreement Standards,
    104
National Quotation Bureau, 7, 303
National Spinning Co., 57
NCNB Corp., 174
New Jersey Resources Corp., 165
Newly issued shares, 23, 49–56, 80
    dilution effects of, 38, 40–41
    growth of employee ownership using,
        51–54
    in a takeover environment, 176
    by year, takeover environment, use of an
        antidilution buyback, type of shares
        used, and dollar value, 313–318
New York Bancorp, 62
New York Daily News, 107
New York Stock Exchange (NYSE), 3, 7, 46,
    95, 107, 162, 302
NFS Financial Corp., 62
Nonleveraged employee ownership, 3, 23, 72,
    80. See also Employee stock-purchase
    plans; Employee share-purchase plans
Nonqualified-stock options (NSOs), 27
Norfolk Southern, 89
Norlin Corp., 155, 162, 220
Norris, S. David, 58
North American Phillips, 212
North Bay Financial Corp., 62
Northbay Financial Corp., 62
Northern Trust Inc., 49, 51
Northwest Airlines, 103
Northwestern Steel & Wire, 58, 64, 105, 229,
    252

O'Dea, Dennis, 170
Odetics Inc., 161
Ogden Corp., 63
Old Stone Bank, 34
Ombudsperson, 221
Optical Coating Laboratories, 67, 173
Oregon Metallurgical Corp. (OREMET), 61,
    64, 105
Oregon Steel Mills Inc., 60
Outsider five- or ten-percent owners, 191
Over-The-Counter Market (OTC), 7, 46, 95,
    303
Ownership culture, 196
Ownership replacement, 38, 39, 80, 180. See
    also Cashing out large shareholders;
    Employee ownership, buybacks
Ownership structure, revolution in, 35–37, 79

Pace, Rooney, 162
Pamida Company, 57
Pan Am, 101, 102
Par put, 56, 86
Parsons Inc., 58
Participatory culture, 212, 215, 227–230, 235
Part-time employees, 12, 13
Partridge, William D., 3, 109
Pass-through voting provision, 163, 173, 230
Paternalism, 5, 91, 196, 218
Pattison Canadian, 89
Paul Getty Museum, 68
Pay-at-risk philosophy, 222
Pennzoil Corporation, 185–186
Pension Benefit Guarantee Corporation
    (PBGC), U.S., 22, 246
Pension plans:
  conventional, 26
  private *vs.* direct employee ownership, 71
  termination of, 108
  types of, 22–28
  See also Defined-benefit plans
People Express Airlines, 61, 104
Peoples Federal Savings of Dekalb City, 47
PepsiCo, 90, 123–124
Performance-based pay, 5
Perini, Bonfilio, 213
Perini Corporation, 213
Petro-Lewis Corporation, 166
Philadelphia Stock Exchange (PSE), 303
Phillips, Kevin, 132, 254
Phillips Petroleum, 158–159, 164, 165, 244
Pickens, T. Boone, 164, 185, 244
Piezo Electric Products Corp., 162
Pink-sheet firms, 7, 248, 257, 302, 303
Pioneer Federal Savings Bank, 62
Pittsburgh Forgings, 63, 64
Poison pills, 142, 155, 167, 177, 219
Polaroid Inc., 43, 70, 106, 127, 140,
    176, 178–179, 189, 194, 229,
    244, 245, 251
Polifly Financial Corp., 47
Portsmouth Bank Shares Inc., 62
Posner, Victor, 162
Postretirement medical benefits, 115–119
  as an expected benefit, 92
  funding retiree health plans with
    employee-held company stock,
    116, 117
  plans benefiting employers *vs.* plans
    benefiting employees, 116–118
  takeovers and, 116
Poughkeepsie Savings Bank, 110

Pound, John, 177, 233
Preferred stock, 78
Price-earnings (P-E) ratio, 38
Primark Corp., 110
Principal-agent problem, 149, 150, 151,
    235
Principles of Corporate Finance (Brealey
    and Myers), 78
Private companies, 8. *See also* Going private
Private placements, 73–76
Problem-solving teams, 228, 229, 238
Procter & Gamble, 73, 88, 229, 230
Productivity, 91
  employee empowerment, 251–252
  incentives for, 42
  increased employee involvement, 43, 93,
    228
  ownership as a reward for, 28
  and participatory culture, 215
  PepsiCo's Share Power program to inspire,
    90, 123–124
Profitability, 90, 129
Profit-sharing plans, 106
  cash, 25, 28, 114
  cost of, 112
  deferred, 25, 69, 114
  replacing, 111–115
  restructuring with employee ownership, 113,
    114
  tax incentives, 25
Proxy battles, 8, 40, 144, 151, 154,
    155, 179, 183–185, 190, 222,
    233
  implications for employee groups, 197
  role of employee ownership in, 160
Proxy contests, 150, 153, 159, 189, 236
Proxy solicitation, 185, 190, 193, 233
Proxy statements, 216, 235, 238
Proxy voting, 190
Prudential-Bache Securities Inc., 165
Public capital market, 7, 76–77
  examples of, 76
Public companies, 7–8
  in the American economy, 8, 9
  changes in capital sources, 34, 78
Public companies going private with employee
    ownership, 319
Public Company Employee Ownership
    Database, 6–7, 29, 72
Purolator Courier Corp., 66, 110, 177

Quaker Oats Company, 111, 112, 114
Quality circles, 34, 239

Quality improvement programs, 251
Quest for Value, The (Stewart), 195

Radiation System Inc., 114
Railroads, 146
Ralston Purina, 117, 118
Rath Packing Company, 63, 98, 100
Raymond International, 57
Reagan, President Ronald, 73, 78
Real wages, 21, 93, 94, 252
Recapitalization, 164, 165–166, 170–171, 172
Reed, Travis, 103, 104
Regan, Edward V., 48
Regional Bancorp Inc., 62
Reliance Electric, 167
Remaking the Public Corporation from Within
      (Stewart), 196, 197
Reorganization, 43, 55, 68
Republic Airlines, 101, 103
Republic Container, 64
Republic Storage, 64
Resdel Industries, 167
Resolution Trust Corp., 219
Resorts International, 166
Retirement benefits, tax deductibility of, 21
Rexnord Corporation, 165
Rhoads, D. D., 164
Riese Organization, 171
Rights, 5
Risk, 225
    as an abuse of employee ownership, 246
    company quality and, 118
    contribution, 4
    of defined-contribution *vs.* defined-benefit
        plans, 22
    for employees, 71, 131, 133
    government attempts to limit, 4
    inflation, 4
    investment, 3
    longevity, 3–4
    for managers, 133
    as the price of employee power, 3
Robert M. Bass Group, 172, 244
Rochester Community Savings Bank, 122
Roessner, Gilbert, 218
Rohm & Haas Co., 48
Rollover, 107, 108
Ropak Corporation, 167
Roper Corporation, 110
Rosen, Corey, 214. *See also* National Center
      for Employee Ownership
Ruddick Inc., 223
Ryder/P-I-E, 101

Salomon Brothers, 48, 75, 88, 106, 242
Salomon Inc., 88–89
Salwen, Al, 222
Saporito, Bill, 227
Sarah Getty Trust, 68
Sara-Lee Corp., 223
Savings plans, 24, 49, 69, 72
    company matching contributions to,
        119–123
Schaeffer, Bernie, 124, 230
Scholes, Myron S., 28
Science Application International, 71, 125,
        212, 253. *See also* Robert Beyster
Scott & Fetzer Inc., 58
Scotty's Inc., 162
Sears, Roebuck & Co., 11, 64, 114, 223
Second World of Employee Ownership,
        247
Section 133 tax incentive, 73, 75
Section 423 plans, 27
Securities Exchange Act of 1934, 159, 192,
        199
Securities and Exchange Commission (SEC):
    complaints by, 172
    filings required by, 6, 62, 191–192, 216,
        220, 249, 250, 304–305
    Forms 10-K and 10-Q, 192
    Forms 13D, 13F, and 13G, 191–192
    proxy solicitations, 185, 190
    regulations, 233
    Rule 144a, 75–76
    as a source of employee-ownership
        information, 304
Security American Financial Enterprises,
        58
Self-funding insurance plans, 93
Self-liquidating credit, 79
Shamrock Corp., 140, 244
Shamrock Holdings, 48, 166, 178
Share dividends, 199
Share Economy, The (Weitzman), 247
Shareholder activism, 155, 233
Shareholder culture, 235
Shareholder-employee relations, 249–250
Shareholder-management relations:
    arguments over the market for corporate
        control, 151–152
    courts' opposition to second-guessing
        management, 152–154
    declining loyalty of shareholders, 147–148
    distribution of power in corporations through
        corporate law, 148–149
    electing and testing agents, 150–151

management as agents of shareholders, 149–150
principal-agent problem, 150, 151
shareholder defense *vs.* management entrenchment, 155
split between ownership and control, 146–147
Shareholder neutral, 106, 170, 175, 176, 180, 194, 218
Shareholder relations, 71, 175
Shareholder rights, 172, 177, 190, 215, 219, 228, 231, 233, 234, 236
Shareholders:
board representation by, 151
disclosures to, 150
limited role of, 149–150
loyalty of, 147–148
options available to, 150
Shareholder value, 91
Share Power program (PepsiCo), 90, 123–124
Share-purchase plans. *See* Employee stock-purchase plans
Share repurchases, 26, 43–44
and dilution, 52, 174–177, 313–318, 325–329, 330–336
Shark repellents, 155
Shearson Lehman Hutton, 61, 76
Simmons, Harold, 142, 174, 184, 186
Skadden, Arps, Meagher & Flom, 102
Smale, John G., 88
SMC, 167
Smith, James, 106
Smith, Randall, 184
Smith Transfer, 101
Smithburg, William D., 111
Social Security, 21, 35, 94
Sole proprietorships, 8
Soros, George, 171
South Bend Lathe, 64
Southeastern Public Service Company, 162
Sperry Rand Corp., 63
SPX Corp., 174
Standard Brands, 229
Standard Brands Paint Company, 173
Standard & Poor's:
credit ratings by, 70, 128, 147
list of risky banks, 248
Standard & Poor's Composite Index, 225
Standard & Poor's 500, 181, 182
Statistical Process Control, 34
Steel industry, 105–106
Steinberg, Saul, 167
Steinway, Henry W. T., 142, 143

Steinway & Sons, 142–144
Steinway v. *Steinway*, 194
Stern, Stewart & Co., 79
Stewart, G. Bennett, 79, 195, 196, 197
Stock-bonus plans, 26, 69
Stock buybacks. *See* Employee ownership, buybacks
Stock exchanges, three major, 7
and representation of Employee Ownership 1000, 257, 302
Stockholders' equity, 78
Stock-option plans, 27–28
and executive performance, 124
increasing interest in, 124
results of surveys on, 124
trends in, 125
upper-level management and, 124
Stock-ownership patterns, 36, 253–255
Stock price, 38, 128–129
impact of employee-ownership plans on sponsoring companies, 181–183
Stock purchases, individual employee, 26–27
Swank Inc., 166
Syncor International Corp., 122
System Roundtable, 213

Takeover-defense silent majority, 143–146, 190–191
Takeover-defense unknown minority, 191–193
Takeover environment, 78, 81–82, 116, 120, 206
and buybacks, 45
and cashing out large shareholders, 49
company experimentation with employee ownership in, 166–167
court actions concerning, 167–168, 173–174
disclosure crisis, 191–193
employee ownership adopted or proposed in, 157–158
employee-ownership buybacks and, 45, 81–82
employees in, 163–164, 197
evolution of employee ownership in, 155–179
going private and, 58
growth of employee ownerships in, 161–163
impact of state and federal actions, 186–190
list of public companies using employee ownership in, 330–337
new developments in, 181–193
newly issued shares in, 51, 176
from 1973–1984, 158–164
from 1985–1987, 165–168

Takeover environment (*continued*)
  from 1988–1990, 170–179
  proxy battles, 183–185
  recapitalization, 165–166
  recent conflicts, 185–186
  scorecard for 1973–1987, 168–170
  scorecard for 1988–1990, 179–181
  in setting up the employer-ownership
    transaction, 127
  wage and benefit restructuring in, 95, 158,
    175–181, 325–329, 330–337
Takeover investor, 17, 197, 206, 233
Takeover laws, 46, 145, 178, 187
  state-by-state comparison, 188
Takeover raiders. *See* Corporate raiders;
  Takeovers, and employee ownership
Takeovers, 53, 129. *See also* Hostile takeovers
  and company matching contributions, 122
  defenses against, 144–145, 154–155,
    165–168
  Delaware law regarding, 46, 145, 178, 187,
    198
  early examples of, 159–161
  and employee ownership, 330–337
    buybacks, 46, 81–82
  and growth of employee ownership,
    243–244
  other state laws regarding, 186–190
  plain-vanilla defense, 144, 198–199
  as a reason for cashing out large holders, 49
  as a reason for employee-ownership stock
    buybacks, 46
  and restructuring of postretirement medical
    benefits, 116
  role of employee benefit plans in, 189
  state and federal actions on, 186–190
  trends in, 179–180
Tandycrafts, 122
Tax benefits, 129
  of employee-paid retirement benefits, 118
Tax incentives, 79–80
  and credit ratings, 70
  deduction of interest income on ESOP loans
    by banks, 73
  of deferred profit-sharing plans, 25
  and dilution, 80
  of employee-ownership buybacks, 46
  of employee stock-ownership plans, 23–24,
    28, 40, 42, 79–80, 85–86
  to encourage retirement plans, 21, 118
  expansion of, 253
  and foreign tax-credit limitations, 32
  of 401(k) plans, 25

  of incentive stock options, 27
  and individual employee stock purchases, 26
  removal of, 75, 76, 252–253
  Section 133, 73, 75
Tax Reform Act of 1986, 32
Team Inc., 114
Tender battles, 144
Tender offers, 8, 145, 150, 155, 160, 161,
    179, 190, 215, 222. *See also* Hostile
    tender offers
Ten-percent rule, 4, 26
Texaco Inc., 11, 122, 174, 176
Texas Air Corporation, 100, 102, 104, 165
Texas American Energy Corp., 165–166
Texas International Airlines, 160
Textileather, 62
Textron, 11
The Limited, 162
Third World of Employee Ownership, 248
Thompson, Virgil, 231
Thompson Bankwatch, 248
Thrift Incentive Plan (Northern Trust Inc.), 49
Thrift plans. *See* Savings plans
Thrifts, conversion of, 62
Tormey, Doug, 124, 217
Total employment, 11
Total Quality Ownership, 212
Towers Financial Corp., 66, 177
Towers Perrin, 124, 217
Trading stock for wages, 89, 97–107. *See also*
    Concession bargaining
  in the airline industry, 100–101, 102–104
  growth of, 107
    by year and stock exchange of company,
      99
  in nonunion companies, 106–107
  in the steel industry, 105–106
  in the trucking industry, 101, 104–105
  in union companies, 98
Training programs, 226
Transcom, 101, 104–105
Transport Workers Union, 103
Travelers Corp., 55
Treasury, U.S. Department of, 187
Treasury stock transfer, 54
Tribune Company, 183
Trucking industry, 101, 104–105
Trustee, role of in employee ownership, 220,
    226
Trusteeship, 4–5, 245
Turner Corp., 55
TWA, 59, 104, 165
Two-tiered offers, 198

Ueberroth, Peter, 102
Underinvesting, 98
Unemployment insurance, 133
Unions, 235, 236
  board representation by, 100
  compared with employee associations, 3
  concession bargaining by, 89, 98, 102,
    103–104
  and defined-benefit pension programs, 109,
    110
  employee benefits to prevent growth of, 91
  and employee buyouts, 64, 65
  evolution of, 133
  exclusion of employees from ownership
    plans, 12
  and the fixed-wage system, 132, 252
  as players in acquiring companies, 213
  private sector decline of, 93, 237, 251
  in the public sector, 237
  in setting up employee-ownership programs,
    127
  union membership compared with
    employee-ownership sector, 13,
    237, 251
Unisys Corp., 76
United Airlines, 141–142, 154, 184, 213,
  244
United Auto Workers (UAW), 100
United Cos. Financial Corporation, 160
United Employee Acquisition Corp. (UEAC),
  141, 184
United Food & Commercial Workers, 98
United Postal Bancorp, 34–35
United Shareholders Association, 185
United Steelworkers of America, 61, 64, 105,
  237
United Technology, 203
Universal Foods Corp., 110
Upjohn, 122
UPS (United Parcel Service), 123
Urban Development Action Grants (UDAGs),
  98
U.S. Steel, 11
U.S. Sugar Company, 33, 58

Value creation, 153
VanFed Bancorp, 62
Vanguard mutual funds, 250
Vermont Asbestos Group, 63
Vitro Sociedad Anoima, 177
Voting power, 38, 40, 43, 56
Voting rights, 44, 57, 134, 179, 189, 231,
  235

Wachtel, Lipton, Rosen, & Katz, 248. *See
    also* Adam Chinn
Wage and benefit restructuring:
  broad-based stock options, 124
  company matching to savings and 401(k)
    plans, 119–123
    trends in, 120, 121
  competitive pressures and, 244, 246
  and dilution, 37–44, 174–181, 325–329,
    330–337
  employee attitudes toward, 94
  and employee ownership, 94–123
    trends in, 96
  funding retiree health plans with
      employee-held company stock, 116,
      117
  last-minute, 105
  major approaches to, 95
  making the employee ownership decision,
    125–130
  for managers, 133
  to maximize shareholder value and avoid
      takeovers, 95
  to offset cost of employee ownership, 42–43
  postretirement medical benefits, 115–119
  replacing defined-benefit plans, 107–111
  replacing profit-sharing plans, 111–115
    trends in, 113
  rising costs of benefits, 93
  risk, 133
  and sale of newly issued shares, 54
  shareholder concerns, 174–175
  trading stock for wages, 97–107
    growth by year and stock exchange of
      company, 99
  trends in, 91, 92, 95, 96, 130–131
  by year, type, presence of takeover
      environment, and other factors,
      325–329
Wage freezes, 98
Wages:
  fixed-wage system, 2, 5, 22, 90–94, 98,
    130–134, 244, 246, 252
Wages and benefits, changes in, 91, 92
Wartzman, Rick, 142
Wealth:
  concentration of, 4, 252, 253–255
  creation of, 79
  risk and, 245–249
Weinberger, Ken, 111, 115
Weirton Steel Corporation, 8, 34, 57, 60,
    212, 229, 231, 233, 252
Weitzmann, Howard, 107

Wertheim Schroeder Inc., 177
Western Airlines, 101, 103
Western Pacific Industries, 162
Wexner, Leslie, 162
Wheeling-Pittsburgh Steel, 105, 106, 109
White knights, 102, 141, 170, 185, 197
Whitman Corporation, 89–90, 115, 119, 174,
    183
Wilcox, John, 185
Wilkus, Malon, 64. *See also* American Capital
    Strategies
William Penn Foundation, 48
William R. Mercer Company, 111, 115, 123,
    222
Williams, Lynn, 106
Williams, Shane, 245
Wolf, Stephen, 1–3

Wolfson, Mark, 28
Workers, defined, 91, 214
Worker shortages, 91
Work rules, 98
Work teams, 212
W. R. Grace and Company, 63
Wright, James O., 48
Wyatt Company, 3, 109

Xerox Corp., 211, 212
Xyvision Inc., 223

Young, Karen, xi. *See also* National Center
    for Employee Ownership
Youngstown Sheet & Tube, 63

Zeus Partners, 89, 174